Auditing

Auditing

8th Edition

A. H. Millichamp

B.A., M.Soc.Sc., F.C.A., F.C.C.A., A.T.I.I.

Alan Millichamp has taught at the Universities of Wolverhampton and Birmingham, at the Open University Business School and in the private sector. He is a former examiner and assessor in auditing to the Chartered Association of Certified Accountants and is currently a member of the examining panel of the ACCA. He is also the author of *Finance for Non-Financial Managers*, published by the Continuum Group, and *Foundation Accounting*.

continuum
LONDON • NEW YORK

Published by
Continuum
Tower Building
11 York Road
London SE1 7NX
www.continuumbooks.com

A CIP Catalogue Record for this book is available from the British Library.

First Edition 1978
Reprinted 1979, 1980
Second Edition 1981
Reprinted 1982, 1983
Third Edition 1984
Reprinted 1985
Fourth Edition 1986
Reprinted 1987, 1988, 1989
Fifth Edition 1990
Reprinted 1991
Sixth Edition 1993
Seventh Edition 1996
Reprinted 1997
Eighth Edition 2002

ISBN 0-8264-58556 (hardback)
ISBN 0-8264-5500X (paperback)

Typeset by YHT Ltd, London

Printed and bound in Great Britain by Martins the Printers, Berwick upon Tweed

Contents

Some auditing problem areas

Current issues

Index

Acknowledgements

The Author wishes to express his thanks to the following for permission to reproduce past examination questions:

Association of Accounting Technicians (AAT)

Chartered Association of Certified Accountants (ACCA)

Institute of Company Accountants (ICA)

Institute of Chartered Accountants in England and Wales (ICAEW)

Institute of Chartered Accountants in Ireland (ICAI)

Institute of Chartered Accountants of Scotland (ICAS)

London Chamber of Commerce (LCC)

Preface

Aims of the manual

1. The primary aim of this manual is to provide a simplified but thorough approach to the understanding of modern auditing theory and practice.

   It is intended for those with little or no knowledge of the subject. However, some knowledge of accounting, company law, and data processing would be an advantage.

   Students who will find this manual essential reading include:

   a. Students studying for the examinations of the Institutes of Chartered Accountants, the Chartered Association of Certified Accountants, the Chartered Institute of Public Finance and Accountancy, the Association of Accounting Technicians, the Institute of Company Accountants and the London Chamber of Commerce.

   b. Students studying auditing as a part of a Foundation Course in a college or university or as part of a BTEC national or higher national course, or as part of the NVQ in Accounting.

   c. Other business students, managers, accountants and members of their staff wishing to gain a knowledge of the new techniques used by the modern auditor.

Need

2. The expansion of the basic core of knowledge required to pass the auditing papers of the professional bodies, has led to a need for a comprehensive, systematic manual in one volume, aimed specifically at the requirements of present day auditing examinations.

3. It is hoped that this manual will provide the student with a clear and succinct exposition of the subject and be sufficiently interesting to encourage even the least conscientious student to proceed in easily digestible stages.

Approach

4. The book has been designed with several uses in mind:

   a. as a textbook, on its own, for specific examinations

   b. for use with a lecturer

   c. as a revision text for those who are taking or retaking examinations.

   The case studies, student self testing questions and exam questions are particularly useful for those taking exams.

Ends of chapters

5. At the end of each chapter is found:

   a. Summary of the chapter.

   b. Points to note. These are used for emphasis and clarification of points which students often misunderstand.

   c. Short case studies. The objective of the case studies is to illuminate the material in the chapter. Readers may find it helpful to ponder on the case study while reading the chapter.

    d. Questions. These are:

        i.   short questions to test comprehension and learning of the material of the chapter and as an aide-memoire

        ii. exercises; and

        iii. examination questions from various bodies.

In addition, the case studies can be seen as questions. Answers to the exam questions are available on the website.

Website

6.   The website contains:

    a. additional questions and case studies

    b. answers to the exam questions and some discussion on the case studies

    c. additional material on matters of current interest

    d. addenda and amendments to the text; and

    e. an opportunity to ask questions and make comments.

Notes to the eighth edition

7.   The eighth edition now takes account of:

    a. all the relevant UK and International Auditing Standards and other official pronouncements, practice notes, bulletins and practice statements extant at the time of writing

    b. all the relevant accounting standards issued to date; and

    c. the new syllabuses of the professional bodies.

    In addition, the opportunity has been taken to prune the text, rewrite some chapters completely and introduce new material. I have updated the exam questions but have found that some questions simply do not date and are relevant for a very long time.

Chapter order

8.   The chapter order follows a logical sequence but I am aware that many users and lecturers would prefer a different order. In fact the Hong Kong version of the text has a very different order. You cannot please all the people all the time! The chapters are self-contained and can be read in any order although most chapters do take account of what has gone before.

Exam syllabuses

9.   Most students who are using the book will be preparing for examinations with specific syllabuses. For some syllabuses all the book is relevant but for many only part of the book may be relevant. Your tutor will advise you on this and the syllabus will be so itemised that you can see which chapters are relevant.

Passing auditing exams

10. Many students have difficulty in passing auditing exams. Often this is simply due to a lack of preparation but it can also be due to a lack of exam technique. I have begun the

book with suggestions on how to pass auditing exams. This has been written from my long experience as a teacher and examiner in auditing. I hope it will be helpful!

Suggestions and criticism

11. The author has received and taken account of many helpful comments on this manual. He would welcome many more so that subsequent editions can be made even more useful to students and teachers alike. He can be contacted by e-mail at auditing8ed@hotmail.com or in case of difficulty through the business editor at the publisher's address.

A.H.M.
April 2001

How to pass auditing examinations

1. There is no simple formula for success. If there were, everybody would be successful. However there are many ways in which you can increase your chances of success. These include:

   a. Being well prepared. There is no real substitute for hard work and application. However reading is not enough. You must practice exam questions. At the end of each chapter there are student self testing questions and exam questions and the case studies. The best way to learn is to write out answers to these in full. It is only by being faced with having to write things down, that you discover the gaps in your knowledge and understanding.

   b. Knowing the syllabus and what you should know. Guidance on this is obtained by reading the relevant syllabus and any other information available from the examining body. Examples are the ACCA study guides. It is also essential to study past exam papers or pilot papers where the exam is a new one. Your study must be purposeful and directed and focused to specific goals. Many examining bodies, such as the ACCA, also publish official answers. These are far more comprehensive than expected student answers but they do give you a clear idea of what is expected.

   c. Time in the exam room. The time in the exam room should be used efficiently and profitably. Specific points here are:

      i. Answer all the questions that you are asked to answer. Given a choice, never spend time finishing a question when there is still a question unanswered. The first few marks on a question are always easy but the last few are always hard to earn.

      ii. Give proper weight to each question and part of a question. There is no point in filling two sides of A4 on a part of a question which earns you 2 marks. Similarly writing two lines on a 20 marks question is clearly not enough. It is a good idea to consider how much time you can allocate to each task. For example in a three hour 100 mark exam, you should not spend more time than 9 minutes per 5 marks.

      iii. Do not omit parts of a question. Even if you do not know the answer, guess and write something.

Tackling a question

2. Here are some general points:

   a. Plan the answer briefly and show your plan.

   b. Answer the question (ATQ). This is a vital point. It is no good answering the question you would have preferred. You must answer exactly the question set. This means reading the question carefully and noting exactly what is required. A good way of doing this is to underline significant words in the question.

   c. Make points. This is the most important thing of all. Some questions say 'List four procedures…'. Obviously four points are wanted. Some say 'State the audit tests that you…'. What is wanted in such questions is as many tests as you can think of.

It does not want long descriptions of two tests. The marking scheme probably says: give 1 mark per valid test.

d. Use all the data given in the question. Many auditing questions have long scenarios before the requirement. This information is not just for idle reading. Then examiner expects you to use it in your answer. It probably contains lots of clues to the answer required.

e. Auditing examiners expect intelligent answers. Try to see the implications in a question. For example a question about audit risk may want a general answer but specific points about audit risk in the particular case will be in the scenario.

f. Markers do not receive princely sums for marking your paper. Keep the answers as short and succinct as possible. When you have made a point using one sentence. Consider whether you really need more sentences. Write legibly and use short sentences and paragraphs. Tabulating and listing is usually acceptable and helps the marker see what you have said. Lengthy prose paragraphs are not normally the best approach.

g. Label each part of your answer. If a question has four parts, a, b, etc., make sure each part is clearly labelled as such.

h. Avoid an anxious display of knowledge (ADK). Answer the question as set. It does not want a recital of all you know on the subject.

i. Explain your terms. Suppose you are faced with a question like 'Explain why external auditors seek to rely on the proper operation of internal controls wherever possible'. First define external auditor and internal controls. You may get marks for it but in any case it will give you clues to how to answer it.

j. Apply lateral thinking. In the internal controls example think about what an external auditor is trying to do or the context in which internal controls are designed or what they are designed to prevent or ensure.

Tackling a question – specific ideas

3. With many questions, you may be faced with making points but not being able to think of many. Here are a few ideas which may trigger points you can make:

a. What Auditing Standards are involved?

b. What Accounting Standards are involved?

c. What Companies Act accounting or auditing requirements are involved?

d. Is business or audit risk relevant?

e. Does the question have any relevance for the letter of engagement?

f. Does the question have any relevance for the auditor's report?

g. What assertions about a figure in the financial statements are implied?

h. Does the question have any relevance to the idea of misstatements in the financial statements.

i. Is materiality worth mentioning?

j. Do ethics have any relevance?

k. What types of audit tests may be applied?

l. What working papers may be needed?

    m. What errors or frauds could occur?

    n. Is going concern an issue?

    o. Is internal audit involved?

Reading through the paper

4. Many students have a moment of panic when they first see the paper. This will pass when you realise how easy the paper really is! Most students read through all the questions briefly first concentrating on the requirements of each question. As you do this jot down any thoughts that occur to you. Do not commit these thoughts to memory but jot them down. While writing this I have random thoughts of relevance to some other part of the book. I always jot them down. Otherwise I forget them unless I write them down straightaway and so will you.

Reviewing your script

5. Some students like to finish early and then proof read their scripts. This is unlikely to add many marks unless you think of new points. Polishing the grammar, spelling and punctuation is very unlikely to add many marks to your score.

How to answer a question

6. It all depends on the question but here are some general ideas:

    a. Read the question.

    b. Read it again.

    c. Underline important words in the question.

    d. Make sure you know exactly what the examiner requires you to do.

    e. Do a. to d. over again.

    f. Jot down the points you want to make, add to these points others as you think of them even while writing the answer out.

    g. Stop and think for a moment.

    h. Draft an outline plan of your answer.

    i. Write your answer referring back continually to the requirements of the question. Take plenty of room, use short sentences and paragraphs. Number your points if you think it appropriate.

    j. Go on to next question.

Common faults in auditing answers

7. Here are some common faults:

Not obeying the questioner's requirements

If it says set out, list, tabulate, to what extent, examine the truth of, state; state concisely; what are the principal matters, discuss, comment on, describe, write a short essay, then:

Do what it says!

Not doing what is says is a more common fault with auditing examinees than lack of knowledge.

Not reading the question carefully

Many students on being asked to audit a partnership will ask for the memorandum and Articles.

Not making enough points

This is very hard to overcome but one good technique is to try to break the question down into sections. A tree approach - roots, trunk, branches, twigs, leaves - is often successful.

Not being specific

'Vouch the cash book' will not often do, 'vouch the entries in the cash book with available supporting documents such as ...' might do.

Being irrelevant

Tied up with not obeying instructions and not reading the question carefully.

Lack of planning, coherence and logic.

Planning an answer should cure this.

Lack of balance

If the examiner asks for five points he does not want four pages on point one and one line each on the others.

Handwriting, grammar, spelling, punctuation

Do not waste your time and opportunities by presenting your work badly or with avoidable errors.

Confusing the role of auditor with that of accountant, tax consultant, etc.

If asked what the auditor should do in certain circumstances, never say 'Alter the accounts' because producing accounts is not the auditor's function. Neither should you advise an action which would save your client tax, you must say what you would do as *auditor*.

Layout and wording of answer

8. a. Use the wording of the question wherever you can.

   b. Answer the question in the sequence requested.

   c. Obey instructions on layout e.g. tabulate.

   d. State any assumptions you make in answering the question. However do not make assumptions which change the question to suit your knowledge.

End of exam procedure

9. a. Have a very quick look at each answer; checking for grammatical errors and badly formed letters. Add any new points if you can think of them.

   b. Ensure each answer sheet has your number on it. Do not leave anything lying on the table.

Conclusions

10. Good technique plays a large part in examination success; this is a fact. Refuse to be panicked, keep your head, and with reasonable preparation you should make it.

   Remember-you don't have to score 100 per cent to pass.

A final point; once you're in the examination room stay there and make use of every minute at your disposal.

Practise your techniques when answering the questions set in the book.

Why do students fail auditing exams?

11. There are four main reasons:
    a. inadequate knowledge
    b. failure to answer the questions set
    c. failure to see the implications of the questions; and
    d. failure to make enough points.

Introduction to auditing

The first chapter introduces you to the idea of stewardship accounting and the need for an independent and competent auditing profession.

1 Introduction to auditing – the why of auditing

Introduction

1. This chapter attempts to explain why auditing exists as a discipline. The chapter first explains the concepts of stewardship and stewardship accounting. The objectives of auditing are next explained with an introduction to auditors' reports and the organisation of the auditing profession. The different types of audit are introduced in the final part of this chapter.

Stewardship

2. Stewardship is the name given to the practice by which productive resources owned by one person or group are managed by another person or group of persons. This has occurred throughout history. For example, in the middle ages, great landowners would not manage their own land but would appoint persons called *stewards* to *manage* the land. Today most business is operated by limited companies which are owned by their *shareholders* and managed by *directors* appointed by the shareholders. Similarly the public own central government resources including the nationalised industries but they are *managed* by the government and persons appointed by the government.

Stewardship accounting

3. Owners who appoint managers to look after the owner's property will be concerned to know what has happened to their property. A famous example of this is in St Matthew's Gospel (Chapter 25) when the rich man went on a journey and delivered his goods to his servants to look after while he was away. On his return he asked each of his servants to *account* for the goods with which he had been entrusted. He was not pleased with the servant who had not *profitably* used the goods he had managed in his master's absence. Today the process whereby the managers of a business account or report to the owners of the business is called *stewardship accounting*. This reporting and accounting is usually done by means of *financial statements*.

Financial statements

4. Financial statements can take many forms. The best known are the profit and loss accounts and balance sheets of businesses. In the specific case of limited companies, financial statements are produced annually and take the form of an 'Annual report and accounts' which include a profit and loss account and balance sheet and also other statements including the directors' report and a cash flow statement.

Parties to financial statements

5. Historically, annual reports and accounts of companies are produced by the directors (as managers) to the shareholders (as owners), and other people were not expected to be interested in them. However, today a much wider range of people are interested in the annual report and accounts of companies and other organisations.

    The following people or groups of people are likely to want to see and use financial statements:

    a. Actual or potential
        i.   Owners or shareholders.
        ii.   Lenders or debenture holders.
        iii. Employees.
        iv.   Customers.
        v.   Suppliers.
    b. People who advise the above – accountants; stockbrokers; credit rating agencies; financial journalists; trade unions; statisticians.
    c. Competitors and people interested in mergers, amalgamations and takeovers.
    d. The government, including the tax authorities, departments concerned with price control, consumer protection, and the control and regulation of business.
    e. The public, including those who are interested in consumer protection, environmental protection, and political and other pressure groups.
    f. Regulatory organisations such as those (e.g. IMRO, PIA) set up under the Financial Services Act 1986.

    All these people must be sure that the financial statements can be relied upon.

Why is there a need for an audit?

6. The problem which has always existed when managers report to owners is – can the owners believe the report?

    The report may:

    a. contain errors
    b. not disclose fraud
    c. be inadvertently misleading
    d. be deliberately misleading
    e. fail to disclose relevant information
    f. fail to conform to regulations.

    The solution to this problem of *credibility* in reports and accounts lies in appointing an independent person called an auditor to investigate the report and report on his findings.

    A further point is that modern companies can be very large with multi-national activities. The preparation of the accounts of such *groups* is a very complex operation involving the bringing together and summarising of accounts of subsidiaries with differing conventions, legal systems and accounting and control systems. The examination of such accounts by independent experts trained in the assessment of financial information is of benefit to those who control and operate such organisations as well as to owners and outsiders.

Many financial statements must conform to statutory or other requirements. The most notable is that all company accounts have to conform to the requirements of the Companies Act 1985 but many other bodies (e.g. charities, building societies, financial services businesses etc.) have detailed accounting requirements. In addition all accounts should conform to the requirements of Financial Reporting Standards (FRSs) and the still relevant Statements of Standard Accounting Practice (SSAPs). It is essential that an audit should be carried out on financial statements to ensure that they conform to these requirements.

Objectives of auditing

7. The auditor should be an independent person who is appointed to investigate the organisation, its records, and the financial statements prepared from them, and thus form an opinion on the accuracy and correctness of the financial statements. The primary aim of an audit is to enable the auditor to say 'these accounts show a true and fair view' or, of course, to say that they do not. The objects of an audit are:

    Primary:

    To produce a report by the auditor of his opinion of the truth and fairness of financial statements so that any person reading and using them can have belief in them.

    Subsidiary:

    a. to detect errors and fraud
    b. to prevent errors and fraud by the deterrent and moral effect of the audit
    c. to provide spin-off effects. The auditor will be able to assist his clients with accounting, systems, taxation, financial, risk management and other problems.

The auditor's report

8. At the end of his audit, when he has examined the organisation, its records, and its financial statements, the auditor produces a *report* addressed to the owners in which he expresses his opinion of the truth and fairness, and sometimes other aspects, of the financial statements.

The auditor's opinion

9. The auditor, in his report, does not say that the financial statements *do* show a true and fair view. He can only say that *in his opinion* the financial statements show a true and fair view. The reader or user of financial statements will know from his knowledge of the auditor whether or not to rely on the auditor's opinion. If the auditor is known to be independent, honest, and competent, then his opinion will be relied upon.

    The vast majority of auditors are well known to be independent. However, a few are perhaps incorrectly thought to be too connected with a client (for example a small firm with a large client) and some may not seem sufficiently competent (again, a small firm with a large client, or an auditor who is not a member of a professional body).

Organisation of the auditing profession

10. A vital part of auditing is that the auditor must be *INDEPENDENT* of the management who are responsible for the accounts and the owners who receive them. In the case of companies, he must not be connected with either the directors or the shareholders. He must also be independent of government agencies or other groups who have contact with the business. For these reasons auditors form themselves into independent firms willing to perform audits for a fee for whoever is able and willing to employ them. Some of these firms are very large with worldwide connections and employing thousands of people. Others are very small with sometimes only one or two principals and a very small staff.

Auditing and other services

11. Auditing firms do not describe themselves as auditors. They describe themselves as *Chartered Accountants* or *Chartered Certified Accountants* or in some cases just as accountants. Auditing firms are composed of accountants who perform audits for their clients. They also perform other services. The small firms especially may spend more time on other services than on auditing.

    The other services may include:

    a. writing up books
    b. balancing books
    c. preparing final accounts
    d. tax negotiations
    e. government form filling
    f. financial advice
    g. management and systems advice
    h. liquidation and receivership work
    i. investigations
    j. risk management
    k. corporate governance.

Qualities required of an auditor

12. An auditor needs to possess the following qualities:

    a. *Independence*

    An auditor cannot give an unbiased opinion unless he is independent of all the parties involved. Total independence is impossible in that the auditor receives his fees from the client. Nonetheless, independence is very important. Not only must the auditor be independent in fact and in attitude of mind but he must also be seen to be independent.

    b. *Competence*

    An auditor must be thoroughly trained and prove his competence before he can sign an audit report. Parliament has decreed that only members of certain professional bodies can become auditors of limited companies. These professional bodies (the three Institutes of Chartered Accountants and the Chartered Association of Certified Accountants) have developed competence in their members by using difficult examinations, post qualifying education, the publication of auditing standards and guidelines and other material. In addition there are requirements before members can become and continue to be *registered auditors.*

c. *Integrity*

Qualified accountants are renowned for their honesty, discretion and tactfulness. Auditors authorised by their professional bodies to conduct audits are known as *Registered Auditors.* Registered auditor firms are supervised and inspected by their professional bodies acting as supervisory bodies.

Types of audit

13. There are four types of audit:

a. *Statutory audits*

These are audits carried out because the law requires them. Statutes which require audits to be done include the Companies Act 1985, the Building Societies Act 1986, the Friendly Societies Acts 1974 and 1992, and others of no examination importance.

b. *Private audits*

A private audit is conducted into a firm's affairs by independent auditors because the owners desire it, not because the law requires it. Examples are audits of the accounts of sole traders and partnerships.

c. *Internal audits*

An internal audit is one conducted by an employee of a business or an outside contractor into any aspect of its affairs.

d. *Others*

Enquiries into specific aspects of an enterprise – management, environmental matters etc. This book is principally about a. and b. but also about internal auditing.

Summary

14. a. Stewardship involves the separation of ownership from control.

b. Stewardship accounting is the means by which those who control report to the owners.

c. The reports produced by those who control to the owners are used by many other people.

d. All those who use the reports need to be able to believe in them.

e. The audit is the means by which this belief is obtained.

f. Auditing is concerned also with the detection and prevention of error and fraud.

g. Auditors form independent firms and carry out numerous other services for their clients.

h. There are statutory, private, internal, and other audits.

Points to note

15. a. The auditor must be independent, a person of integrity and competent.

b. The auditor gives an opinion in his report. He does not certify or guarantee.

c. Auditors often prepare the accounts they audit. For examination purposes, students must assume that the auditor does not do this.

d. The Auditing Practices Board (APB) defines an audit as:

"An audit of financial statements is an exercise whose objective is to enable auditors to express an opinion whether the financial statements give a true and fair view (or equivalent) of the entity's affairs at the period end and of its profit or loss (or income and expenditure) for the period then ended and have been properly prepared in accordance with the applicable reporting framework (for example relevant legislation and applicable accounting standards) or, where statutory or other specific requirements prescribe the term 'present fairly'."

Notes:

– Entity is a general term embracing all types of business, enterprise or undertaking including companies, charities, local authorities, government agencies etc. Some are profit oriented and some are not.

– The reporting framework is for companies the Companies Act 1985 but other statutory and non-statutory provisions may apply to other types of entity.

– The accounting standards apply to nearly all entities.

– 'Present fairly' instead of 'true and fair' applies mainly to local authorities.

A particular point is made of the fact that responsibility for the preparation of the financial statements and the presentation of the information included therein rests with the management of the enterprise (in the case of a company, the directors). The auditor's responsibility is to report on the financial statements as presented by management.

e. A number of auditing issues are becoming subjects of anxious debate and controversy at the time of writing. These include increased accounting regulation of enterprises and the effect on auditors, increased regulation of auditors, the extent of auditors' responsibilities for the detection and prevention of fraud, auditors' responsibilities for ecological matters, the gap between the public's expectations of auditing and the legal position of auditors, risk management, corporate governance, auditor independence, and the whole future of auditing as a professional activity. The accounting press has many articles on these and other auditing issues and students should read as much as possible about them.

Case study 1

Wren, Gibbs and Angelo are partners in a firm of builders specialising in house alteration and improvements. Since commencing in business 15 months ago they have been fairly successful. The books have been kept by Wren who has an HNC in Business Studies as well as in building and Wren has also prepared the first year's Accounts.

The three partners are discussing these Accounts which show a profit in excess of drawings. Gibbs and Angelo suggest that they could draw out the excess but Wren counsels caution, talking about working capital needs, which confuses the others.

Angelo questions Wren on his interpretation of the partnership agreement which is a fairly complicated document and suggests that they should pay to have the Accounts audited. Wren becomes heated and says that would be a waste of money and he is perfectly capable of doing the Accounts and makes no charge to his partners for this work.

Discussion

- What benefits would the partners get from employing an independent auditor?
- Where would they find a suitable auditor?

Student self testing questions *Questions with answers apparent from the text*

1. a. List the people and groups of people who are likely to be interested in financial statements. (5)
    b. What other services do accountants provide in addition to auditing? (11)
    c. State the relationship between the Annual Accounts of a company, the shareholders, the directors, and the auditors. (2, 3, 6)
    d. What may be wrong with an annual report and accounts? (6)
    e. What is the primary objective of an audit? (7)
    f. What other benefits are obtained? (7)
    g. What are the objectives of an audit report? (9)
    h. What qualities are required in an auditor? (12)
    i. Distinguish statutory audits, private audits, internal audits and other audits. (13)
    j. Define an audit. (15)

Exercise

1. Describe the services that a firm of certified accountants might supply to the following clients:
    i.   Intergalactic Oil PLC
    ii. Fred Smith – Butcher
    iii. Go Places Travel Agency Ltd
    iv. Woden Tennis and Squash Club Ltd
    Discuss whether the same firm could carry out all these audits.

Examination question without answer

1. You are approached by one of your friends who says 'You are an auditor! My auditor keeps increasing his fees, he tells me it is because of all the extra work he has to do for me. He doesn't do anything for me – except charge me money'.
    Required:
    Draft a letter to your friend discussing this statement. You should inform him of any benefits you think he derives from the audit.
    (Note: marks will be awarded for style and presentation of the letter.)

(AAT)

Auditing and the Companies Act

1. The majority of statutory audits carried out in the UK are of companies formed under the Companies Act 1985. The Companies Act contains detailed regulations on the conduct of an audit, the accounting records on which the auditor will work, the financial statements on which he will report and on the auditor's relations with the company. The next four chapters summarise the Companies Act rules in this areas.

2. The Companies Act 1985 is a codifying Act. Before this Act there were several Acts in force (those of 1948, 1967, 1976, 1980 and 1981). The 1985 Act effectively re-enacted all the part of the previous Acts which were still in force. Some *amendments* were also made.

3. The Companies Act 1989 made a large number of amendments to Company Law primarily in the areas of Auditing and Group Accounts. The objective was to implement into English Law EEC directives on Company Law.

4. The Companies Act 1985 remains the principal Act and the Companies Act 1989 includes a number of sections which are expressed to be Sections of the principal Act in replacement for the original sections. For example S.235. This section is found in S.9 of the Companies Act 1989 but will be known as S.235 Companies Act 1985.

2 The rights and duties of an auditor under the Companies Act

Introduction

1. The law on the rights and duties of an auditor under the Companies Act is principally laid down in Sections 235, 237 and 390. We will consider each section separately.

2. An additional section of importance is Section 389A and this will be considered next.

3. Finally, the duties, rights and powers of the auditor are summarised and reviewed.

Section 235 – the auditors' report

4. Section 235:

    (1) *A company's auditors shall make a report to the company's members on all annual accounts of the company of which copies are to be laid before the company in general meeting during their tenure of office.*

    (2) *The auditors' report shall state whether in the auditors' opinion the annual accounts have been properly prepared in accordance with this Act, and in particular whether a true and fair view is given –*

        (a) *in the case of an individual balance sheet, of the state of affairs of the company as at the end of the financial year,*

        (b) *in the case of an individual profit and loss account, of the profit or loss of the company for the financial year,*

> (c) *in the case of group accounts, of the state of affairs as at the end of the financial year, and the profit or loss for the financial year, of the undertakings included in the consolidation as a whole, so far as concerns members of the company.*
>
> (3) *The auditors shall consider whether the information given in the directors' report for the financial year for which the annual accounts are prepared is consistent with those accounts; and if they are of opinion that it is not they shall state that fact in their report.*

5. Every company must hold an Annual General Meeting of its members (= shareholders) in each calendar year. At that meeting the Annual Report and Accounts (including the Balance Sheet and Profit and Loss Account and, in the case of holding companies, group accounts) are laid before the meeting.

6. Included in the Annual Report and Accounts, there must be a report by the auditor(s) on the Accounts examined by him/her/them.

7. The auditor is usually appointed at an AGM and holds office from the end of that meeting (say July l9th 20-6) till the end of the following AGM (say July 17th 20-7). That is his tenure of office. He reports on the accounts presented at the AGM of 20-7 which is within his tenure of office.

8. The auditors' report has very specific content viz:

    a. The Act contains very detailed requirements (see Chapter 5) on the form and contents of Accounts.The auditor has to say whether in his opinion the Accounts have been prepared in accordance with the Act.

    b. The Act requires, in Section 226, that the Accounts must give a true and fair view of the state of affairs of the Company (i.e. by the Balance Sheet) and of its profit or loss (i.e. by the Profit and Loss Account).

    The Auditor must say in his report whether, in his opinion, the Accounts give a true and fair view.

    The idea of true and fair is a difficult one and we will consider it in a later chapter.

    For the moment consider that true means what it says – factually correct. For example, if the Balance Sheet includes an item 'cash in hand £875.00' then this can be true or false. If it were untrue the auditor could not say that a *true* and fair view was given. If no depreciation had been applied to buildings in the Accounts then a fair view of the state of affairs would not be given by the Accounts and the auditor could not say that a true and *fair* view was given by the Accounts.

    Finally this section requires the auditor to consider whether there is any inconsistency between the information given in the directors' report and the Annual Accounts. We will deal with it again later in the manual but for the moment realise that the auditor is not asked to give an opinion on the directors' report as such. He is only asked to review the directors' report and to consider whether any information in it, is other than consistent with the Accounts. If he forms an opinion that there is an inconsistency he has to say so in his report. For example, suppose the directors' report states that production at the Bilston Factory has ceased and that the plant there will be sold for scrap. And the Accounts include the Bilston plant at unamortised cost. There is an inconsistency in that the directors' report shows the Bilston plant to have no further use and the Accounts assume further use. If the matter was material (= of significant size) then the auditor would have to detail the inconsistency in this report.

Section 237 – duties

9. Section 237 reads:

   (1) *A company's auditors shall, in preparing their report, carry out such investigations as will enable them to form an opinion as to –*

      (a) *whether proper accounting records have been kept by the company and proper returns adequate for their audit have been received from branches not visited by them, and*

      (b) *whether the company's individual accounts are in agreement with the accounting records and returns.*

   (2) *If the auditors are of opinion that proper accounting records have not been kept, or that proper returns adequate for their audit have not been received from branches not visited by them, or if the company's Individual accounts are not in agreement with the accounting records and returns, the auditors shall state that fact in their report.*

   (3) *If the auditors fail to obtain all the information and explanations which, to the best of their knowledge and belief, are necessary for the purposes of their audit, they shall state that fact in their report.*

   (4) *If the requirements of Schedule 6 (disclosure of information: emoluments and other benefits of directors and others) are not complied with in the annual accounts, the auditors shall include in their report, so far as they are reasonably able to do so, a statement giving the required particulars.*

10. Subsection 1 requires the auditor to carry out investigations to determine if proper accounting records have been kept and proper returns from branches (at least branches not visited by the auditor) have been received.

    What are 'proper accounting records' is considered in Chapter 4.

    The subsection also requires the auditor to investigate whether the Accounts are in agreement with the accounting records and with returns from branches.

11. Subsection 2 requires that if the investigations required by subsection 1 lead the auditor to form a negative opinion on proper accounting records or agreement of Accounts and records then the auditor is given a duty. The duty is to state the fact of his negative opinion in his report. If he forms a positive opinion he need say nothing on the matter in his report.

12. Subsection 3 is another duty. If the auditor fails to get all the information and explanations which are necessary for the purposes of the audit he has to say so in his report. For example if the auditor feels he needs to know if the repairs expense account includes any capital expenditure and the invoices have been lost he has to say so in his report. Or if he asks the directors if they have received any benefits in kind from the firm and they refuse to answer he has to say that in his report.

13. Subsection 4 gives the auditor some more duties. The requirements mentioned are concerned with disclosure in the Accounts of dealings with directors (remuneration, loans, etc.). Directors often do not want these matters disclosed. If the Accounts do not disclose them then the auditor is required to give the necessary facts (so far as he can) in his report. This will make him unpopular with the offending directors but duty is duty.

Auditors' rights

14. Section 389A:

    (1) *The auditors of a company have a right of access at all times to the company's books, accounts and vouchers, and are entitled to require from the company's officers such information and explanation as they think necessary for the performance of their duties as auditors.*

    This section gives the auditor some rights. He has a right of access at all times to the company's books, accounts and vouchers. In practice this right is exercised with courtesy and reasonableness. Auditors do not appear at their client's premises at two in the morning demanding to see the petty cash book.

15. There is also the right to require from the company's officer such information and explanations as he (the auditor) thinks necessary for the performance of the auditor's duties. The company's officers can refuse to give information or explanation but that leads to subsection 3 of S.237 (see above). The company's officers can also lie or mislead but that may be a criminal action – see Section 389A(2) later in the chapter.

Publication of the auditors' report

16. The Companies Act has a number of rules for publicising the auditors' report:

    a. Firstly Section 238:

       (1) *A copy of the company's annual accounts, together with a copy of the directors' report for that financial year and of the auditors' report on those accounts. shall be sent to –*

          (a) *every member of the company,*

          (b) *every holder of the company's debentures, and*

          (c) *every person who is entitled to receive notice of general meetings.*

          not less than 21 days before the date of the meeting at which copies of those documents are to be laid in accordance with Section 241.

    b. Secondly Section 239:

       (1) *Any member of a company and any holder of a company's debentures is entitled to be furnished. on demand and without charge, with a copy of the company's last annual accounts and directors' report and a copy of the auditors' report on those accounts.*

    c. Thirdly Section 240:

       (1) *If a company publishes any of its statutory accounts, they must be accompanied by the relevant auditors' report under Section 235.*

       (4) *For the purposes of this section a company shall be regarded as publishing a document if it publishes, issues or circulates it or otherwise makes it available for public inspection in a manner calculated to invite members of the public generally, or any class of members of the public, to read it.*

    d. Fourthly Section 241:

       (1) *The directors of a company shall in respect of each financial year lay before the company in general meeting copies of the company's annual accounts. the directors' report and the auditors' report on those accounts.*

e. Finally Section 242:

> (1) *The directors of a company shall in respect of each financial year deliver to the registrar a copy of the company's annual accounts together with a copy of the directors' report for that year and a copy of the auditors' report on those accounts.*

Thus whenever the Annual Accounts are sent to members and other entitled persons, published, laid before the company in general meeting, or delivered to the Registrar of Companies then the auditor's report has to be included.

Every company has a file at Companies House and the Accounts sent to the Registrar are included in the file. The file is open to inspection by members of the public. Thus any interested person has access to the file without the company being aware of the enquiry.

Auditors' rights to attend meetings

17. Section 390 establishes the right of an auditor to receive notice of and attend at meetings:

> (1) *A company's auditors are entitled –*
>
> (a) *to receive all notices of, and other communications relating to, any general meeting which a member of the company is entitled to receive*
>
> (b) *to attend any general meeting of the company; and*
>
> (c) *to be heard at any general meeting which they attend on any part of the business of the meeting which concerns them as auditors.*

In practice the auditor usually attends the AGM and speaks if he is asked to do so. The right to attend at meetings is of little use if the directors wilfully refuse to send him notice of the date, time and place of a meeting.

In addition, the auditor has rights to attend any meeting at which it is proposed to remove him from office – we shall deal with this in the next chapter.

False statements to auditors

18. Section 389A:

> (2) *An officer of a company commits an offence if he knowingly or recklessly makes to the company's auditors a statement (whether written or oral) which –*
>
> (a) *conveys or purports to convey any information or explanations which the auditors require, or are entitled to require, as auditors of the company, and*
>
> (b) *is misleading, false or deceptive in a material particular.*
>
> *A person guilty of an offence under this subsection is liable to imprisonment or a fine, or both.*

Auditors might remind the officers of a company of the Section when asking questions. However very few do.

It would seem that fear of committing a criminal offence should prevent an officer of a company from lying to or misleading the auditor. However there are few prosecutions and the Section cannot be relied on by an auditor.

Sadly, directors and officers of companies and other enterprises do sometimes lie to or mislead their auditors and are sometimes economical with the truth.

Powers of an auditor

19. An auditor of a limited company is given burdensome duties by the Companies Act. He is required to make a report on, amongst other things, the truth and fairness of the Annual Accounts. If he is negligent in any way and fails to discover that the Accounts contain an untruth or do not fairly present the position then he may be legally required to compensate from his own pocket any persons who lose money as a result of actions taken as a result of the false Accounts.

20. Because of these onerous duties the Act has given the auditor extensive rights. However he is given no legal powers to assist him in his work. It might be said that the right to report, for example, that the directors have not given him all the information he needs, is a power. But it is not really so as the directors can refuse to publish his report. If they so refuse then there are legal consequences but fundamentally the auditor has no POWER to MAKE anybody do any particular action. There are some powers given in the event of the auditor resigning and these are in the next chapter.

Summary

21. a. The Companies Act has laid down substantial duties for auditors of companies primarily in Sections 235 and 237.

   b. The duties of an auditor include:

   – making a report on all Accounts presented to shareholders

   – including in the report his opinion on whether the Accounts comply with the Act and give a true and fair view

   – investigating whether proper accounting records, proper returns from branches (not visited by the auditor) have been kept and whether the Accounts are in agreement with the accounting records

   – stating in his report IF any of the last three things are not so

   – stating in his report if he has not obtained all the information and explanations that he needs

   – giving certain information about directors if the information is not given in the Accounts

   – some duties re the directors' report.

   c. The Act ensures that the auditors' report is widely publicised by requiring it to be attached when the Annual Accounts are sent to shareholders and others, laid before the Company at the AGM and filed at Companies House.

   d. Some small assistance is given to an auditor by Section 389A which makes it a criminal offence to give false or misleading information to an auditor.

Points to note

22. a. Note the idea of the tenure of office of an auditor and how it ends at the end of an AGM. The auditor has to report on the Accounts presented at that meeting.

   b. The duties described in this chapter are the principal statutory duties of auditors of companies. There are a number of other duties in special circumstances. For example duties are imposed on the auditor of a private company that is re-registering as a public company.

c. You will have noticed references in the sections to subsidiary companies and to group accounts. These will be dealt with in a later chapter. The Companies Act 1989 has extensively added to the law on these matters.

d. It is essential to grasp the central purposes of an audit of a company:

–   Do the Accounts give a true and fair view?

–   Do the Accounts conform to the requirements of the Companies Act?

It is easy to get lost in the minutiae of auditing and of auditing techniques. Always remember why an audit test is performed.

e. The subsidiary requirement of the Act re proper accounting records is often overlooked. All audit tests are partially aimed at determining if proper accounting records have been kept.

f. The Act prescribes numerous penalties (fines and imprisonment) for contravention of most of the rules laid out in this chapter.

g. There are some modifications of the rules for small and medium-sized companies and these are dealt with in the chapter on small companies.

h. There are a number of exceptions and exemptions from these regulations for small and medium-sized companies. These will be dealt with in the chapter on small companies.

Case study 1

Ananias is the auditor of Shady Deals Ltd. During the audit of the company for the year ending 31st December 20-6 the following matters came to light:

a. £50,000 cheques had been drawn on 31.12.-6 and entered then in the cash book. These cheques were not mailed until 17.1.-7.

b. Plant and Machinery appear in the fixed assets section of the Balance Sheet without showing the original cost and accumulated depreciation, but just the net carrying value.

c. The turnover in the profit and loss account is reduced from the figures in the accounting records by a large amount of bad debts incurred in the year.

d. The auditor was refused access to the directors' minute book on the grounds that it contained personal information about the company's staff.

e. The Chairman's report states that the company were expected to have lower profits in 20-7 owing to unfavourable settlement of a two year old dispute with a customer. No provision appears in the balance sheet regarding this matter.

f. Ananias asked Elm, a director, if he had been supplied with free timber by the company for an extension to his house. He assured Ananias that this was not so. However Ananias could trace no invoice to Elm but noticed that discarded company packing material was in Elm's garage.

g. The company sell on credit to a number of sub-contractors to the building trade but keep no record of their names or addresses. However all seem to pay satisfactorily despite the invoices stating only Pat or Mick.

Discussion

The company have had the Accounts printed and refuse to alter them. Ignoring questions of materiality what does the Companies Act say about Ananias' duty in respect of these matters?

Student self testing questions *Questions with answers apparent from the text*

1. a. What Act of Parliament codified company law? (1)
    b. What must be contained in the Auditor's report? (4–15)
    c. What is the tenure of office of an auditor? (7)
    d. Which set of Accounts must an auditor report on? (7)
    e. What investigations must an auditor make? (9)
    f. Summarise the duties of an auditor. (4, 9)
    g. What duty has an auditor toward the directors' report? (4)
    h. In what ways must an auditor's report be publicised? (16)
    i. Summarise an auditor's rights. (4, 9, 14, 17)
    j. Summarise Section 389(A). (18)
    k. What is the auditor's duty if he discovers that the directors have failed to disclose the remuneration of directors in the Accounts? (9, 13)
    l. What does the Companies Act see as the main purposes of an audit? (4)
    m. Summarise Sections 235, and 237 Companies Act 1985. (4, 9)

Exercises

What are the auditor's duties in the following circumstances:

a. The accounts contain an item land and buildings at cost £340,000 when in fact the land and buildings had cost £360,000 and had been depreciated by £20,000.

b. The accounts contain an item debtors £390,000. In fact this item includes a probable bad debt of £30,000.

c. The accounts show a profit after tax of £200,000. The directors' report states that the profit was £330,000 compared with £240,000 the previous year. It does not say that the £330,000 is the profit before tax or that the £240,000 was the profit after tax.

d. The directors' remuneration is stated at £200,000 without any breakdown.

e. The auditors were not allowed to attend the stocktaking.

f. The company did not have a detailed breakdown of new plant and machinery. The total was obtained from a computer file which was overwritten. The details could with much difficulty be resurrected from the original invoices which are filed with other invoices in supplier name order.

g. A director informed the auditor that the company owned a warehouse in South Africa which had been paid for by the company at £50,000. In fact the director had fraudulently misappropriated the money. The auditor could not go to South Africa and had no other evidence on the warehouse.

h. The auditor had not visited the branch at Glasgow and she found that no returns had been received from that branch and the figures included in the accounts were those of the previous year.

3 The auditor and the Companies Act

Introduction

1. Most statutory audits are conducted for companies and are governed by the rules of the Companies Act 1985, as amended by the Companies Act 1989.

   This chapter sets out the rules on the requirements:

   - of a company to have an auditor
   - on the appointment of an auditor
   - on the remuneration of an auditor
   - on the removal of an auditor
   - on the resignation of an auditor
   - on who can be an auditor of a company.

   Finally the current professional body rules on *registered auditors* are discussed.

Appointment of auditors

2. Section 384 states that every company shall appoint an auditor. The only exceptions to this rule are that certain small companies and *dormant companies* do not need an auditor. A dormant (= sleeping) company is one where in a period no significant accounting transaction occurred. Small company exemption is dealt with in the chapter on small companies.

3. Section 385 states how auditors of companies are to be appointed:

   a. The company shall, at each general meeting at which Accounts are presented (usually at each Annual General Meeting [AGM]), appoint an auditor or auditors. Note that it is the company (i.e. the shareholders) who appoint the auditor.

   b. The appointment is for the period of time known as the *tenure of office* and that is from the conclusion of the meeting to the conclusion of the following general meeting at which accounts are laid (= presented at the meeting).

   c. On the commencement of a new company the directors may appoint the auditor at any time before the first AGM.

   d. There are some exemptions for private companies which are dealt with in the chapter on small companies.

   e. In the event of no auditor being appointed as required, Section 387 states that the company must inform the Secretary of State within one week. The Secretary of State may then make an appointment.

   f. Casual vacancies in the office of auditor (perhaps caused by death) may be filled by the directors.

Remuneration of an auditor

4. Under Section 390A the remuneration of an auditor is fixed by the person/persons appointing. Usually this is the company in General Meeting and many company AGM agendas include something like:

'To re-appoint the auditors Fussy & Co. as the company's auditors until the conclusion of the next AGM of the Company, and to authorise the Board to fix the auditors' remuneration.'

You will notice that the independence of the auditor is honoured by an appointment by the members in General Meeting but may appear to be compromised by the delegation of the fixing of their remuneration to the Board.

5. Section 390A goes on to require that the remuneration of the auditor shall be stated in a note in the company's accounts. Remuneration disclosable is for auditing services only (i.e. excluding other services e.g. taxation) but must include sums paid in respect of expenses and the money value and nature of any benefit in kind.

    Under *The Companies Act 1985 (Disclosure of Remuneration for Non-Audit Work) Regulations 1991*, disclosure in the Accounts must also be made of remuneration (including benefits in kind) paid to the auditor for non-audit work (preparing accounts, tax, consultancy etc.) Inclusion must be made of the remuneration from non-audit work paid to associates of the audit firm (e.g. management consultancy firms which are connected with the auditors) and for work done for subsidiaries of the client. The auditors must supply the necessary information to the company. This requirement does not apply to small and medium-sized companies.

    Thus auditors' remuneration must be disclosed to members and other users of the accounts and cannot be hidden by including it in a global figure such as administration expenses. Look it up every time you see a copy of a company's Annual Report and Accounts.

The removal of an auditor

6. The Companies Act takes a serious view of the removal of an auditor and there are a number of special procedures and rules to go through in order to effect a change of auditor.

    Suppose that the directors prepare the accounts with the inclusion of some unusual accounting policy in order to increase profits in a particular year. The auditors (Fussy & Co.), being honourable people, may feel that the unusual policy is not acceptable and inform the Directors that they would qualify their report if the policy is not changed. The directors may decide to abandon the policy for this year and change the auditors to Flexible & Co. in order that in future years the unusual policy may be adopted. Flexible & Co. may privately indicate that the unusual policy is acceptable to them.

    Company law takes the view that company auditors must be capable of being changed if the MEMBERS wish it but is designed:

    −   to ensure that the reality of the usual company situation, where the appointment of the auditor which is nominally by the members, cannot be manipulated by the directors to change an auditor who is doing his duty but who does not please the directors.

    −   to ensure that maximum publicity is given to any proposed change of auditor so that members are aware of the matter and can make informed choices

    −   to give an auditor who the directors would like to remove every opportunity to state his case.

7. The Companies Act legislation is:

    a. Section 391 states that a company may remove its auditor by ordinary resolution (a simple majority) notwithstanding anything in any agreement between it and him.

The Section also requires that the company shall give notice of the resolution to the registrar within 14 days on pain of a fine.

   b. Section 391A requires that:

– special notice (28 days) must be given to the company of intention to move a resolution to remove an auditor or appoint some person other than the retiring auditor. However most such resolutions are moved by the directors.

– on receipt of such an intended resolution the company shall forthwith send a copy to the auditor who may be removed and also to the intended new auditor. At least the removal cannot be done behind the auditor's back.

– the auditor, proposed to be removed, may make with respect to the intended resolution, *representations* in writing to the company and request their notification to members. Thus the auditor who does not wish to be removed can state his case and require it to be sent to the members. Note that representations may not exceed a reasonable length.

– the company must do two things (unless the representations are received too late): state the fact of representations being received in any notice of the resolution and: send a copy to every member of the company to whom notice of the meeting has been or will be sent.

– the auditor has a general right to speak at the meeting on the subject of his intended removal and, if the representations have not been sent to the members he/she has the right to have them read out at the meeting.

Note:

   i. The object of these rules is not to prevent the auditor being removed, if the members wish to remove him, but to ensure that he has adequate opportunity to put his case to the members before they vote on the resolution.

   ii. Section 391A allows the company to seek an injunction against the auditor to restrain him from using his representations as a vehicle for needless publicity for defamatory matter.

   c. In the case of private companies where an election is in force to dispense with annual appointment of auditors then Section 393 says:

– any member may deposit notice in writing at the registered office proposing that the appointment of the company's auditors be brought to an end.

– the directors must then convene a meeting of the company within 28 days and propose a resolution to decide the matter.

– if the directors do not convene a meeting then the proposer may do so himself.

In these cases the rules of Sections 391 and 391A still apply.

Resignation of auditors

8. Auditors can resign. There are two main reasons why they may wish to do so. These are:

   a. The obvious reasons: ill health, the company have grown too large for a small audit firm, the fee is inadequate etc.

   b. Where the auditor concludes that because of fraud or other irregularity the accounts do not show a true and fair view and there is no immediate opportunity to report to members. He would be unable to report to members if the entity refused to issue its financial statements, or at another stage in the year the auditor has considerable doubts about management's integrity.

9. Procedures are:

   a. Section 392:

     – an auditor may resign by depositing a notice in writing to that effect at the registered office. This is not effective unless accompanied by a *statement of circumstances*.

     – the company must send a copy of the notice of resignation to the Registrar of Companies within 14 days on pain of a fine. Thus any person searching the file will have notice of the resignation.

   b. Section 394:

     – The statement of circumstances should contain a statement of any circumstances (e.g. fraudulent trading) which he/she considers should be brought to the attention of members or *creditors* or if he/she considers that there are no such circumstances then a statement that there are none.

     – the auditor can cease to be auditor by simply not seeking re-election. However in that case he must still deposit a statement of circumstances and there are time limits for this.

     – if the statement of circumstances contains matters which the auditor considers should be brought to the attention of members or creditors then the company must within 14 days of receipt of it send a copy to all persons entitled to receive copies of the accounts or apply to the court.

     – the court may order that the statement may not be sent out if it thinks the statement is seeking needless publicity for defamatory matter but otherwise the statement must be sent out.

     – the auditor must send his statement to the Registrar.

   Section 392A gives further rights and duties to the resigning auditor:

     – the auditor may deposit with his notice of resignation and his statement of circumstances, a notice calling on the company to convene an Extraordinary Meeting.

     – the directors must call such a meeting within 21 days on pain of a fine and must send out copies of the statement and if they fail to do so the auditor can require that the statement be read at the meeting.

There are the usual caveats re the court and defamatory matters.

Who can be an auditor?

10. The Companies Act 1989 radically changed the law in relation to who can be an auditor. The object of the changes was to incorporate into English Law EC directives and to increase regulation of the auditing profession in line with the general modern tendency to regulate everything that moves.

The sections involved are of the 1989 Act Sections 24 to 54.

11. Section 24 states the general purpose of the law which is to:

'secure that only persons who are properly supervised and appropriately qualified are appointed auditors, and that audits by persons so appointed are carried out properly and with integrity and with a proper degree of independence.'

12. Section 25:

    (1) A person is eligible for appointment as a company auditor only if he –

    (a) is a member of a recognised supervisory body, and

    (b) is eligible for the appointment under the rules of that body.

    The Section goes on to allow either individuals or firms to be appointed a company auditor.

13. Section 34 concerns auditors who are not members of professional bodies recognised by the Companies 1967. They retain rights to audit individual unquoted companies as a consequence of being in office when the Companies Act 1967 came into force. There are still some of these accountants around and many are now members of The Association of Authorised Public Accountants which is a recognised supervisory body. The Association is responsible for regulating its members but in fact has subcontracted the actual monitoring to the Chartered Association of Certified Accountants.

14. Section 27 repeats earlier legislation but with modifications and states that certain persons with connections to a company are ineligible to act as auditor to that company. These persons are:

    – officers and employees of the company.

    – partners or employees of such persons or a partnership of which such a person is a partner.

    – Persons who have connection with the company or where the company has a connection with an associate of his of any description specified in regulations made by the Secretary of State.

    Note that:

    a. Persons who are ineligible to act as auditor of a particular company are also ineligible to act as auditor of a parent, subsidiary, or fellow subsidiary of that company.

    b. The whole purpose of this sections is to secure the *independence* of the auditor from the company.

15. Section 28 makes it an offence for a person to act as a company auditor if he is ineligible and requires vacation of office if he becomes ineligible.

16. Section 29 gives the Secretary of State power to require a second audit if the first was carried out by an ineligible auditor. It is likely that this will be a very rare occurrence.

17. Section 30 is on supervisory bodies.

    A supervisory body is a body established in the UK which maintains and enforces rules as to the eligibility of persons seeking appointments as company auditors and the conduct of audit work which are binding on such persons because they are members of such bodies or subject to its control.

    Recognition will only be given to a supervisory body if the body has rules on: holding of appropriate qualifications, professional integrity and independence, technical standards, investigation of complaints and meeting of claims arising out of audit work.

There are currently five *supervisory bodies*: the three Institutes of Chartered Accountants, the Chartered Association of Certified Accountants and the Association of Authorised Public Accountants. The last is responsible for regulating its members but in fact has subcontracted the actual monitoring to the Chartered Association of Certified Accountants.

18. Section 31 sets out the persons who hold appropriate qualifications. Essentially the only persons so qualified are members of the three Institutes of Chartered Accountants and the Chartered Association of Certified Accountants plus pre-1967 auditors of certain unquoted companies.

19. Section 32 considers *qualifying bodies*. A qualifying body means a body established in the UK which offers a professional qualification in accountancy. The body must have enforceable rules on: admission to or expulsion from a course of study leading to a qualification, the award or deprivation of a qualification, the approval of a person for the purposes of giving practical training or the withdrawal of such approval, entry requirements, courses of instruction, professional experience, examination and practical training.

The currently recognised qualifying bodies are the three Institutes of Chartered Accountants and the Chartered Association of Certified Accountants.

The Act recognises a distinction between supervisory bodies and qualifying bodies but in practice all bodies except the AAPA are both.

20. Sections 35 and 36 require supervisory bodies to maintain a *register* of persons and firms which are eligible to be company auditors and to make the register available to the public.

Professional body rules

21. The professional bodies have strict rules on granting *practising certificates*. Members of the professional bodies cannot practise or be an auditor unless they have a *practising certificate*. It may also be necessary to have *registered auditor* status. Obtaining a *practising certificate* or *registered auditor* status is difficult and the rules about experience are strictly enforced. The precise rules change regularly and can be obtained by enquiry of the relevant professional body.

Summary

22. a. Every company (except dormant companies and some exempt small companies) must appoint an auditor.

   b. Auditors are normally elected by the members (shareholders) at the Annual General Meeting when Accounts are presented.

   c. Tenure of office is usually till the end of the next AGM so that they can report on the accounts presented at that AGM.

   d. Directors may appoint the first auditor of a company and may fill a casual vacancy.

   e. Special rules apply to private companies who have elected to dispense with the laying of accounts at an AGM and /or have elected to dispense with the holding of AGMs.

   f. It is possible for private companies to elect to dispense with annual appointment of auditors.

   g. In certain circumstances the Secretary of State may appoint an auditor.

h. The remuneration of the auditor is normally fixed by the persons/groups appointing the auditor. Full disclosure of remuneration in the accounts is required.

i. An auditor can be removed from office but the detailed rules must be followed. An auditor, who it is proposed to remove, has rights including the making of representations and the requisitioning of a meeting.

j. An auditor can resign either because he wishes to for his own reasons or to draw attention to some matter (e.g. illegal conduct) relating to the company. He must then write a statement of circumstances or a statement that there are no notable circumstances and this must be circulated to members and the Registrar of Companies.

k. The statement of circumstances rules apply to any situation where an auditor leaves office.

l. The Companies Act prohibits certain persons who have personal connections with the company from also being its auditor.

m. The Companies Act 1989 radically changed rules as to who can be an auditor in order to ensure that only persons who are properly supervised and appropriately qualified are appointed auditors, and that audits by persons so appointed are carried out properly and with integrity and with a proper degree of independence.

n. The Act established the idea of recognised supervisory bodies and recognised qualifying bodies. Only persons who are members of and authorised by supervisory bodies can be company auditors.

o. The supervisory bodies have set up Registers of eligible company auditors.

p. The supervisory bodies have complex rules for authorising Registered Auditors and have supervisory regimes in force. These include requirements for Professional Indemnity Insurance and Continuing Professional Education and monitoring visits.

Points to note

23. a. The rules require all company auditors to be supervised by a supervisory body. Currently the supervisory bodies are the three Institutes of Chartered Accountants, the Chartered Association of Certified Accountants and the Association of Authorised Public Accountants. All but the last are qualifying bodies. The rules are complex and need not detain students too long until they have qualified and seek to become Registered Auditors.

b. EU auditors can seek membership of, and authorisation by, the ACCA. There are safeguards on the competence of such persons.

c. The ICAEW authorises firms and ACCA individual members.

d. The Companies Act 1989 ended the prohibition on corporate bodies (e.g. companies) being auditors. This means that professional firms could at least in law incorporate as limited companies.

e. Schedule 11 (on the subject of supervisory bodies) requires that any firm appointed as auditors must be controlled by qualified persons. This means that firms of accountants may have unqualified members or partners but that a majority of the partners/Board of Directors/ shareholdings must be qualified persons. The supervisory bodies have complex rules to cover this point.

f. The objects of all these rules are to:
    – ensure all company auditors are fit and proper persons
    – ensure professional integrity and independence

- have technical standards
- have procedures to maintain competence
- ensure practitioners have insurance
- investigate complaints
- maintain a register of eligible auditors
- monitor and enforce the rules.

g. These rules apply to companies registered under the Companies Act 1985. However similar rules apply also to many other bodies. These include bodies registered under other Acts of Parliament e.g. Building Societies, Financial Service Companies, Clubs and Societies registered under the Friendly Societies Act, Associations registered under the Industrial and Provident Societies Act, Solicitors, members of the Association of British Travel Agents etc.

Special rules apply to Charities under the Charities Act 1993 and we will deal with these in a later chapter.

Other bodies may have rules in their constitutions which require the audit to be by a Registered Auditor.

h. The rules in this chapter both directly under statute and by the professional bodies as required by statute are very complex. The ACCA publish annual reports to the President of the Board of Trade which report among other matters the shortcomings of firms visited under the monitoring visits. Presumably these shortcomings will be remedied and so the new rules will have raised standards. Whether the rules have improved the independence of auditors is still an open question. The basic structure where auditors are appointed by the shareholders remains but this is manipulated by directors in many cases. They can do this because of the inertia of shareholders. The delegation of auditor's remuneration to the Directors also mitigates against true independence in that it leaves the auditor beholden to the directors for his remuneration and that may affect his attitude in any dispute with the directors. Hopefully auditors maintain an independent attitude in any circumstances.

i. The rules have a large economic cost. Better auditing (e.g. circularisation of debtors which was not often done in the audit of small companies) has an economic cost but it is less clear if it has any economic benefit. Regulation may seem to be wholly good but in practice bad auditors still manage to survive and not all business people want the burdens of more audit regulation. The impact of extra regulation may be that many businesses do not incorporate and thus lose the benefit of limited liability. The impact of any extra regulation is to change at least some economic behaviour, whether for good or ill is a matter for discussion.

Student self testing questions *Questions with answers apparent from the text*

1. a. Must every company have an auditor? (2)
   b. Who may appoint a company's auditor? (3)
   c. What period of time is covered by an auditor's tenure of office? (3)
   d. Outline the rules when a private company has:
      - elected to dispense with the requirement to hold AGMs
      - elected to dispense with the requirement to lay accounts at the AGM
        elected not to appoint its auditor annually. (3)
   e. How is the remuneration of an auditor fixed? (4)

f. Outline the rules on disclosure of an auditor's remuneration. (5)
g. How can an auditor be removed from office? (7)
h. What rights has an auditor whose removal is proposed? (7)
i. Why may an auditor wish to resign? (8)
j. What are the rules re the resignation of an auditor? (9)
k. Who cannot be a company's auditor? (12–14)
l. What is a supervisory body and which bodies are so recognised? (17)
m. What rules must such bodies have? (17)
n. What is a qualifying body and which bodies are so recognised? (19)
o. What rules must such bodies have? (21)

Case study 1

Associated Gargoyles Ltd is a private company with only three shareholders, all of whom are directors. They wish to reduce company formalities to a minimum.

Discuss how this may be done.

They wish to appoint Ted as auditor, a director's brother who is a chartered accountant working for British Gas PLC.

Can they do this? They want, in any case, to remove Harry, the present auditor. How can this be done and what rights and duties does Harry have?

Examination questions

1. Growfast plc was formed on 1 August 1990 in order to manufacture minicomputers. The directors are unsure as to their responsibilities, and the nature of their relationship with the external auditors. The audit partner has asked you to visit the client and explain to the directors the more fundamental aspects of the accountability of the company and their relationship with the auditor.

   Required:

   Explain to the directors of Growfast PLC

   a. Why there is a need for an audit. (5 marks)
   b. How the auditor of a public company may be appointed under the Companies Act 1985. (5 marks)
   c. What the auditor's rights are under the Companies Act 1985. (6 marks)
   d. The responsibilities of the directors in relation to the accounting function of the company. (4 marks)

   (ACCA) (20 marks)

2. The Companies Act includes provisions regarding the appointment, duties and powers of a company's auditor.

   Required:

   a. State the ways in which an auditor can be appointed; (5 marks)
   b. Detail the statutory duties imposed on an auditor; (5 marks)
   c. Specify the statutory powers given to the auditor to enable him to carry out his work. (5 marks)

   (AAT) (Total 15 marks)

4 Accounting records

Introduction

1. This chapter details the Companies Act requirements on the keeping of accounting records by companies.

2. An auditor must know these rules because he has to carry out investigations to enable him to form an opinion on whether the company has kept proper accounting records and has proper returns from branches not visited by the auditor. Further, if he forms an opinion that the company have not kept proper accounting records, he has to say so in his report. The word 'proper' here means in accordance with custom or appropriate to the circumstances.

3. Note that the responsibility for keeping proper accounting records lies wholly with the directors.

4. The Companies Act 1989 made some minor amendments to the principal Act (The Companies Act 1985) and it is the amended version that is reproduced here.

5. The chapter also lists the statutory books.

Section 221:

(1) Every company shall keep accounting records which are sufficient to show and explain the company's transactions and are such as to –

(a) disclose with reasonable accuracy, at any time, the financial position of the company at that time, and

(b) enable the directors to ensure that any balance sheet and profit and loss account prepared under this Part complies with the requirements of this Act.

(2) The accounting records shall in particular contain –

(a) entries from day to day of all sums of money received and expended by the company, and the matters in respect of which the receipt and expenditure takes place, and

(b) a record of the assets and liabilities of the company.

(3) If the company's business involves dealing in goods, the accounting records shall contain –

(a) statements of stock held by the company at the end of each financial year of the company,

(b) all statements of stocktakings from which any such statement of stock as is mentioned in paragraph (a) has been or is to be prepared, and

(c) except in the case of goods sold by way of ordinary retail trade, statements of all goods sold and purchased, showing the goods and the buyers and sellers in sufficient detail to enable all these to be identified.

(4) A parent company which has a subsidiary undertaking in relation to which the above requirements do not apply shall take reasonable steps to secure that the undertaking keeps such accounting records as to enable the directors of the parent company to ensure that any balance sheet and profit and loss account prepared under this Part complies with the requirements of this Act.

(5) If a company fails to comply with any provision of this section, every officer of the company who is in default is guilty of an offence unless he shows that he acted honestly and that in the circumstances in which the company's business was carried on the default was excusable.

(6) A person guilty of an offence under this section is liable to imprisonment or a fine, or both.

Subject matter

6. a. Sums of money received and expended and the matters about which the receipts or payments took place – *a cash book.*

  b. A record of assets and liabilities – presumably including sales and bought ledgers.

  c. Where the company deals in goods then:

  i. Statements of stock held at each year end

  ii. Statements of stock takings from which (i) are prepared

  iii. Except for ordinary retail sales (= cash sales over the counter) statements of all goods purchased and sold, showing the buyers and sellers and identifying them – sales and purchase day books.

7. a. The accounting records must be sufficient to disclose with reasonable accuracy, at any time, the financial position of the company at that time.

  It must be pointed out that a Balance Sheet could only be produced if stock was taken and that is only required at year ends.

  b. Enable the directors to ensure that any balance sheet and profit and loss account comply with the Act.

8. Subsection (4) is concerned with subsidiary undertakings abroad.

9. The company's accounting records can be kept wherever the directors think fit.

  Special rules relate to accounting records kept outside Great Britain:

  a. Accounts and *returns* in respect of such business shall be sent to Great Britain.

  b. These accounts and returns sent to Great Britain must be such as to:

  i. Disclose with reasonable accuracy the financial position of the overseas business at intervals not exceeding *six months.*

  ii. Enable the directors to ensure that Accounts comply with the Act as to *form* and *content.*

Statutory books

10. The Companies Act requires a company to keep the following books:

  a. Proper accounting records – Section 221.

  b. A register of directors and secretaries – Sections 288, 289.

  c. A register of charges (fixed and floating) – Section 407.

  d. Minute books of meetings of the company, meetings of its directors and meetings of its managers – Section 382.

  e. An indexed register of members – Sections 352–354.

  f. An indexed register of each director's interest in shares and debentures of the company and those of his spouse, infant children and some other persons, trusts and companies connected with him – Sections 324–328.

  g. Public companies must keep a register of shareholders who have an interest of 3% or more in the nominal value of the voting share capital – Section 211.

The auditor's interest in the statutory books

11. The auditor is interested in the statutory books being properly maintained because:–

    a. They are directly concerned with the Accounts (especially a. and c.).

    b. They are audit evidence to be used in verifying detailed items in the accounts; for example the total share capital shown by the sum of the individual share holdings in the register of members must agree with the share capital recorded in the books of account.

    c. Failure to maintain proper records of any sort casts doubt upon the accuracy and reliability of the records generally.

Summary

12. a. The Companies Act lays down rules for keeping of proper accounting records and for proper returns from branches including those overseas.

    b. The Companies Act also requires a company to keep a range of additional records called the statutory books.

    c. The directors are responsible for the maintenance of accounting records and statutory books.

    d. The auditor has a duty to investigate and form an opinion on whether proper accounting records have been kept.

Points to note

13. a. The Companies Act lays down rules for the keeping of proper accounting records and proper returns from branches overseas.

    b. The directors have the responsibility for seeing that the company obeys the rules.

    c. Failure to obey the rules may mean that:

        i. Proper books of account have not been kept.

        ii Proper returns have not been received.

        iii. Sufficient information may not be available for the proper disclosure of matters of which the Companies Acts require detailed disclosure.

        iv. Insufficient evidence may be available for confirmation of items in the accounts.

    All these matters are of direct concern to the auditor who may have to consider a qualified report.

    d. Returns in the context of this chapter are of two types:

        i. Those from branches in the UK. The auditors must see that proper returns have been received by head office when he has not himself visited the branches. Some companies have numerous branches, e.g. Woolworths. The auditor cannot be expected to visit them all.

        ii. Those from branches overseas. These are subject to special statutory requirements but the auditor has the same duty to satisfy himself on overseas branch matters as he does for UK branches.

    e. The company law referred to in this chapter may seem very tedious but examiners in auditing frequently require knowledge of these matters.

    f. There are penalties for failing to keep proper accounting records or statutory books.

g. Particular problems that may cause the auditor to reflect on whether proper accounting records have been kept include:

- delays in writing up the records
- frequent alterations in records
- exceptionally large numbers of errors found by the auditor
- audit trail difficulties (audit trail is the ability to follow a transaction through the records and documentation. It may be lost in some computer systems)
- computer problems including failure of software, chaos, hardware breakdowns, changes of computer staff, viruses, loss of data etc.

h. Organisations other than companies may have specific statutory requirements re accounting records (e.g. financial service companies) and the auditor needs to ensure that these have been complied with.

i. Note the requirement in Section 221(1)(a) 'at any time'.

Case study 1

Mr and Mrs Seamus O'Neill jointly own a company, O'Neill Fashion Shirts Ltd operating in London. The company buy from a range of suppliers and sell on credit to retail shops nationwide. Copy sales invoices are retained and when the customer pays, the invoice is so marked. A proper cash book is kept. Output VAT is obtained by adding up the VAT on the invoices using an add-listing machine. All this is done neatly and accurately. Incoming purchase invoices are placed in a box and when paid are marked paid and filed in a proper file. Input VAT is obtained from an analysis column in the cash book. The company have a branch in Dublin run by Mrs O'Neill's sister. The branch operates exactly the same system. At the end of each year a summary of the books is sent to London where accounts are prepared and an audit done by O'Connor, a certified accountant.

Seamus asks O'Connor whether his books of account are adequate. O'Connor also maintains the company's statutory books and makes a separate charge for so doing. To justify the charge O'Connor takes Seamus through the statutory books and explains why they are kept.

Discussion

Are the books adequate?

Does a private company need all the statutory books?

Student self testing questions *Questions with answers apparent from the text*

1. a. What must appear in books of account? (5)
    b. List the statutory books. (10)
    c. Who are responsible for maintaining the books of account and the statutory books? (3)
    d. What is the auditor's interest in these documents? (11)

Exercise

1. List the accounting records that Positron Electrical Wholesalers Ltd should keep.

5 Accounting requirements of the Companies Act

Introduction

1. This chapter outlines the Companies Act requirements on the accounting reference date, the form and content of company accounts, the procedure on the completion of the accounts, modified accounts and the publication of full and abridged accounts.

2. An auditor must know these rules because:

    a. The majority of audits are company audits.

    b. The principal objective of the audit is to report on the truth and fairness of the financial statements.

    c. Section 235 requires the auditor to state in his report whether, in his opinion, the Accounts have been properly prepared in accordance with the Act.

    d. Examiners in auditing require this knowledge in students.

3. The responsibility for preparing financial statements, laying them before the company (= presenting them to shareholders) and delivering them to Companies House lies wholly with the directors.

Accounting reference date

4. Every company has to have a year end and the profit and loss account is for the year ending on that date and the balance sheet is made up as at that date. A company's year end is known as the *accounting reference date* and the financial statements are made up for the *accounting reference periods* ending on that date.

5. Sections 223 to 225 give the law on this matter in unbelievable length. In short:

    a. the company can give notice to the Registrar of its chosen date.

    b. if this is not done then the date is the last day of the month in which the anniversary of its incorporation falls (or 31 March for companies formed before 1990).

    c. the date can be changed by going through the prescribed procedures.

6. The company must prepare accounts for each and every accounting reference period. The actual date used may be up to seven days either side of the accounting reference date.

Financial statements required

7. The following financial statements must be prepared:

    a. A Profit and Loss account for each accounting reference period – Section 226.

    b. A Balance Sheet as at the accounting reference date – Section 226.

    c. If the company is a holding company then group accounts must also be prepared – Section 227. It is permissible and is the common practice not to publish the company's own profit and loss account but to publish a consolidated profit and loss account which shows how much of the consolidated profit or loss for the financial year is dealt with in the company's individual accounts – Section 230.

   d. Notes attached to and forming part of the Accounts:

     i   Giving the detailed information required by Schedule 4 without cluttering the financial statements.

     ii. Giving certain required additional information (e.g. the emoluments of directors) – Section 232 and Schedule 6.

   e. A directors' report – Section 234.

   f. The auditors' report – Section 235.

Form of company accounts

8. a. The balance sheet must follow either of the two *formats* included in Schedule 4.

    b. The profit and loss account must follow one of the four formats given in Schedule 4.

    c. There are complex rules on the interpretation and variation of the format rules in Schedule 4.

    d. It is possible to depart from the formats only if special circumstances require departure in order that the overriding requirement of a true and fair view be met. In practice departure from the formats is very rare.

Accounting principles

9. The 4th Schedule paragraphs 9 to 15:

ACCOUNTING PRINCIPLES

Preliminary

9. *Subject to paragraph 15 below, the amounts to be included in respect of all items shown in a company's accounts shall be determined in accordance with the principles set out in paragraphs 10 to 14.*

Accounting principles

10. *The company shall be presumed to be carrying on business as a going concern.*

11. *Accounting policies shall be applied consistently within the same accounts and from one financial year to the next.*

12. *The amount of any item shall be determined on a prudent basis, and in particular –*

    (a) only profits realised at the balance sheet date shall be included in the profit and loss account; and

    (b) all liabilities and losses which have arisen or are likely to arise in respect of the financial year to which the accounts relate or a previous financial year shall be taken into account, including those which only become apparent between the balance sheet date and the date on which it is signed on behalf of the board of directors in pursuance of Section 238 of this Act.

13. *All income and charges relating to the financial year to which the accounts relate shall be taken into account, without regard to the date of receipt or payment.*

14 . *In determining the aggregate amount of any item the amount of each individual asset or liability that fails to be taken into account shall be determined separately.*

Departure from the accounting principles

15. *If it appears to the directors of a company that there are special reasons for departing from any of the principles stated above in preparing the company's accounts in respect of any financial*

year they may do so, but particulars of the departure, the reasons for it and its effect shall be given in a note to the accounts.

The accounting principles required are:

a. going concern

b. consistency

c. prudence/conservatism

d. realisation/accruals.

The principle enunciated in para 14 does not seem to have a name in the accounting literature. It could be applied to stocks – the concept of lower of cost and net realisable value must be applied to individual items of stock and not to stock as a whole.

10. Detailed rules on the application of the accounting principles are also given in Schedule 4 both for *historical* accounts and for *alternative* accounting (current cost, i.e. adjusting for inflation). For example there are rules or guidance on valuing fixed assets, the value of manufactured work in progress and finished goods and FIFO, LIFO, etc. for fungible items.

Content – detailed disclosure requirements

11. Schedule 4 gives extensive detailed rules on the *minimum* information which must be given in the Accounts or in notes attached to them.

There is no objection made against Accounts giving *more* information than the minimum but in practice most Accounts just disclose the minimum required by the law.

Procedure on completion of the Accounts

12. a. The Accounts comprising:
    - the balance sheet
    - the profit and loss account
    - the directors' report
    - the auditor's report
    - the group accounts where required.

    must be approved by the board and then the balance sheet must be signed by a director of the company on behalf of the board – Section 233.

    b. A copy of the Accounts must be sent to all persons entitled at least 21 days before the AGM – Section 238.

    c. Copies of the Accounts must be *laid before* the company in general meeting (usually the AGM) – Section 241.

    d. A copy of the Accounts must be *delivered* to the registrar of companies – Section 242.

Period allowed for laying and delivering accounts

13. The directors of a company are required by the Act (Section 242) to *lay* and *deliver* the Accounts in accordance with a timescale as:

    a. Private companies – within 10 months after the end of the accounting reference period.

    b. Public companies – within 7 months after the end of the accounting reference period.

These times may be extended by three months in companies with overseas interests.

Abbreviated accounts

14. Sections 246 and 247 and The Companies Act 1985 (Accounts of Small and Medium-Sized Enterprises and Publication of Accounts in ECUs) Regulations 1992 gives a number of *exemptions* to small and medium-sized companies. These are:

    a. exemption for both small and medium-sized companies from the requirement of *disclosure* of whether the accounts have been prepared in accordance with applicable accounting standards.

    b. small companies need only produce a slightly reduced form of Balance Sheet.

    c. small companies are exempt from some filing requirements. Notably they need only file an abbreviated Balance Sheet and need not include many of the notes to the accounts. They do not need to file a Profit and Loss Account or the directors' report.

    d. medium-sized companies can file a slightly abbreviated Profit and Loss Account and there is no need for the note analysing turnover over classes and markets.

15. Small and medium-sized companies are defined as companies which satisfy two or more of the following:

	Small	Medium-sized
i. Turnover does not exceed	£2.8 million	£11.2 million
ii. Balance Sheet total does not exceed	£1.4 million	£5.6 million
iv. Average number of employees does not exceed	50	250

    The exemptions do not apply to a company if in the year it is:

    − a public company

    − a banking or insurance company

    − an authorised person under the Financial Services Act 1986

    − a member of an ineligible group.

    An ineligible group is one in which any of its members is:

    − a public company

    − an authorised institution under the Banking Act 1987

    − an Insurance company to which part II of the Insurance Companies Act 1982 applies

    − an authorised person under the Financial Services Act 1986.

    In addition, a parent company does not qualify as small or medium-sized unless the group headed by it qualifies as a small or medium-sized group (see chapter on group accounts).

16. There are formalities to be gone through if abbreviated accounts are filed:

    a. The Balance Sheet shall contain:

       − a statement that advantage is taken of the exemptions

       − a statement of the grounds on which, in the directors' opinion, the company is entitled to those exemptions.

    b. Inclusion of a special report by the auditor stating that in his opinion:

       i. the directors are entitled to deliver abbreviated accounts;

    ii.   the accounts have been properly prepared as abbreviated accounts.

The full text of the auditor's report must be included in the special report.

Publication of accounts

17. Section 240 has some rules on the publication of accounts.

A company may publish its statutory accounts. When it does so, it must also publish its auditors' report. Statutory accounts means the full accounts or the reduced accounts allowed to small or medium-sized companies.

Companies may also publish non-statutory accounts (formerly called abridged accounts) (Section 240). When it does, then it must also publish a statement:

    a.   that the accounts are not statutory accounts

    b.   whether statutory accounts have been delivered to the Registrar

    c.   whether the auditors have made a report

    d.   whether any such report has been qualified.

Dormant companies

18. Section 250 has some rules on dormant companies:

A company is dormant in a period if during the period no significant accounting transaction occurred. Such companies need not appoint an auditor but must still lay and deliver accounts.

Listed public companies

19. Section 251 has some special rules for limited public companies.

These are new in the Companies Act 1989 and the rules are:

    a.   Listed companies need not send full accounts to their shareholders but may instead send them a summary financial statement.

    b.   The company must send full accounts to members who require them.

    c.   There are regulations as to what must be included in the summary accounts derived from the full accounts.

    d.   The summary accounts must contain a statement that they are only a summary and also contain a statement from the *auditors* to whether the summary is consistent with the full accounts. The auditors' statement must also state whether their report was qualified or unqualified and if it was qualified give their report in full.

Summary

20. a.   The Companies Acts lay down very detailed rules on:

        i.   What financial statements are required.

       ii.   The form of the financial statements.

     iii.   The accounting principles to be followed.

     iv.   Detailed information to be disclosed.

      v.   Accounting period and time limits for laying and delivering accounts.

    b.   Specified exemptions from these rules are given to small and medium-sized companies.

c. Listed companies may send out summary financial statements.

Points to note

21. a. The Companies Act rules are voluminous and complex. They are properly the subject of texts in accounting or publications devoted to them and this chapter gives only a brief summary. Auditors must know the rules because their duties laid down by the Act include a requirement to report on the true and fair view and compliance with statute of the Accounts. Auditors also have specified duties in connection with the abbreviated accounts of small and medium-sized companies.

b. Auditing examinees are sometimes required to show specific and detailed knowledge of the rules.

c. In addition to the Companies Act requirements on Accounts, there are also two other sets of requirements to be fulfilled. These are:

   i. The Statements of Standard Accounting Practice and the Financial Reporting Standards. The detail of these is dealt with in a later chapter. However note that the SSAP and the FRS specify detailed principles of preparation, and disclosure requirements of the Profit and Loss Account and Balance Sheet but they also require additional financial statements.

   ii. Requirements under the Stock Exchange Listing Agreement for listed companies (and similarly for the Alternative Investment Market). There are also new requirements in the listing agreement concerning corporate governance.

d. Note the distinction between:

   i. *Laying* Accounts before the company. These must be full but there are some modifications for small and medium-sized companies. (See Statutory Instrument 1992/2452.)

   ii. *Delivering* (filing at Companies House). These can be, for small and medium-sized companies, abbreviated.

   iii. *Publication.* These can be *abridged.*

e. The Companies Act 1989 formally recognised the accounting standards and companies are now required to state, with their statement of accounting policies, whether the accounts have been prepared in accordance with applicable accounting standards and give particulars of any material departure from those standards and the reasons for any such departure.

f. Accounts must give a true and fair view. Note Section 226:

   (4) Where compliance with the provisions of that Schedule, and the other provisions of this Act as to the matters to be included in a company's individual accounts or in notes to those accounts, would not be sufficient to give a true and fair view, the necessary additional information shall be given in the accounts or in a note to them.

   (5) If in special circumstances compliance with any of those provisions is inconsistent with the requirement to give a true and fair view, the directors shall depart from that provision to the extent necessary to give a true and fair view.

   Particulars of any such departure, the reasons for it and its effect shall be given in a note to the accounts.

Case study 1

Pansy Retail Fashions Ltd was formed and began trading on 6 April 19-5 together with a subsidiary, Fairy Fashions Ltd.

At 31.3.-6 the company and its subsidiary had figures as:

	Pansy	Fairy
Turnover	£1.2 million	£1.4 million
Balance Sheet total	£1.6 million	£0.2 million
Average number of employees	65	20

Discussion

The directors have written to you with a series of questions:

a. What reference date they should use?

b. What financial statements they should prepare?

c. Which formats they should use for the accounts?

d. What is the latest date for the first annual general meeting (the company have a branch in Paris)?

e. Whether full accounts have to be sent to the shareholders and the registrar of companies?

Reply to them in the form of a letter.

Student self testing questions *Questions with answers apparent from the text*

1. a. What financial statements must be prepared? (7)
   b. What are the time limits for laying and delivery of accounts? (13)
   c. Define small and medium-sized companies. (15)
   d. What exemptions are available to them? (14)
   e. What are the rules on publishing accounts in abridged form? (17)
   f. What are the rules on sending out accounts in summary form? (19)
   g. What additional reports are required from an auditor? (16, 19)

Exercises

1. Hannah plc have both ordinary and preference shares, some of which have been redeemed out of profits in the year. They have also revalued the company's freehold property in the year and included the new figure in the accounts.
   State the Companies Act requirements on disclosure of these items.

2. Shineton Supplies PLC was formed many years ago by a group of retailers as a supplier of widgets. It is now one of many such suppliers and it is run by Glenk who sees it as his own private property. The shareholding is however very diverse (with 40 shareholders) and Glenk has only a small number of shares. The company is a PLC but is not listed. This year, its turnover was £2.2 million, its Balance Sheet total £1.7 million and it has 20 employees.
   Required
   a. What exemptions on preparing, filing and laying accounts are available? Glenk is

anxious to give as little information as posssible to his shareholders or his competitors.

b. What options are open to the company to secure yet more exemptions?

Professional rules

The next part of the book is concerned with various rules and guidelines on auditing and auditors laid down by the professional accounting bodies. There are chapters on the auditing standards and guidelines, accounting standards, professional conduct, and finally, the letter of engagement.

6 Auditing standards and guidelines

Introduction

1. The professional accounting bodies are very anxious to improve and maintain high standards in the conduct of audits. To that end they have set up the Auditing Practices Board. This authoritative body issues Statements of Auditing Standards (SASs) which are mandatory and Practice Notes which are helpful and indicative of good practice.

    In addition there is an International Auditing Practices Committee (IAPC) which is a committee of the International Federation of Accountants (IFAC). This committee issues International Standards on Auditing (ISAs) and International Auditing Practice Statements. Generally the UK SASs cover the same ground as the ISAs and most UK SASs state that compliance with this SAS ensures also compliance with a stated ISA. There is some current movement towards convergence of UK and international standards.

Statements of auditing standards

2. Each SAS has two types of material:
    a. Basic principles and essential procedures with which auditors are required to comply. These tend to be general. For example in SAS140, there is a basic procedure – auditors should ensure that the engagement letter documents and confirms their acceptance of the appointment, and includes a summary of the responsibilities of the directors and of the auditors, the scope of the engagement and the form of any reports. Each basic principle and essential procedure statement within an SAS is given a number. For example SAS 440.2 – auditors should obtain evidence that the directors acknowledge their collective responsibility for the preparation of the financial statements and have approved the financial statements.
    b. Explanatory and other material which, rather than being prescriptive is designed to assist auditors in interpreting and applying auditing standards. For example an essential procedure in SAS 430 is that auditors should, when determining sample sizes, consider sampling risk, the amount of error that would be acceptable and the extent to which they expect to find errors. These terms (sampling risk etc.) are then explained at length and advice given on their interpretation in practice.

    Auditors must comply with the numbered Statements of Auditing Standards. Apparent failure to comply may be enquired into by the appropriate committee of the relevant accountancy body and may lead to disciplinary or regulatory action. The professional body may withdraw registration from an auditor, who cannot then conduct company audits and is thus partly deprived of his livelihood. In addition the courts may take into account the SASs when considering if audit work was adequate in negligence cases. The explanatory and other material has less authority in theory but not much less in practice.

3. Current SASs are: (with corresponding ISA number in brackets):

100. Objectives and general principles governing an audit of financial statements (200)

110. Fraud and error (240)

120. Consideration of law and regulations (250)

130. The going concern basis in financial statements (570)

140. Engagement letters (210)

150. Subsequent events (560)

160. Other information in documents containing audited financial statements (revised 1999) (720)

200. Planning (300)

210. Knowledge of the business (310)

220. Materiality and the audit (320)

230. Working papers (230)

240. Quality control for audit work (revised 2000) (220)

300. Accounting and internal control systems and audit risk assessments (400)

400. Audit evidence (500 and 501)

410. Analytical procedures (520)

420. Audit of accounting estimates (540)

430. Audit sampling (530)

440. Management representations (580)

450. Opening balances and comparatives (510 and 710)

460. Related parties (550)

470. Overall review of financial statements

480. Service organisations (issued 1999) (402)

500. Considering the work of internal audit (610)

510. The relationship between principal auditors and other auditors (600)

520. Using the work of an expert (505 and 620)

600. Auditors' reports on financial statements (700)

601. Imposed limitation of audit scope (issued 1999) (700)

610. Communication of audit matters to those charged with governance (revised 2001) (260)

620. The auditors' right and duty to report to regulators in the financial sector.

There are some IASs which do not have corresponding SASs. These are:

100. Assurance engagements

401. Auditing in a computer information systems environment

800. The auditor's report on special purpose audit engagement

810. The examination of prospective financial information

910. Engagements to review financial statements

920. Engagements to perform agreed-upon procedures regarding financial information

930. Engagements to compile financial information.

Both the APB and the IAPC have glossaries of terms used.

Probable future SASs include: Independent professional review; Public sector entities.

Practice Notes

4. The APB also issues Practice Notes which are designed to assist auditors in applying Auditing Standards of general application to particular circumstances and industries. They are persuasive rather than prescriptive and have similar status to the explanatory material in the SASs. Practice Notes may later be developed into or be included in SASs.

Current ones of importance are:

PN5. The auditor's right and duty to report to SAB and other regulators of investment businesses

PN8. Reports by auditors under company legislation in the UK

PN10. The Audit of Financial Statements of Public Sector Entities in the UK

PN11. The audit of charities

PN12. Money laundering

PN13. The audit of small businesses

PN14. The audit of registered social landlords in the UK

PN15. The audit of occupational pension schemes in the UK

PN16. Bank reports for audit purposes

PN19. Banks in the UK

PN20. The audit of insurers in the UK

PN21. The audit of investment businesses in the UK.

The IAPC issue *International Auditing Practice Statements* which provide practical assistance to auditors on implementing the ISAs.

Current ones include guidance on microcomputers, on-line computer systems, database systems, communication between auditors and regulators, audit of small entities, communications with management, computer assisted audit techniques, and environmental matters.

Bulletins

5. The APB also issues bulletins. These are likely to be developed into, or be included within, SASs or Practice Notes. They are issued to provide auditors with timely advice on new or emerging issues and, like Practice Notes are persuasive rather than prescriptive.

   Current bulletins include:

   - Review of interim financial information
   - The combines code (re corporate governance)
   - The Summary Financial Statement
   - Departures from SORPs
   - Electronic publication of auditors' reports
   - Revisions to the wording of auditors' reports
   - Auditors' reports on abbreviated accounts
   - The FRS on small enterprises
   - Preliminary announcements
   - Proforma financial information
   - E-business: identifying financial statement risks.

Other APB documents

6. Other APB documents include The Scope and Authority of APB pronouncements and the SSRA *Audit Exemption Reports* covered in Chapter 42 of this book. The Scope document outlines the purposes of the APB and scope and authority of APB pronouncements. Most of its points have been dealt with in this chapter but it also says that it will issue Exposure Drafts from time to time and may issue other consultative documents.

Summary

7. a. In 1991 the Auditing Practices Board was formed which issues SASs, Practice Notes, Bulletins and other pronouncements.

   b. The CCAB bodies have undertaken to adopt all SASs promulgated by the APB.

   c. Apparent failures by auditors in the UK to comply with the Auditing Standards contained in the SASs may be investigated and may lead to penalties. The penalties may include withdrawal of registration.

   d. The Auditing Standards are likely to be taken into account in a court of law where the adequacy of an auditor's work is being considered. For example if an auditor is being proceeded against for the recovery of damages caused by his/her alleged negligence. All the APB pronouncements are in practice likely to be taken into account in this way.

   e. The SASs contain numbered Auditing Standards which are mandatory and also explanatory and other material which is persuasive.

Points to note

8. a. There have been suggestions that the APB should become an independent body not connected with the six members of the CCAB. Future legislation may bring this about.

b. There can be no doubt that auditing has improved as a result of the mandatory standards. In particular accountants who both prepared and audited the accounts of small enterprises have to change their thinking and see that preparation of figures is not a substitute for auditing them. The economic cost of this extra auditing has probably been heavy but has been relieved to some extent by the exemption from audit of some small companies.

Case study 1

Blameless & Co. have just taken over the audit of Widget Machines Ltd, a company in the machine tool industry. Preliminary indications are that the company has a turnover of £1 million and is owned and run by Jack Martinet, who keeps tight control over day to day operations. It seems that the company is in financial trouble. The Accounts of previous years have been subject to a qualification of the auditor's report due to non compliance with SSAP's, inefficiencies in the company's computer system and difficulties in the measurement of work in progress.

Discussion

List the SASs, Practice Notes and Bulletins that may be relevant to this audit.

Case study 2

Earthshake PLC are a construction company controlled by the major shareholder and director Bill. The company have been accused of bribing a foreign government official and the trial is expected shortly. The auditors have been asked to give a report on the environmental record of the company. During the audit the auditor finds that the work in progress in the previous year contained a major error. Several of the overseas subsidiaries are audited by other firms.

Discussion

List the SASs, ISAs and other documents that may be relevant to this audit.

Student self testing questions *Questions with answers apparent from the text*
1. a. What documents are issued by the APB? (3–6)
   b. What material is contained in a Statement of Auditing Standards? (3)

7 Accounting standards and the auditor

Introduction

1. In general, published accounts are required to conform to the accounting standards. Part of the auditor's duties is to assess whether or not the financial statements he is auditing do comply in general and in detail with the accounting standards. This book is about auditing and cannot include a detailed description of all the accounting standards. For a detailed understanding my readers will need to consult an accounting textbook or perhaps they are already conversant with the accounting standards – FRSs and SSAPs and/or the International Accounting Standards (IASs).

Accounting standard setting

2. The accounting standards are issued by the Accounting Standards Board (ASB) which is a subsidiary of the Financial Reporting Council (FRC). A subcommittee of the ASB is the Urgent Issues Task Force (UITF) which issues UITF Abstracts. These abstracts are regarded as accepted practice in the area in question and financial statements should generally conform to them. There is another subsidiary of the FRC – the Financial Reporting Review Panel (FRRP) which examines departures (when referred to them) from the accounting standards.

    Some industries have Statements of Recommended Practice. These are not approved by the ASB but they do approve the bodies who issue them. The financial statements of relevant industries would normally comply with the appropriate SORP.

    The ASB issues a Financial Reporting Exposure Draft (FRED) on matters on which a new FRS is intended and sometimes a discussion paper before the FRED. FREDs have no standing but often give an understanding of current best practice.

Current Accounting Standards

3. Auditing students should be aware of and familiar with the accounting standards required for the syllabuses they are studying. They should also be aware that new standards are being issued all the time and the up-to-date situation must be known.

Small companies and the accounting standards

4. The accounting standards are on a continuum from basic accounting (SSAPs 9 and 12, FRS 10) to arcane issues, such as FRS 13, which affect only large companies. It is still a matter of contention and discussion as to whether all the accounting standards should apply to small companies. The matter has been largely resolved by the issue of the FRRSE – Financial Reporting Standard for Smaller Entities. However this is currently under review.

    Students should also be aware of the Statement of Principles for Financial Reporting (ASB) and/or the Framework for the Preparation and Presentation of Financial Statements (IASC).

The relevance of accounting standards to auditing

5. Auditors must include in their reports their opinion on whether the financial statements they report on give a true and fair view.

    The abstract concept of the true and fair view is discussed at length in a later chapter. However it is enough to say at this stage that, in general, in order that accounts show a true and fair view, accounts must comply with the accounting standards. There can be situations where a true and fair view will not be given if an accounting standard is followed but these will be extremely rare.

    The Companies Act 1989 formally recognised the accounting standards and required (Schedule 4 (36A)) that with Disclosure of Accounting Policies there should also be a statement as to whether the accounts have been prepared in accordance with applicable accounting standards.

    Thus an auditor is, in effect, being asked to give an opinion on whether all accounting standards have been complied with in the preparation of the accounts he is auditing. This means that auditors must know and understand the accounting standards in detail.

Auditing students are also expected to know the accounting standards in detail. Many auditing questions in examinations require this knowledge and examinees are advised to quote from the accounting standards and state which of the accounting standards are relevant to their answer. For example questions involving depreciation will require mention of SSAP 12 and FRS 15 and questions on Groups will require mention of FRS 2.

Summary

6. a. The accounting standards are essential knowledge for auditing students.

    b. Among the requirements for a true and fair view is compliance with the accounting standards.

    c. The FRSs and those SSAPs and/or IASs which are still current are essential knowledge

    d. The UITF abstracts are also relevant to auditing students.

    e. All financial statements must give a true and fair view.

Points to note

7. a. Departures from the accounting standards are now rare as they have achieved full recognition by business. In addition the FRRP may pick up undisclosed departures. Normally when the FRRP finds against a company the company restates its next set of accounts to adjust the wrong treatment but the FRRP can take a company to court if it declines to do so. A recourse to the court has not yet happened. Under the panel's procedures, the facts of cases requiring changes to the accounts are handed on to the professional body of the auditors and this body may take disciplinary action.

    b. The ASB approves bodies who produce SORPs rather than the SORPs themselves. SORPs are normally issued with regard to the accounts of specialised bodies (e.g. universities, pension schemes). SORPs are not mandatory but accounts for a body where a relevant SORP exists are unlikely to show a true and fair view if the SORP is not followed. Examiners do not normally expect students to know the SORPs.

    c. Accounting standards are mandatory except where a true and fair view would not be given which is very unlikely. FREDs and Discussion documents are not mandatory until they have become FRSs but the discussion in them may indicate what present opinion is on what is a true and fair view. However a present accounting standard must be complied with until it is superseded.

    d. In an opinion for the APB in 1993, Mary Arden QC (now Mrs Justice Arden) said that the courts are likely to treat accounting standards as legally binding and that compliance with them is likely to be found necessary if the true and fair view requirement in company accounts is to be met.

Case study 1

Shirley is the auditor of Earthy Products Ltd, a small company in Walsall. She is reviewing the accounts for the year ending 31 March 20-6 and notes the following facts:

    a. The stock is valued at marginal cost whereas the stock in the previous year was valued at direct cost.

    b. Cost of sales includes the costs of closure of the branch at Warley.

c. The company have some shares in a public company supplier and the dividends received are in the accounts as cash received.

d. There is no cash flow statement.

e. The company's freehold factory has not been depreciated.

f. The company have not provided for corporation tax as they have unused capital allowances.

g. The accounts make no mention of uninsured loss of stock in a fire on 6 April 20-6.

h. Certain development expenditure written off in the 20-4/5 accounts has been reinstated in the 20-5/6 accounts.

i. A contingent gain has been omitted from the accounts as its effects are almost equal but opposite to an unrelated contingent loss which is also omitted.

j. Some 25% of the sterling amount of trade debtors includes loans to customers which are recoverable only when the customer ceases trading with Earthy Products.

Discussion

What are the implications of these facts for the audit?

Case study 2

Worldweary PLC is a listed company. The company's financial statements for 20-3 include:

A very large debt which is payable in four instalments over the next 2 years is included in the sundry debtors without comment. The company value stocks in the USA under LIFO and in the UK under FIFO. This is stated in the accounting policies.

Discussion

What are the implications of these facts for the audit?

Student self testing questions

8. a. What do the FRRP do? (2)

b. What is a SORP? (2)

c. What is the relevance of FREDs for auditors? (2)

d. In the audit of small companies what accounting standard is specially important? (4)

e. Why are accounting standards important to auditors? (5)

8 Rules of professional conduct

Introduction

1. Auditing is carried out by accountants in public practice. Accountancy is a profession. Professions have certain characteristics including an ethical code and rules of conduct. This chapter is concerned with the rules of conduct prescribed by the professional accounting bodies.

2. Professional conduct is frequently found in auditing examinations, as examiners see auditing papers as a suitable vehicle for examining ethics, even when they do not specifically relate to auditing.

3. The rules are found in the handbooks issued to all members. The Association publishes the rules in one volume – The Rule Book – and all students are advised to obtain a copy.

4. In this chapter we will look at:

   - fundamental principles
   - confidentiality
   - money laundering
   - whistleblowing
   - ethics
   - independence

   - conflicts of interest
   - advertising
   - publicity
   - obtaining professional work
   - remuneration
   - insider dealing.

5. Fraud, changes in professional appointments (professional etiquette) and professional liability are dealt with in separate chapters.

Fundamental Principles

6. The Fundamental Principles apply to all members of the ACCA (and similar ideas apply to other professional bodies).

7. The five Fundamental Principles are:

   a. Members should behave with integrity in all professional, business and personal financial relationships. Integrity implies not merely honesty but fair dealing and truthfulness.

   b. Members should strive for objectivity in all professional and business judgements. Objectivity is the state of mind which has regard to all considerations relevant to the task in hand but no other. It presupposes intellectual honesty.

   c. Members should not accept or perform work which they are not *competent* to undertake unless they obtain such advice and assistance as will enable them competently to carry out the work.

   d. Members should carry out their professional work with due *skill, care, diligence* and expedition and with proper regard for the technical and professional standards expected of them as members.

   e. Members should behave with *courtesy and consideration* to all with whom they come into contact during the course of performing their work.

   Frequently these ideas can be incorporated into auditing answers. Look out for these opportunities!

Ethics – general rules

8. Professional accountants are required to observe proper standards of professional conduct whether or not the standards required are written in the rules or are unwritten. They are specifically required to refrain from misconduct which is difficult to define precisely but which includes any act or default which is likely to bring discredit on himself, his professional body or the profession generally.

Several general points can be made:

a. Professional independence is exceedingly important. This is very much an attitude of mind rather than a set of rules but there are many rules which we will describe later.

b. Integrity is vital. Synonyms for integrity include honesty, uprightness, probity, moral sounness, rectitude.

c. Accountants must not only be people of integrity and independence; they must also be seen to be so. Any interest (e.g. owning shares in a client company) which might diminish an accountant's objectivity of approach or which might appear to to others, must be avoided.

d. When an accountant has ethical difficulties or is unsure of what course of conduct to follow, he should consult his professional body or take legal advice. If in doubt always seek advice.

Independence

9. An auditor's objectivity must be beyond question when conducting an audit. An auditor must always approach his work with integrity and objectivity. The approach must be in a spirit of independence of mind.

There are a number of matters which may threaten or appear to threaten the independence of an auditor. These include:

a. Undue dependence on an audit client. Public perception of independence may be put in jeopardy if the fees from any one client or group of connected clients exceed 15% of gross practice income or 10% in the case of listed or other public interest companies. This general observation needs modifying in the cases of new practices.

b. Family or other personal relationships. It is desirable to avoid professional relationships where personal relationships exist. Examples of personal relationships include mutual business interests with members of the group comprising the client, the audit firm, officers or employees of the client, partners or members of staff of the audit firm.

c. Beneficial interests in shares and other investments. In general, partners, their spouses, and minor children should not hold shares in or have other investments in client companies. An audit staff member should not be employed on an audit if the staff member or some person connected with him has a beneficial interest in the audit client. Some company articles require the auditor to have a qualifying shareholding. In such cases the minimum only should be held and the holding should be disclosed in the accounts.

d. Loans to and from clients. An auditing practice or anyone closely connected with it should not make loans to its clients nor receive loans from clients. The same applies to guarantees. Overdue fees may in some circumstances constitute a loan.

e. Acceptance of goods and services. Goods and services should not be accepted by a practice or by anyone closely connected with it unless the value of any benefit is modest. Acceptance of undue hospitality poses a similar threat. A bottle of Scotch at Christmas is acceptable but a weekend in Paris would probably not be.

f.   Actual or threatened litigation. Litigation or threatened litigation (e.g. on auditor negligence) between a client company and an audit firm would mean the parties being placed in an adversarial situation which clearly undermines the auditor's objectivity.

g.   Influences outside the practice. There is a risk of loss of objectivity due to pressures from associated practices, bankers, solicitors, government or those introducing business.

h.   Provision of other services. This is acceptable in principle but care must be taken and this is reviewed in the next paragraph.

i.   Auditors should not allow their judgement to be swayed by the receipt of a commission, fee or other reward from a third party as a result of advising a client to pursue one course rather than another. If a commission is to be received the accountant should either give it to the client or, with the client's express or implied consent, retain it. If it is to be retained then the fact of a payment of commission, and the amount or how it is to be calculated, should be disclosed to the client, preferably in the letter of engagement. The client must assent to retention.

Audit firms should review on an annual basis every client to determine if it is proper to accept or continue an audit engagement, bearing in mind actual or apparent threats to audit objectivity. The rules of the Financial Services Act must always be followed.

Conflicts of interest

10. Conflicts of interest can arise between an accountant and his client. Conflicts of interest can arise between a client and another client, and an accountant should not act for both parties if the parties are in dispute. For example the accountant may be called upon to advise two clients who are tendering for the same contract. Or he may be advising a company and one of its directors who are in dispute. In all such cases the accountant should not accept assignments where he is put in a position where he must advise both sides. On the other hand he may well be able to put forward proposals to settle the dispute.

Specific examples of conflict of interest include:

a.   Provision of other services to audit clients. It is customary for auditors in many cases to provide other services as well as the audit, for example preparing accounts. This is perfectly acceptable providing the service does not involve performing executive functions or making executive decisions. For example discussing the annual dividend decision with the board would be an executive action and hence unacceptable.

b.   Preparation of accounting records. Care should be taken that the client takes responsibility for the work done and that objectivity in auditing is not impaired. The accounting records of public company clients should not be prepared by the auditor.

c.   A practice should not report on a company if a company associated with the practice is the company secretary to the client. However it is acceptable to provide assistance to the company secretary.

d.   No person in an accounting firm should take part in the reporting function (i.e. take part in the audit) if he or she has in the accounting period or in the previous two years been an officer or employee of that company.

e.   Receivership, liquidation and audits. In general auditors should not accept receiverships or liquidatorships of client companies without a three year gap between the assignments. Clearly a liquidator of a company would be inhibited from taking a negligence action against the auditor if he had himself been the auditor.

Advertising

11. There are still considerable restrictions on advertising including:

    any advertisement should not:

    a. bring into disrepute himself, any member of his professional body, his firm or the accountancy profession generally;

    b. discredit the services of others by for example claiming superiority;

    c. contain comparisons with other members or firms;

    d. be misleading, either directly or by implication;

    e. fall short of the Advertising Standards Authority as to legality, decency, honesty and truthfulness.

    f. Adverts *may* refer to the basis on which fees are calculated. However, no hourly or other charging rates are permissible. 'This month's special cheap offer' will not appear in accountants' adverts.

    None of this means that accountants' advertisements need be dull or unimaginative. Many firms have put out exciting adverts but whether they are also 'attractive' is not yet clear.

    Enterprises in all sectors of the economy have sought to reduce costs in recent years. A major cost is the audit fee and other fees paid to the auditor for other work. Many enterprises have asked several firms to tender for the audit and other work. This has led to the practice of "lowballing" or tendering low to get the work. Whether this has had a deleterious effect on the quality of auditing is arguable.

Publicity

12. In the past, accountants were required to be very anonymous in public matters. The rules are now less restrictive but there are still some prohibitions. A general prohibition is on any publicity which would bring the accountant, his professional body or the profession, into disrepute. Presumably, an accountant appearing on a chat show and introduced as John Ticker, certified accountant would be acceptable. But if the conversation revealed him to be a transvestite satanist, it might not.

Obtaining professional work

13. Accountants may now advertise for work and engage in other forms of publicity, for example by posters or hoardings or on motor vehicles, on sportswear or by sports sponsorship. However accountants may not give any commission, fee or reward to a third party for introducing clients. Such commissions may, however, be paid to his employees or other practising accountants.

Remuneration

14. The normal basis for charging for professional work, is on the time spent on the work calculated at appropriate hourly rates for principals, senior and other staff. The hourly rate may vary according to the difficulty or complexity of the work involved. It is up to

the accountant to decide upon his hourly rates depending on his cost structure, greed, market conditions, etc. It is not permissible to charge:

a. On a percentage basis except where statute or custom allows, e.g. in liquidation and receivership work. Many accountants are jealous of the percentage charging methods of estate agents, architects, solicitors, etc., but these professional people generally do not have recurring work from clients and continually need to seek new clients. In any event other professionals also charge flat rates nowadays.

b. On a contingency basis. This means accountants cannot accept work on a percentage of tax saved basis or anything similar.

   It is possible to charge on a contingency basis where the client's capacity to pay is dependent on the success or failure of the venture. Examples could be advising on a management buy-out or the raising of venture capital.

Accountants who receive commissions from stockbrokers, insurance brokers, etc. for transactions effected for clients or for trusts of which the accountant is a trustee should either:

a. Pass on the commissions to the client or trust by deducting the amounts received from his fee invoice and showing the deduction.

b. Keep the commissions if he has been specifically authorised to do so by the client.

Insider dealing

15. Insider dealing is illegal. It is also contrary to the ethical rules. People who during the course of their work come across 'unpublished price sensitive information' are prohibited from dealing in securities to which that information relates. Unpublished price sensitive information covers specific matters not generally known to those who normally deal on the stock exchange but which if it were known to them would alter the prices of those securities to which the information relates. The prohibition applies to anyone who has a connection at present or at any time in the previous six months and to any third person who the insider may wish to instruct.

Auditors with their close connection with the accounts of a public company client are often in possession of insider information. For example they may know that the profit is £12 million when the market is expecting only £10 million. They must not take advantage of this information by buying shares in the company on the expectation of a rise in the price when the accounts are published.

Other matters

16. In addition to the matters mentioned in this chapter, there are rules on professional conduct in the following areas:

a. Descriptions of members of professional bodies and their designatory letters.

b. Activities through corporate and non-corporate organisations.

c. The obligations of consultants. Alan, an accountant consults Bertha, an accountant with special knowledge of taxation, on behalf of Colin, a client. Bertha should not then obtain further work from Colin unless:

   i.   Alan consents, or

   ii. three years has elapsed since the end of the consultancy engagement, or

    iii. exceptionally, if the interests of Colin might be prejudiced.

    This is to allay the fears of accountants that if they consult experts, they may lose the client.

d. Membership of trade unions. Accountants may belong to trade unions and go on strike.

e. The incapacity or death of a sole practitioner. Arrangements must be made for continuity of a practice.

f. Client's money. Clients' money should be paid into a separate general client account or into an account opened for the particular client. Such moneys should only be used to cover disbursements on behalf of the client, payments made on the instructions of the client and to pay fees to the accountant. Such fees must have been agreed with the client and an invoice raised. Deposit account interest on clients' accounts belongs to the clients.

g. Estates of deceased persons. This is concerned with the division of work between accountants and solicitors.

Money laundering

17. The Money Laundering Regulations 1993 require that accountants who engage in investment business must comply with the regulations. Money laundering is the process by which criminals try to make the proceeds of their crimes appear 'clean'. To do this, they need the services of others such as banks, accountants, and lawyers. Accountants may not assist others to retain the benefit of criminal conduct and they must report knowledge or suspicion of money laundering relating to drug trafficking or terrorism.

Accountants normally have procedures to identify prospective clients and to ensure they are what they purport to be. Partners and staff need training to recognise suspicious clients and transactions. Evidence of identity of clients should be kept for at least five years and many firms have a 'Money Laundering Reporting Officer' to deal with the whole matter.

Whistleblowing

18. Whistleblowing means informing the proper authorities of some breach of law or regulation. It is an issue for any employee who feels compelled to tell the proper authorities of some wrong doing by his employers but fears being dismissed if he does. It is also an issue for auditors. There are three issues for auditors:

a. Breaches of law or regulation may have an impact on the financial statements.

b. Breaches of law or regulation may need to be reported to the proper authorities in the public interest.

c. Breaches of law or regulation may in certain circumstances need to be reported immediately to the proper authorities as a statutory requirement.

The rulebook spells out requirement for b. and c. and SASs 120 and 620 have detailed requirements.

19. There are statutory duties to report immediately any breach of law or regulation in connection with money laundering and to regulators under the Financial Services Act. Failure to report may be a criminal offence.

20. Where the auditor comes across a situation where a breach of law or regulation has occurred and she feels that this should be reported to the proper authorities in the public interest but there is no specific statutory duty report, the auditor should:

    a. Take legal advice.

    b. Discuss the matter with the Board of Directors.

    c. Request that the Board disclose the matter to the proper authorities.

    d. If they fail to do so, inform the proper authorities themselves.

Summary

21. a. The professional bodies require their members and students to behave in an ethical manner.

    b. In some areas, the codes of ethics and conduct are spelt out in detail.

    c. Independence is of particular importance and detailed guidance is issued to members.

Points to note

22. a. The ethical codes are in some areas mandatory. For example a certified accountant cannot describe himself as a 'certified accountant and auditor'.

    b. In some areas they give guidance only. For example in the independence ethical guide, the 15% fees rule is for guidance only, a client giving 10% of gross fees may influence an auditor who fears the loss of income if he loses the client.

    c. In all these ethical matters, an accountant must not only behave correctly, he must also be seen to be behaving correctly.

    d. These matters are occasionally tested in examinations. In recent examinations, independence rules, advertising, remuneration method, and insider dealing have appeared.

    e. Ethics are taken very seriously by professional accountants.

    f. Professional accountants are not allowed to give investment advice or conduct investment business unless they are authorised to do so by their professional body under the Financial Services Act 1986.

    g. Auditors become privy to all sorts of information in the course of their work. I well remember being surprised at the very large investment account of a family friend in the Building Society I was auditing as a trainee. Similarly I was interested to discover the amount paid by a neighbour for his house and his method of financing it when I audited a firm of solicitors (to say nothing of divorce cases). Auditors and their staff must regard all such information as totally privileged and not disclose it to third parties except in circumstances where there is a legal right or duty to disclose it. They may not also use such information for personal gain, e.g. by insider trading.

    h. Partners and staff of audit firms can become so familiar with the management or staff of a client company that they lose their objectivity. This must be avoided perhaps by rotating the partners and staff involved.

    i. Independence is a big issue at the time of writing and the practice of audit firms performing other services for their audit clients has come into some criticism. Warnings are made in the ethical guides of the professional bodies of the risks to objectivity in performing these services but these all fall a long way short of prohibition. The real question is whether an audit firm can offer a totally dispassionate opinion if it and/or an associated firm are supplying services like:

- bookkeeping
- preparing the annual accounts
- taxation
- advice on company secretarial matters
- management consultancy
- obtaining staff
- selecting computer systems
- litigation support
- corporate financial advice e.g. on capital raising or takeovers.

In a particular situation an auditor may well feel that he or she is a professional person and is quite capable of giving an independent audit opinion even though:

- the fee for the opinion is fixed by the directors
- the directors can engineer a change of auditor if they wish
- the senior conducting the audit prepared the final accounts
- the firm advised the firm on the choice of a computer firm for the supply of new hardware and software
- the firm investigated a company which the client company purchased
- the firm advised the client on a complex scheme for tax avoidance.

I leave you to think about this.

j. Firms of auditors make a lot of money by giving advice and performing other services for their audit clients. This may or may not seem to compromise their objectivity in carrying out an audit. The Companies Act and the rulebooks have much to say on this. The EC have a discussion paper on the issue as part of a desire to harmonise rules throughout the EC.

They recognise that economics must necessarily require that some services (e.g. finalising the financial statements) should be performed by the auditor in many circumstances. However any such assistance should be *solely of a technical or mechanical nature or the advice given must be of an informative nature only*. The auditor can advise on issues such as provisions but may not take part in *management decisions*. The overriding rule is that the auditor should not be involved in decision making and, where there is a threat to independence, the risk has to be reduced to an acceptable level.

Case study 1

Philip has been in practice for many years. At the present time he is anxious to develop more income to send his sons through university. Amongst the new ventures he has been offered are:

a. the audit of his brother's new company;
b. a 25% share in a new company being formed by a client to market computer software;

c. an agency with a building society who want him to agree to an illuminated sign in his office window;

d. a back duty case client has offered him 20% of the sum saved if he will negotiate a reduction in the estimated assessment.

George, his assistant, has been offered a part-time job, by a company client, keeping the client's books.

Discussion

a. How might Philip enlarge his practice?

b. How should he deal with the matters mentioned above?

Case study 2

Brown is the auditor of Tricky PLC. The directors have asked him to prepare the financial statements for the year ending 31 December 20-3 as well as audit them. They have also asked him to help them install a new computer system, select a new chief executive and discuss at a board meeting the dividend to be paid. The company is also subject to a probable take-over bid and wants Brown to act for them in rebutting statements made by the take-over bidder.

On the audit, Brown finds that the company are systematically breaching rules on exporting goods to a certain middle east country, contrary to the law and he suspects that some cash receipts in a subsidiary may be bogus.

Discussion

What jobs can Brown accept? What should Brown do about the exports and the cash receipts?

Student self testing questions

a. List the fundamental principles? (7)

b. What general ethical rules are there? (8)

c. What should an accountant do if faced with an ethical dilemma? (8)

d. Enumerate the guidelines to independence. (9)

e. What should an accountant do about commissions? (9)

f. Enumerate the areas where conflict of interest may occur. (10)

g. What restrictions are there on advertising? (11)

h. How can an accountant obtain publicity in an ethical manner? (12)

j. What are the rules on accountants' remuneration? (14)

k. What is insider dealing? What does an audit clerk do when he knows his mother has shares in Risky PLC and that, while on the audit of Risky, he discovers that company's new pharmaceutical product of which the market expects much, has been banned as unsafe? An announcement of the ban will be made next week. (15)

l. What is money laundering? (17)

m. What is whistleblowing? When may an auditor inform the proper authorities of a breach of the law? (19, 20)

n. What criteria apply to the decision of an auditor as to whether he can assist his client in non-audit ways? (22)

Examination questions

1. Your auditing practice is a firm of 3 partners and 10 staff. Your firm has been offered the appointment as auditor of a new client company which is a large manufacturer of agricultural machinery. The client has 5 manufacturing centres and has computerised accounting systems.

   Required:
   a. State 5 considerations which might influence your decision whether to accept the appointment. (10 marks)
   b. Describe 4 steps which your firm should take before accepting the appointment.
   (4 marks)
   (LCCI)

2. It is important that an auditor's independence is beyond question and that he should behave with integrity and objectivity in all professional and business situations. The following are a series of questions which were asked by auditors at a recent update seminar on professional ethics.
   a. Can I audit my brother's company? (4 marks)
   b. A B and Co. the previous auditors, will not give my firm professional clearance or the usual handover information because they are still owed fees. Should I accept the client's offer of appointment? (5 marks)
   c. Can I prepare the financial statements of a public company and still remain as auditor? (4 marks)
   d. My client has threatened to sue the firm for negligence. Can I still continue to act as auditor? (5 marks)
   e. I am a student of the Chartered Association of Certified Accountants. Am I bound by the ethical guidelines of the Association? (2 marks)
   Required:
   Discuss the answers you would give to the above questions posed by the auditors.
   (20 marks)
   (ACCA)

9 Letters of engagement

Introduction

1. Before commencing any professional work, an accountant should agree, in writing, the precise scope and nature of the work to be undertaken. This is done through the medium of an engagement letter.

2. There is a Statement of Auditing Standards SAS 140 *Engagement letters* and an ISA 210 *Terms of Audit Engagement.*

Purposes

3. a. To define clearly the extent of the auditor's responsibilities.

   b. To minimise misunderstandings between auditor firm and client.

   c. To confirm in writing verbal arrangements.

   d. To confirm acceptance by the auditor of his engagement.

   e. To inform and educate the client.

   f. Unless the terms of engagement are agreed in writing there may be an implied contract arising out of the Articles of Association or previous conduct of the auditor. The terms of such an implied contract may not be to the auditor's liking.

When to send a letter

4. a. To all NEW clients before any professional work has been started.

   b. To all existing clients who have not previously had such a letter.

   c. Whenever there is a change of circumstances (e.g. extra duties, a significant new auditing guideline, or a major change in ownership or management). The engagement letter should be reviewed every year to see if there is a need for a revised letter.

   d. In the case of groups an engagement letter should be sent to each member company of the group that is to be audited by the firm. Or if a standard letter is satisfactory then a letter to the group Board requesting that the letter be sent to all group members and that acknowledgement be received from all of them.

Procedure

5. a. On or before acceptance of a new client, discuss the precise terms with the management (the Board in the case of a company).

   b. Draft and sign the letter before commencing any part of the assignment.

   c. Receive the client's written acceptance.

   d. Every year review the letter and consider if revision is necessary.

Principal contents

6. The letter should outline the clients' statutory duties (e.g. on accounting records) and the auditors' statutory (e.g. to report) and professional (e.g. to follow the auditing standards) responsibilities. The sections may include:

   a. The Board's responsibilities regarding proper accounting records and financial statements which show a true and fair view and comply with the Act. Also the

Board's responsibility to make available to the auditors all the accounting records, other relevant records and related information and minutes of meetings.

b. The auditor's responsibility to report on the financial statements and on the consistency of view of the directors' report. Also a list of Companies Act responsibilities (S.235 and S.237).

c. The scope of the auditor's work:
   - auditing standards
   - accounting systems review
   - collection of audit evidence
   - tests and reliance on internal controls.

d. The sending of a letter of weakness to the management.

e. Any special factors:
   - relations with internal audit
   - audit of divisions or branches
   - any overseas location problems
   - other auditors if any
   - significant reliance on supervision of the directors in small proprietory companies.

f. The need for a letter of representation from the management.

g. Irregularities and fraud
   - the directors' primary responsibility
   - the auditors' planning of his audit to have a reasonable expectation of discovering MATERIAL misstatements in the ACCOUNTS
   - non-reliance on the auditor to uncover irregularities and frauds.

h. Any agreement for the auditors to carry out work of a bookkeeping or accounting nature – this could be covered in a separate letter.

i. Any agreement for the auditor to provide taxation services – this could also be a separate letter.

j. Where accounting or tax services are carried out the staff may be different from those engaged on audit work and so information given to tax or accounting staff is not thereby given to audit staff. This is known as the CHINESE WALL idea.

k. The fees and the basis on which they are charged.

l. A request for written acknowledgement of the letter and that it creates contractual obligations. In the case of a company the letter of acknowledgement should be signed on behalf of the Board.

Example

7. Here is an example:

QUIBBLE, QUERY & CO.
CHARTERED ACCOUNTANTS   28 Feb 20-6
to THE DIRECTORS
HEDONITE LTD

GENTLEMEN

The purpose of this letter is to set out the basis on which we are to act as auditors of your company and the respective areas of responsibility of ourselves and yourselves.

AUDIT

a. You are responsible for maintaining proper accounting records, preparing financial statements which give a true and fair view and which comply with the Companies Act, supplying us with the records and with such explanations and information as we may require.

b. We are responsible for giving an opinion on the truth and fairness and compliance with statute of those financial statements in a report.

c. We are required to consider and if necessary report on:

   – whether proper accounting records have been kept

   – whether the Accounts are in agreement with the records

   – whether we have received all the information and explanations we think necessary

   – whether the information in the directors' report is consistent with the financial statements.

d. We have a professional duty to report if the financial statements do not conform to the Accounting Standards.

e. Our audit will be conducted in accordance with the auditing standards. We shall gather such relevant and reliable evidence as is sufficient to draw reasonable conclusions therefrom. We shall assess your systems of accounting and internal control and our tests will vary according to that assessment. We may wish to place reliance on the system of internal control. We shall report any significant weaknesses in the systems to you.

f. We may request you to provide written confirmation of oral representations given to us.

g. We shall require sight of all documents to be issued with the Accounts and we will wish to receive notice of and attend all general meetings.

h. The responsibility for prevention and detection of fraud and irregularities rests with yourselves. We shall endeavour to plan our audit to detect material misstatements in the Accounts but we cannot be relied upon to disclose frauds or other irregularities which may exist.

ACCOUNTING

We shall prepare the Accounts based on the accounting records maintained by you.

TAXATION

a. We shall agree the corporation tax liabilities of the company with the Inspector of Taxes.

b. You will be responsible for all other tax matters including returns, payment of advance corporation tax and forms P11D.

FEES

Our fees are based on the time necessarily spent by our partners and staff at a level commensurate with the skill and responsibility involved. The audit work will be billed separately from other work.

AGREEMENT OF TERMS

We will be grateful if you would confirm in writing your acceptance of the terms of this letter.

Yours faithfully

Note: This letter has been slightly abbreviated from the usual length of real letters.

It may be desirable to have separate letters for the audit, other services and the giving of investment advice.

Some accountants may also include clauses on any complaints the client may have about the service offered and a note of the country by whose laws the engagement is governed.

Summary

8. a. All assignments given to accountants should be subject to an engagement letter agreeing the terms of the assignment with the client.

    b. SAS 140 and ISA 210 govern this subject.

Points to note

9. The letter of engagement has assumed more importance in recent years as clients have become more litigious and accountants take on new duties such as assurance engagements. Students should look for opportunities to put 'agree a letter of engagement' in many answers.

Case study 1

Juliet, a certified accountant, receives a telephone call from Chateaubriand who is starting up in business as a restaurateur specialising in the business trade. He wishes to appoint Juliet as his accountant. Juliet requests him to call.

Discussion

    a.   What matters should be discussed at the meeting?

    b.   In the light of a. draft an engagement letter.

    c.   What might be the consequences of omissions from the letter?

Student self testing questions *Questions with answers apparent from the text*

1.   a.   List the purposes of an engagement letter. (3)

    b.   What are the procedures connected with engagement letters? (5)

    c.   List the principal contents. (6)

    d.   Write out an engagement letter for a public company client. (7)

Examination questions

1.   You are the external auditor to Fleeting & Flotsam, a large firm of international architects with branches worldwide. The basis of your audit is an engagement letter.

    Give reasons suggesting the desirability of frequent renewal of your engagement letter.

(LCC) (10 marks)

2.   Effective audit planning is essential to ensure both quality of service to the client and the minimising of risk to the practitioner.

    Required

    a.   What general points should an auditor consider before accepting a new audit client?

(3 marks)

    b.   What is the purpose of the letter of engagement; what major matters should it refer to?   (12 marks)

(AAT) (Total 15 Marks)

The modern audit

The next part of the manual explains in outline how an audit is conducted, and the timing of audit work.

10 The modern audit – stages

Introduction

1. An audit can be carried out on enterprises both large and small, and both new and well established. The audit of smaller enterprises has special features that are dealt with in Chapter 42 and the first audit of a new business and first audit by a newly appointed auditor of an established business presents special features which are dealt with in Chapter 41.

2. This chapter describes the stages in the audit of an established client enterprise which is big enough to have a comprehensive system of accounting and record keeping and a system of controls over those records.

Outline stages in the audit

3. The stages in the modern audit can be summarised as:
   - Background research
   - Preparation of the audit plan
   - Accounting system review
   - Internal control system review
   - Substantive testing
   - Analytical review techniques
   - Analytical review of financial statements
   - Preparation and signing of report.

The stages explained

4. **Background research**

   Before commencing the audit proper the auditor must discover as much as possible about:

   a. The present condition and future prospects of the *industry* of which his client is a part.

   b. The past history and the present condition and future prospects of his *client*.

   c. The management and key *personnel* of his client and any recent changes.

   d. The *products* and manufacturing and trading *processes* of the client and any recent changes.

   e. The *locations* of all his client's operations.

f. Any *difficulties* encountered by the client in manufacturing, trading, expanding, contracting, labour relations or financing.

g. Any problems in *accounting* or in *internal control systems*.

h. Any problems in *accounting measurement* e.g. in stock valuation or income recognition.

i. Any problems likely to lead to *audit risk* e.g. the difficulty of assessing the value of long-term contracts in a civil engineering business.

j. Any problems likely to be met in *carrying out* the audit e.g. distant locations, tight timing problems, or large staff requirements on stocktaking attendance.

k. Any *changes* in *law* or *accounting practice* which may affect the client.

This background research will be done by reading or interviewing:

i. Previous years audit files.

ii. Audit staff who have been previously engaged on the audit.

iii. Published material concerning the client company and the industry.

iv. The company's interim, internal and management accounts.

v. The management of the enterprise.

In order to carry out a comprehensive and effective audit which is nevertheless efficient in terms of time spent, the modern auditor must focus his audit on areas of particular difficulty and risk. In addition the evaluation of many areas in the financial statements, must entail a consideration of the whole circumstances of a client. As simple examples, the evaluation of the life of fixed assets liable to obsolescence or the value of the investment in a subsidiary company can only be effected by a knowledge of all factors having a bearing on the matter and many of these factors are external to the company. For these reasons, the modern audit requires a more detailed knowledge of the client company and its problems than was required in earlier years. This does make auditing more interesting and rewarding to the auditor and potentially also to the client.

5. There is a comprehensive Statement of Auditing Standards SAS 210 *Knowledge of the Business* and an ISA 310 *Knowledge of the Business*. Among the points it makes are:

a. Auditors should obtain a *knowledge of the business* which is sufficient to enable them to *identify* and *understand the events, transactions and practices that may have a significant effect on the* financial statements and the audit thereof.

b. This knowledge may be used in assessing *risks of error*, planning the *nature, timing and extent* of audit procedures, and considering the *consistency and reliability* of financial statements.

c. There are a seemingly infinite number of sources for such knowledge. Examples include the previous experience of persons engaged on the audit, visits to the entity, trade journals, promotional literature and even job advertisements by the company.

d. Specific instances of use of knowledge of the business include recognising conflicting information, recognising the reasonableness of answers given to questions, assessing the effectiveness of internal controls by considering management's whole attitude to the control environment.

e. Matters to consider in relation to knowledge of the business. There is an appendix which sets out over 50 matters to consider. A questionnaire derived from this and other matters would enable a very comprehensive picture of an audit client to be gained.

An example

6. Jane is about to start to plan the audit of Metalbash Pressings Ltd, a company which manufactures parts for two UK lorry manufacturers. She will need to research the background as:

- the industry. She finds that UK lorry output is 75% of normal and she considers the problems for higher unit costs and greater competition resulting in lower prices for component suppliers.

- the company. The company may be suffering from price and cost squeezes, plant closures and redundancies. She finds that a factory has closed and 50 workers have been made redundant. However the company have purchased for cash (with a bank loan) the business of a company in receivership which is in a related industry. This business has a factory in a neighbouring town and Jane has to plan visits there.

- management and personnel. Any changes may weaken controls, change policies or worsen accounting records. Jane finds that there is now a new chief accountant.

- products and processes. These may have changed with possible consequences in stock values or the value of redundant equipment.

- locations. Closures may involve closure costs with disclosure problems from FRS 3.

- difficulties experienced by the client (e.g. on labour relations or cost and quality control) may impact on internal controls. Jane finds that the new accountant has streamlined several accounting processes and controls may be weaker.

- accounting systems change frequently nowadays as a consequence of new information technology. The accounting records of the new business have been incorporated into existing systems and some teething problems have occurred.

- accounting measurement problems may arise in product costs, redundant stocks, closure costs, redundancy costs, lives of fixed assets etc.

- audit risk. Some lorry makers have gone into receivership and there is a risk of Metalbash losing its business or incurring fatal bad debts. Jane will need to concentrate consequently upon the value of debtors and the going concern applicability. There may be risks of wrong values of stocks and fixed assets. Cuts in staffing may give a risk of weakening in systems or controls.

- in planning the audit, Jane will need to consider locations, timing problems, staff requirements, and the quality of audit staff needed for some of the risky areas including a possible need to look into and assess new systems.

She will do all this by reading the previous years' files, talking to the staff member responsible for last year's audit, talking to the management, reading minutes, management accounts, newspaper and magazine articles and the previous annual report and accounts.

7. **The audit plan**

The auditor must plan his audit in some detail and the plan will involve preparation of an overall audit plan showing:

   a.   an outline of the audit work to be done on each area of the client's systems and financial statements.

   b.   the staff who will do the work

   c.   the location of the audit

   d.   the timing of the work to be done

   e.   a budget of time and costs.

The plan must be made to fit in with the client's timing requirement and with the client's ability to produce necessary analyses and summaries.

8. **The example of Metalbash**

In preparing the audit plan, Jane will need to complete the following:

- ensure there is an up-to-date engagement letter and ensure the plan encompasses all the work required by the letter of engagement.

- update the permanent file (all the details about the client which are of permanent significance) with details of changes in nature of trade, areas of activity, organisation, accounting systems, internal controls and personalities.

- identify the areas of high risk, that is, areas where material errors may occur and plan accordingly. We have already seen some of these.

- consider materiality limits. Essentially this means that some things are too small or trivial to be worth any audit effort. In practice this is difficult and we will come back to it.

At the planning stage a number of actual audit actions need to be planned (e.g. attendance at stock take) but we will look at these as we discuss the later stages of the audit.

9. **Accounting system review**

The auditor must:

   a.   ascertain by asking questions

   b.   record on paper

   c.   corroborate his record (confirm that the record is correct)

   d.   review for adequacy and for planning of tests

   e.   test to determine that it always works as it is supposed to

   f.   evaluate

   g.   form a conclusion on the adequacy of the client's system for documenting and recording the transactions, assets and liabilities of the client in the books of account and other records. This is because:

      i.   the Companies Act requires the auditor to investigate and report on the company keeping of 'proper' accounting records

      ii.   the books of account and other records form the basis for the preparation of the financial statements.

10. **The example of Metalbash**

Jane will need to be sure that the company has maintained adequate accounting records throughout the year both as a specific Companies Act requirement and also to ensure that the records form a reliable basis for the preparation of the annual accounts.

She will need to review the integration of the new business records with the old and ensure that all the records adequately enable the directors to produce true and fair accounts. Especial care will be needed with stock records which are also a Companies Act requirement.

11. **Internal control system review**

    The auditor should:

    a. ascertain
    b. record
    c. corroborate the record
    d. review
    e. test
    f. evaluate
    g. form a conclusion on the adequacy of the client's system of internal control.

    Internal control is exhaustively explored in Chapter 14 but, in short, internal controls are *procedures* which ensure that *all* transactions, assets and liabilities are recorded *correctly*.

12. The objectives of the accounting systems and internal control systems investigations are to enable the auditor to have *evidence* that:

    a. The client maintains adequate books and records.
    b. The client has a system of internal controls over the processing and recording of transactions such that *all* transactions are recorded *correctly* both numerically and in principle.
    c. The books of account can be relied on to form a reliable basis for the preparation of the Accounts.

    Thus it is not necessary for the auditor to *vouch* every transaction recorded in the books. He will rely upon the system. If the system is satisfactory then he can substitute an investigation and test of the system for a detailed examination of every entry. This is both more economical and is more effective because only by examining the system can he have evidence that *all* the transactions are recorded.

13. In practice in some areas of the firm internal controls may not exist or may be weak. In such cases the auditor cannot rely on the controls and other evidence needs to be sought for the completeness and accuracy of the record. The basic audit process today is for the auditor to consider the internal controls and if she wishes to place reliance on any of them, she must then ascertain and evaluate them and perform compliance tests on them. Compliance tests will be considered again but are those tests which seek to provide evidence that internal control procedures are being applied as prescribed.

14. **The example of Metalbash**

    Jane finds that there have been many areas in the client's business where her predecessors have placed reliance on internal controls. She finds now that she needs to investigate, document, and evaluate the controls operating currently especially with regard to the records of the new business. The controls on which she considers that reliance may be placed need to be compliance tested.

As an example a series of controls are applied to ensure invoices are passed for payment are all for goods or services which have been authorised, delivered, inspected and approved. Jane will compliance test these controls.

15. **Substantive testing**

Substantive testing is defined in the auditing standards as:

'Those tests of transactions and balances, and other procedures such as analytical review, which seek to provide audit evidence as to the completeness, accuracy and validity of the information contained in the accounting records or in the financial statements.'

We have seen that the reliability of the records is established by the auditor by him investigating the system. However not all data can be verified in this *indirect* way and some transactions, balances and items in the financial statements must be verified with *direct* evidence.

In particular substantive tests are applied to:

a. Transaction records where internal controls are weak or non-existent and where the *system cannot be relied on.*

b. Unusual, extraordinary or one-off transactions and transactions which are not covered by a system. For example if the client sold a part of its premises, this transaction is clearly rare and the client will not have a system for dealing with it and thus the auditor must seek evidence that the transaction was fully and accurately recorded and was carried out with proper authority.

c. All assets and liabilities at the balance sheet date. For some assets (e.g. debtors and creditors) the *system* will provide good audit evidence, but additional audit evidence is always sought.

In practice an auditor has to consider on grounds of effectiveness and cost whether to rely on systems controls or whether to carry out substantive tests in each area of the audit. In some areas sufficient evidence can be obtained by analytical review. In many areas a combination of internal control reliance, substantive testing and analytical review provides the necessary audit evidence.

16. **The example of Metalbash**

Much of the audit consists of substantive testing and examples could be culled from any of the assets or liabilities or elsewhere. We will consider one important area. The valuation of finished goods stocks. She must seek evidence that prices used are in accordance with the requirements of SSAP 9. This will be a practical problem as the build up of costs will be very detailed. And this will also be a conceptual problem as fixed overheads may need to be added in accordance with normal level of activity and the idea of normal may be difficult to assess.

17. **Analytical review techniques**

This is defined as:

The study of relationships between elements of financial information expected to conform to a predictable pattern based on the organisation's experience and between financial and non-financial information. Information is compared with compatible information for a prior period or periods, with anticipated results and with information relating to similar organisations.

In general audit evidence is gained from internal control, from substantive tests and increasingly from analytical review.

For example, the wages item in the accounts of a company may be investigated firstly by analytical review. Supposing that:

- no problems had been encountered in the past in this area
- the total payments were within 2% of budgets adjusted for output variation and global wage awards
- the records and the financial statements and the notes attached to them all agree
- inter-firm comparison indicated that gross wage payments were within 3% of mean wage costs of firms of this turnover.

The auditor now has valid evidence that wages are correctly stated within materiality limits. He/she may well feel that some substantive testing to supplement the analytical review may be desirable but that internal control investigation is unnecessary.

18. **The example of Metalbash**

Analytical review is an economical and powerful way of obtaining audit evidence. However in times where upheavals have occurred with disposals and acquisitions and plant closures and redundancies, patterns are harder to find. Nonetheless, industrial wages may be an area where analytical review may be helpful.

19. **Analytical review of financial statements**

At the conclusion of the detailed work of the audit, when all the systems testing and substantive testing has been done, the auditor will have audit evidence that:

a. proper books of account have been kept which form a reliable basis for the preparation of the Accounts.

b. the Accounts have been properly drawn up from those books.

c. all assets, liabilities and transactions, balances and items in the account have been confirmed indirectly by systems investigation and/or directly by substantive testing.

Nonetheless, the auditor will then subject the Financial Statements to an overall *final analytical review* to determine whether:

a. Acceptable, consistent and appropriate *accounting policies* have been applied. For example, the Accounts would not show a true and *fair* view if the depreciation policy had been changed from straight line to reducing balance without this being disclosed or the stock had been valued at marginal cost contrary to the requirements of SSAP 9.

b. All the information in the Financial Statements is *compatible* with all other information. For example, an industrial firm using straight line depreciation may have items of plant which have been fully depreciated. However in determining product cost for valuing work in progress and finished goods, notional depreciation on fully depreciated plant may have been taken.

c. All items in the Accounts are compatible with the auditor's knowledge of the enterprise and its circumstances. For example, the auditor may have read in the press that new processes have been invented in a client's industry which makes some of the client's plant obsolete.

d. There is adequate disclosure of all items requiring disclosure. Numerous disclosure requirements are in the Companies Act and also some items may require special disclosure for proper understanding of the accounts. For example, if farm product sales have been changed from free market credit sales to a purchasing cooperative giving regular monthly cheques, then the change in the debtors/sales ratio may mislead readers unless the change is disclosed.

e. The accounting requirements of the Companies Act and other regulations have been complied with.

f. Overall, whether the auditor has sufficient evidence to enable him to give an opinion on the truth and fairness of the Accounts.

20. **The example of Metalbash**

Jane will need to ensure a wide range of things including:

- adequate audit evidence for all account items
- proper accounting records
- appropriate accounting policies
- Companies Act compliance
- SSAP and FRS compliance
- adequate disclosure of all items

and many others.

She might find that her firm have a series of audit working papers including checklists which enable her to be sure she has covered everything.

21. **Preparation and signing of the report**

The ultimate aim of an audit is the report by the auditor to his client. This is a formal statement giving:

a. a title identifying the persons to whom the report is addressed (e.g. Auditors' Report to the Members of XYZ PLC)

b. an introductory paragraph identifying the financial statements audited (e.g. Profit and Loss Account, Balance Sheet etc.)

c. separate sections, appropriately headed, dealing with:

   i. respective responsibilities of directors and auditors

   ii. the basis of the auditors' opinion (we conducted our audit in accordance with auditing standards ...)

   iii. the auditors' opinion (e.g. the financial statements give a true and fair view ...)

d. the manuscript or printed signature of the auditors

e. the date of the report.

22. **The example of Metalbash**

Jane will use a checklist to confirm that she has thought of everything in preparing the report of the auditor. She may have to consider a qualified report if there are areas of the accounts for which she has insufficient evidence or if she disagrees with any material aspect of the accounts. However before qualifying an audit report much agonising would occur with her and the partners in the firm.

Summary

23. The modern audit can be seen as having the following stages:

   a. Background research into the client's place in the economy generally and its industry in particular, the client's constitution, history, operations and personnel.

   b. Preparation of an audit plan.

   c. Accounting system review.

   d. Internal control system review.

   e. Substantive testing including analytical review techniques.

   f. Analytical review of financial statements.

   g. Preparation and signing of the auditor's report.

Points to note

24. a. The audit as outlined in this chapter is sometimes called the systems audit approach or the Balance Sheet audit approach. This idea of a systems based audit is still current. However, a newer idea – the risk based audit – is now prevalent because of its inclusion in the new Statement of Auditing Standards. Risk based audits still involve investigation of systems and usually some reliance on internal control.

   b. The idea to grasp is that, in the past, auditors had the time and resources to vouch or verify every transaction. The modern view is that this approach was both inefficient (expensive on time and resources) and ineffective (no certainty that all transactions had been entered).

   c. The modern auditor is not concerned with individual routine transactions but with the system for documenting and recording them. He is still concerned with material non-routine transactions.

   d. The modern audit is characterised by the search for audit evidence. Some evidence is obtained directly. For example, evidence that a building exists is best obtained by direct inspection of the building. Some evidence is obtained by indirect means. For example, evidence that all deliveries of goods to customers in a period have been followed by the sending of an invoice is best obtained by verifying that a system exists which is good in principle, works in practice and has worked throughout the period. The system will include such ideas as raising pre-numbered advice notes, prohibition of goods leaving the factory without an advice note, and regular comparisons of advice notes issued with invoices issued.

   e. In the modern literature on auditing, the system of accounting is seen as separate from the system of internal controls over the books and records. For example, in setting up a system for continuous inventory (stock records) the elements of the system would include use of goods inwards notes, stores requisitions, stock cards etc. To ensure that the records were complete and accurate, internal controls such as pre-numbering documents with sequence checks to ensure all items were accounted for and regular independent comparisons of actual stock items with the corresponding record to ensure accuracy of recording would be superimposed.

   The auditor would obviously examine the whole system together, viz both the accounting and the controls over the accounting. However it is essential to appreciate that there is a difference.

f. In this chapter I have described the stages in a modern systems based audit. However, the audit is not done all at one time but is spread out over a period of time. The timing of audit work is discussed in the next chapter.

g. The modern audit is concerned largely with a search for evidence. Evidence can be of several kinds including:
    – internal control reliance
    – substantive testing
    – analytical review.

    The costs of modern audits and the pressure on fees has meant that audit firms have sought greater effectiveness in their audit procedures together with greater efficiency. This has led to:

    i.   Greater use of combinations of evidence from all three sources.

    ii. Greater reliance on analytical review.

    iii. Greater reliance on substantive tests where internal control review and testing have been considered too expensive for the degree of reliance gained.

h. The definition of substantive testing includes analytical review but analytical review can also be viewed as a separate evidence collecting technique.

i. The concept of audit risk is also now very important. It is covered in a later chapter but for the moment note that auditors now try to identify areas of high risk (e.g. bad debts, wrong valuations of stock, inappropriate presentation of continuing and discontinuing business under FRS 3, going concern etc., in the case of Metalbash). The auditor can concentrate resources on the areas of high risk but of course all areas have to be covered.

j. As a by-product of the investigation of records and systems, the auditor usually sends a letter to the company pointing out weaknesses in the system. Such letters of weakness have their own chapter in this manual.

k. The latest idea in auditing is the business risk approach but we will leave that to a later chapter.

Case study 1

Carnac Computers PLC are a company making, importing, and retailing computers and computer software. They have branches in several European countries. They have recently suffered from falling sales and excess stocking of outdated hard and software and have survived by cutbacks and reducing staff, both management and workers.

The auditors, Earnest and Worried, are planning the audit of the Accounts for the ensuing year.

Discussion

Outline the stages required in the audit of the Accounts of Carnac noting, in particular, difficulties or requirements which this audit will entail.

Case study 2

Dream Boatbuilders PLC are builders of large luxury yachts. Many of their boats are built to order mainly for the export market when the boats' prices are quoted in US dollars. Some boats are built without orders in the hope of obtaining buyers. The company is experiencing trading difficulties and is heavily indebted to the bank. To improve trading a new managing director was appointed on 1.4.-8. You have been asked to conduct the audit by your firm. The company's year end is 31.12.-8. The date is now 2.6.-8. On reading the previous audit file you find that the company has always had weak internal controls.

Discussion

Outline the stages in the audit of the company noting any particular difficulties or requirements that this audit will entail.

Student self testing questions *Questions with answers apparent from the text*

1. a. List the stages in the modern audit. (3)
    b. What background facts must an auditor discover? (4)
    c. How will the background facts be determined? (4)
    d. What will be included in an audit planning memorandum? (7)
    e. What are the steps in an accounting system review? (9)
    f. What are the steps in an internal control systems review? (11)
    g. Define substantive testing. (15)
    h. What are the objectives of analytical review? (17)
    i. What are the objectives of analytical review of financial statements? (19)
    j. What are the contents of the auditor's report? (21)
    k. What forms of evidence are available to an auditor? (24)
    l. Why and in what ways has the search for audit evidence changed over the years? (24)
    m. Distinguish between direct and indirect evidence. (24)
    n. When are substantive tests used? (24)
    o. In what circumstances can an auditor not place reliance on internal controls? (24, 15)

11 The timing of audit work

Introduction

1. Audit work on the records and financial statements relating to a financial year are carried out at various times during, at the end and after the end of the financial year. This chapter discusses the timing of audit work usually found in practice.

Audit visits

2. In all but the very smallest of audits, the audit work will be carried on at the client's premises. Where the client has branches, this can create problems of travelling for the

auditor but in such cases some branches are visited as samples or all the branches are visited by rotation.

3. In the majority of cases, three extended visits are made by the auditor to the client's premises to carry out audit work:

   a. During the year – the *interim* audit.

   b. At the year end.

   c. After the year end – the *final* audit.

Interim audit

4. The interim audit will be carried out during the financial year. Very often the interim audit will be about two-thirds of the way through the year e.g. September or October for a December year end.

5. The work done will be:

   a. Ascertain the system of accounting and internal control.

   b. Record the system by flow chart or other method.

   c. Evaluate the systems for adequacy and presence of apparent weaknesses.

   d. Design and carry out compliance tests to determine if the system is operated at all times in accordance with the description of the system evaluated by the auditor.

   e. Design and carry out tests to determine if, in areas where controls are weak or non existent, the records can be relied upon.

   f. Draw conclusions on the adequacy of the systems and hence of the reliability of the books of account and other records.

   g. Seek evidence, by substantive tests, that unusual or one-off transactions have been fully and correctly recorded.

   h. Where possible carry out tests on assets and liabilities. Tests on assets and liabilities should be carried out *after* the year end but with clients with strong systems, some verification can be done at the interim stage. Examples are physical verification of stock records and debtors circularisation.

On modern audits a decision has to be taken on whether to place reliance on internal controls. If there is to be a decision to rely on analytical review and/or substantive tests instead then a detailed review of the internal control system will be wasted. Consequently the auditor at some stage in his examination of the accounting records has to decide on whether to complete his examination and review and do compliance tests or to go no further than becoming sure that proper accounting records are being kept.

Year-end work

6. On the last day of the client's year end it will be possible to verify some year-end assets and liabilities in a way impossible at any other time. Thus attendance will be required for:

   a. Observation and testing of the stock count.

   b. Observation and testing of cut-off procedures.

   c. Counting of cash balances.

   d. Inspection of investments, for example, share and loan certificates.

Final audit

7. The final audit will take place after the year end and is designed to seek evidence that financial statements give a true and fair view and comply with statutory and other requirements.

8. The timing of the final audit varies from client to client. Some final audits are commenced within days of the year end and the financial statements are published within as short a period as two months after the year end. Others are commenced many months after the year end. The advantage of an early audit and early publication of the Accounts is that the information given to members and others is up-to-date. From the audit point of view, transactions in progress at the year end are often not resolved and estimates of outcome have to be made and evaluated. The advantage of a late audit is that transactions in progress at the year end are often resolved and fewer estimates need to be made. For example, after a few months it will have become clear whether or not a doubtful debt is in fact bad. The disadvantage of a late audit is that information reaching members and others is out of date. The Accounts will have become truly historical.

9. The work carried out after the year end will be:
   a. Updating of the auditor's review of the systems of accounting and internal control. This will involve:
      i. Determining if the systems changed between the interim audit and the year end by interviewing officials and a few 'walk through' checks.
      ii. Thoroughly testing new systems.
      iii. Compliance tests of the unchanged systems from the interim audit to the year end.
   b. Drawing conclusions on:
      i. Adequacy of the accounting system and the system of internal controls thereon.
      ii. Whether proper books of account have been kept.
      iii. Whether the book of account and other records form a reliable base for the preparation of the Accounts.
   c. Comparing the financial statements with the underlying records and books of account to see that they correspond.
   d. Performing substantive tests on all assets and liabilities.
   e. Performing the final analytical review.
   f. Preparing and signing the auditor's report.

Summary

10. a. Audit work is usually accomplished on several visits to the client's premises.
    b. The work is usually distributed between
       i. An interim audit during the financial year.
       ii. A year-end attendance.
       iii. A final audit after the year end.
    c. The interim audit is principally for the investigation and testing of the systems of recording and internal control.

d. The year-end work is mainly for the observation and testing of the stock count but also the examination of cash balances and investment certificates.

e. The final audit is all the rest of the work and includes:

   i. testing systems for the period from the interim audit to the year end

   ii. substantive testing of transactions and balances

   iii. the analytical review

   iv. preparation and signing of the report.

Points to note

11. The timing of audit work depends upon many factors including:

   a. Deadlines fixed by the client. For example the client may arrange an AGM for three months after the year end.

   b. The organisation of the accountant's office. For example bunching of client year ends around certain dates (e.g. 31 December) can create severe problems.

   c. The extent to which the client can provide schedules and analyses. If these are not available more time is required on the final audit.

   d. The extent to which the client has very strong systems in routine areas such as debtors, creditors, stock control, fixed asset registers. Where the systems are very reliable substantive tests can often be performed at the interim instead of the final audit. For example debtors and creditors circularisation and comparison of physical stock or fixed assets with records can be performed mainly at the interim with only small samples being tested at the final.

   e. When an audit is carried out for the first time on a new client, an additional visit may be necessary, in order that the auditor may obtain knowledge of the client, its background, personnel, accounting problems, audit risk areas, etc. Following this visit the audit plan, which will be carried out on the other visits, can be prepared.

   f. In some very large audits, the audit work is so great that audit staff are on the client's premises the whole year round. This is called a *continuous* audit.

   g. In some large audits with very highly computerised records, audit evidence is sometimes available on a temporary basis only. For example where internal control (say over the credit worthiness of customers) is operated by a computer program which is changed at intervals. Then the auditor needs to be present at fairly frequent intervals to test the functioning of the controls on which he wishes to rely.

Case study 1

Automated Manufacturing PLC are a very large manufacturer of electrical appliances with factories in the Midlands and the North. The company prides itself on the excellence of its systems and its very tight financial control run by its large staff of qualified accountants. The year end is 31 December and stock is taken during the Christmas holidays while the factories are closed. The Annual General Meeting is held before the end of February.

Discussion

Give an outline audit plan for use by Pooter Brothers, the auditors, noting specially the timing of the audit work.

What special problems may arise in this audit?

Case study 2

O. Nix Ltd is a family owned chain of some 12 jewellers shops in Birmingham and the West and East Midlands. Their year end is 31 January. The company buy some stock centrally but delivery is always direct to the branches. Each branch has the power to buy on its own account but all bills are settled centrally. Some stock is transferred between branches depending on demand. The books are reasonably well kept by a member of the family who is a part qualified accountant. She prepares draft annual accounts which are ready by the end of April each year.

Discussion

Give an outline audit plan for use by Hex and Co. of Darlaston, the auditors, noting particularly the timing.

Student self testing questions *Questions with answers apparent from the text*

1. a. What work will be done on an interim audit? (5)
   b. What work will be done at the year end? (6)
   c. What work will be done at the final audit? (9)
   d. What factors determine the timing of particular audit work? (11)

Examination questions

1. You are a manager in a medium-sized auditing firm and you have just been informed by one of the partners that you are to be responsible for the audit of Solstice Ltd, a newly acquired client. Solstice Ltd has just incorporated as a limited company after trading for many years as an unincorporated business.

   It is expected that Solstice Ltd will have a turnover of about £10 million in its first year as a limited company and, as such, will be one of your largest clients. The Managing Director has written to you asking about the current year audit and, in particular, about the audit process.

   Requirement

   Prepare a draft letter to the Managing Director of Solstice Ltd explaining each of the following:

   a. The reasons why an audit is necessary. (2 marks)
   b. The effects that the audit requirement will have on his company. (4 marks)
   c. The different stages of the audit process. (18 marks)

   (ICAI) (Total 24 marks)

2. You are the auditor of Rigney Ltd, a company involved in the manufacture and distribution of bathroom fittings. Currently, the company is experiencing trading difficulties resulting in cash flow problems. The bank requires the signed year-end accounts by 31 January in order to be able to review the present overdraft facility.

   As the company's year-end is 31 December, you have agreed with the Finance Director that a roll forward type of audit approach would be the most appropriate. You have decided to start the audit in early December, carry out the necessary audit procedures based upon the 30 November management accounts, and then finish the audit in the last two weeks in January.

Requirement

a. Set out the audit procedures that you would carry out at both stages of the audit, assuming that you plan to rely on internal controls. (16 marks)

b. With regard to the approach considered appropriate in relation to (a) above, outline the amendments that would be necessary, if you did not plan to rely on internal controls. (4 marks)

(ICAI) (Total 20 marks)

*N.B. You are **not** required to detail the specific procedures to be carried out in the individual balance sheet or profit and loss account areas.*

12 Objectives and general principles

Introduction

1. There is a Statement of Auditing Standards SAS 100 *Objectives and General Principles Governing an Audit of Financial Statements* and ISA 200 *Objectives and General Principles Governing an Audit of Financial Statements*. This chapter is derived from that SAS and offers some commentary on its requirements.

Objectives

2. SAS 100 begins with a statement of the objective of an audit. The objective of an audit of financial statements is to enable auditors to give an opinion on those financial statements taken as a whole and thereby to provide reasonable assurance that the financial statements give a true and fair view (where relevant) and have been prepared in accordance with relevant accounting or other requirements. Let us look at this.

   a. **Opinion** – not a guarantee or a certificate just an opinion – see paragraph 9 of Chapter 1.

   b. **Taken as a whole**. This is a difficult point. Essentially there is a degree of imprecision in all but the very simplest of financial statements because they contain accounting estimates about uncertainties and unresolved transactions. There may even be some non-material misstatements in some of the individual items. However we hope that the auditor's activities provide an opinion that the overall view given by the financial statements is a true and fair one (or that it is not).

   c. **Reasonable assurance**. This is also difficult! An audit enhances the *credibility* of financial statements. However the user cannot assume that the auditor's opinion is a guarantee as to the *future viability* of the enterprise nor an assurance as to the *efficiency or effectiveness* with which management has conducted the affairs of the enterprise. Reasonable, as a word, contrasts with absolute.

   d. **True and fair view**. This is a difficult concept too – see Chapter 31. Note that some financial statements (e.g. those of local authorities) have different requirements from true and fair view.

   e. **Relevant accounting and other requirements**. These usually include Statutes (e.g. the Companies Act) and the Accounting Standards but may also include various industry specific SORPs (e.g. those of colleges) and Codes of Practice (e.g. those of local authorities).

Required procedures

3. SAS 100 *requires* that, in undertaking an audit of financial statements, auditors should:

    a. Carry out procedures designed to obtain sufficient appropriate audit evidence, in accordance with Auditing Standards to determine with reasonable confidence whether the financial statements are free of *material misstatement*.

    b. Evaluate the overall presentation of the financial statements, in order to ascertain whether they have been prepared in accordance with relevant legislation and accounting standards.

    c. Issue a report containing a clear expression of their opinion on the financial statements.

    Some comments:

    i. **Sufficient appropriate audit evidence.** This is a phrase to be committed to memory. It looks right in most auditing answers! Audit evidence is the whole thrust of this book but it is the special subject of Chapter 24. The gathering of evidence is a matter of judgement in deciding on the *nature, timing and extent* of audit procedures. Even when evidence has been gathered it is a matter of judgement what conclusions are drawn from the evidence. For example an auditor may gather much evidence on the future useful life of some plant and machinery – its natural life, the possibility of obsolescence, the cost of repairs as against replacement etc. but still has to determine whether he thinks the life selected by the directors is reasonable in the circumstances.

    ii. **The auditing standards**. These are discussed and listed in Chapter 6 and are to be found throughout the book.

    iii. **Reasonable confidence**. A problem with this idea is that not all auditors will see an audit problem in the same way. In any event the view given by financial statements is a mixture of fact (true) and judgement (fair). As a result financial statements cannot be correct. There are no absolute right treatments, judgements or accounting policies.

    iv. **Free of material misstatement**. Materiality is discussed in Chapter 36. Misstatement is usually in terms of fact. For example the creditors item does not include an actual creditor or the development expenditure carried forward does not comply with SSAP 13 or the requirements of the Companies Act re fixed assets have not been fully complied with.

    v. **Report.** The auditors' report is discussed in Chapters 35 to 40.

Influences on an audit

4. There are many influences on how an actual audit is conducted. These include:

    a. The Statements of Auditing Standards. These have to be complied with – see Chapter 6.

    b. Professional body rules – see Chapter 8. These are now very extensive.

    c. Legislation – for companies this is The Companies Act 1985 but most enterprises seem to be affected by some legislation or other. We live in a very regulated age.

d. The terms of the engagement – see Chapter 9.

e. Codes of practice. Some audits are influenced by codes of practice – local authorities are an example.

f. Audit risk – see Chapter 26. Risk (the possibility that an auditor may give an inappropriate audit opinion e.g. say the accounts give a true and fair view when they do not) permeates all auditing. Risk arises due to:

   i. Inherent risk in some areas. For example the risk of obsolescence in hi-tec industries, or the viability of construction companies in an industry in depression with excessive competition.

   ii. Control risk. The risk that internal controls fail to prevent or detect some misstatement. No system is perfect and human failings amongst other reasons may lead to some inability to detect or prevent some error or fraud.

   iii. The impracticality of examining all items within an *account balance* or *class of transactions*. Auditors test check or sample most populations of items. This raises the possibility of detection risk which is the possibility that the auditors' procedures may fail to detect some misstatement.

   iv. The possibility of some fraud or misrepresentation which is committed with *collusion* by staff or management.

   v. Audit evidence is usually persuasive rather than conclusive. Auditors do not expect a standard of evidence like that in a criminal trial where the decision as to a person's guilt has to be beyond all reasonable doubt. As a result an auditor may give an inappropriate opinion.

g. Fear of litigation. Actions under the law of tort to recover losses alleged to be caused by the negligence of auditors are common and very expensive for auditors in terms of cost, time and loss of clients and reputation. – see Chapter 46.

h. Ethics. SAS 100 requires that in the conduct of any audit of financial statements auditors should comply with the ethical guidance issued by their relevant professional bodies. These guides are now fairly extensive – see Chapter 8. Relevant matters include integrity, objectivity, independence, professional competence, due care, professional behaviour and confidentiality.

i. The individual auditing manual of the firm of auditors. These may be influenced by quality control standards.

Summary

5. a. SAS 100 and ISA 200 *Objectives and General Principles Governing an Audit of Financial Statements* is a general statement which governs all audits.

  b. SAS 100 has a statement of the objective of an audit. This should be learned by heart.

  c. SAS 100 requires certain procedures. These can be summarised as obtain evidence, evaluate the financial statements for truth and fairness, compliance with statutes and for compliance with accounting standards and finally make a report.

  d. There are numerous influences on the actual conduct of an audit including the risk of giving an inappropriate audit opinion.

Points to note

6. a. SAS 100 is a very important (if rather general) Statement of Auditing Standards. Many of the phrases should be memorised and reproduced in auditing answers.

    b. SAS 100 appears to be prescriptive in requiring auditors to do certain things (like gather evidence) and the requirements are expanded in detail in all the other SASs. However the reality is that the role of judgement is still paramount in auditing. Note words like sufficient, reasonable, risk, judgement, imprecision, uncertainties, opinion, material, conclusions.

    c. Note that financial statements are drawn up by the directors (or other managing bodies) who take full responsibility for them.

Case study 1

Dracula Stoneware LTD are a small company retailing gravestones in a small town. Their auditors are Simple & Co. Bram Simple, a partner, performs the audit like this:

–   After the year end John Goole, a senior audit clerk. is sent to the company's premises.

–   He finds that the books are in excellent shape but that no postings have been made to the nominal ledger which in fact is kept at the accountants.

–   He reconciles the cash book to the bank statements, prepares and balances total accounts for the sales and purchase ledgers, reconciles the VAT, PAYE and NI payments, posts the nominal ledger, extracts a trial balance, prepares a list of prepayments, accruals and other adjustments, prepares the Annual Accounts, directors' report etc.

–   He then shows drafts to the directors, settles any queries and returns to Simple & Co. where Mr Simple glances through the drafts comparing the figures with previous years.

–   The Accounts are then typed and copies sent to the client and to the Inland Revenue.

Discussion

Relate this approach to the standard.

Can the standard be applied to audits such as that of Dracula?

How could Simple & Co's office organisation be adapted to the requirements of the standard?

Does this have any bearing on costs and welfare economics?

Case study 2

Boffin is the junior technical partner of Wood, Tree & Co., Certified Accountants. His partners have asked him to draw up a statement contrasting and comparing the audit work required by the Companies Act and by SAS 100.

Discussion

Draw up the statement.

Case study 3

Delbert is about to commence the audit of Sandcastle PLC. This a company in the construction and speculative housing industry which has expanded greatly in recent years. It is run by Gogetter who is known as a very autocratic but charismatic entrepreneur. He has expanded the company rapidly by both acquisition and internal growth. The company is heavily geared and the share price has fallen from an absurd high to a very low figure in the past two years.

Discussion

a. In what ways is there a risk of misstatement in the auditor's opinion on the financial statements?
b. What influences would act on Delbert in conducting the audit?

Student self testing questions *Questions with answers apparent from the text*

1. a. Define the objective of an audit. (2)
   b. What is meant by opinion, taken as a whole, reasonable assurance, true and fair view? (2)
   c. State the procedures required by SAS 100. (3)
   d. List possible influences on the conduct of an audit. (4)
   e. What risks are relevant to an auditor? (3)
   f. Why is an audit not just a set of mechanical procedures? (5)

Examination question

1. You are the partner in charge of the audit of Q Limited for the year ending 30 September 1984. Q Limited is a small company which has expanded rapidly during the last year. Turnover has increased by 80% from £1M to £1.8M, trading profit by 65% from £120,000 to £198,000 and net assets by 90% from £1.7M to £3.23M. The share capital is entirely owned by the Smith family with Mr James Smith and his two sons managing the business on a day-to-day basis.

   As a result of the increased activity during the last year the accounting staff has increased from 2 clerks under the control of Mr James Smith to four staff comprising a qualified chief accountant under the supervision of Mr James Smith and three clerks. As a result of the increased accounting workload and staff numbers, sales and wages systems have been introduced. Purchases are still dealt with on a purely manual cash book basis.

   You have indicated to Mr James Smith that you have to request an increase in the audit fee. Mr Smith has always considered the audit of his family company unnecessary and considers this request for an increased fee as being a complete waste of money.

   Required:
   a. i. Explain to Mr. Smith why an audit is required. (2 marks)
      ii. Outline the basis for determining the fee which your firm would charge. (2 marks)
   b. Describe in outline the stages of the audit of Mr Smith's company indicating in what order the audit work would be carried out. (8 marks)
   c. Describe the benefits of the audit and give FOUR specific uses of audited accounts. (8 marks)

   (ACCA)

The conduct of the audit

1. The next section of the book describes the auditor's interest in his client's system of accounting and internal control (Chapters 13 and 14). Chapters 15 and 16 explain audit testing of the books and records of an enterprise and Chapter 17 describes the manner in which an auditor records and documents his work.

2. At the conclusion of a session of audit testing, an auditor will usually discover a number of weaknesses in the way his client is recording, documenting and controlling his transactions. The penultimate chapter in this section shows how an auditor informs his client of these weaknesses.

3. The final chapter deals with an old subject which has recently received renewed attention – the auditor's duty toward error and fraud.

13 Accounting systems

Introduction

1. This chapter considers:
   a. The auditor's interest in a client's accounting system.
   b. The management's interest in the accounting system.
   c. The need for controls over the system.
   d. The auditor's procedures concerning the accounting system.

   The relevant Statement of Auditing Standards is SAS 300 *Accounting and Internal Control Systems and Audit Risk Assessments*.

The auditor's interest in a client's accounting system

2. The auditor's interest in a client's accounting system comes from two sources:
   a. SAS 300 requires that auditors should obtain an understanding of the accounting and internal control systems sufficient to plan the audit and develop an effective audit approach. Further SAS 300 requires that auditors should, in planning the audit obtain and document an understanding of the accounting system and control environment sufficient to determine their audit approach.
   b. The Companies Act 1985 Section 237 states:

   (1) A company's auditors shall, in preparing their report, carry out such investigations as will enable them to form an opinion as to:

   (a) whether proper accounting records have been kept by the company and proper returns adequate for their audit have been received from branches not visited by them,

   (b) whether the company's balance sheet and (if not consolidated) its profit and loss account are in agreement with the accounting records and returns.

   If the auditors form a contrary opinion, they must state the fact in their report.

The management's interest in an accounting system

3. The management of an enterprise need *complete* and accurate accounting and other records because:
   a. the business cannot otherwise be controlled
   b. day-to-day records of debtors and creditors are indispensable
   c. assets can only be safeguarded if a proper record of them is made
   d. financial statements which are required for numerous purposes can only be prepared if adequate primary records exist
   e. statutes (e.g. the Companies Act) often have specific requirements on record keeping for specific types of business
   f. record keeping for PAYE, NHI, VAT and statutory sick pay an statutory maternity pay is also a statutory requirement.

4. What constitutes an adequate system of accounting depends on the circumstances. A small shopkeeper may find that a 'Simplex' book and a spike for unpaid invoices may suffice but an international company clearly needs rather more sophisticated records. The basic needs of a system is that it provides for the orderly assembly of accounting information to enable the financial statements to be prepared but all the other requirements of paragraph 3 must be borne in mind.

The need for controls over the system

5. A system of accounting and record keeping will not succeed in completely and accurately processing all transactions unless controls, known as internal controls, are built into the system. The purposes of such internal controls are:
   a. to ensure transactions are executed in accordance with proper general or specific *authorisation*
   b. to ensure all transactions are *promptly recorded* at the *correct amount*, in the *appropriate accounts* and in the proper *accounting period* so as to permit preparation of *financial statements* in accordance with relevant legislation and accounting standards
   c. to ensure *access to assets* is permitted only in accordance with proper authorisation
   d. to ensure recorded assets are compared with the existing assets at reasonable intervals and appropriate action is taken with regard to any differences
   e. to ensure errors and irregularities are avoided or made apparent.

Auditor's procedures

6. The auditor's procedures will depend on the circumstances but may include:
   a. Obtaining an understanding of the enterprise as a whole in order to see the accounting system in context and thus being able to assess the system's effectiveness and appropriateness.
   b. Ascertaining the complete system by enquiry, use of an internal control questionnaire or requesting the client to supply full details.
   c. Recording the system in the form of flowcharts, narrative notes, check lists or in the answers to the Internal Control Questionnaire. ICQs are explained in Chapter 17.

d. If the auditor intends to rely on the internal controls, he should record the system of controls in especial detail.

e. If the system specification was supplied by the client, then perform walk-through checks to confirm the correctness of the description.

f. Perform a preliminary evaluation of the system.

g. If the system of controls seems adequate and the auditor is able to and wishes to rely upon the controls, then design and perform compliance tests.

h. If the auditor does not feel able to rely on the controls then perform substantive tests on the records. In any case, some substantive tests must be planned and performed on all material items.

i. Evaluate his evidence and form an opinion on whether proper books of account have been kept and whether the records form a reliable basis for the preparation of financial statements.

SAS 300 requires that auditors should obtain and *document* an understanding of the accounting system and control environment sufficient to determine their approach. This does not mean that a detailed knowledge of the accounting system or internal controls is required. However SAS 300 suggests that what is required is an understanding of the system sufficient to enable them to identify and understand:

a. major classes of transactions in the entity's operations

b. how such transactions are initiated

c. significant accounting records, supporting documents and accounts in the financial statements

d. the accounting and financial process, from the initiation of significant transactions and other events to their conclusion in the financial statements.

This seems to be very comprehensive! However note the words major and significant.

More detailed knowledge of internal controls may be required if the auditor, after evaluating risk matters, decides that her approach is to rely on some internal controls as audit evidence. In practice an understanding of accounting records often goes hand in hand with an understanding of internal controls. In any event the auditor needs to have evidence on The Companies Act 1985 S 237 requirements.

International Auditing Standard 400

7. International Standard on Auditing 400 Risk Assessments and Internal Control includes the following requirements which are not reflected in SAS 300:

a. The auditor should obtain an understanding of the accounting system sufficient to identify and understand:

i   major classes of transactions in the entity's operations

ii how such transactions are initiated

iii significant accounting records, supporting documents and accounts in the financial statements

iv the accounting and financial reporting process, from the initiation of significant transactions and other events to their inclusion in the financial statements.

b. The auditor should obtain an understanding of the *control environment* sufficient to assess directors' and management's attitudes, awareness and actions regarding internal controls and their importance in the entity.

c. The auditor should obtain an understanding of the control procedures sufficient to develop the audit plan.

Summary

8. a. The auditor needs to evaluate the accounting system in order to form a conclusion on whether the records form a reliable basis for the preparation of the Accounts and whether proper books of account have been kept.

b. Authority for this view comes from The Companies Act 1985 S.237 and from SAS 300.

c. No enterprise can be managed and controlled successfully without adequate records.

d. Adequate accounting systems must incorporate internal controls to ensure authority, completeness and accuracy and to prevent or uncover error and fraud.

e. Auditors need to investigate, record, test and form an opinion on the accounting system.

Points to note

9. a. The expression 'accounting systems' must be seen as wider than books of account. It encompasses all the procedures necessary to record transactions in the form of documents (e.g. goods inward notes, clock cards etc.) as well as the actual books of account.

b. In recent auditing literature, internal controls have been seen as a separate system superimposed upon the accounting system. In practice the accounting system and the system of internal controls are really one system and investigation and testing of both systems is carried out simultaneously.

c. It is essential to realise that auditors are interested in accounting systems not only as a step along the way of forming an opinion on the truth and fairness and compliance with statute but also as an audit aim in itself.

d. Commit to memory the phrase 'whether or not the accounting records form a reliable basis for the preparation of the accounts'.

Case study 1

Sunbeam Ltd own a garage in Hightown. They sell imported Yaki cars, have a spares service for Yaki, and offer servicing, petrol and motor accessories to the public.

The records are:

All cash sales are recorded daily for each section in a giant cash book. Credit sales are evidenced by copy invoices. Each invoice is marked 'paid' on the date when it is paid. No sales ledger is kept.

Incoming invoices are placed on a spike. When they are paid, they are marked as such and filed away.

Cheques are entered consecutively in the cash book.

There is a wages book and a rudimentary petty cash book.

A private ledger is written up annually by Manuel Day & Co., Certified Accountants the auditors.

Discussion

Relate this system to the requirements of Section 237 Companies Act 1985.

Student self testing questions *Questions with answers apparent from the text*

1. a. Detail the auditor's interest in a client's accounting records. (2)
    b. Why should management maintain good accounting records? (3)
    c. Why are internal controls necessary? (5)
    d. Summarise the auditor's procedures in connection with a client's accounting systems. (6)

Examination question

1. The external auditor has duties in connection with the client's accounting system.
    a. What are these duties?
    b. What procedures does an auditor adopt to discharge these duties?

(LCCI)

14 Internal controls

Introduction

1. This chapter considers the auditors' approach to internal control systems as outlined in SAS 300 and then considers what internal control is and then gives a detailed review of internal control in specific areas. At the end we take a look at the ideas on control environment and control procedures and consider the limitations of internal control.

The auditor and internal control

2. SAS 300 and ISA 400 requires auditors:
    a. to obtain an understanding of the accounting and internal control systems sufficient to plan the audit and develop an effective audit approach
    b. in planning the audit, to obtain and document an understanding of the accounting system and control environment sufficient to determine their audit approach
    c. if after obtaining an understanding of the accounting systems and control environment, they expect to be able to rely on their assessment of control risk to reduce the extent of their substantive procedures, they should make a preliminary assessment of control risk for material financial statement assertions, and should plan and perform tests of control to support that assessment.

    Control risk is defined as the risk that a misstatement that could occur in an account balance or class of transactions and that could be material, either individually or when aggregated with misstatements in other balances or classes, would not be prevented, or detected and corrected on a timely basis, by the accounting and internal control systems.

Tests of control are tests to obtain audit evidence about the effective operation of the accounting and internal control systems, that is, that properly designed controls – identified in the preliminary assessment of control risk – exist in fact and have operated effectively throughout the relevant period. Such tests are also called *compliance tests*.

3. Suppose the auditor, Rosemary, of Sheinton Widgets Ltd is starting her audit. She explores and obtains an understanding of the accounting and internal control system of the whole company but we will consider sales. She is concerned that the figure for sales is complete and that no sales have been omitted. In effect we can say that the directors in putting sales at £x in the Profit and Loss Account are asserting things about sales including that all are included. Our auditor needs to have evidence of this.

   She considers the internal controls applied to sales and assesses that they seem well designed and effective in theory. However there is a control risk that a misstatement (a material amount of sales are omitted) may occur and that the internal control system will not prevent it or detect it and correct it. Rosemary decides that part of her audit evidence on the completeness of sales will be reliance on the internal controls applied to sales. Rosemary now has to design, perform, document and draw conclusions from tests of control.

   A notable point from SAS 300 is that 'regardless of the assessed levels of inherent and control risks, auditors should perform some substantive procedures for financial statement assertions of material account balances and transactions classes.' In this case possible omission of sales is a material matter and Rosemary will need to perform some substantive tests as well as testing the controls.

Definition

4. Internal control is defined as:

   'Internal control system – the whole system of controls, financial and otherwise, established by the management in order to carry on the business of the enterprise in an orderly and efficient manner, ensure adherence to management policies, safeguard the assets and secure as far as possible the completeness and accuracy of the records. The individual components of an internal control system are known as 'controls' or 'internal controls.'

5. In this paragraph, we will consider the definition in detail:

   a. **The whole system**. Internal controls can be seen as single procedures (e.g. Clerk A checks the calculations performed by Clerk B) or as a whole system. The whole system should be more than the sum of the parts.

   b. **Financial and otherwise**. The distinction is not important. Perhaps *financial* would include the use of control accounts and *otherwise* may include physical access restrictions to computer terminals.

   c. **Established by the management**. Internal control systems are established by the management, either directly or by means of external consultants, internal audit, or accounting personnel. External auditors may be asked to advise on the setting up of systems.

   d. **'Carry on … efficient manner.'** Clearly the converse is unacceptable in any business.

e. **Ensure adherence to management policies**. Not all management have *expressed* policies. But as an example a budget is an expression of management policy and adherence to the budget can be achieved by procedures such as variance analysis. Another example might be the selling prices of the enterprise's products being laid down by management and controls existing to ensure that these prices are adhered to.

f. **Safeguard the assets**. Obviously allowing assets to be broken, lost or stolen, is unacceptable and procedures are always devised to safeguard them. Examples are locks and keys, the keeping of a plant register, regular reviews of debtor balances etc. An aspect of this which is often overlooked is that payment where no benefits have been received, as payment for piece work not done, or the setting up of liabilities where no benefit has been received – as in fraudulent purchase and subsequent embezzlement of goods by employees – are both examples of failure to safeguard assets.

g. **Secure ... completeness**. It is especially important that *all* transactions are recorded and processed. Procedures which do this include checks that no goods leave the factory without a delivery note followed by regular comparison of invoices with delivery notes to see that no goods sold (always evidenced by a delivery note) have failed to result in an invoice.

h. **And accuracy of the records**. Again, the converse is unacceptable. Examples of procedures to achieve this include checking of the work of one clerk by another or, the use of control accounts, independent comparison of two sets of records e.g. stock records and stock, or piecework payments and good work put into store.

Types of internal control

6. The types of internal control can be categorised as:

a. **Organisation**. An enterprise should:

i. have a plan of organisation which should –

ii. define and allocate responsibilities – every function should be in the charge of a specified person who might be called the *responsible official*. Thus the keeping of petty cash should be entrusted to a particular person who is then responsible (and hence answerable) for that function

iii. identify lines of reporting.

In all cases, the *delegation of authority* and responsibility should be clearly specified.

An employee should always know the precise powers delegated to him, the extent of his authority and to whom he should report. Two examples:

1. Responsibility for approving the purchase of items of plant may be retained by the Board of Directors for items over £X and within the competence of the works manager for a budgeted amount agreed by the board.

2. Responsibility for the correct operation of internal controls may be delegated by the board to specific management personnel and to the internal audit department.

b. **Segregation of duties**.

i. No one person should be responsible for the recording and processing of a complete transaction.

    ii.   The involvement of several people reduces the risk of intentional manipulation or accidental error and increases the element of checking of work.

    iii. Functions which for a given transaction should be separated include initiation (e.g. the works foreman decides the firm needs more lubricating oil), authorisation (the works manager approves the purchase), execution (the buying department order the oil), custody (on arrival the oil is taken in by the goods-in section and passed with appropriate goods-in documentation to the stores department) and recording (the arrival is documented by the goods inward section and the invoice is compared with the original order and goods-in note by the accounts department, and recorded by them in the books).

Another example is the area of sales where initiation is by a representative, authorisation by credit control and the sales manager, execution is by the finished goods warehouse staff who physically send the goods, custody is transferred from the warehouse staff to the transport department, and the transaction is recorded by the goods outward section, the invoicing section and the accounts department.

c. **Physical**.

    i.   This concerns physical custody of assets and involves procedures designed to limit access to authorised personnel only.

    ii. Access can be direct, e.g. being able to enter the warehouse or indirect, that is by documentation e.g. personnel knowing the correct procedures, may be able to extract goods by doing the right paper work.

    iii. These controls are especially important in the case of valuable, portable, exchangeable or desirable assets. Examples are the locking of securities (share certificates etc.) in a safe *with procedures for the custody of use of the keys*, use of passes to restrict access to the warehouse, use of password to restrict access to particular computer files.

d. **Authorisation and approval**. This is a special case of type a. above. All transactions should require authorisation or approval by an appropriate person. The limits to these authorisations should be specified. Examples:

    i.   All credit sales must be approved by the credit control department.

    ii. All overtime must be approved by the works manager.

    iii. All individual office stationery purchases may be approved by the office manager up to a limit of £n. Higher purchases must be approved by the chief accountant.

e. **Arithmetical and accounting**.

    i.   These are the controls in the recording function which *check* that the transactions have been *authorised*, that they are *all* included and that they are *correctly* recorded and *accurately* processed.

    ii. Procedures include checking the arithmetical accuracy of the records, the maintenance and checking of totals, reconciliations, control accounts, trial balances, accounting for documents (sometimes known as sequence checks or continuity checks) and preview. Preview means that before an important action involving the company's property is taken, the person concerned should review the documentation available to see that all that should have been done, has been done. Examples of all these:

1. Clerk A checking the extensions of a sales invoice, the extensions having been made by Clerk B.

2. The purchases invoices checked by the purchase invoice section of the accounting department being prelisted by that section before sending them to the computer department for processing.

3. An official in the accounting department independent of the cash book officials, making a *bank reconciliation*.

4. An accountant, independent of the sales ledger function, making a sales ledger control account.

5. A clerk in the buying department examining purchase requisitions to ensure that they are correct, complete and authorised before making out an order.

6. A clerk in the accounting department comparing the incoming purchase invoices with copy order forms and goods inwards notes.

7. An accounting official going through the goods outward records to verify that all have been followed by an invoice.

8. Checking that the copy cash sales invoices are in numerical sequence. (If one is missing a clerk may have made a sale and misappropriated the cash received.)

f. **Personnel.**

   i. Procedures should be designed to ensure that personnel operating a system are competent and motivated to carry out the tasks assigned to them, as the proper functioning of a system depends upon the competence and integrity of the operating personnel.

   ii. Measures include appropriate remuneration and promotion and career development prospects, selection of people with appropriate personal characteristics and training, and assignment to tasks of the right level.

g. **Supervision.** All actions by all levels of staff should be supervised. The responsibility for supervision should be clearly laid down and communicated to the person being supervised.

h. **Management.**

   i. These are controls, exercised by management which are outside and over and above the day-to-day routine of the system.

   ii. They include overall supervisory controls, review of management accounts, comparisons with budgets, internal audit and any other special review procedures.

   Examples:

   1. Senior management must be aware of day-to-day activities and be seen by staff to be so. Glaring failures of control (stock thefts, excess stocking, unnecessary overtime) will become apparent and staff will be motivated to perform well.

2. Management accounts should be designed to summarise performance in fine detail. Any anomalies (cost overruns, travelling expense fiddles) should become apparent.

3. Budgeting and variance analysis is a management tool which should prevent or at least detect departure from management's intended plans.

7. In addition to the above, two other categories are

a. **Acknowledgement of performance**. Persons performing data processing operations should acknowledge their activities by means of signatures, initials, rubber stamps, etc. For example, if invoice calculations have to be checked, the checker should initial each invoice. Acknowledgement of performance not only allows blame to be ascribed but also has a powerful psychological effect. Audit clerks usually initial the audit programme when they have completed a part of the work. Even audit clerks are reluctant to confirm in writing that they have examined a thousand credit notes when they have looked at only one hundred!

b. **Budgeting**. A common technique used in business is the use of budgets, which can be defined as quantitative plans of action. Budgets having been agreed, can be compared with actual turn-out and differences investigated.

Design of systems of accounting and internal control

8. The design of accounting and control systems is a specialised activity and an auditing manual is not the place for a detailed description of the processes involved. However we will look at one example. Luso Books Ltd run a small mail order operation selling specialist books. The firm advertise and the customers send in their requirements through the post with cheques. Clearly there is a risk of employees misappropriating the cheques and other problems and to avoid these a system like this may be installed:

1. All post to be opened by one member of an authorised group of staff in the presence of another.

2. All orders are transcribed onto a pre-printed form (the blank forms are numbered consecutively).

3. Cheques are entered into a 'post cash book' which is totalled daily and initialled by all staff members present.

4. Cheques are sent to the cashier for banking and accounting in the computer system.

5. Orders are sent to dispatch for processing.

6. Other mail is sent to the appropriate manager.

7. Totals banked shown on a print-out are compared weekly with the sales invoices prepared by dispatch and with the bank paying in slip and the post cash book by a senior manager.

8. The completed forms are checked for consecutivity by a senior manager.

9. In practice this system will have complications – what happens to orders without cheques or cheques for the wrong amount etc. etc.? Clearly there are other parts to the whole system of the company. However you may be able to discern some features of the system:

– organisation – specified responsibilities, specified procedures

- segregation of duties – several people are involved and no one person has complete charge of all aspects of the transactions
- arithmetic – reconciliations of post cash book, sales invoices and bankings. Also numerical sequence checks.

Internal control in specific areas of a business

10. This section is divided up into the areas of activity usually found in a business. At the beginning of each area are stated the objectives of internal control in the area and some measures then follow which will achieve the objectives.

a. **Internal control generally**

Objectives

To carry on the business in an orderly and efficient manner, to ensure adherence to management policies, safeguard its assets, and secure the accuracy and reliability of the records.

Measures

1. An appropriate and integrated system of accounts and records.
2. Internal controls over those accounts and records.
3. Financial supervision and control by management, including budgetary control, management accounting reports, and interim accounts.
4. Safeguarding and if necessary duplicating records.
5. Engaging, training, allocating to specific duties staff who are capable of fulfilling their responsibilities. *Rotation* of duties and cover for absences.

b. **Cash and cheques received by post**

Objectives

To ensure that *all* cash and cheques received by post are accounted for and accurately recorded in the books.

To ensure all such receipts are *promptly* and *intactly* deposited in the bank.

Measures

1. Measures to prevent interception of mail between receipt and opening.
2. Appointment of an official to be responsible for the opening of the post.
3. Two persons to be present at the opening of the post.
4. All cheques and other negotiable instruments to be immediately given a restrictive crossing eg account payee only, not negotiable.
5. Immediate entry of the details of the receipts (date, payer, amount, cash, cheque, or other) in a 'rough cash book' or post list of money received. The list should be signed by both parties present.
6. Regular independent comparison of the post list with banking records. The tests should be of total, detail and dating to detect teeming and lading at a later stage in the processing.

c. **Cash sales and collections**

Objectives

To ensure that all cash, to which the enterprise is entitled, is received.

To ensure that all such cash is properly accounted for and entered in the records.

To ensure that all such cash is promptly and intactly deposited.

Measures

1. Prescribing and limiting the number of persons who are authorised to receive cash e.g. sales assistants, cashiers, roundsmen, travellers etc.

2. Establishing a means of evidencing cash receipts e.g. pre-numbered duplicate receipt forms, cash registers with sealed till rolls. The duplicate receipt form books should be securely held and issue controlled.

3. Ensuring that customers are aware that they must receive a receipt form or ensuring that the amount rung up on the cash register is clearly visible to the customer.

4. Appointment of officers with responsibility for emptying cash registers at prescribed intervals, and agreeing the amount present with till roll totals or internal registers. Such collections should be evidenced in writing and be initialled by the assistant and the supervisor.

5. Immediate and intact banking. Payments out should be from funds drawn from the bank on an imprest system.

6. Investigation of shorts and overs.

7. Independent comparison of agreed till roll totals with subsequent banking records.

8. Persons handling cash should not have access to other cash funds or to bought or sales ledger records.

9. Rotation of duties and cover for holidays (which should be compulsory) and sickness.

10. Collections by roundsmen and travellers should be banked intact daily. There should be independent comparison of the amounts banked with records (e.g. duplicate receipt books) of the roundsmen and salesmen.

11. Wherever possible roundsmen should have a controlled issue of merchandise with a check, on their return, that they have cash or goods to the value of the controlled issue on the lines of an imprest system.

d. **Payments into bank**

Objectives

To ensure that all cash and cheques received are banked intact.

To ensure that all cash and cheques received are banked without delay at prescribed intervals, preferably daily.

To ensure that all cash and cheques received are accounted for and recorded accurately.

Measures

1. Cash and cheques should be banked intact.

2. Cash and cheques should be banked without delay preferably daily.

3. The bank paying-in slip should be prepared by an official with no access to cash collection points, bought or sales ledgers.

4. Bankings should be made with security in mind e.g. for large cash sums, security guards should be used.

5. There should be independent comparison of paying-in slips with collection records, post lists and sales ledger records.

e. **Cash balances**

Objectives

To prevent misappropriation of cash balances.

To prevent unauthorised cash payments.

Measures

1. Establishment of cash floats of specified amounts and locations.

2. Appointment of officials responsible for each cash balance.

3. Arrangement of security measures including use of safes and restriction of access.

4. Use of imprest system with rules on reimbursement only against authorised vouchers.

5. Strict rules on the authorising of cash payments.

6. Independent cash counts on a regular and a surprise basis.

7. Insurance arrangements e.g. for cash balances and fidelity guarantee.

8. Special rules for IOUs. Preferably these should not be permitted.

f. **Bank balances**

Objectives

To prevent misappropriation of bank balances.

To prevent teeming and lading.

Measures

1. Reconciliations should be prepared at prescribed frequency.

2. They should be performed by independent personnel.

3. Arrangements should be made for bank statements to be sent direct to the person responsible for the reconciliations.

4. Work on reconciliations should include:

A comparison of each debit and credit in the cash book with the corresponding entries in the bank statements.

A comparison of returned cheques with the cash book entries noting dates, payees and amounts.

A test of the detailed paying-in slips with the cash book.

The dates of credits in the bank statements should be carefully compared with the cash book to detect any delays.

All outstanding cheques and lodgements should be traced through to the next period and their validity verified.

Any unusual items e.g. contras or dishonoured cheques should be investigated.

5. The balances at the bank should be independently verified with the bank at intervals.

6. Special arrangements should be instituted on the controls and recording of trust monies e.g. employees' sick pay or holiday funds, attachment of earnings.

g. **Cheque payments**

Objectives

To prevent unauthorised payments being made from bank accounts.

Measures

1. Control over custody and issue of unused cheque books. A register should be kept if necessary.

2. Appointment of an official to be responsible for the preparation of cheques or traders credits.

3. Rules should be established for the presentation of supporting documents before cheques can be made out. Such supporting documents may include GRNs, orders, invoices, etc.

4. All such documents should be stamped 'paid by cheque no. ...' with date.

5. Establishment of who can sign cheques. All cheques should be signed by at least two persons, with no person being permitted to sign if he is a payee.

6. No cheques should be made out to bearer except for the collection of wages or reimbursement of cash funds.

7. All cheques should be restrictively crossed.

8. The signing of blank cheques must be prohibited.

9. Special safeguards should be implemented where cheques are signed mechanically or have pre-printed signatures. Such signings are often made for dividend payments, salary cheques and other reasons.

10. Rules to ensure prompt despatch and to prevent interception or misappropriation.

11. Measures to ensure cash discounts are obtained.

12. Special rules for authorising and checking direct debits and standing orders.

13. Separation of duties: custody, recording and initiation of cheque payments: cash records and other areas e.g. debtors and creditors.

h. **Wages and salaries**

Objectives

To ensure that wages and salaries are paid only to actual employees at authorised rates of pay.

To ensure that all wages and salaries are computed in accordance with records of work performed whether in respect of time, output, sales made or other criteria.

To ensure that payrolls are correctly calculated.

To ensure that payments are made only to the correct employees.

To ensure that payroll deductions are correctly accounted for and paid over to the appropriate third parties.

To ensure that all transactions are correctly recorded in the books of account.

Measures

1. There should be separate records kept for each employee. The records should contain such matters as date of engagement, age, next of kin, agreed deductions, skills, department, and specimen signature. Ideally these records should be maintained by a separate personnel department.

2. Procedures for, and specified officials responsible for, engagements, retirements, dismissals, fixing and changing rates of pay. Procedures should be laid down for notification of these matters to the personnel and wage roll preparation departments.

3. Time records should be kept, preferably by means of supervised clock card recording. These should be approved and approval acknowledged. All overtime should be authorised.

4. Output or piecework records should be properly controlled and authorised. Procedures should exist for reconciling output or piecework records with production records.

5. The payroll should be prepared by personnel unconnected with other wage duties. Special procedures should exist for dealing with advances, holiday pay, lay-off pay, luncheon vouchers, new employees, employees leaving, sickness and other absences and bonuses.

6. The payroll should be checked by separate personnel. All work on the preparation and checking of the payroll should be initialled. All such work should be supervised and the payroll scrutinised and approved by a senior official.

7. The net amount due to be paid out in cash should be drawn after a coin analysis. Tight security should be imposed on the security of cash, both on collection from the bank and at all times up to the receipt of pay envelopes by the workforce. Ideally collection of cash from the bank should be by a security organisation.

8. Wage envelopes should be made up by personnel independent of the wage roll preparation team.

9. Specified times should be laid down for distribution of wage packets. These should either be acknowledged by the recipients or distribution should be made in the presence of (but not by) foremen or others capable of identifying employees.

10. Surprise attendance at payouts should be made at intervals by internal audit or by a senior official.

11. Unclaimed wages should be subject to special procedures. These should include a record to be maintained of unclaimed wages, safe custody of such pay packets, a requirement for investigation, subsequent payout only after proof of entitlement, breaking down and rebanking after a specified period of time.

12. Payments by cheque and credit transfer should be subject to special procedures. These could include maintenance of a separate bank account with regular reconciliation.

13. Deductions such as PAYE, national insurance, pension contributions, save as you earn, and union dues should be subject to prompt payment over to the institutions concerned. Control totals subject to frequent review should be kept.

Independent comparisons of such totals with records such as tax deduction cards should be performed regularly.

14. Regular independent comparisons should be made between personnel records and wages records.

15. Regular independent comparisons of payrolls at different dates.

16. Regular independent comparisons of wages paid with budgets and investigation of variances.

17. Surprise investigation of wage records and procedures by internal audit or senior officials.

18. An independent official should be appointed to be responsible for settling queries.

19. Wage records should conform to the requirements of Statutory Sick Pay.

Note that most firms now credit employees bank accounts through the banking system.

i. **Purchases and trade creditors**

Objectives

To ensure that goods and services are only ordered in the quantity, of the quality, and at the best terms available after appropriate requisition and approval.

To ensure that goods and services received are inspected and only acceptable items are accepted.

To ensure that all invoices are checked against authorised orders and receipt of the subject matter in good condition.

To ensure that all goods and services invoiced are properly recorded in the books.

Measures

1. There should be procedures for the requisitioning of goods and services only by specified personnel on specified forms with space for acknowledgement of performance.

2. Order forms should be pre-numbered and kept in safe custody. Issue of blank order form books should be controlled and recorded.

3. Order procedures should include requirements for obtaining tenders, estimates or competitive bids.

4. Sequence checks of order forms should be performed regularly by a senior official and missing items investigated.

5. All goods received should be recorded on goods received notes (preferably pre-numbered) or in a special book.

6. All goods should be inspected for condition and agreement with order and counted on receipt. The inspection should be acknowledged. Procedures for dealing with rejected goods or services should include the creation of debit notes (pre-numbered) with subsequent sequence checks and follow up of receipt of suppliers' credit notes.

7. At intervals, a listing of unfulfilled orders should be made and investigated.

8. Invoices should be checked for arithmetical accuracy, pricing, correct treatment of VAT and trade discount, and agreement with order and goods-in records. These checks should be acknowledged by the performer preferably on spaces marked by a rubber stamp on the invoices.

9. Invoices should have consecutive numbers put on them and batches should be pre-listed.

10. Totals of entries in the invoice register or day book should be regularly checked with the pre-lists.

11. Responsibility for purchase ledger entries should be vested in personnel separate from personnel responsible for ordering, receipt of goods and the invoice register.

12. The purchase ledger should be subject to frequent reconciliations in total by or be checked by an independent senior official.

13. Ledger account balances should be regularly compared with suppliers' statements of account.

14. All goods and service procurement should be controlled by budgetary techniques. Orders should only be placed that are within budget limits. There should be frequent comparisons of actual purchases with budgets and investigation into variances.

15. Cut-off procedures at the year end are essential.

16. A proper coding system is required for purchase of goods and services so that the correct nominal accounts are debited.

j. **Sales and debtors**

Objectives

To ensure that all customers orders are promptly executed.

To ensure that sales on credit are made only to bona fide good credit risks.

To ensure that all sales on credit are invoiced, that authorised prices are charged and that before issue all invoices are completed and checked as regards price, trade discounts and VAT.

To ensure that all invoices raised are entered in the books.

To ensure that all customers claims are fully investigated before credit notes are issued.

To ensure that every effort is made to collect all debts.

To ensure that no unauthorised credits are made to debtors accounts.

Measures

1. Incoming orders should be recorded, and if necessary, acknowledged, on pre-numbered forms. Orders should be matched with invoices and lists prepared at intervals of outstanding orders for management action. Sequence checks should be made regularly by a senior official.

2. Credit control. There should be procedures laid down for verifying the credit worthiness of all persons or institutions requesting goods on credit. For existing customers, credit worthiness data should be kept up-to-date and checks made that outstanding balances plus a new sale does not cause the pre-set credit limit

to be exceeded. For new customers, investigative techniques should be applied including enquiry of trade protection organisations, credit rating agencies, referees, the company's file with the Registrar of Companies, etc. A credit limit should be established. This may be fixed at two levels, a higher one such that further sales are not made and a lower one such that management are informed and a judgement made on granting credit.

3. Selling prices should be prescribed. Policies should be laid down on credit terms, trade and cash discounts, and special prices.

4. Despatch of goods should only be on properly evidenced authority. Goods out should be recorded either in a register or using pre-numbered despatch notes. Unissued blocks of despatch notes should be safeguarded and issue recorded. Sequence checks of despatch notes should be made regularly by a senior official. Where appropriate acknowledgement of receipt of goods should be made by customers on copy despatch notes.

5. Invoicing should be carried out by a separate department or by sales staff. Invoices should be pre-numbered and the custody and issue of unused invoice blocks controlled and recorded. Sequence checks should be regularly made by a senior official and missing or spoiled invoices investigated.

6. All invoices should be independently checked for agreement with customer order, with the goods despatched record, for pricing, discounts, VAT and other details. All actions should be acknowledged by signature or initials.

7. Accounting for sales and debtors should be segregated by employing separate staff for cash, invoice register, sales ledger entries and statement preparation.

8. Sales invoices should be pre-listed before entry into the invoice register or day book and the pre-list total independently compared with the total of the register.

9. Customer claims should be recorded and investigated. Similar controls (e.g. pre-numbering) should be applied to credit notes. At the year end, uncleared claims should be carefully investigated and assessed. All credit notes should be subject to acknowledged approval by a senior official.

10. A control account should be regularly and independently prepared.

11. Debtors statements should be prepared by personnel separate from the sales ledger personnel. Posting should be subject to safeguards so that no statements are misappropriated before posting.

12. Procedures must exist for identifying and chasing slow payers. Very overdue balances should be brought to the attention of senior management for legal or other action to be taken.

13. All balances must be reviewed regularly by an independent official to identify and investigate overdue accounts, debtors paying by instalments or round sums, and accounts where payments do not match invoices.

14. Bad debts should only be written off after due investigation and acknowledged authorisation by senior management.

15. At the year end, an aged analysis of debtors should be prepared to evaluate the need for a doubtful debt provision.

16. Also at the year end, cut off procedure will be required. Particular attention will be paid to orders despatched but not invoiced.

k. Stock and work in progress

Objectives

To ensure that stock is adequately protected against loss or misuse.

Measures

1. Separate arrangements for each type of stock e.g. raw materials, components, work in progress, finished goods, consumable stores.

2. Control over the receipt of goods (see under purchases).

3. Stock should be stored under conditions which deter deterioration due to physical causes e.g. heat, cold, damp, microbial action. Special arrangement for stock which is dangerous or classified secret.

4. Stock should be safeguarded against loss by theft by appropriate physical controls including restriction of access.

5. Where appropriate, stock records should be maintained. Entries should be made by personnel independent of staff responsible for purchasing and custody of goods.

6. Documentation should be controlled by the use of controlled pre-numbered forms with regular sequence checks.

7. Work in progress and finished goods stocks may be subject to recording by value including the charging of material, labour and overhead costs. Control over the latter items can be exercised by the use of control accounts and reconciliation with payroll or records of machine hours.

8. Stock records should be continuously compared with actual stocks held by independent officials. All differences should be corrected and causes investigated.

9. Ideally all stock items should be subject to established maximum and minimum stock levels with re-order levels.

10. Special arrangements should be applied to returnable containers, other's stock on our premises, our stock on other's premises, scrap and waste.

11. Whether or not a continuous inventory is maintained, there should at least be an annual stock take. Procedures should be prescribed for this with emphasis on identifying damaged, slow moving, and obsolete stock and on cut-off procedures.

l. Fixed assets

Objectives

To ensure that fixed assets are only acquired with proper authority.

To ensure that fixed assets are properly maintained and used only in the business.

To ensure that fixed assets are properly accounted for and recorded.

To ensure that disposals are properly authorised and that proceeds of disposals are accounted for and recorded.

Measures

1. Capital expenditure should be subject to authorisation procedures which in all cases should be evidenced. In appropriate cases (e.g. new products or produc-

tion methods), capital investment appraisal techniques should be applied to acquisitions. It may be desirable in such cases for proposed expenditure to be reviewed by a special committee and for board authority to be required. Other capital expenditures (e.g. replacement of equipment) may be subject to requests on specified forms with board approval. In yet other cases (e.g. motor vehicles) the board may lay down overall policy and detailed approval may be given by a designated senior official (e.g. transport manager) subject to review by or reports to the board. In other cases (e.g. routine replacement or update of equipment) the expenditure may be subject to budget limits with actual expenditure approved by a senior official after review that the proposed expenditure is within the budget.

2. All capital expenditure should be monitored by a senior official (e.g. chief accountant) with approvals; and any excess expenditure investigated and approval sought.

3. Allocation of expenditure between capital and revenue should be approved.

4. Adequate recording of fixed assets should be made with detailed breakdowns as necessary. In many cases (e.g. for plant, vehicles or buildings) detailed registers should be maintained.

5. Where registers are maintained, frequent and regular review of the record with actual assets should be made by senior independent officials. Where necessary (e.g. land and buildings) this should include a check of documents of title. In all cases, condition and use should be checked.

6. Disposals whether by scrapping, sale, or trade-in should be subject to authorisation procedures. Receipt of and assessment of reasonableness of proceeds should be monitored by a senior official (e.g. chief accountant).

7. Arrangements to see that fixed assets are properly maintained by regular inspection and reporting of location, operation and condition. This can be combined with the physical verification of the asset registers.

8. Depreciation policy should be laid down by the board (subject to a minute). Policy should accord with the requirement of FRS 15. Officials should be appointed to calculate and check the actual calculations.

Control environment and control procedures

11. In this chapter I have continued the definition and understanding of internal controls used in previous editions of this book. SAS 300 has introduced a new analysis and we will consider it now. This new analysis is useful but perhaps not as clear cut as older analyses.

The control environment means the overall attitude, awareness and actions of directors and management regarding internal controls and their importance in the entity. The control environment encompasses the management style, and corporate culture and values shared by all employees. Factors reflected in this idea include:

– the philosophy and operating style of the directors and management

– the entity's organisational structure and methods of assigning authority and responsibility (including segregation of duties and supervisory controls) and

– the directors' methods of imposing control, including the internal audit function, the functions of the board of directors and personnel policies and procedures.

Control procedures are those policies and procedures in addition to the control environment which are established to achieve the entity's specific objectives. They include in particular procedures designed to prevent or detect and correct errors. Specific control procedures include:

– approval and control of documents (e.g. custody and use of purchase orders)
– controls over computerised applications and the information technology environment (see Chapter 50)
– checking the arithmetical accuracy of the records (e.g. checking sales invoice calculations)
– maintaining and reviewing control accounts and trial balances
– reconciliations
– comparing the results of cash, security and stock counts with accounting records
– comparing internal data with external sources of information (e.g. bank statements, customers remittance advices, suppliers statements of account)
– limiting direct physical access to assets and records (e.g. passwords and locks and keys).

Auditors are expected to make an assessment of the control environment in a client. A good control environment may well mean that internal control is strong but nonetheless internal control may be weak at the level of control procedures. It is generally felt that a poor control environment will mean unreliable control procedures but not necessarily so.

Limitations of internal controls

12. Internal controls are essential features of any organisation that is run efficiently. However it is important to realise (especially for an auditor) that internal controls have inherent limitations which include:

– a requirement that the cost of an internal control is not disproportionate to the potential loss which may result from its absence
– internal controls tend to be directed at routine transactions. The one-off or unusual transaction tends not to be the subject of internal control
– potential human error caused by stress of work-load, alcohol, carelessness, distraction, mistakes of judgement, cussedness, and the misunderstanding of instructions
– the possibility of circumvention of controls either alone or through *collusion* with parties outside or inside the entity
– abuse of responsibility
– management override of controls
– fraud
– changes in environment making controls inadequate
– human cleverness – however secure the computer code designed to prevent access, there is always some hacker who gets in !

SAS 300 requires that auditors must always perform some substantive tests of material items as well as relying on internal controls. The inherent limitations of internal controls are the reason.

Summary

13. a. Internal control is defined as the whole system of controls, financial and otherwise, established by the management in order to carry on the business of the enterprise in an orderly and efficient manner, ensure adherence to management policies, safeguard the assets and secure as far as possible the completeness and accuracy of the records.

    b. The types of internal control include:

        i. organisation

        ii. segregation of duties

        iii. physical controls

        iv. authorisation and approval

        v. arithmetic and accounting

        vi. personnel

        vii. supervision

        viii. management controls

        ix. acknowledgement of performance

        x. budgeting.

    c. The control environment is a new concept in auditing.

    d. Internal controls have limitations.

Points to note

14. a. The definition of internal control should be memorised.

    b. All entities have some sort of accounting system with some internal controls over the transactions. Indeed listed companies are required to have systems and report on them in accordance with the Combined Code on Corporate Governance (see chapter 48). Auditors may rely on these controls as evidence of prevention or detection and correction of errors and irregularities but whether or not they do so depends on their assessment of the risks attached. In any event some substantive tests must be performed on all material balances and classes of transaction.

Case study 1

Jason, Ian and Caroline Ltd operate a large shop in the centre of North Bromwich. They sell expensive reproduction antique furniture. Normally customers see the furniture in the shop and place an order for delivery in the company van within four weeks. The delay occurs because each sale results in a purchase order for one of the suppliers. On placing the order the customer pays by cash, cheque, credit card or signs a hire purchase agreement. There are four sales assistants, a van driver and a cashier in the shop. Accounting and purchasing is done by the manager and a part-time bookkeeper.

The three directors all have other businesses and review the company operations once a month at an all-day board meeting.

Discussion

Devise an internal control system for the shop.

Relate your system to the definition of internal control.

Identify the types of internal controls in your system.

Identify some costs of control that the auditor could perform.

Consider the auditor's attitude to the system.

Student self testing questions *Questions with answers apparent from the text*

1. a. Define internal control (4) and control risk and tests of control. (2)
   b. List the types of internal controls. (6)
   c. What categories of internal controls are comprised in the term 'organisation'? (6)
   d. What functions should be segregated so that no two are under the control of one person? (6)
   e. What kinds of access to assets and records are there? (6)
   f. What types of arithmetical and accounting controls are possible? (6)
   g. What are the internal control objectives of personnel policies? (6)
   h. What personnel policies achieve these ends? (6)
   i. List some management controls. (6)
   j. What are the effects of acknowledgement of performance? (7)
   k. What budgeting benefits have internal control implications? (7)
   l. When are physical controls especially important? (6)
   m. List some physical controls. (6)
   n. How can theft of cheques in the post be prevented/detected? (10)
   o. How can theft of cash sales be prevented/detected? (10)
   p. How can teeming and lading be prevented? (10)
   q. List suitable controls over a petty cash system. (10)
   r. How can the issue of fraudulent cheques be prevented? (10)
   s. List some possible wages frauds. (10)
   t. A PLC pays B, a cousin of C who is an employee of A PLC, for goods not supplied. How could this be engineered and how can it be prevented? (10)
   u. E Ltd supplies F with goods but these are not charged to him. What measures could prevent this? (10)
   v. List the benefits of a stock control system and how the benefits are achieved. (10)
   w. How can the accuracy of a fixed asset register be assured? (10)
   x. What is a control environment? (11)
   y. List some limitations of internal control. (12)

Exercises

1. Devise detailed internal control systems for the following:

   a. **Cheques through the post and over the counter**

      Joe's Garage Ltd repair and service cars and vans. About half the customers are given credit and pay by cheque through the post. The garage also deal with new and used cars and sell petrol. Customers for these items pay by cash or credit card. There are some five clerical staff in the firm.

b. **Cash tills in a public house**

The Bull and Bear has a single bar/lounge and usually there are some four bar staff on duty sometimes including the manager. Bar meals are also sold.

c. **Cheque payments**

Scarecrow Fashions Mfg Ltd have some 100 suppliers and a healthy balance at the bank. Many suppliers offer settlement discount. The four directors are often away on business and the office staff is run, in the absence of the financial director, by Mrs Tan who is a part-qualified accountant. She has six staff.

d. **Wages**

Dolerite Builders Ltd carry out repairs and extensions to domestic and business premises. They have 50 workmen all of whom are paid weekly in cash and some 30 firms of subcontractors who are paid weekly by cheque. The company have some six office staff. Turnover of workmen and sub-contractors is fairly rapid as the company do not pay well.

e. **Sales and debtors**

Caxgut Publishers Ltd publish books (some 150 titles). The books are kept in a large warehouse. Orders are received by post and telephone from bookshops and from individuals.

f. **Plant and machinery**

OBSO Manufacturing manufacture electrical apparatus using a mix of sophisticated and traditional machinery (lathes, presses etc.). The company regularly change the sophisticated machinery as items become obsolete and also have a need for constant servicing and maintenance of the plant. The company have some 10 clerical staff.

2. a. In Smoothe Tyres Ltd, a company that supplies and fits new tyres to customers' cars, a year-end purchase/sales./stock reconciliation revealed that over 200 tyres valued at £11,000 were missing. There are no continuous stock records and the seven tyre fitters select the tyres from stock, fit them and make out the invoices at the computer terminal.

b. Jezebel is the cashier of Gungho Ltd, a company which supplies security services. She is in sole charge of payments of expense claims by security personnel. On examining the draft annual accounts, Saif, the chief executive is appalled to find that the total of expenses claims is double that of the previous year when turnover was only 5% lower.

c. The gross profit of Sundree Ltd, a firm of wholesalers was lower than expected. An investigation revealed that Margaret who produced the sales invoices (using a computerised system) had priced many invoices in the East Anglian region at below the correct prices. Her husband, Michael, is the sales rep for that region and his commission had increased by 50% in the year.

d. The treasurer of St Mary's Church confessed to the newly appointed honorary auditor (a certified accountant) that she had misappropriated the weekly offering envelopes of several parishioners over a period of years. The Church Wardens always counted and banked the notes and coins in the collections but handed the envelopes to the treasurer.

e. The newly appointed auditor of Tinpot PLC, a small manufacturing company attempted to reconcile the individual items of plant with purchases and disposals since the last such reconciliation five years previously. This revealed some forty machines were unaccounted for.

What might have happened in each of these cases?

Design internal control procedures to prevent recurrence.

Examination questions

1. In the accounts department of your client, Merchants PLC, there is a section devoted to the calculation and authorisation of discounts, and allowances for returned goods, to customers.

    i.   What internal control would you recommend for this section?   (12 marks)

    ii. How far is the external auditor concerned with this section?   (3 marks)

    (LCC) (Total 15 marks)

2. As a senior partner in the auditors to Fat & Thin PLC, you are concerned about the efficiency of your client's internal control covering the acquisition of small tools.

    Prepare an Internal Control Questionnaire, covering the acquisition of small tools.

    (13 marks)

    (LCCI)

15 Audit testing

Introduction

1. This chapter discusses the vocabulary of audit testing and describes the purposes and uses of the different types of testing.

Walk-through checks

2. The modern audit requires the auditor to have in his working papers a record of the accounting system and its associated internal controls. This record may be in the form of simple written descriptions, the answers to an Internal Control Questionnaire or as flow charts, checklists or a combination of these.

3. Auditors need to have an understanding of a client's accounting system and control environment. From this initial understanding it is possible to plan the audit and determine the audit approach. The audit approach may be to rely on substantive tests alone or, in some areas, to rely partly on internal control evidence as well as substantive tests. The problem is how to gain an initial understanding of the accounting system and associated control environment. One way is to use walk-through tests.

    Walk-through tests are defined as tracing one or more transactions through the accounting system and observing the application of relevant aspects of the internal control system. For example the auditor might look at the sales system in a wholesaler and trace a sale from its initiation through to the sales figure in the Profit and Loss Account. This will involve looking at customers orders, how the orders are documented and recorded, credit control approval, how the goods are selected and packed, raising of an advice note and /or delivery note, invoicing procedures, recording the invoice in the books of account and so on. At each stage the controls applied (for example applying consecutive numbers to customer order documents and subsequent sequence checks to ensure all orders are invoiced) are examined.

4. When the auditor has done the audit for several years then the audit files will contain a record of the systems but each year the auditor needs to confirm her understanding by:

   – enquiries of supervisory and other staff at all levels of the enterprise

   – inspection of client documentation such as procedure manuals, job descriptions and systems descriptions. You will appreciate that a lack of these may imply a weak control environment. Note that the existence of procedure manuals etc. does not necessarily imply that the prescriptions in them are actually carried out in practice!

   – inspection of relevant documents and records produced by the system

   – observation of the entity's activities and operations including watching personnel actually performing procedures.

5. If the preliminary understanding of the systems and control environment leads the auditor to plan the audit to include some internal control reliance then the system needs to be investigated in more depth than the knowledge provided by walk-through tests. See Chapter 17 for ICQs and flow charts etc.

6. Walk-through checks will also be applied:

   a. In any situation where the auditor has not obtained his description of the system from a personal investigation of the system by questioning operating staff and examining documents and records.

   b. At the final audit when he needs to review the system from the date of the interim completion to the year end. He must first determine if the system has changed and walk-through checks will achieve this.

Tests of control

7. Tests of control are tests to obtain audit evidence about the effective operation of the accounting and control systems – that is, that properly designed controls identified in the preliminary assessment of control risk exist in fact and have operated throughout the relevant period.

   Tests of control are sometimes called *compliance tests*.

8. The first stage in the auditor's assessment of the reliability of a system is a preliminary review of the effectiveness of the system by using an internal control evaluation questionnaire which contains key questions. For example, to test the effectiveness of the wages system, he would ask questions including:

   Can wages be paid to piecework personnel for work not done?

   The system would then be inspected to see if it included procedures to ensure that this could not happen.

9. If the system appears to be defective or weak then the auditor may need to abandon the systems approach and apply substantive tests. If the system is effective, then the next stage is for the auditor to obtain evidence that the system is applied as in his description *at all times*. This evidence is obtained by examining a sample of the transactions to deter-

mine if each has been treated as required by the system, i.e. to see if the system has been complied with.

10. Two points must be made about compliance tests:

   a. It is the application of the system that is being tested not the transaction although the testing is through the medium of the transactions.

   b. If discovery is made that the system was not complied with in a particular way then:

      i. he may need to revise his system description and re-appraise its effectiveness

      ii. he will need to determine if the failure of compliance was an isolated instance or was symptomatic.

   It may be that a larger sample may need to be taken.

11. As an example of a test of control, suppose that a system provided that all credit notes issued by the client had to be approved by the sales manager and that a space was provided on each credit note for his initials. Then the auditor would inspect a sample of the credit notes to determine if all of them had been initialled. In practice other internal controls (e.g. checking of calculations or coding) would be tested on the same credit notes.

Substantive tests

12. Substantive procedures are tests to obtain audit evidence to detect material misstatement in the financial statements. They are generally of two types:

   a. analytical procedures – see Chapter 16.

   b. other substantive procedures, such as tests of details of transactions and balances, reviews of minutes of directors' meetings and enquiry.

13. From this definition, you may deduce that all audit work comes within the compass of substantive testing. However it is usually used to mean all tests other than tests of control. A substantive test is any test which seeks *direct evidence* of the correct treatment of a transaction, a balance, an asset, a liability, or any item in the books or the Accounts. Analytical review is also seen as a separate type of test.

14. Some examples:

   a. Of a transaction – the sale of a piece of plant will require the auditor to examine the copy invoice, the authorisation, the entry in the plant register and other books, the accounting treatment and some evidence that the price obtained was reasonable.

   b. Of a balance – direct confirmation of the balance in a deposit account obtained from the bank.

   c. Analytical review – evidence of the correctness of cut-off by examining the gross profit ratio.

   d. Completeness of information – obtaining confirmation from a client's legal adviser that all potential payments from current litigation had been considered.

   e. Accuracy of information – obtaining from each director a confirmation that an accurate statement of remuneration and expenses had been obtained.

   f. Validity of information – validity means based on evidence that can be supported. For example, a provision for future warranty claims may be extremely difficult to estimate in precise monetary terms. If such a provision is made in the Accounts, the auditor would need to apply substantive tests to determine its validity, i.e. that it was supported by adequate evidence.

Techniques of audit testing

15. There are several categories of auditing test technique:

a. **Inspection** – reviewing or examining records, documents or tangible assets. Examples are:

 i. Examining a sample of piecework records for evidence of inspection by inspection staff and approval by the works manager, gives evidence of compliance with the system presented.

 ii. Examining copy sales invoices for initials of the member of staff charged with checking invoice calculations, gives evidence of compliance with a system which prevents calculation errors.

 iii. Inspecting buildings provides evidence of the existence (but not ownership or value) of the building.

b. **Observation** – looking at an operation or procedure being performed by others with a view to determining the manner of its performance.

 Examples:

 i. Observing the giving out of wage packets to see that internal control procedures are adhered to.

 ii. Observing the counting of stock at the year end with the same end in view.

 Observation gives evidence of how the procedures are performed at the time of observation but perhaps not at any other time. It is a general truth that actions are rarely performed in the presence of the observer without the observer affecting the operation in some way.

c. **Enquiry** – seeking relevant information from knowledgeable persons inside or outside the enterprise, whether formally or informally, orally or in writing.

 Examples are:

 i. Routine queries to client staff such as 'Why is invoice copy 643 missing?'.

 ii. Seeking formal representations from management on the value of a large subsidiary company in a volatile country.

 iii. Circularising debtors.

d. **Computation** – checking the arithmetical accuracy of accounting records or performing independent calculations.

 Examples:

 i. Checking (by sampling!) the accuracy of stock extensions (quantity × cost price).

 ii. Verifying the accuracy of detailed interest calculations by a global calculation.

Rotational tests

16. Rotational tests are of two kinds:

a. Rotation of audit emphasis – the auditor performs a systems audit on all areas of the client's business every year but each year he selects one area (wages, sales, stock control, purchasing, etc.) for special in-depth testing.

b. Visit rotation – where the client has numerous branches, factories, locations, etc., it may be impractical to visit them all each year. In such cases the auditor visits them in rotation so that while each will not be visited every year, all will be visited over a period of years.

17. There is an opinion that each yearly audit is independent of all others and adequate evidence must be found in all areas each year. However, auditors normally serve for many years and rotational testing makes sense in terms of effectiveness and efficiency.

18. It is vital that rotational tests are carried out randomly so that client staff do not know which areas or locations will be selected in any one year.

Summary

19. a. The language of audit testing includes the following definitions:

   i. Walk-through tests are defined as tracing one or more transactions through the accounting system and observing the application of relevant aspects of the internal control system.

   ii. Tests of control are tests to obtain audit evidence about the effective operation of the accounting and control systems – that is, that properly designed controls identified in the preliminary assessment of control risk exist in fact and have operated throughout the relevant period.

   iii. Substantive procedures are tests to obtain audit evidence to detect material misstatement in the financial statements

   iv. Rotational tests are tests carried out on the assumption that the auditor will be in office for several years and can in any individual year bring to bear special emphasis on a particular area of the affairs of his client or visit particular branches.

b. Techniques of audit testing include:

   i. Inspection – looking at records, documents and tangible assets.

   ii. Observation – looking at procedures actually taking place.

   iii. Enquiry – seeking relevant information by asking questions, orally or in writing, to persons or institutions inside or outside the clients.

   iv. Computation – checking or performing calculations.

Points to note

20. a. The language of audit testing varies from firm to firm but in this manual I have followed the words used in the auditing standards.

b. The language used is less important that understanding the *purpose* of a test. One common audit test is the checking of codings put on purchase and expense invoices. Such codings are extremely important because an error may lead to mis-analysis between capital and revenue expenditure. The auditor may check a large random sample. By so doing he may be:

i.   Testing that the *system* works. Various controls may be applied to the coding. Do the controls work? A good way of seeking evidence that the controls are applied (compliance testing) may be to verify a sample of the results.

ii. Seeking direct evidence that the accounting records correctly reflect the nature of expenditure incurred. This will be a substantive test. The difference is a little subtle but it is important in practice that the auditor knows precisely what evidence he is getting from a test.

c. The distinction between *inspection* and *observation* should be noted. Use observation to mean only the looking at the actual performance of an operation or procedure.

Inspection has a much wider meaning including that of inspecting written records to obtain evidence that an operation or procedure did take place. Another word for observation is witnessing.

d. Two old words, still much used are depth tests and block tests. These words describe what auditors do but do not explain why they are doing the tests. As many audit staff follow audit programmes without really knowing what they are doing, these words are best avoided.

e. The definition of the various types of tests should be commited to memory.

f. The extent of use of each type of test can be summarised as:

–   Walk-through tests are used in making the preliminary assessment of the accounting system and control environment.

–   All items should be subject to substantive tests but the extent of such tests depends on the materiality of the item and the inherent risk of misstatement attached to the item. As an example of materiality consider petty cash which, even if grossly wrong, may be unlikely to affect the view given by the financial statements. As an example of inherent risk, consider the evaluation of the value of work in progress in a civil engineering company. The valuation may be critical to the financial statements yet it may be very difficult to establish precisely.

–   The auditors may expect to be able to rely upon their preliminary assessment of control risk to reduce the extent of their substantive procedures. In such cases they should make a preliminary assessment of control risk for material financial statement assertions and should then plan and perform tests of control to support that assessment. For example the preliminary walk-through tests might indicate good controls over fees in a college. The auditors may then assess the control risk attached to the assertion that all fees, that should have been invoiced, have been invoiced. Tests of control should then be planned and performed to support that assessment. If such tests do support the assessment, then the extent of substantive tests can be reduced.

–   In particular cases (especially small enterprises) the auditors may conclude that accounting and internal control systems are not effective or they may conclude that it is likely to be inefficient to adopt an audit approach which relies on tests of control.

g. Tests of control may include:

–   Corroborative enquiries about, and observation of, internal control functions. For example being present at the post opening of a mail order firm.

- Inspection of documents supporting controls or events to gain audit evidence that internal controls have operated properly. For example inspecting works manager approval for capital expenditure and reports of completed installation of new plant before payment was made.
- Examination of management reviews. For example examination of minutes of management where salary rates were decided upon.
- Testing of the internal controls operating on specific computerised applications – see Chapter 50.
- Reperformance of control procedures. For example, making sequence tests or re-reconciling bank statements to the cash book.

Case study 1

Foley Widgets Ltd are a wholly owned subsidiary of a German group. Foley trade as stockists of the German parent's products and sell to engineering companies all over the UK and the Republic of Ireland. All sales are on credit. Tiswas & Co. are the newly appointed auditors and are planning their audit of the sales area. The system is as laid down in a manual (in English) which has been given to Tiswas. The system in essence is:

a. Orders are received by telephone, telex or through the company's four representatives.

b. Orders are first cleared to a list of acceptable customers provided weekly by credit control.

c. Accepted orders are transcribed onto pre-numbered order forms. These are in triplicate – 1 retained, 2 to accounts, 3 to warehouse.

d. Warehouse pack the goods and send them with the order and pre-numbered despatch note to the despatch section. The despatch note is in quadruplicate (1 to retain in packing, 2 to customer, 3 to accounts, 4 to retain in despatch).

e. Despatch send goods by carrier.

f. Accounts invoice the goods – pricing and VAT are added at this point. Invoice is in triplicate – 1 retained, 2 customer, 3 sales. You may invent or assume controls added to this outline.

Discussion

What audit tests would be done on this system?

What audit evidence would be obtained from these tests?

Relate these tests to the overall audit objectives.

Student self testing questions *Questions with answers apparent from the text*

1. a. Define walk-through checks. (3)
   b. What is the purpose of a walk-through check? (3)
   c. Define test of control. (7)
   d. What is the purpose of a test of control? (9)
   e. Define substantive test. (12)
   f. List the techniques of audit testing. (15)
   g. When are walk-through tests used? (4, 6)
   h. What is tested by a test of control? (10)

j.   What might an auditor do if tests of control show that a control, on which he wishes to rely, is not always complied with? (10)

k.   Give examples of a substantive test:
     –   of a transaction
     –   of a balance
     –   in analytical review
     –   for completeness of information
     –   for accuracy of information
     –   for validity of information. (14)

l.   Distinguish inspection and observation. (15, 20)

m.   List the sub-categories of enquiry (15)

n.   When are rotational tests used? (16)

o.   What two views of auditing are involved in the decision to or to not test rotationally? (17)

Exercises

1.   Devise audit tests in the following situations:

a.   *Industrial wages.* Gong Manufacturing PLC are makers of motor car parts in a factory in North Bromwich. They employ 500 factory workers paying on a mixture of time, piecework and bonus systems. They have a sophisticated system of budgetary control and standard costing. They have a very good personnel department with full records and excellent systems of internal control over wages.

b.   *Industrial wages.* Backward Ltd are an engineering company, also in North Bromwich. They have 100 workers and pay by a mixture of time and piecework. They have no system of budgetary control or standard costing. Pricing is by an ad hoc system of rather rudimentary costing and market-based pricing. They are none the less profitable. They have no personnel department but the wages department have a wages system which holds some information about each employee. Basically the wage calculation/payment is:

The wage department has 4 staff (who do have other duties not connected with accounting). Each Monday morning they take the previous week's clock cards from the gate (which is well supervised). The piecework cards are taken from the works manager who signs them as approved. They are completed by the various foremen who also sign them.

The cards and piecework sheets are summarised by Angela and Jill and then exchanged and checked. Brian then enters the data on duplicate wage sheets and calculates the wages due and the deductions. Philip checks a sample of the calculations and does the totalling. New employees/leavers are subject to a system of weekly reports from the works manager (pre-numbered).

Georgia, the chief accountant checks the totalling and prepares the cheque for signature by two directors, both of whom inspect the wages sheets. The cheque is cashed by Simon the security guard using a different car and route each week.

The wages envelopes are made up by Walter and Ellen the sales ledger clerks in a locked room and the copy wage slips inserted in the envelopes.

Payment to the workers is made by Henry, a director in the presence of the foreman. A signature is obtained from each worker in a special book.

c. *Sales and debtors.* Ficab Ltd sell office furniture on credit from a large warehouse in Dudley to industrial and commercial customers.

Orders are obtained through representatives, agents and directly from customers. Deliveries are by the company's own pantechnicons. The system is:

- Orders are received by various means and transcribed onto quadruplicate prenumbered sales order forms SOFs with details for customer name etc., codes and description of furniture and also source of order (important for commission).

- Firstly a credit check is made. New customers are credit enquired and the SOF is held until completed or the customer is rejected. Existing customers are enquired into as to outstanding amounts.

- The goods are always in stock as all catalogue items are held.

- Copy 1 of the order is sent to accounts for invoicing using a micro computer which produces a disc (daily) with details of each invoice including a consecutive number.

- Print outs are made of each invoice in duplicate with top copy going to the customer. The computer also produces a daybook listing. The disc is used to update the sales ledger disc and also to calculate commissions. Copy invoices are filed with the SOF.

- The second and third copies of the SOF are sent to the warehouse where the goods are assembled for despatch. Goods are labelled with the SOF number. The second copy is retained in the warehouse on a file. The third and fourth copies go with the goods to the customer. The third copy is signed by the customer and is brought back for attachment to the second copy. The gatekeeper ensures that no goods leave the factory without a label and a SOF.

- Cheques are received through the post and paid into bank. Bankings are put on disc. The disc is used to update the sales ledger file. Matched invoices and cheques and discounts are eliminated after customers statements of account are printed out in duplicate. Copy 1 to customer, copy 2 retained.

- The chief accountant lists the totals of the statements and prepares a monthly control account using the invoice listing and the cash book listing. He also reviews and actions any overdue accounts.

(This exercise can also be used as a flowchart exercise.)

2. *Purchases.* Steel is in charge (with two assistants: Thicke, who is his cousin and Thynne, who is his next-door neighbour) of the components warehouse of Pieces Manufacturing Ltd. Dodd is the chief buyer (he also has two assistants) and Peck is the works manager. Tulp is in charge of the bought ledger. The system for purchases of components is:

a. Peck's secretary makes out requisitions on a word processor for new components and Steel does the same for stocks of components where the bins are nearly empty. Dodd or his assistants make out purchases orders on duplicate forms which are preprinted. They order from the firms that normally supply the components but obtain tenders for new components after discussion with Peck. Most of the components are standard things that many firms can supply. Dodd puts consecutive numbers on the order forms and the top copy goes to the supplier and the bottom copy is sent to Steel. Peck or Dodd usually chase overdue orders when they have difficulties because of shortages.

When the goods arrive, they are signed for by Lewis, the gatekeeper, who sends them through to Steel. Steel checks them against the order and sends the delivery note to Tulp. Tulp checks the invoice, when it arrives, against the delivery note and enters the details in the computer. The computer gives each invoice a consecutive number. At the end of the month the computer adds invoices due for payment to each supplier and prints out a cheque and a remittance advice. The remittance advices and the cheques are sent to Britten who is the very busy chief executive. She signs them and Tulp sends them off.

Short deliveries etc. are taken up with the suppliers by Steel. Tulp ignores creditors' statements.

Required:

a. Enumerate the weaknesses in this system and the possible consequences.
b. Suggest some improvements.
c. What are the audit objectives in connection with the purchase of components?
d. What controls might be relied upon by Mills, the auditor?
e. How might these be tested by Mills?
f. What other audit tests might Mills apply to detect any misstatement in the Profit and Loss Account figure for purchases of components?

Note: after Chapter 17, you should also be able to flow chart this system.

Examination questions without answers

1. The senior audit clerk in charge of the audit of a small company observes from the previous year's flow chart that Mr Lennonserp was the only staff member authorised to make changes in rates of pay for the company's salaried and weekly staff. Half way through the current year, Mr Lennonserp retired and this particular function was not allocated to anyone else.

   What action should the senior audit clerk take?

   (LCC) (15 marks)

2. Draft out an Audit Programme to cover that part of the wages audit of a large manufacturing company that relates to the *actual payment of wages*.

   Note: you are not required to deal with the collection of information for wages, preparation of wage sheets, or calculation of wages.

   (LCC) (12 marks)

3. You are a senior working on the audit of a large chemical engineering company. One of your assistants on the audit has heard you mentioning the term 'audit objectives' and is confused as to exactly what the different audit objectives are in relation to various account balances.

   Requirement:

   a. Identify the seven audit objectives which are applicable to all account balances and classes of transactions. Define and illustrate each objective by reference to:
      i. trade debtors and sales; and
      ii. trade creditors and purchases.
   b. Select *any five* of the audit objectives identified at (a) (i) above. *For each one* of the five audit objectives selected, describe briefly *any* two audit tests that would provide the auditor with sufficient evidence to achieve the specific audit objective selected.

   (ICAI)

16 Analytical review techniques

Introduction

1. Auditors are required to carry out procedures designed to obtain sufficient appropriate audit evidence to determine with reasonable confidence whether the financial statements are free of material misstatement. They are also required to evaluate the overall presentation of the financial statements, in order to ascertain whether they have been prepared in accordance with relevant legislation and accounting standards. The auditors have to give an opinion on whether the accounts give a true and fair view and comply with regulations.

2. Amongst the methods of obtaining audit evidence are internal control reliance, substantive tests and analytical review. This chapter is about analytical review.

3. There is an SAS 410 and an ISA 520 *Analytical Procedures.* These standards require that auditors should apply analytical procedures at the planning and overall review stages of the audit. It also suggests that analytical procedures can be applied as *substantive procedures designed to obtain audit evidence directly.*

Definition

4. Analytical review can be defined as:

> The study of relationships between elements of financial information expected to conform to a predictable pattern based on the organisation's experience and between financial information and non-financial information. Information is compared with comparable information for a prior period or periods, with anticipated results and with information relating to similar organisations.

In addition, analytical review involves:

a. Investigating unexpected variations identified by analytical review.

b. Obtaining and *substantiating* explanations for such variations.

c. Evaluating the results of analytical review with other audit evidence obtained e.g. by systems and substantive tests.

5. In an actual case this definition might be applied by examining:

   - increases in magnitude corresponding to inflation
   - changes in amounts consequent on changes in output levels
   - comparisons with previous periods
   - trends and ratios
   - comparisons with budgets and forecasts
   - comparisons with other, similar, organisations e.g. by inter-firm comparison.

6. Similar techniques are also applied by management, investment analysts and internal auditors to provide information on the performance of an entity, the efficiency of its operations or the quality of its management. Note that in performing these techniques an auditor has a quite different purpose.

7. Analytical review can be simple tests comparing absolute magnitudes of different years, comparing ratios with earlier years, budgets and industry averages but also:

    a.   using computer audit software

    b.   using advanced statistical techniques e.g. multiple regression analysis.

Timing

8.   Analytical review techniques will be applied throughout the audit but specific occasions include:

    a.   At the planning stage. The auditor will hope to identify areas of potential risk or new developments so that he can plan his other audit procedures in these areas. As a simple example, the auditor might discover that the gross profit ratio in a retail organisation had changed from the 28–30% of previous years to 24%. Or he might discover that a sales analysis revealed that exports had increased from 3% to 26% of turnover.

    b.   Obtaining evidence. Modern audits with their emphasis on efficiency and economy depend heavily on analytical review as a valid audit technique used alone or in conjunction with internal control reliance and substantive testing.

       It can be reasonable to obtain assurance of the completeness, accuracy and validity of the transactions and balances by analytical review as by other types of audit evidence. For example, if the relative amounts under different expense headings repeat the pattern of previous years the auditor has evidence of the accuracy of expense invoice coding.

    c.   At the final review stage of the audit. Analytical review techniques can provide support for the conclusions arrived at as a result of other work. For example, indications from external sources that profit margins have declined by 10% may support the declined profit figure in a segment of the company whose figures have been audited by other means and found to be correct. The techniques are also used to assess the overall reasonableness of the financial statements as a whole.

Extent of use

9.   Factors which might influence the extent of use of analytical review include:

    a.   The *nature* of the entity and its operations. A long-established chain of similar shops which have changed little in the period under review will offer many opportunities for analytical review to be used as the primary source of audit evidence. Conversely a newly established manufacturer of high-tech products will not.

    b.   Knowledge gained in *previous audits* of the enterprise. The auditor will have experience of those areas where errors and difficulties arose and of those areas of greatest audit risk.

    c.   *Management's* own use of analytical review procedures. If management has a reliable system of budgetary control then the auditor will have a ready made source of explanation for variance. Also the reliability of information prepared for management will be a factor. Information subject to internal audit will be an example of reliable information.

    d.   Availability of *non-financial information* to back up financial information. Many companies record non-financial statistics (e.g. on production, input mixes etc.). Some companies have to make returns of output (e.g. newspapers on circulation, dairies on gallonage etc.). All this data can be used as evidence by an auditor.

e. The reliability, relevance and *comparability* of the information available. Clients that take part in inter-firm comparison exercises will be especially appropriate for analytical review evidence.

f. The *cost effectiveness* of the use of analytical review in relation to other forms of evidence. In general, analytical review is cheap but requires high quality (and therefore expensive) staff. Some analytical review techniques can be expensive if for example they involve complex statistical techniques (e.g. multiple regression) and computer audit software.

g. The availability of staff. Analytical review requires high quality staff with much intelligence, experience and training.

h. SAS 410 has a mandatory requirement that auditors should apply analytical procedures at the *planning* stage to assist in *understanding the entity's business,* in identifying areas of *potential audit risk* and in planning the *nature, timing and extent* of other audit procedures.

Procedures

10. The following remarks can be made:

a. Analytical review procedure can best be carried out on particular segments of the organisation e.g. the branch at Walsall or the paint division or the subsidiary in France. They can also be used on individual account areas such as creditors or fixed asset depreciation.

b. Analytical review is a *breaking down* of data into sub divisions for analysis over time, by product, by location, by management responsibility etc.

c. Analytical review techniques are not effective in reviewing an entity as a whole unless it is very small. The greater the *disaggregation* the better.

d. One approach is to identify the *factors* likely to have an effect on items in the accounts; to ascertain or assess the probable *relationship* with these factors and items; and then to *predict* the value of the items in the light of the factors. Then the predicted value of the items can be *compared* with the *actual* recorded amounts. As an example, gas consumption is a function of temperature. A knowledge of daily temperature will permit an auditor to estimate gas consumption. If actual consumption is similar to that expected the auditor has evidence of the correctness of the sales value of gas.

e. The auditor should consider the implications of significant *fluctuations,* unusual items or relationships that are unexpected or inconsistent with evidence from other sources. Similarly he should consider the implications of predicted fluctuations that fail to occur.

The expense of heating oil consumed at the Bridgnorth factory increased by 6% over the previous year. The auditor knows that in the period heating oil prices were 23% on average lower than in the previous period.

f. Any significant variations should be discussed with management who usually have an explanation for them. Independent evidence must then be sought.

g. The auditor's reactions to significant fluctuations or unexpected values will vary according to the stage of the audit:

   – at the planning stage, the auditor will plan suitable substantive tests

- at the testing stage of the audit, further tests and other techniques will be indicated
- at the final stage the unexpected should not happen!

h. All fluctuations and unexpected values must be fully investigated and sufficient audit evidence obtained.

i. As with all audit work, analytical procedures should be fully documented in the working papers. The files should include:
- the information examined, the sources of that information and the factors considered in establishing the reliability of the information
- the extent and nature of material variations found
- the *sources* and *level* of management from which explanations were sought and obtained
- the *verification* of those explanations
- any further action taken e.g. further audit testing
- the *conclusions drawn by the auditor*.

Example of use of analytical techniques

11. Zilpha Fashion Shops PLC own a chain of high fashion shops in major towns. Each shop is operated by a separate subsidiary company. All subsidiaries buy from the parent. The auditor of the Covhampton shop is reviewing the accounts for the year ending 31.1.-6 before starting the audit.

These reveal (in extract):

(all in £'000)	20-5	20-6	budget 20-7
turnover	600	638	640
cost of sales	400	459	425
gross profit	200	179	215
wages	78	71	70
overheads	70	75	74
net profit	52	33	71
stock	58	53	62
creditors	71	79	74

External data known to Fiona the auditor includes:

- rate of inflation – 5%
- a University survey of the traders in the precinct in which the shop is situated indicates a 5% growth in real terms
- the rate of gross profit achieved by other shops in the group was 34% and average stock was 45 days worth
- creditors in three other shops averaged 13% of turnover
- wages in the other shops averaged 13% of turnover.

12. From all this data, Fiona could:

a. Compute estimated turnover as 600*1.05*1.05 = 661. The actual turnover is significantly less. The difference must be investigated.

b. Gross profit from the turnover should be 638*.34 = 217. Actual rate of gross profit is only 28%.

c. Stock should be about 45 days worth – 459*45/365 = 56. Actual is lower but not materially so.

d. Creditors should be 459*65/365 = 82. This confirms the figure. In any case this figure can be confirmed by head office.

e. Wages perhaps ought to be 638*.13 = 83. If the direction of causation was reversed turnover should be 71*100/13 = 546. Wages do agree with budget and should be confirmable by considering the numbers on the staff.

f. Other expenses should perhaps have risen by 5% but they should be reviewed after disaggregation.

Conclusions:

a. Stock and creditors are in line with expectations.

b. Globally other overheads are out of line and disaggregation is required.

c. Sales are lower than expected. Causes may be misappropriation of stock or cash. Close investigation is required.

d. Gross profit is way out of line. This does not appear to be cut-off errors as stock and creditors seem to be about right. Debtors are negligible in this type of retail business. (Customers pay by cash, cheque or credit card.) It seems that misappropriation of stock or cash has occurred. Full investigation is required. It may be of course that the management have other explanations – burglary losses, excessive shoplifting, price competition, sales of old stock at low prices etc.

Summary

13. a. Amongst the procedures for obtaining audit evidence available to an auditor are analytical review techniques.

b. Analytical review can be and should be carried out at all stages of the audit from planning to final review.

c. The extent of use of analytical review depends on:
   - nature and operations of the client
   - knowledge from previous audit
   - management's use of similar techniques
   - availability of non-financial information
   - reliability, relevance and comparability of available information
   - cost effectiveness of analytical review techniques in comparison with other audit techniques
   - quality of audit staff.

d. Procedures include:
   - disaggregation
   - concentration on segments or single areas
   - identifying influences, assessing mathematical relationships, predicting values, comparing predictions with actual

    – examining unexpected values and seeking explanations which must be fully verified.

Points to note

14. a. Any relationship perceived between variables must be plausible. Thus debtors and sales have a plausible relationship. The relationship found should be reasonable. The relationship in this example is clearly relevant to audit objectives. However no plausible relationship can be established between say selling expenses and work in progress in a manufacturing company.

    b. Reliable substantive evidence of the correctness of the magnitude of an item might be established by comparing it with another magnitude e.g. salaries from staffing numbers. However both magnitudes may be wrong.

    c. The nature of analytical review includes a comparison over time and the use of past experience on the audit. Therefore it is desirable to build up a picture of the organisation and the relationship between magnitudes in the permanent files.

    d. There is a relationship between the use of analytical review and the reliability of the information being reviewed. Information which is subject to good control procedures is clearly more susceptible to analytical review techniques than other information.

    e. Materiality is very important here. The auditor will often rely largely or wholly on analytical review techniques in areas judged to be not material. He would normally rely on a combination of analytical review, substantive testing and internal controls for material items.

    f. Finding that the gross profit ratio is unchanged from one year to the next is not of itself good audit evidence of the correctness of that ratio. All years may have the same built-in errors.

    g. Analytical review is especially useful in obtaining evidence of *completeness* of accounting magnitudes.

    h. If anomalies are found and inadequate explanations are received then further audit work will be necessary. If doubts remain and cannot be resolved then the auditor may consider qualifying his report for uncertainty.

Case study 1

Odo Einstein MBA, FCA is about to embark on the audit of Hosiah Wholesale Health Foods Ltd. The company have been established for 5 years and have been modestly successful. Einstein has not encountered many problems in the past except for debt collection problems and bad debts. A feature of the accounts each year has been the large amount of stock. The management is good and monthly accounts are prepared by Hortensia Goodbody FCCA who was head hunted from the auditors. The accounts are disaggregated for management purposes into dried goods, tinned goods and specialty imports.

Discussion

    a. To what extent can Odo engage in analytical techniques?

b. Devise analytical techniques using financial and non-financial data for verifying the expense 'motor van running expenses'. The company have 20 vans.

c. Devise analytical techniques for verifying sales figures. Odo is particularly worried that he has no systems assurance that all sales have been invoiced.

Case study 2

The annual accounts of Dorb Paints PLC are being audited by Ann Tick of Sooper Brothers, Certified Accountants. She is investigating the item salaries and national insurance. There is also an item wages and national insurance. The company is large (turnover £40 million) and salaries is material. The company have separate personnel and wages departments with extensive records.

Discussion

Devise a selection of analytical review procedures to enable Ann to avoid detailed investigation of the salaries area.

Student self testing questions *Questions with answers apparent from the text*

1. a. What methods of obtaining audit evidence are there? (2)
   b. Define analytical review. (4)
   c. When can analytical review be used? (8)
   d. What factors influence the extent of use of analytical review? (9)
   e. List the procedures that can be used. (10)
   f. List some analytical review procedures. (5)
   g. What actions can an auditor take if he finds fluctuations or unexpected magnitudes? (10)

Exercises *(on Chapters 15 and 16)*

1. Aleph Ltd import and then wholesale widget fittings. Turnover is £3 million and the company is fully computerised and has an excellent system of budgetary control. They also subscribe to the inter-firm comparison scheme of the national association of widget importers and traders.

   Devise analytical review tests for the following items:
   a. total sales ·
   b. wages
   c. stocks
   d. debtors
   e. bad debts (this item is material)
   f. motor expenses
   g. petty cash expenditure.

2. Cheepo Animal Feeds Ltd wholesale animal feed in sacks to farmers and wholesalers. Sales are obtained largely through agents and some 20,000 invoices a year are put through with commission being due on about 15,000. There are some 80 agents.

   Most orders are telephoned to the company but a few come by post or fax. Many of the orders are phoned through by the agent concerned but much repeat business (on which commission is due) is phoned in by the customer. The sales department clerks make out a sales order form and perform the following work:

a. Check customer is approved or perform credit control checks for new customers.
b. Check goods are in stock (form is held until stock is in).
c. Mark SOF with name and code number of agent if commission is due. This is obtained from a list of customers with agent (if any) stated. The credit control procedure includes adding customer and agent to this list.

All SOFs are checked and countersigned by the sales manager or his assistant. They include a check on the agent coding.

The SOFs go to despatch and a good system exists to ensure all goods are invoiced. The invoices are made out by computer from details input from the SOF. All such inputs must have an agent code and invoices where no commission is payable must have code 00 input to be accepted.

The invoice disc is used to make out commission statements for the agents monthly.

Required:

a. The commission is 10% of sales price and is material to the company. What aspects of the item 'sales commission' appearing in the accounts would the auditor seek evidence on?
b. What audit tests could be devised to acquire such evidence?

3. Nixon Ltd is a second-hand car dealer. He acquires cars from auctions, from other dealers, from the public, and from trade-ins. He always pays by cheque and maintains a cash book and a file of vouchers appertaining to these purchases.

Sales are made to the general public and occasionally to other dealers. The money from these sales comes in the form of cash, cheques or from hire purchase companies. All sales are on invoices which are consecutively numbered. He obtains a commission from the hire purchase companies which comes by cheques monthly with commission statements.

All purchases are entered in a stock book with details of the car, the supplier and the price. Any repairs etc. required are done and invoiced by another company and paid by cheque monthly against a monthly statement. Such repairs are noted in the stock book also.

Sales are entered in the stock book with details of price, customer etc.

Some 500 cars are sold annually.

Required:

a. What aspects of the items 'sales', 'purchases' and 'stocks' would require audit evidence?
b. What audit tests would tend to provide such audit evidence?

Examination question

1. In the course of your audit review of the accounts of Ramos PLC, you have tabulated the following statistics:

Year	Gross Profit Ratio	Stock Turnover
49	19.8%	12.0 times
50	18.5%	11.3 times
51	18.6%	11.3 times

52	25.7%	9.4 times
53	30.6%	8.6 times

Required:

a. What conclusions may be drawn from the above statistics? (6 marks)

b. As a consequence, what auditing procedures would you consider undertaking? (9 marks)

(LCCI) (Total 15 marks)

2. a. Explain how analytical review procedures can contribute to an audit,

b. explain how the results of analytical review can influence the nature and extent of other audit work, and

c. give THREE specific examples of analytical review procedures that might be carried out as part of the audit of a company that operations a chain of departmental stores.

(ICAEW) (12 marks)

3. An important aspect of any audit is an analytical review of the financial statements.

a. Explain how you think the analytical review can potentially assist each stage of the audit.

b. Explain how ratios or other steps in the analytical review could draw the auditor's attention to the following possible problems:

i. an overstatement of the stock in trade;

ii. misclassification of repairs expenditure as fixed assets;

iii. substantial misappropriation of sales takings or amounts received from debtors.

(IComA)

17 Working papers

Introduction

1. An audit has been defined as a process by which the auditor amasses paper. The more paper he has collected the better the audit he has done. This view is by no means a totally frivolous one for modern audits do involve the collection of papers in such large numbers that an index is invariably required. Note that working papers may in part be held in computer form.

2. There is a Statement of Auditing Standards SAS 230 *Working Papers* and an ISA 230 *Documentation*. The SAS requires that:

   – auditors should document in their working papers matters which are important in supporting their report

   – working papers should record the auditors' *planning, the nature, timing and extent* of the audit procedures performed, and the *conclusions* drawn from the audit evidence obtained

   – auditors should record in their working papers their *reasoning* on all significant matters which require the exercise of judgement and their *conclusions* thereon.

Purposes

3. Audit working papers are produced and collected for several reasons. These include:

   a. To control the current year's work. A record of work done is essential for:

      i. The audit clerk to see that he has done all that he should.

      ii. His supervisor, manager, the partner to whom he is responsible, and other persons who will review the work he had done.

      iii. Enabling evidence to be available in the *final overall review* stage of an audit so that it can be considered whether the Accounts show a true and fair view and comply with statutory requirements.

      iv. Working papers collected in the investigation of one part of an enterprise may be used in the verification process for another part.

      v. The audit of one part of an enterprise is not conducted in isolation. The whole is not just the sum of the parts. Audit verification includes a review of each part in the context of the whole. This is considered further in Chapter 30.

   b. To form a basis for the plan of the audit of the following year. Clearly a starting point for a year's audit is a review of the previous year's work. However, a slavish following of the previous year's work must be avoided and new initiatives taken. Rigidly following the same audit procedures year after year can lead to:

      i. Client staff getting to know the procedures.

      ii. Client staff designing frauds which the procedures will not uncover.

   c. **Evidence of work carried out**

      i. Audit clerks need to provide evidence to their superiors that they have carried out work.

      ii. More importantly in recent years, evidence that work was carried out may need to be provided in a court of law. *For example,* if a company becomes insolvent and is put into liquidation, the liquidator ought to consider if the company has a justification for action against any person to recover some of the losses. Company A has severe trading losses but shows a profit in its accounts by the inclusion in stock of non-existent stock. Out of this false profit it pays a dividend. The following year the company becomes insolvent and the assets are found to be negligible in relation to the liabilities. Clearly the dividend should not have been paid and if it had not been paid then more money would be available to the creditors. Somebody was to blame for the wrong payment of the dividend and the liquidator can sue the guilty parties and make them compensate the company for the loss. Who is to blame? Presumably the directors, who are responsible for the stocktake and the preparation of the Accounts, are primarily to blame. But what about the auditors? They would have to prove in court they did all that they should have done which would include their attendance at the stocktake. The evidence they would need to produce would be from their working papers showing the work they did on attendance at the stocktake. It would seem obvious in the case mentioned (based on an actual case) that they failed to carry out their duties conscientiously, but all auditors should remember that working papers are evidence of the work they have done and may need to be presented in court.

Nature and content

4. Audit working papers should be sufficiently complete and detailed to enable an experienced auditor with no previous connection with the audit subsequently to ascertain from them what work was performed and to support the conclusions reached.

5. In the case of *significant* matters that may require the exercise of judgement, the working papers should contain:

   a. Details of the matter and all information available.

   b. The management's conclusions on the matter.

   c. The auditors' conclusions on the matter.

   This is because:

   i. the auditor's judgement may be questioned later

   ii. by someone with the benefit of hindsight

   iii. it will be important to be able to tell what facts were known at the time when the auditor reached his opinion

   iv. it may be necessary to demonstrate that, based on the then known facts, the conclusions were reasonable.

   For example, the matter in doubt may be the amount expected to be paid under a guarantee given by the client company to a bank which has lent money to a related company which is in financial difficulty. The working papers should contain:

   i. All the facts with copies or extracts from relevant documents (the related company's financial statements, the document containing the guarantee).

   ii. The management's conclusions. Perhaps that the related company will survive and meet its commitments so that no payment will be required of the client company. The reasons for this conclusion will be summarised.

   iii. The auditor's conclusions. Perhaps that a payment of £x will be required. Again reasoning will be spelt out in detail.

6. The auditors' working papers will consist of:

   a. Information and documents which are of continuing importance to each annual audit.

   b. Audit planning and control information.

   c. Details of the client's systems and records with the auditor's evaluation of them.

   d. Schedules in support of the accounts additional to, or summarising the detail in the client's books.

   e. Details of the audit work carried out, notes of queries raised with action taken thereon and the conclusion drawn by the audit staff concerned.

   f. Evidence that the work of the audit staff has been properly reviewed by more senior people.

   g. A summary of significant points affecting the financial statements and the audit report (e.g. the guarantee above), showing how these points were dealt with.

   h. Evidence of the inherent and control risk assessments and any changes thereto (see Chapter 26).

    i.   Evidence of the auditors' consideration of the work of internal audit and their conclusions thereon.

7.   Working papers can be in any form desired by the auditor but a usual division is between the *permanent* file and the current file.

The permanent file

8.   The permanent file usually contains documents and matters of continuing importance which will be required for more than one audit. It will usually be *indexed*.

    a.   **Statutory material** governing the conduct, accounts, and audit of the enterprise. For example, if auditing a Building Society, one would need a copy of the Building Societies Act 1986 and subsequent regulations. In the case of companies this would not be necessary as all auditors know the Companies Act by heart! However, a copy of the Stock Exchange regulations may be required.

    b.   **The Rules and Regulations** of the enterprise. For companies, this means the Memorandum and Articles of Association. For partnerships, it means the partnership agreement; for sports clubs, the club rules, and so on.

    c.   **Copies of documents** of continuing importance and relevance to the auditor. Examples are:

        i.   Letter of engagement and minutes of appointment of the auditor. This is particularly important in non-statutory audits as it embodies the auditor's instructions.

        ii.   Trade, licence, and royalty agreements entered into by the client.

        iii.   Debenture deeds.

        iv.   Leases.

        v.   Guarantees and indemnities entered into.

    d.   **Addresses** of the registered office and all other premises, with a short description of the work carried on at each.

    e.   An organisation chart showing:

        i.   The principal departments and sub-divisions thereof, with a note of the numbers of people involved.

        ii.   The names of responsible officials showing lines of responsibility. Extra details should be given for accounting departments.

    f.   **List of books and other records** and where they are kept. Names, positions, specimens of signatures and initials of persons responsible for books and documents should also be included. Account codes and classifications should also be held.

    g.   **An outline history** of the organisation. Special mention must be made of the history of reserves, provisions, share capital, prospectuses, and acquisition of subsidiaries and businesses. There should also be a record of important accounting ratios.

    h.   **List of accounting matters** of importance. Accounting policies used for material areas such as stock, work in progress, depreciation, research and development.

    i.   Notes of interviews and correspondence re *internal control* matters and all past letters of weakness.

    j.   A note of the position of the company in *the group* and of all subsidiaries and associated companies with holdings therein.

k. Clients' *internal audit* and accounting instructions.

l. A list of the *directors*, their shareholdings, and service contracts.

m. A list of the company's *properties and investments* with notes on verification.

n. A list of the company's *advisors* – bankers, merchant bankers, stockbrokers, solicitors, valuers, insurance brokers, etc.

o. A list of the company's *insurances*.

This is rather a longer list than some authorities suggest but it does have the merit of reasonable completeness. It will be seen that a reading of the permanent file will be an excellent introduction for staff coming new to an audit. It is very important that on the occasion of each audit, the permanent file is updated.

The current file

9. The current file will contain matters pertinent to the current year's audit. It will contain:

a. A *copy of the Accounts* being audited, authenticated by director's signatures.

b. An *index* to the file.

c. A description of the *internal control* system in the form of an Internal Control Questionnaire (ICQ; see later in this chapter), flow charts, or written description together with specimen documents.

d. An *audit programme*. This will contain:

    i. A list of work to be carried out by audit staff.

    ii. A list with details of the tests actually carried out.

    iii. The results of the tests and the conclusions drawn from them.

    iv. Cross reference to the internal control records and letter of weakness.

    v. Where rotational testing over a period of years is used, reference to the appropriate part of the permanent file.

e. A *schedule* for each item in the *balance sheet*. Each schedule should show:

    i. The item at the beginning of the year, changes during the year, and the balance at the end.

    ii. Details of how its existence, ownership, value and appropriate disclosure have been verified.

    iii. Documents of external verification e.g. a bank letter.

f. A *schedule* for each item in the *Profit and Loss Account* showing its make up.

g. Checklists for compliance with statutory disclosure requirements. Accounting Standards, Auditing Standards etc.

h. A records showing *queries* raised during the audit and coming forward from previous years. This record will show how the queries have been dealt with, by whom (i.e. audit clerks, supervisor, manager or partner) and, if not satisfactorily answered, the treatment adopted, which may be a qualification of the auditor's report.

i. A *schedule* of important *statistics*. These will include quantitative matters such as output, sales composition, employment, and also accounting ratios such as return on capital employed, gross and net profit ratios, and liquidity ratios. Comparison of these statistics with those of previous years (noted in the permanent file) must be made to determine significant variations. These variations need to be investigated and explanations sought.

j. A *record* or *abstract* from the *Minutes* of:

   i.   the company

   ii. the directors

   iii. any internal committee of the company whose deliberations are important to the auditor. Examples might be an Internal Audit Committee, a Budget Committee, a Capital Expenditure Committee, the Audit Committee, the Remuneration Committee etc.

k. Copies of *letters to the client* setting out internal control weaknesses.

l. *Letters of Representation.* These are letters written by the *directors* (or equivalent in organisations other than companies) to the auditors, being written confirmation of information given or opinions expressed by the directors on such matters as the value of stock, value of properties, uncertain obligations, and contingent liabilities.

It will be seen that both permanent and current files contain material on internal control. It is a matter of opinion where this data is filed; some audit firms adopt a filing system whereby internal control matters are stored in a third file, the *internal control file*.

Throughout the current file, reference should be made as to how each item is used as audit evidence. Conversely, for each type of transaction and balance, the nature of the audit evidence supporting it should be demonstrated. This evidence may be from internal control reliance, substantive testing or from analytical review or from a combination of these sources.

Internal control questionnaires

10. These documents can have several functions:

   a. A method of *ascertainment* of the system.

   b. Enabling the auditor to *review* and *assess* the adequacy of the system.

   c. Enabling the auditor to identify areas of *weakness*.

   d. Enabling the auditor to *design a series of tests*. In effect this means enabling the auditor to draw up his audit programme.

   e. Enabling audit staff to *familiarise* themselves with the system quickly and comprehensively.

The advantage of using an ICQ are implicit in the functions just stated but in addition they include:

   i.   The use of *standardised* ICQ ensures that *all* the important questions are asked and the important characteristics of a system are brought out.

   ii. The ICQ is a comprehensive, all in, inclusive method of ascertaining, recording, and evaluating a system of internal control.

Next follows an example of a part of an ICQ. Note the separate columns for:

   i.   Questions.

   ii. Answers – if possible Yes/No.

   iii. Assessment of internal control strength.

   iv. Disposal of weaknesses.

   v.   Cross reference to audit programme.

Internal control questionnaires (extracts)

Client name: **HEDONITE MANUFACTURING LTD**
Subject area: **BANK RECONCILIATIONS**

Symbols: Satisfactory ✔
Weakness ✗

Q No.	Questions	Answers	Assessment	Weakness dealt with	Audit programme
1	How often is a bank reconciliation prepared?	4 weekly	✔		S(a)
2 (a)	Is the person responsible for function independent of the receipts and payment function?	Yes	✔		S(a)
(b)	Alternatively is the reconciliation independently checked?	n/a	✔		
3	Where the reconciliation is prepared as in 2(a) above does he obtain statements direct from the bank and retain them until the reconciliation is effected?	Yes	✔		S(a)
4	Does the independent reconciliation include:				S(a)
(a)	A comparison of the debits and credits shown on the bank statements with the cash book?	Yes	✔		
(b)	A comparison of paid cheques with the cash book as to names, dates and amounts?	Yes	✔		
(c)	A test of the detailed paying-in slips with the cash book?	No	✗	Letter of weakness 12.1.x2.	
(d)	An enquiry into any contra items?	Yes	✔		
(e)	Are items more than one month old investigated to establish that they are genuine?	Yes	✔		S(a)

Subject area: UNCLAIMED WAGES				
Q No. Questions	Answers	Assessment	Weakness dealt with	Audit programme
1 What records are maintained of unclaimed wages?	Entered in unclaimed wages book by Mr Smith ✓			14(c)
2 When are unclaimed wages recorded?	After pay out, on return to wages department ✓			14(c)
3 To whom are unclaimed wages packets handed for safe keeping?	Wages dept. manager ✓			14(c)
4(a) Is he responsible for any other cash funds?	Yes	✓		14(c)
(b) If so, which?	Wages	✓		14(c)
5 Is the authenticity of each unclaimed wage envelope or container investigated by a person independent of the payroll preparation?	Yes	✓		14(c)
6 How long after the pay-out are unclaimed wages broken down and rebanked?	At intervals	X	Letter of weakness 12.1.x2	14(c)
7 Who authorises payment of unclaimed wages?	Wages dept. manager	✓		14(c)
8(a) Are receipts obtained?	Yes	✓		14(c)
(b) If not, how are employees identified?	n/a			
9 Is an authority required before an employee can collect unclaimed wages on behalf of another?	Yes	✓		14(c)
10 Is the unclaimed wages record signed by:				
(a) The employee receiving the payment?	Yes	✓		14(c)
(b) The person making the payment.	Yes	✓		

Internal control evaluation questionnaires

11. Some audit firms use ICQs exclusively, others prefer to ascertain the system by questioning staff and recording the system by means of flow charts or by written notes. With all methods, specimen documents and other exhibits are also collected. If the flow chart and written notes method of recording the system is adopted, it is necessary to evaluate the system's strengths and weaknesses. An ideal method of doing this is by means of an *internal control evaluation questionnaire*. This is a standardised set of questions

which has the advantage, like the ICQ, of ensuring all the right questions are asked and the strengths and weaknesses of a system are brought out.

The basic questions in an ICEQ are called control questions. An example from the sales area is 'can sales be invoiced but not recorded in the books?'. Each control question requires an answer yes or no. To determine the answer, a series of detailed questions are then asked. To answer the control question referred to, the back-up questions would be:

a. Are invoices pre-numbered?

b. Is there an independent sequence check of the ledger posting copy of the invoice with acknowledgement of performance?

c. Are there procedures for spoilt and cancelled invoices?

d. Is there control over 'sale or return' goods?

e. Is there control over 'pro forma' invoices?

Here is an example of an ICEQ and a list of control questions.

Internal control evaluation questionnaire (extract)

Subject area: **PURCHASES**

Control Question	Criteria	Answer	Might weakness be material?
CAN ORDERS BE PLACED FOR GOODS (OR SERVICES) WHICH ARE NOT AUTHORISED	1. Control over custody of unused requisitions.		
	2. Specified authority for requisitions.		
	3. Limits to authority for issue of requisitions.		
	4. Custody of unused purchase orders.		
	5. Measures for issue of purchase orders.		
	6. Purchase orders pre-numbered.	No	Yes
	7. Purchase orders complete with specification and prices.		
	8. Purchase orders valued and compared with budgets.		
	9. Segregation of duties between officials responsible for, requisition, orders and other sections.		
	10. Requisitions matched with orders and subsequent documents.		

List of control questions to be used in an ICEQ (extracts)

General

1. Is the business conducted in an orderly manner?
2. Are the records accurate and reliable?
3. Are the assets safeguarded?

Cash and bank

1. Can monies be received but not accounted for?
2. Can cash balances, bank accounts or negotiable instruments be misappropriated?
3. Can unauthorised payments be made?
4. Can wage payments be made for work not done?
5. Can the payroll be inflated?

Purchases and creditors

1. Can orders be placed for goods or services which are not authorised?
2. Can goods or services be accepted without being ordered?
3. Can goods or services be accepted without inspection?
4. Can goods or services be paid for without being received?

Sales

1. Can goods be despatched to a bad credit risk?
2. Can goods be despatched but not invoiced?
3. Can goods be invoiced but not recorded in the books?
4. Can debtors' accounts be improperly credited?
5. Can debtors' accounts remain uncollected?

Stocks

1. Are stocks protected against loss or misuse?
2. Are period end stocks properly evaluated as to quantity, condition, and value?

Fixed assets

1. Can fixed assets be acquired or disposed of without proper authority or record?

Investments

1. Can investments be acquired, disposed of or pledged without proper authority or record?
2. Can documents of title be lost or misappropriated?
3. Can income fail to be collected or be misappropriated?

Flow charts

12. Flow charts are a method of recording internal control systems from the auditor's standpoint.
13. The *advantages* of flow charts are as follows:
    a. Flow charts enable the system to be recorded in such a way that it can be *understood* by:
        i. New staff coming to the audit.
        ii. Supervisors, managers and partners.
        iii. Client staff, who can have weaknesses pointed out more easily.

b. The *overall* picture of a firm can be seen, and in particular the auditor can be assured he has the whole picture as flowlines going nowhere can be easily spotted.

c. Flowcharting is a *consistent* system of recording.

d. Flowcharting is a *disciplined* method of recording. Full understanding must be gained to draw them.

e. Flowcharting highlights the *relationships* between different parts of a system.

f. *Weaknesses* are easier to spot.

g. *Superfluous* forms and bottlenecks are easily spotted. This is really of use to organisation and method study practitioners but auditors often help their clients in this area.

h. Flow charts are a permanent record but are easily *updated*.

i. In complex cases, flowcharting is the only way to gain an understanding of a system.

14. The *disadvantages* of flowcharting are:

a. Their creation can be very *time consuming*.

b. They can become a *fetish* i.e. ends in themselves.

c. They are of little use in systems (e.g. small concerns) where internal control is ineffective or very simple.

d. Numerous symbol systems abound which can cause confusion.

15. When preparing flow charts the following points should be borne in mind:

a. An *organisation chart* is an essential concomitant.

b. *Simplicity and clarity* are fundamental.

c. Flow charts must not be congested. Use separate charts for sub-procedures, exceptional procedures etc. *Small congested charts lose examination marks.*

d. Use only *horizontal and vertical lines*.

e. Chart the flow of *goods and documents* on separate charts.

f. *Serial number* operations.

g. *Cross reference* to ICQ, ICEQ, audit programme, letter of weakness, etc.

h. Charts must *show*:

   i. Initiation of each document and operation.

   ii. Sequence of all operations on documents and all copies of documents, especially operations of control, inspecting, checking, comparing and approving.

   iii. The sections or individuals who perform operations.

   iv. The ultimate destination, i.e. where is it filed?

   v. Explanatory notes where required.

i. Use flow chart symbols only, if possible. There is not usually a need for verbal description *and* symbols.

j. Specimens of documents should be attached and cross referenced.

The objective of a flow chart is that it is complete in itself and can be read and understood quickly and comprehensibly. However this takes practice. A verbal description of the system might be:

a. The company has a number of separate departments (e.g. sales, credit control). This is important for separation of duties.

b. Orders are received from customers in various forms.

c. All orders are transcribed onto prenumbered official 'sales order forms'. Prenumbering ensures all orders will be fulfilled or discovered as unfulfilled.

d. The blank order forms are kept locked in the manager's safe. Order forms are important as they key the release of goods.

e. The sales order forms are in duplicate. One copy is attached to the original customer order and filed in a temporary file.

f. The second copy is sent to credit control. Credit control check that the customer is credit worthy by reference to their records and the customer's ledger account printout (to see the customer is not overdue or has not exceeded his credit limit).

g. If credit is not approved then the sub-routine. The sub-routine is on another Flow Chart which I have not included.

h. The order is then sent to the warehouse. There, the goods on the order are checked for availability. If the goods are not available then a routine is operated (presumably to order more from the supplier).

i. A despatch note in triplicate is made out from the details in the sales order form. This despatch note is prenumbered.

j. One copy of the despatch note is put with the goods (which are presumably picked off the shelves and packed) and signed by the goods-out foreman who compares the goods with the despatch note.

k. This copy is attached to the sales order form and filed in despatch note number order in the warehouse.

l. The second copy of the despatch note is checked against the goods and sent with the goods to the customer.

m. The third copy is used to make out the invoice. It is subsequently attached to a copy of the invoice and filed in invoice number order in the invoice section. But before being so attached it is checked for sequence (to see none are missing, meaning goods were despatched but not invoiced) by the invoice section manager.

n. The invoice has four copies. The top copy is sent to the customer.

o. The third copy has been dealt with (see m.).

p. This copy is checked for accuracy and initialled by the checker. The second copy is batched daily. From the batch a prelist is made out in duplicate. The top copy is filed in numerical sequence in the invoice department.

q. The second copy of the prelist is sent with the batch of copy invoices daily to computer input (this is yet another Flow Chart. I have not included it).

r. The fourth copy of the sales invoice is sent to the sales department.

s. From the order forms and the invoice copies, a schedule of outstanding orders is made out weekly in duplicate.

t. The matched order forms and invoices are attached to each other and filed monthly in alphabetical order of customer.

u. The top copy of the schedule is filed. The second copy is sent to the managing director.

Note:

i. The symbols used are explained below and the internal control features listed.

ii. You may well feel that the flow chart explains the system in a much more digestible manner than the narrative above.

Flow Chart for audit purposes

Gremlin Wholesale Co. Ltd – Flow Chart of Sales Orders and Invoicing Procedures

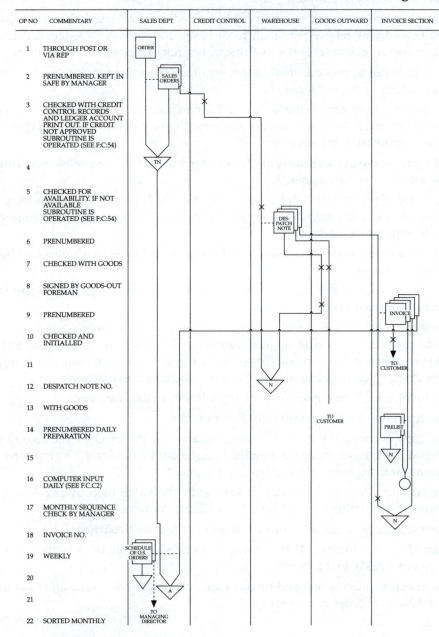

OP NO	COMMENTARY	SALES DEPT	CREDIT CONTROL	WAREHOUSE	GOODS OUTWARD	INVOICE SECTION
1	THROUGH POST OR VIA REP	ORDER				
2	PRENUMBERED. KEPT IN SAFE BY MANAGER	SALES ORDERS				
3	CHECKED WITH CREDIT CONTROL RECORDS AND LEDGER ACCOUNT PRINT OUT. IF CREDIT NOT APPROVED SUBROUTINE IS OPERATED (SEE F:C:54)					
4		TN				
5	CHECKED FOR AVAILABILITY. IF NOT AVAILABLE SUBROUTINE IS OPERATED (SEE F:C:54)			DESPATCH NOTE		
6	PRENUMBERED					
7	CHECKED WITH GOODS					
8	SIGNED BY GOODS-OUT FOREMAN					
9	PRENUMBERED					INVOICE
10	CHECKED AND INITIALLED					
11						TO CUSTOMER
12	DESPATCH NOTE NO.			N		
13	WITH GOODS					
14	PRENUMBERED DAILY PREPARATION				TO CUSTOMER	PRELIST
15						N
16	COMPUTER INPUT DAILY (SEE F.C.C2)					
17	MONTHLY SEQUENCE CHECK BY MANAGER					N
18	INVOICE NO.					
19	WEEKLY	SCHEDULE OF O.S. ORDERS				
20						
21		A				
22	SORTED MONTHLY	TO MANAGING DIRECTOR				

Notes to flowchart

1. Symbols used are:

Document	☐
Prepared using details in	- - - - -
Action or Check	✕
File	▽

T   Temporary
A   Alphabetical order
N   Numerical order
D   Date order

To another flow chart   ◯

2. Note incidence of:
   a. Separation of duties:
      – initiation (by customer)
      – authorisation (credit control)
      – custody (warehouse)
      – documentation and recording.
   b. Specified organisation structure.
   c. Proof measures (prelist).
   d. Acknowledgement of performance (invoice checking).
   e. Protective devices (blank sales order forms kept in safe).
   f. Formal transfer of goods (warehouse to goods out).
   g. Pre-review (by credit control).
   h. Post review (sequence checks).

   Notes to student:
   1. This is, of course, incomplete. The warehouse, goods-out section etc., have not been included.
   2. Further detail could be included if desired, e.g. actual names of officials, their location, etc.

Audit programmes

16. An audit programme is simply a list of the work an auditor does on the occasion of his audit. At one time, an audit programme would contain entries like:

    'Vouch three months' wages'

    There would be columns for the periods selected and for the initials of the audit clerk and the date of the test. In the modern audit programme these columns would still be found but the tests would be different, being designed to test the internal control system or to substantiate balances or transactions rather than the authenticity of individual entries. The results of tests, particularly if based on statistical sampling, would need some evaluation and the audit programme would provide space for this.

17. The advantage of using audit programmes are:

   a. They provide a clear set of *instructions* on the work to be carried out.

   b. They provide a clear *record* of the work carried out and by whom.

   c. Work can be *reviewed* by supervisors, managers etc.

   d. Work will not be *duplicated*.

   e. No important work will be *overlooked*.

   f. *Evidence* of work done is available for use in defending actions for negligence, etc.

18. The disadvantages of audit programmes are:

   a. Work may become *mechanical*.

   b. Parts may be executed without regard to the *whole* scheme.

   c. Programmes are *rigidly* adhered to although client personnel and systems may have changed.

   d. *Initiative* may be stifled.

   e. There is an audit theory that when an auditor's suspicions are aroused (the usual term is *put upon enquiry*) he should *probe the matter to the bottom*. A fixed audit programme and limited time tend to inhibit such probings.

   f. If work is performed to a pre-determined plan, client staff may become aware of the fact and fraud is facilitated.

Here are examples of audit programmes.

Extract from a procedural audit programme

Client: Hedonite Manufacturing Ltd
Year end: 31 January 20-2
Area: Purchases

Tests	**Signature**	**Date**
1. Select randomly 25 invoices and 10 credit notes for detailed checking in the manner described in the following paragraphs. The items selected for test should include the following types of transaction:		

   production purchases
   production services
   capital expenditure
   non-production goods and services
   imports.

2. Obtain up-to-date specimen signatures and initials of all officials operating in this area. This should be obtainable from the permanent file.

3. Prepare a schedule of the items selected together with the tests to be applied. On conclusion of each test, the results should be entered on the schedule.

4. For each item selected (where applicable):

   a. Verify that each invoice is supported by a properly signed requisition.

b. Verify that each invoice is supported by a properly signed copy order.

c. Verify that each invoice for goods is supported by a goods received note (GRN) bearing evidence that the goods have been inspected and approved as being in good condition and order and in agreement with the purchase order.

d. Verify that invoices for services have been approved by the person requisitioning the service.

e. Verify that capital expenditure requisitions have been made within authorised limits.

f. Verify that prices are as authorised by examining priced copy, orders, estimates, tenders or other evidence.

g. Verify calculations and additions have been checked.

h. Check calculations, extensions, and additions.

i. Check that invoices have been correctly expense and cost record coded and that entries in the invoice register and cost records correctly reflect the coding.

j. Verify that credit notes are supported by a goods returned note or by other authority if they are for services or adjustments.

k. Verify that appropriate acknowledgements in the form of initials or signatures appear on each document.

l. Verify that each invoice has been passed for payment and that invoices on which cash discounts can be claimed have been correctly treated.

m. Check postings from the invoice register to the purchase ledger accounts.

n. Verify correct treatment of VAT.

5. Verify sequence of:

   orders
   goods received notes
   copy orders
   invoice numbers applied internally.

6. Enquire into missing numbers.

7. Enquire into outstanding orders.

8. Enquire into unmatched GRNs.

9. Enquire into unprocessed invoices.

10. Examine pre-lists for control accounts.

11. Test additions and crosscasts of invoice register.

12. Test postings to nominal ledger.

13. Scrutinise the invoice register and the file of invoices for unusual and extraordinary items.

After test review

Did the tests reveal:

a. Any changes in the system of internal control?

b. Any weaknesses in the system of internal control?

c. Any instances of the system being short-circuited or not being followed?

d. Any delays in processing which may affect:

 i. efficiency of the system?

 ii. year-end cut-off?

e. Any evidence of fraud?

f. Any matter that should put the auditor on enquiry?

After review action

Does the review require any of the following actions?

a. Updating the ICQ and Flowcharts.

b. Revision of the audit programme.

c. Further tests.

d. Queries to raise with the management which could not be answered at the time.

e. Matters to be cleared with supervisor, manager, or partner.

Extract from a vouching audit programme

Client: Smallfry Manufacturing Ltd
Year end: 31 July 20-1
Area: Industrial wages

	Number Examined	Signature	Date

1. Select one week's wages sheets from each month and:

 a. Check additions of each column.

 b. Trace totals to summaries.

 c. Check additions and cross casts of summaries.

 d. Trace summary totals to nominal ledger.

 e. Vouch totals with actual payments recorded in the cash book.

2. Vouch data recorded on wage sheets for calculation of gross pay with:

 a. Time clock cards.

 b. Piecework records.

 c. Overtime authorisation.

3. Vouch gross pay with tax records.

4. Vouch employees' names with personnel records and contracts of employment.

5. Select 20 employees in one week of each quarter (all departments should be covered) and vouch:

 a. Hours worked with time records.

 b. Piecework with records.

 c. Overtime with authorities.

    d.   Other gross pay (e.g. lay-off pay) with authority.

    e.   Rates of pay with union or other agreements or with authority.

    f.   Check calculations of gross pay and all deductions.

    g.   Trace deductions through to separate records of each deduction (e.g. income tax, national insurance, pension contributions, union dues, savings schemes).

    h.   Inspect receipts where these were given.

    i.   Inspect authority for non-statutory deductions.

    j.   Investigate any advances of pay ('subs').

6. Select five employees at random and vouch holiday pay paid to them.

7. Investigate five payments of sick pay.

8. Investigate statutory sick pay records.

9. Verify that the procedure for dealing with unclaimed wages has been applied correctly by vouching the unclaimed wages book.

10. At intervals averaging three years witness wages pay-out procedure by:

    a.   Attending at the pay-out of wages.

    b.   Inspecting the application of physical controls over wage packets.

    c.   Verifying that wage packets are handed over to identified workmen.

    d.   Counting the cash in some selected wage packets and verifying with net wages recorded.

    e.   Verifying treatment of unclaimed wages.

Overall tests

1. Select two dates some three months apart and compare wages sheets to identify new employees and leavers:

    a.   Verify correct employment of new employees by examining tax records, personnel records, and other documentation.

    b.   Verify procedures have been correctly carried out when employees have left including a test of redundancy pay, correct notice, etc.

2. Compare wage payments in total and by department with budgets and costing records and obtain explanations for differences.

Internal control

1. Do the procedures as investigated by the above audit programme:

a.	Prevent employees being paid for work not done?	Yes/No
b.	Allow the payroll to be inflated in any way?	Yes/No
c.	Prevent errors occurring in the wage calculation?	Yes/No
2. a.	Is there adequate evidence of time worked and piecework performed?	Yes/No

b.	Is the adequate evidence for rates of pay?	Yes/No
c.	Are there independent checks on the arithmetical accuracy of the payroll?	Yes/No
d.	Is the payroll presented to check signatories as support for the cheque?	Yes/No
e.	Can 'dummy' men be paid?	Yes/No

Conclusions

1.	Have proper accounting records been kept in this area?	Yes/No
2.	Does the figure for industrial wages give a true and fair view?	Yes/No

Other working papers

19. Other audit working papers may be mentioned:

   a. *Manuals.* Most audit firms of any size have printed audit manuals which complement internal instruction given to staff. They contain general instructions on the firm's method of auditing in each area and on the audit firm's procedures generally.

   b. *Audit note books.* These were common at one time but now most notes made by audit staff are incorporated in the current or permanent files.

   c. *Time sheets.* These are not strictly a part of the audit working papers but are of great importance in controlling the work of audit staff and making a proper charge to the client.

   d. *Audit control and review sheets.* These, again, are usually incorporated in the working files.

   They are papers which are concerned with a review of the work done by audit staff and acceptance of the work by supervisors, managers, partners, and reviewing committees. This is further discussed in Chapter 34.

Standardisation of working papers

20. Most firms adopt a system of standard working papers which can be used on all audits. This has many advantages including:

   a. efficiency

   b. staff become familiar with them

   c. matters are not overlooked

   d. they help to instruct staff

   e. work can be delegated to lower level staff

   f. work can more easily be controlled and reviewed.

21. The disadvantages are:

   a. work becomes mechanical

   b. work also becomes standard

   c. client staff may become familiar with the method

   d. initiative may be stifled

   e. the exercise of necessary professional judgement is reduced.

Ownership of books and papers

22. The ownership of the working papers of an accountant hinges on whether the accountant is acting as an agent for the client. The leading case is Chantrey Martin & Co. v Martin 1953.

    The general rules are:

    a. Where the relationship is that of client and professional man, then all documents are the property of the accountant. The only exceptions are original documents, e.g. bank statements, invoices etc., which remain the property of the client.

    b. Where the relationship is that of principal or agent. This relationship will exist in situations like dealing with the inland revenue, negotiating loans, and arranging the sale or purchase of a business or other property. In these cases all the papers are likely to be the property of the client.

    The ownership of working papers may not seem important, but it may be relevant in situations such as changes in professional appointments, legal proceedings for the recovery of documents, negligence actions etc.

Accountant's lien

23. Accountants are considered to have a particular lien over any books of account, files and papers which their clients have delivered to them and also over any documents which have come into their possession in the course of their ordinary professional work.

    A particular lien gives the possessor the right to retain goods until a debt arising in connection with those goods is paid.

    The leading case is Woodworth v Conroy 1976.

Retention of working papers

24. It is a general principle that working papers should be retained for as long a period as possible. The precise period is dependent on a number of factors including:

    a. Prospectus requirements are for accounts for the preceding six years.

    b. Tax assessments can be made up to six years after the end of the chargeable period but in fraud cases, can be made at any time.

    c. Actions based on contract or tort (e.g. professional negligence) must be brought within six years.

Summary

25. a. Working paper collection is an essential part of an audit.

    b. The reasons for collecting working papers include:

       i. The reporting partner needs to satisfy himself that all audit work has been properly performed. He does this by reviewing the working papers.

       ii. Working papers provide for future reference, details of work preformed, problems encountered, and conclusions drawn. Future reference needs may include a court hearing.

       iii. The preparation of working papers encourages the audit staff to adopt a methodical approach.

    c. Audit working papers will typically contain:

i. Information and documents of continuing importance to the audit.

ii. Audit planning information.

iii. The auditor's assessment of the client's accounting system *and* if appropriate, a review and assessment of internal controls.

iv. Details of all audit work undertaken, problems and errors met and of all conclusions drawn.

v. Evidence that all audit work by the staff has been reviewed by more senior staff and/or a partner.

vi. Records of relevant balances and other financial information including summaries and analyses of all items in the Accounts.

vii. A summary of significant points affecting the Accounts and the auditor's report, and how they were dealt with.

viii. The working papers detail what evidence has been obtained for each class of transaction and balance.

d. Working papers are often divided into permanent and current files.

e. Working papers will include:

Internal control questionnaires.

Internal control evaluation forms.

Flowcharts.

Audit programmes.

Points to note

26. a. The actual conduct of any audit where internal control is relied on is fundamentally the same but the detailed methods vary from firm to firm. The collecting of working papers is universal but the precise labels to these vary as do the detailed audit methods. Here is a summary of the standard audit method showing how some of the working papers might fit in:

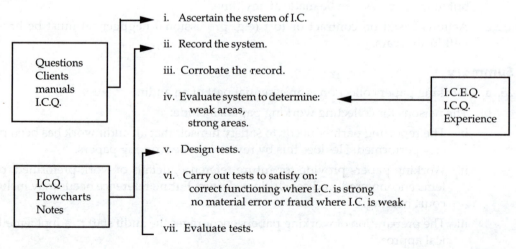

i. Ascertain the system of I.C.

ii. Record the system.

iii. Corrobate the record.

iv. Evaluate system to determine:
weak areas,
strong areas.

Questions
Clients
manuals
I.C.Q.

I.C.E.Q.
I.C.Q.
Experience

v. Design tests.

vi. Carry out tests to satisfy on:
correct functioning where I.C. is strong
no material error or fraud where I.C. is weak.

I.C.Q.
Flowcharts
Notes

vii. Evaluate tests.

viii. Substantive tests.

b. Modern Accounts are subject to much regulation (by companies or other acts and by accounting standards). Modern audits are regulated by the professional bodies acting as supervisory bodies. It is essential that auditors perform all the tests and reviews that are necessary to ensure that Accounts comply with the regulations and that the audit is comprehensive and that nothing has been overlooked. All actions must be fully recorded. One way of ensuring that all is done is to have checklists which must be completed, signed and reviewed by managers and partners.

c. Working papers can be stored in a choice of media – paper, film, electronic or other.

d. Auditors use many schedules, analyses and other documentation prepared by the client. It is essential that there is adequate audit evidence that such information is properly prepared. This is especially true of computer print-outs.

e. SAS 230 requires that auditors should adopt appropriate procedures for maintaining the *confidentiality* and *safe custody* of their working papers.

f. Auditors should retain their working papers for some years at least. They may be needed for a prospectus or for regulatory requirements or even in inland revenue investigations.

Case study 1

Charlatan Furniture Ltd are a large company engaged in the manufacture and import of self-assembly furniture kits. Their system for the placing of purchase orders is:

a. Requisitions are drawn up by production control, by marketing and by stores accounting who keep stores records on a micro computer. Requisitions are not pre-numbered.

b. All requisitions must be cost allocation coded and be signed as approved by a departmental manager. Certain codes (e.g. capital expenditure) are excluded from this process.

c. Requisitions are passed to the purchasing department. They approve requisitions and complete purchase orders. Orders are placed with approved suppliers. There is an ongoing programme to find the optimal suppliers.

d. The orders are in triplicate – 1 retained, 2 to requisitioner and 3 to the supplier. Orders are pre-numbered and are valued. Cost codes and total purchases for that cost code are entered on the order together with budgeted allowance for that code.

e. The orders are checked and signed by the purchasing manager.

Discussion

a. Flow chart this system.

b. Evaluate its strengths and weaknesses (you may use the ICEQ in this chapter).

c. What audit tests could be applied?

d. Relate this system to the overall audit objectives.

Case study 2

During the final audit of the Accounts of Zap Pesticides PLC it appeared that large quantities of Anophocide had been sent to customers in certain African countries on sale or return terms. Only a small proportion has been sold and cash received. Payment is due in US dollars. The banks have reported that several of the countries concerned have difficulties with foreign currencies. There is a strong rumour that the chemical causes environmental damage and that its use may be banned in the US and other countries.

Discussion

What problems are identifiable in determining the choices open to the company's directors in accounting for this item on the annual accounts?

How would the auditor deal with the matter with special reference to his working papers?

Student self testing questions *Questions with answers apparent from the text*

1. a. What are the objectives of working papers? (3)
   b. List the contents of working papers. (4, 5, 6)
   c. List the contents of a permanent file. (8)
   d. List the content of a current file. (9)
   e. What are the functions of an ICQ? (10)
   f. What are the functions of internal control evaluation questionnaires or forms? (11)
   g. Enumerate the advantages and disadvantages of flowcharting. (12, 14)
   h. Who owns an accountant's working papers? (22)
   i. What is a lien and why might it be important to an accountant? (23)
   j. How long should an auditor retain his working papers? (24)
   k. In the case of significant matters that require the exercise of judgement, what should working papers do? (5)
   l. List the advantages and disadvantages of standardising working papers. (20, 21)
   m. What should an auditor do if his suspicions are aroused? (18)
   n. Distinguish an ICQ from an ICEQ. (10, 11)

Exercises

1. Rapidrise Ltd are a firm of plumbers' and electricians' merchants which has expanded very rapidly to a turnover of some £3 million in five years. There are three founder director/shareholders and some 20 staff + six clerical staff including Ted who is a part-qualified accountant. The system for ordering and paying for incoming goods is:

   Each morning Ted visits the warehouse and the foreman and his deputy tell him precisely what to order in order to replace existing stocks and to obtain new lines. New lines are usually suggested by the directors. Ted telephones through the orders to the regular suppliers. Some suppliers require a written order and for them he writes out an order from a duplicate pad which is not sequentially numbered.

   On arrival of the goods, the goods are checked by the foreman or his deputy and the delivery note marked 'OK' and passed to Ted. Ted places the delivery notes in a file. When the invoices arrive they are placed in a box. Approximately once a week, Jean, a clerk, compares the invoices with the delivery notes, settles queries and staples the invoices to the matching delivery notes. She then enters the details of the invoices (supplier, net, gross, VAT) into a micro-computer floppy disc used only for this purpose. At the end of each month the file is printed out and a listing obtained of the outstanding invoices in supplier name order. When the monthly statements are received, Jean compares them with the print-out and settles any queries over the phone with the supplier or with the foreman.

She then passes the statements to Ted who decides which items are to be paid (the company has cash flow difficulties caused by its rapid expansion). He marks the items to be paid and gives the lot back to Jean. Jean makes out cheques for these items and sends them to Ted. He signs the cheques (only his is required) and Jean hands them to Mary who sends out the post.

Jean enters the cheques in the invoice disc. The computer system also:

-   prints out lists of invoices (and credit notes)
-   prints out lists of cheques drawn
-   updates the cash book disc which is used by Ted to control the bank overdraft
-   matches cheques with items and eliminates them where possible.

Jean journalises entries to match and eliminate invoices where several are settled with one cheque.

Jean has no other duties apart from some typing and the keeping of the petty cash.

There are no stock control systems and the warehouse is open during the day to all staff and to customers. Good security operates at night and at weekends.

Required:

a. Flow chart this system.
b. Identify and list the weaknesses in this system.
c. List the possible consequences of these weaknesses. These should include possible frauds as well as errors.
d. Suggest a better system.

2. Alset Ltd have 12 electrical appliance shops in the Midlands. The company maintains a warehouse in Bilston and supplies goods to the branches using 2 lorries. There is a central accounts department at the warehouse with five staff under the chief accountant Louise.

    Supplies are ordered for the central warehouse from specific suppliers (these are changed as necessary and a director Toby is in charge of an effective system for selecting suppliers) using an effective system. A stock control system is used in the central warehouse which works well.

    The 12 shops are in the charge of individual managers who have autonomy over most aspects of the shop including hiring staff. They are expected to indent for supplies from the central warehouse but are permitted to buy some supplies elsewhere if the central warehouse does not stock items and there is customer demand. Prices for items supplied from head office are fixed by head office as there is central advertising with prices (low) given.

    The accounting system is:

    -   Shop managers send in a weekly form of requisition for supplies to the central warehouse. The supplies are invoiced to the shops at cost and the invoices form input for the warehouse stock control system.
    -   Supplies bought for individual shops are paid for by head office when the invoices and delivery notes are sent to head office with a covering letter from each manager stating why they were purchased.
    -   Sales are made in the shops for cash or cheque (no credit cards). These are recorded in till rolls and the managers count the takings daily each morning and bank the proceeds. They agree the till rolls and retain the bank paying in counterfoils and the

till rolls. Petty cash and wages are taken out of takings before banking. Each manager maintains his own wages records but payments to the inland revenue are made centrally. A weekly return is sent to head office showing takings and payments made from takings.

- Overheads of the branches such as rent, rates and electricity are paid for centrally.
- Stock is counted half yearly by the managers and accounts prepared for each shop based on the data at head office. Action is taken if the profit margins are less than expected.
- Some sales are made on hire purchase. The managers fill in the HP forms and keep the recording in the branches. They collect the instalments which are normally paid in cash. Full details are sent to head office on the weekly return. Some HP customers pay direct to head office bank account by standing order.
- Each shop manager is remunerated up to 50% by a commission on the net profit of the shop he/she manages.

Required:

a. List the weaknesses in this system indicating the possible frauds and errors that could occur.

b. Prepare a flow chart/flow charts of a system which would prevent/detect errors and frauds.

c. Devise auditing tests for the existing system indicating whether these are compliance tests, substantive tests or analytical review.

d. Devise auditing tests on the system you have designed for b.

Examination questions

1. Your firm has recently been appointed auditor of Falmouth Manufacturing Ltd, a small manufacturing company that employs 100 staff in the production department (divided into four sections of 25 staff in each) and administration staff of 35 (including 10 office staff). The personnel department consists of a manager and secretary. The wages department prepares manual wages records, employing two wage clerks who are responsible for making up pay-packets and the payment of wages. The production staff work a single eight-hour daytime shift with overtime. All employees clock in and out each day. The section foremen authorise overtime and calculate the weekly bonus payable to employees based on the weekly production of the department; the bonus is calculated at a standard rate and is sent to the wages department on a standard form. In addition to PAYE and National Insurance (Social Security) deductions, certain employees also have trade union dues, holiday fund and staff saving schemes contributions deducted from their wages. Wages are paid each week on a Thursday based on the time worked in the week to the previous Friday.

Required:

a. Design an internal control evaluation questionnaire to apply to the above system.

(5 marks)

b. Draft an audit programme to audit the existing production wages system.

(10 marks)

(AAT) (Total 15 marks)

2. a. Why is it important to ascertain and review a client company's system of internal control?

b. Give *five* types of internal control and explain their importance to the client's business.

c. A number of techniques are available to an external auditor to ascertain the client's internal control procedures. Give *five* examples of these techniques and briefly explain them. At least two of your examples should be suitable for use for a smaller client company (indicate which).

d. What action may an external auditor take if the ascertainment procedures reveal weaknesses in the control systems?

(IComA)

3. a. For what purposes do auditors prepare and retain working papers?   (12 marks)

b. What are the rights of an auditor to exercise a lien over a company's books for unpaid fees?   (8 marks)

(ICA) (Total 20 marks)

4. You are the audit partner in charge of the audit of Watson Manufacturing PLC. The audit senior who conducted the audit presents you with the files on completion of the audit for the year ended 31 March 1992.

Required

a. List FOUR reasons why audit working papers are prepared.   (4 marks)

b. List the categories of items that will be included in a complete set of audit working papers.   (3 marks)

c. Briefly state the advantages and disadvantages of following pre-prepared audit programmes.   (8 marks)

(AAT) (Total 15 marks)

18 Reports to directors or management

Introduction

1. Auditors *may* consider that they should report some matters which come to their attention during the audit to the directors (or other governing body) including any audit committee or to management. The object of the report is to assist the directors and managers. It is in no way a substitute for a qualified audit report. The practice of issuing such a report now seems to be universal.

2. This chapter outlines the purposes, the timing, the procedures, the addressees, the contents and the format and presentation of such letters.

3. There is a Statement of Auditing Standards SAS 610 *Communication of Audit Matters to those Charged with Corporate Governance*. There is an International Auditing Practice Statement 1007 *Communications with Management*.

4. The title of letter to management varies from firm to firm. Such titles include: letter of weakness, management letter, post audit letter, letter of comment, letter of recommendation, internal control letter, follow-up letter.

Purposes

5. These include:

   a. To enable the auditor to give his comments on the accounting records, systems and controls.

   b. To enable the auditor to bring to the attention of management areas of weakness that might lead to material errors.

   c. In some audit engagements there is a requirement to make a report. These include local authorities, stock exchange firms, housing associations and the financial services sector.

   d. To enable the auditor to communicate matters that may have an impact on future audits.

   e. To enable the management to put right matters that may otherwise have led to audit report qualification.

   f. To enable the auditor to point out areas where management could be more efficient or more effective or where economies could be made or resources used more effectively. For example unnecessarily large balances may occur occasionally in the bank. The auditor could point out that facilities exist in the banking sector for short-term investment of surplus funds. This is clearly outside the audit assignment but can be very helpful to management and may well make the audit fee more palatable.

   The letter can also be used to advertise the other services available from the audit firm.

Timing

6. a. As the report is a natural by-product of the audit the production of the report to management should be incorporated in the audit plan.

   b. The report should be sent as soon as possible after the end of the audit procedures out of which the report arises.

   c. Where the audit is spread over several visits then it may be appropriate to send a report after each visit. Frequently two reports are sent – one after the interim and one after the final.

   d. Where procedures need to be improved before the year end (e.g. on stock control or identification of doubtful debts or undisclosed liabilities) then the report must be sent as soon as the weaknesses are identified by the auditor.

Procedures

7. a. As weaknesses or breakdowns are identified they should be discussed in detail with the operating staff involved and/or with more senior management. It is vital that the auditor has his facts right.

   b. The report should then be written, and discussed with the addressee.

   c. The report should then be sent.

   d. An acknowledgement should be obtained from management stating what they propose to do about the weaknesses.

   e. The weaknesses should be followed up on the next visit.

Addresses

8. It is usual to address the report to the Board or the audit committee who may then choose to send it down the line for action. Alternatively with the agreement of the Board the report may be sent to the management of the appropriate section, branch, division, region, etc. In some cases separate reports are prepared for the Board and for line management.

Contents

9. The report will include:

   a. A list of weaknesses in the structure of accounting systems and internal controls. This means where the client has records or controls which are ill-designed or inadequate. For example there may be no serial numbering of sales invoices so that it is possible for sales invoices to be lost and not be entered in the records.

   b. A list of deficiencies in operation of the records or controls. In principle good records and controls have been designed but they may be by-passed or not always carried out. For example the system in a department store may require all credit notes to be approved by a departmental manager. But in practice the auditor may find that not all credit notes are so approved so that fraudulent credit notes may be issued.

   c. Unsuitable accounting policies and practices.

   d. Non-compliance with accounting standards or legislation.

   e. Explanations of the risks arising from each weakness. For example the possibility of non-collection of the sum due on an invoice or the issue of a fraudulent credit note.

   f. Comments on inefficiencies as well as weaknesses.

   g. Recommendations for improvement. In some cases the required changes may be complex and the auditor should not delay his report if suggestions cannot be made quickly. Also improvements may require much research and in such cases the auditor would not be able to recommend specific action.

Note that items a., c. and d. may require the auditor to qualify his report to the MEMBERS as required by statutes (e.g. the Companies Act on proper accounting records, accounting requirements and true and fair view and a professional duty re compliance with Accounting Standards). The report to management is not a substitute for the auditor's report.

Format

10. The report should be clear, constructive and concise. It should contain:

   – an opening paragraph explaining the purpose of the report

   – a note that it contains only those matters which came to the auditor's attention and cannot be a comprehensive list of all weaknesses

   – if required the report may be tiered by having major weaknesses separated from minor weaknesses

   – a request that the management should reply to each point made.

Response

11. It is essential that the auditor should obtain a response from his client on each point in the report. The auditor should expect an acknowledgement of receipt, a note of the actions to be taken and in some important cases the directors' discussions should be recorded in their minutes.

The report and third parties

12. At the present time auditors are much frightened of legal actions for negligence and are also much concerned with confidentiality. The auditor should not himself disclose the report to any third party without permission from the client.

It may be that the client may disclose the report to others (e.g. the bank, regulatory bodies). The report may be relied upon by the third party and the auditor may then have a potential claim for damages arising out of his negligence. The auditor may include paragraphs stating that the report has been produced for the private use of his client only and/or requesting that it not be shown to third parties without permission from the auditor.

As the report may be critical of individuals, care should be taken that all its contents are factually accurate and that there are no gratuitously derogatory remarks.

13. The new revision of SAS (revised June 2001) 610 makes a number of points. These include:

- Relevant matters should be communicated to those charged with the manage–ment of the enterprise promptly enough to enable those persons to take appro–priate action.

- Auditors should communicate to those charged with the management of the enterprise an outline of the nature, scope and limitations of the work they intend to undertake and the form of the reports they expect to make. This will normally be done through the medium of the letter of engagement.

- Auditors should communicate to those charged with the management of the enterprise their findings from the audit. These findings will include expected modifications to the auditor's report, unadjusted misstatements in the financial statements, material weaknesses in accounting and internal controls, their views on the qualitative aspects of the entity's accounting policies and financial reporting, matters specifically required by other auditing standards to be communicated, and any other relevant matters.

- Discussion and communication of various matters is required in several SASs, including SAS 120, SAS 130, SAS 140, SAS 150, SAS 160, SAS 440, SAS 460 and SAS 620.

•Examples

14. <h2 style="text-align:center">Internal control letter following interim audit</h2>

Albert Hall, Esq., FCA
Financial Director
Hedonite Manufacturing Ltd
Cloghampton   17th October 20-4

Dear Sir

<h3 style="text-align:center">Internal Control</h3>

During our interim audit we examined the accounting records of your company and the system of internal control over those records established in your company. This system was designed to ensure accurate and reliable records and to safeguard the company's assets.

As discussed in our meeting on 14 October 20-4 we set out below the principal weaknesses in the system which we found together with our recommendation for improvement. We also attach a schedule of minor weaknesses.

We must point out that our examination was necessarily limited by considerations of cost and time and that the matters dealt with in this letter are not necessarily all the shortcomings in your company's system.

Sales

The system incorporates measures to ensure that all goods leaving the factory are subject to goods outward notes and are invoiced. On checking the GONs. with the copy invoices, we discovered six instances of goods leaving the factory without corresponding invoices. It appeared on closer investigation that all these items were sales of scrap with a corresponding receipt of notes and coin recorded in the cash book. It was not possible to confirm that the receipt corresponded to the amounts charged. Scrap sales are material in amount and we recommend that:

a. Scrap sales be subject to the invoicing procedure.

b. A responsible official should have the task of comparing goods outward notes with invoices at specified intervals.

Credit control

The system requires that among other procedures the sales ledger account is consulted before credit is granted to category 2 customers (not regular customers but customers who have dealt with the company previously). In our investigations we came across two material instances where credit was granted to a customer from whom sums had been due for more than the allowed credit period. We recommend that the clerk checking the creditworthiness of each customer should initial the sales order to confirm that all procedures have been gone through with satisfactory results.

Wages

We detected some errors in keying in the number of hours worked by hourly-paid operatives. As a result some workers were overpaid and these errors were not corrected. Some workers were underpaid and these errors were detected as the workers concerned complained. There is some propensity for fraud in these circumstances and we recommend that the keying in be checked or verified in some way such as the use of hash totals or prelisting.

Cheque payments

We would also like to point out that the company's system for dealing with cheque payments is slow and cumbersome although effective. Several cash discounts taken for early payment were disallowed by the suppliers for being out of time. We suggest that the system of payments be examined in detail to consider if it could be speeded up and made more efficient in terms of administrative time.

Raw materials

In previous years raw material stock has been priced on the highest price of the year basis. The difference globally between this basis and acceptable bases such as FIFO has been not material. However prices have fluctuated to a greater extent this year and the difference may be material. We recommend that the computer programme extracting this data be amended to value stock on a FIFO basis.

We should be glad if you would tell us in due course what measures you decide to adopt about these matters. We should also like to be informed about any changes you make to the system.

Yours faithfully

Quibble, Query & Co.

Schedule of minor weaknesses.

1. We recommend that the functions of (a) ordering, (b) recording and (c) passing invoices for payment, of catering supplies in the directors' dining room should be performed by separate persons.

2. It is not clear who is responsible for hiring coaches for the works football team and controlling this cost. We recommend that specific responsibility should be ascribed to specified personnel.

3. Purchase invoices are checked as to casts and extensions by Miss Robinson and Miss Smith. No acknowledgement of this check appears on the invoice and we recommend that the rubber stamp should be extended to provide for such an acknowledgement.

4. Small tools such as electric drills are frequently lent by one department to another with no documentation recording these transfers. We recommend that a simple pre-numbered transfer form with spaces for signatures of both parties be used.

5. The petty cash drawer containing up to £200 is kept in Mr Williams' desk with the key left in the lock during his temporary absences. We recommend that more rigorous control be kept over the key to the petty cash holding.

6. Cash sales of small items at the company's branch at Great Bromwich are evidenced by a book kept at the branch. No review is made as to how these sales correspond with the cash banked and we recommend that such a review is instituted.

15. **Internal control letter following the final audit**

Albert Hall, Esq., FCA
Financial Director
Hedonite Manufacturing Ltd
Cloghampton   30th April 20-5

Dear Sir

Internal control

At the conclusion of our interim audit we wrote to you pointing out certain weaknesses in your company's system of internal control. We have now completed the final audit and wish to confirm in writing our discussions on March 14 concerning three more matters.

1. Stocktaking

   Stock sheets were issued by the Chief Accountant and were returned to him. The stock-taking instructions require that these should be numbered to ensure all had been accounted for. This was not done and there is therefore no assurance that all completed stock sheets were returned to the Chief Accountant.

2. Plant

   Our investigation of the physical items of plant with the records revealed two machines which had been scrapped and some parts used to repair other machines. No record of the scrappings had been made in the accounting records.

3. Loans to employees

   It is the company's practice to make loans to employees for car purchase etc., and approval for each loan must be granted by the board. Four loans included in the debtors at the year end had been made to employees who left the company between the making of the loans and the year end. Each of these debtors had ceased to make payments on leaving the company.

We recommend:

1. Stock sheets be pre-numbered.
2. a. Scrapping of machinery be approved by the board.
   b. A plant register should be instituted with regular comparison with actual and record.
3. a. Loans outstanding by employees leaving should, where possible, be deducted from out-standing remuneration.
   b. A senior official should supervise the collection of all employees' loans.
   c. Consideration should be given to employees giving security for loans made to them.

Please tell us in due course, what action you have taken on these matters.

Yours faithfully,
Quibble, Query & Co.

Note that both these reports (Paras 13 and 14) should contain disclaimers of liability.

Summary

16. a. A report to directors or management has several purposes:

    i.   Constructive advice to client on economies or more efficient use of resources.

    ii. Formal request to client to rectify weaknesses which, if not rectified, may require the auditor to qualify his report.

    iii. To enable the auditor to comment on accounting, records, systems and controls with weaknesses and recommendations for improvement.

    iv. To communicate matters that have come to the auditor's attention that might have an impact on future audits.

    v. Formal information to directors to make clear that they know their legal responsibilities for the consequences of weakness in internal control.

b. The usual procedure is:

    i. Verbal discussion.

    ii. Formal letter.

    iii. Follow up.

c. Letters of weakness can be after interim or final audit or both.

d. The contents should be:

    i. Note of purpose of letter.

    ii. Note of purpose of internal control investigation.

    iii. Disclaimer.

    iv. Weaknesses – primary and secondary.

    v. Recommendations for improvement.

    vi. Request for information on remedial action.

Points to note

17 a. Clearly distinguish the auditors' report required by Section 235 Companies Act 1985 and the subject of this chapter which is on a report to management.

b. The audit plan should include the preparation of the report to management and a review of actions taken (if any) on previous reports.

c. In some cases the weaknesses are not material enough to merit a full scale report or the auditor chooses not to send a report. In these cases the auditor should reduce the discussions to writing, agree them with the management, supply a copy to management and file a copy with the audit working papers.

d. Make sure that the weakness really is a weakness. The auditor must be sure that he really understands the system not only in detail but as a whole. A well known example is the multiple retail store which abandoned detailed stock control on the grounds of cost. The weakness of the system (or lack of it) is in the possibility of stock losses. Statistical analysis showed that the cost of losses were less than the cost of a control system. It is also a fact that sampling procedures can be as effective as a fully controlled system.

e. A notable misapprehension is that the letter of weakness can absolve the auditor from blame and hence a legal responsibility to pay for any losses which flow from weakness in internal control. If a weakness is discovered by an auditor and he is unable to satisfy himself that to a material extent:

    i. losses have not occurred,

ii. The records can be relied upon,

he must qualify his report.

Case study

Folly Manufacturing PLC are a multi-product manufacturing company with four factories around the country. The auditors Careful & Co. have completed the interim audit for the year ending 31.12.-6 in September 20-6 and are considering their report to management.

The matters they have discovered include:

a. Each factory has a separate bank account. Sometimes the individual accounts are overdrawn but the bank have agreed to set-off for interest calculation. At times there is a net credit balance.

b. The factory at Tipton shares the policy of straight line depreciation for its plant but unlike the others does not keep a plant register.

c. The factory in Oldham buys large quantities of scrap copper from scrap merchants paying by cash. Each purchase is approved in writing by the plant works manager but there is no regular check of the cash balance kept to make these purchases.

d. The stock of finished goods at Oldham is valued at total absorption cost using budgeted global direct wages for overheads purposes. The other factories use a more sophisticated system of departmental overhead recovery based on machine hours.

e. In all the factories about half the manual workers are paid in cash. Their wages packets are simply given to the foremen to hand out with no formalities.

f. The factories each use a computerised sales ledger system with complex analytical facilities. One facility, to analyse sales on a month to month and year by year basis for each customer is not used.

Discussion

How should these matters be treated in a report/reports to management? Draft such a report/reports.

Student self testing questions *Questions with answers apparent from the text*

1. a.   What reports should be made to management? (5)
    b.   When should these reports be made? (6)
    c.   What names are given to these reports? (4)
    d.   List the contents of such reports. (9)

Examination questions

1. A normal audit procedure is for an external auditor to send a 'management letter' (letter of weakness) to a client.
    a.   What is a letter of weakness? (2 marks)
    b.   When should an auditor send a letter of weakness to a client? (2 marks)
    c.   Why is it important for the client to reply to the letter? (2 marks)
    d.   What is the difference between a letter of weakness and an internal audit report? (6 marks)   *(LCCI)*

2. At the end of the audit of a company the auditor presents the statutory audit report to the members. He or she will also make a report to the management of the company covering points which have arisen during the audit and which should be brought to the attention of management.

You are required to:

a. explain the purposes of a management letter
b. explain the types of matter which are likely to be raised in a management letter, and
c. give *two* examples, with brief details, of specific matters which might be raised in relation to the purchasing department of a manufacturing company.

(IComA 94)

19 The auditor and errors and frauds

Introduction

1. There is a difference of perception between the public and the auditing profession in relation to an auditor's duty regarding errors and fraud.

2. The auditor sees his duty as:

   'the independent examination of, and expression of opinion on, the financial statements of an enterprise by an appointed auditor in pursuance of that appointment and in compliance with any relevant statutory obligation'.

   The emphasis is on the financial statements. However the public, including much of the business community, tend to see an auditor's duties in terms of the detection and possibly prevention of fraud and error. This chapter explores the relationship which an auditor has with the prevention, discovery and reporting of fraud and also error.

3. There is a lengthy Statement of Auditing Standards SAS 110 *Fraud and Error* and an ISA 240 *Fraud and Error*.

Error

4. Errors can be described as *unintentional mistakes*. Errors can occur at any stage in business transaction processing: transaction occurrence, documentation, record of prime entry, double entry record, summarising process and financial statement production. Errors can be of any of a multitude of kinds – mathematical or clerical, or in the application of accounting principles. There can be mistakes of commission or mistakes of omission, or errors in the interpretation of facts.

5. Auditors are primarily interested in the prevention, detection and disclosure of errors for the following reasons:

a. The existence of errors may indicate to an auditor that the accounting records of his client are unreliable and thus are not satisfactory as a basis from which to prepare financial statements. The existence of a material number of errors may lead the auditor to conclude that proper accounting records, as required by Section 221 CA

1985, have not been kept. This is a ground for qualification of the auditor's report under Section 237(2).

b. If the auditor wishes to place reliance on any internal control, he should ascertain and evaluate those controls and perform compliance tests on their operations. If compliance tests indicate a material number of errors then the auditor may be unable to place reliance on internal control. For example, a client invoices goods of both zero rated and standard rated VAT supplies, the VAT is calculated by Clerk A on a calculator and checked by Clerk B. The auditor tests the control by reperforming a sample of the calculations and a significant number of errors are found. The auditor cannot rely upon the control.

c. If errors are of sufficient magnitude they may be sufficient to affect the *truth* and *fairness* of the view given by the financial statements. If errors in VAT calculation are made then the liability to HM Customs and Excise will be incorrect. The affect of the total number of errors may not be *material* enough to affect the true and fair view. In that case, the auditor is not concerned with the error, except that he will inform his client in the management letter. However, the auditor has to have good *evidence* that the effect of the errors is not *material*.

Fraud and other irregularities

6. The term 'fraud and other irregularities' is used for several sins including:
    a. Fraud, which involves the use of deception to obtain an unjust or illegal financial advantage. An example of fraud might be the action of J. the principal shareholder and director of J Ltd in intentionally stating stock to be larger than it actually was. This may be criminal deception in that he is intending to obtain an illegal advantage for J Ltd by continuing to receive trade credit from K Ltd who have reviewed J Ltd's accounts. There is a possibility that J Ltd may not be able to fulfil its obligations under the continued credit line.
    b. Intentional misstatements in, or omissions of amounts or disclosures from, an entity's accounting records or financial statements.
    c. Theft. whether or not accompanied by misstatements of accounting records or financial statements.

    Illegal acts is another term. This is any act which is contrary to law. It may be committed intentionally or inadvertently. In our over-regulated society acts contravening laws relating to planning, health and safety, pollution, employment etc. are easy to commit either intentionally or in ignorance of the law.

    The auditor may be concerned with a known or proven fraud or other irregularity but the problems arise mainly with suspected frauds and situations where the auditor suspects wrongdoing but has no hard data.

7. The auditor's responsibility towards fraud and other irregularities is not dissimilar to that in relation to errors:
    a. Irregularities may mean that proper accounting records have not been kept. For example, the financial position of the company may be unable to be disclosed with reasonable accuracy S.221(1)(a) or *all* sums of money received are not entered in the accounting records, S.221(2)(a).

b. The existence of irregularities may indicate that some internal controls are not effective and that the auditor cannot place reliance on those internal controls.

c. Irregularities may exist which prevent the financial statements from showing a true and fair view and complying with Companies Act requirements. Examples:

    i. Theft of stock by employees and the public from a supermarket chain is commonplace and readers of financial statements presume that some thefts will have occurred. Providing the thefts are within normal tolerances, the accounts do not need to show the fact of or the amount (always unknown) of such thefts.

    However, a *material* theft of cash concealed by suppression of copy invoices, in one particular year, by the company accountant would need to be *disclosed* in the accounts. Otherwise, readers would have a wrong view of the annual profits in relation to trends in annual profits.

    ii. Intentional inclusion in the accounts of debts which are known by the directors to be bad would lead to a wrong view being given to readers of the accounts, of profits and capital.

Materiality

8. A true and fair view may be given by financial statements of Huge PLC with or without disclosure of a minor petty cash defalcation. On the other hand, a theft by an employee of £50,000 from Small Ltd, would have to be disclosed if the profits were reported as £45,000. The latter is material to the accounts and the former is not.

9. Materiality is discussed elsewhere and should be fully understood by my readers. However, if an auditor, knows or suspects that an error or irregularity has occurred or exists, then he cannot apply materiality consideration until he had sufficient evidence of the *extent* of the error or irregularity. Consequently, investigations may need to be made (by the auditor or by the client) into all errors and irregularities so that the auditor can have evidence of the materiality of the matter concerned.

Responsibility for prevention and detection of errors and irregularities

10. Primary responsibility for the prevention and detection of errors and irregularities rests with management. This responsibility arises out of a contractual duty of care by directors and managers and also because directors and other managers act in a stewardship capacity with regard to the property entrusted to them by the shareholders or other owners. How they exercise this duty of care is a matter for them, but in most cases their duty may be discharged by instituting and maintaining a strong system of internal control.

There are many ways the Board can discharge their duty toward prevention and detection of fraud and error. These include:

- complying with the Combined Code on Corporate Governance
- developing a Code of Conduct, monitoring compliance and taking action against breaches
- establishing systems of internal control, monitoring effectiveness and taking corrective action
- establishing an internal audit function
- establishing a compliance function, that is a separate department of the enterprise specifically charged with ensuring compliance with regulations of all sorts
- having an audit committee.

11. The auditor is not required to assist the directors in this task but the guideline does suggest that an auditor should remind directors of director responsibilities of this kind, (in the engagement letter or other communication) and of the need to have a system of internal control as a *deterrent* to errors and irregularities.

12. The auditor, however, must obtain sufficient relevant reliable audit evidence to support his opinion. In regard to errors and irregularities he should have sufficient evidence that no material errors and irregularities have occurred or if they have occurred, then they have been either corrected and/or been properly disclosed in the financial statements.

    The auditor's responsibility is to properly plan, perform, and evaluate his audit work so as to have a reasonable expectation of detecting material misstatements in the financial statements, whether they are caused by fraud, other irregularities or errors.

Audit planning

13. Before preparing the audit plan, the auditor should appraise the risk of material errors and irregularities having taken place. Factors to take into account would include the situation facing the client (e.g. financial difficulties) or known problems with internal controls. The whole approach to the audit may be coloured by the risks involved.

14. In detail, the matters to be considered might involve:

    – The nature of the business, its services and its products (which may be susceptible to misappropriation). Organisations which involve cash takings (e.g. retailers) and easily portable and valuable assets (e.g. jewellers) are particularly at risk. As also are organisations where assets are held in a fiduciary capacity (e.g. solicitors who hold clients monies before handling them on to the appropriate persons).

    – Circumstances which may induce management to understate profits e.g. the impact of taxation on profits.

    – Circumstances which may induce management to overstate profits (or understate losses) e.g. to retain the confidence of investors, bankers or creditors, to meet profit forecasts, to increase profit related remuneration or to stave off the threat of insolvency proceedings, or where management have shares or share options.

    – The known strength, quality and effectiveness of management.

    – The internal control environment including the degree of management involvement and supervision and the degree of segregation of duties, and where there is excessive authority vested in a senior officer.

    – The ability of the management to override otherwise effective controls.

    – The existence and effectiveness of internal audit.

    – The accounting record type. Changeovers to computers are notorious for giving opportunity for error and fraud.

15. In particular account area matters to consider include:

    – The susceptibility of an area to irregularity e.g. cash sales, portable and valuable stock, exclusion of liabilities.

    – Unusual transactions.

    – Related party transactions.

    – Materiality.

16. The information on the matters outlined above will come from prior experience and the annual review of the business and environment. Weight given will depend upon:
    – The type of error or irregularity that may occur or is known to have occurred.
    – The relative risk of occurrence.
    – Materiality.
    – The relative effectiveness of the different audit tests available.

Internal control

17. Internal controls are designed, in part, to prevent and deter errors and irregularities. The auditor has a duty to ascertain the enterprise's system of recording and processing transactions and assess its adequacy as a basis for the preparation of financial statements. In so doing, he will inevitably also examine the internal controls since they are inextricably linked with the system of recording and processing. The auditor may wish to place reliance on some internal controls and must then ascertain and evaluate those controls and perform compliance tests on their operation. Thus the auditor is most likely to acquire some knowledge of the existence and effectiveness of internal controls and this knowledge may be very extensive.

18. This review of internal control may indicate potential or actual instances of fraud and error which may lead to the auditor determining by audit tests if fraud or error has taken place and to what extent. In any event, the auditor should inform his client of any potential fraud or error in the management letter.

19. The auditor does not have a specific responsibility by statute to consider internal controls except as outlined in Para. 17 above.

Indications of irregularities

20. Possible indications of the existence of irregularities include:
    a. Missing vouchers or documents. An employee may destroy an invoice copy and pocket the cash paid in connection with the invoice.
    b. Evidence of falsified documents. Note the Thomas Gerrard case where invoice dates were altered to place the documents in a different year to bolster profits.
    c. Unsatisfactory explanations. Auditors should always say 'show me' and insist on hard evidence when asking for explanations.
    d. Evidence of disputes. Late or partial payments by debtors may indicate disputed invoices.
    e. Unexplained items on reconciliation or suspense accounts. Differences on bought and sales ledger control accounts may indicate trivial non-material errors but may indicate real fraud or major errors.
    f. Evidence that internal control is not operating as it is intended to. Explanations that short cuts have been made to achieve greater efficiency may in fact have been made to facilitate fraudulent conversion.
    g. Evidence of unduly lavish life styles by officers and employees. Suspicion may be in order but other explanations (e.g. inheritances) may be possible.

h. Failure of figures to agree with expectations produced by analytical review. An unexpectedly low gross profit ratio or a surprisingly high breakage rate in a glass factory may hide defalcations.

i. Investigation by government department or the police, or a regulatory authority.

j. Substantial fees, commissions or other payments which are larger or smaller than is usual or are to consultants or advisers for unspecified services.

k. Transactions with overseas 'shell' or tax haven companies or numbered bank accounts.

l. Payments made to officials of home or overseas governments.

Companies may be involved in frauds on investors, creditors, or governments or may be involved in 'laundering' monies from criminal, drug dealing or mafia activities.

Audit tests and irregularities

21. Audit tests may unearth irregularities although their primary purpose is to simply obtain audit evidence. Compliance tests are designed to seek evidence that the controls, which the auditor may desire to place reliance upon, are effective. Compliance tests may also reveal actual or possible irregularities. Substantive tests are designed to obtain audit evidence of the completeness, accuracy and validity of information. Again irregularities may be revealed as a by-product of the tests.

22. Some audit tests are designed to detect irregularities in addition to obtaining audit evidence. For example, tests may be designed to reveal understatements of liabilities or overstatement of assets such as stock and debtors.

23. In general, an auditor is a watchdog not a bloodhound and tests designed specifically and uniquely to detect irregularities will be performed only when the auditor's suspicions are aroused.

Action to be taken on discovery by an auditor of potential errors or irregularities

24. The following sequence of actions may be appropriate:

a. Consider materiality. If the matter could not be material in the context of the accounts then take no further action apart from informing management. Consider again Para. 9 above.

b. If the matter may be material, perform appropriate additional tests.

c. If it appears that irregularities or errors have occurred, and may be material, then consider the effects on the financial statements and ensure that these have been prepared with such adjustments and amendments (and disclosures) as may be required.

d. If further investigations are required and the accounts cannot be delayed, then the auditors' report may have to be qualified for uncertainty.

e. In events where errors or irregularities have occurred ensure top management are aware of such events.

f. Any weakness in the system of accounting and internal control which may give or have given rise to error or irregularity should be fully discussed with, and reported to, management.

Reporting

25. a. *To members.* Errors and irregularities need not be reported to members as such. But if financial statements or any part of them do not or may not give a true and fair view or conform to statute or if proper accounting records have not been kept, then the auditor has his statutory duties under Sections 236 and 237.

 b. *To top management.* In the event of the auditor suspecting that management may be involved in or condoning irregularities, then a report to the main board or the audit committee may be necessary.

 c. *To management.* All actual or potential irregularities discovered should be in the management letter, with recommendations for changes.

 d. *To third parties.* This is a very difficult area and has been covered in the chapter on unlawful acts of clients and their staffs.

 The auditor should:

   i. Take legal advice or advice from his professional body.

   ii. Ensure the accounts give a true and fair view.

   iii. Disclosure to third parties (e.g. the police) only matters where he has a clear public duty to disclose (e.g. if a serious crime is contemplated).

   iv. Consider resignation and its effects under Section 392. SAS 110 considers resignation as the step of last resort.

Requirements of SAS 110

26. SAS 110 has a number of specific requirements:

 a. Auditors should plan and perform their audit procedures and evaluate and report the results thereof *recognising* that fraud or error may materially affect the financial statements.

 b. When planning the audit the auditors should assess the *risk* that fraud or error may cause the financial statements to contain material *misstatements.*

 c. Based on their *risk* assessment, the auditors should design audit procedures so as to have a reasonable expectation of detecting *misstatements* arising from fraud or error which are *material* to the *financial statements.*

 d. When auditors become *aware* of information which indicates that fraud or error may exist, they should obtain an *understanding* of the nature of the event and the circumstances in which it has occurred, and sufficient other information to evaluate the possible effect on the *financial statements*. If the auditors believe that the indicated fraud or error could have a *material* effect on the financial statements, they should perform appropriate modified or additional procedures

 e. When the auditors become aware of, or suspect that there may be, instances of error or fraudulent conduct, they should *document* their findings and, subject to any *requirement to report them direct to a third party*, discuss them with the *appropriate level* of management.

 f. The auditor should consider the *implications* of suspected or actual error or fraudulent conduct in relation to *other aspects* of the audit, particularly the reliability of management representations.

g. The auditors should as soon as practicable *communicate* their findings to the appropriate level of management, the board or the audit committee if:
    – they suspect or discover fraud, even if the potential effect on the financial statements is *immaterial*
    – material fraud is actually found to exist.

h. Where the auditors conclude that the view given by the financial statements could be affected by a level of *uncertainty* concerning the consequences of a suspected or actual fraud which, in their opinion, is *fundamental*, they should include an *explanatory paragraph* in their report.

i. Where the auditors conclude that that a suspected or actual instance of fraud or error has a material effect on the financial statements and they *disagree* with the accounting treatment or with the extent, or the *lack of disclosure* in the financial statements they should issue an *adverse or qualified* opinion.

j. If the auditors are unable to determine whether fraud or error has occurred because of *limitation of scope* of their work, they should issue a *disclaimer or a qualified* opinion.

k. Where the auditors become aware of a suspected or actual fraud they should:
    – *consider* whether the matter may be one that ought to be reported to a *proper authority* in the public interest; and where this is the case
    – except where there is possible director involvement, *discuss* the matter with the board including any audit committee.

l. Where, having *considered* any views expressed on behalf of the entity and in the light of any *legal advice* obtained, the auditors conclude that the matter ought to be reported to the proper authority in the public interest, they should notify the directors in writing of their view and, if the entity does not do so voluntarily itself or is unable to provide evidence that the matter has been reported, they should *report* it themselves.

m. When a suspected or actual instance of fraud casts doubt on the *integrity* of the directors auditors should make a report direct to a proper authority in the public interest without delay and without informing the directors in advance.

Notes:
– a proper authority may be the Serious Fraud Office, the Police, the Securities and Investments Board, the Bank of England or many others
– qualified auditors' reports are covered by Chapter 36
– fraud is a delicate matter and before doing anything precipitate an auditor should take legal advice and discuss the matter with her professional body.

Summary

27. a. There is a difference in perception of auditor's duties on errors and fraud between auditors and the public.

    b. An auditor's duty is to give his opinion on the truth and fairness etc., of financial statements.

    c. Discovery of some errors and frauds may be a by-product of the audit.

    d. Discovery of the existence of and disclosure of errors and fraud may be essential to the true and fair view.

e.   Errors are unintentional misstatements in, or omissions of amounts or disclosures from, an entity's accounting records or financial statements. Frauds and other irregularities include frauds (which involves the use of deception to obtain an unjust or illegal financial advantage), intentional misstatements in or omissions of amounts or disclosures from, an entity's accounting records or financial statements and theft as defined in the Theft Act 1968.

f.   Materiality is an important concept in this area and the auditor must have evidence that a matter is not material.

g.   Audit planning must take into account the risk of material misstatement due to errors or irregularities.

h.   Auditors should disclose irregularities to their clients, should ensure their responsibilities under Statute have been observed but should not, in general, disclose irregularities to third parties.

Points to note

28. a.   Some audits under statutes or regulations other than the Companies Act give auditors more extensive duties towards internal control and irregularities. For example, the Building Societies Act 1986 requires the auditor to review and report on a society's establishment and maintenance of a system of control, supervision and inspection. The Local Government Finance Act 1982 requires the auditor of a local authority to actively seek out irregularities and to certify losses due from persons responsible and to recover the sum from them.

b.   The engagement letter should educate the client in the true nature of an audit and outline the auditor's duties towards irregularity and fraud. The letter should say that the auditor will endeavour to plan his audit so that he has a reasonable expectation of detecting material mis-statements in the financial statements resulting from irregularities or fraud, but that the examination should not be relied upon to disclose all irregularities and frauds which may exist. Some clients may desire a special examination for irregularities and fraud outside the audit.

c.   In some audits, the possibility of fraud is especially high (e.g. banks and other financial service businesses). In these types of businesses reliance on the work of the internal auditor may be very important.

d.   Irregularities in the form of falsifying financial statements are a special risk in companies with going concern problems. The auditor must always be aware of temptations of management to dress or falsify their financial statements to present an untrue but desirable view of the results and position.

e.   An auditor has the right to require from management any information and explanations he may need. It is reasonable for an auditor to ask management if any irregularities have occurred and, if any are discovered, for the full facts. Section 389A may be helpful here.

If the auditor feels that he has not been given all the information and explanations that he needs then *the scope of his audit has been restricted* and he should consider qualifying his report.

In extreme cases he should resign and invoke the Companies Act rules outlined in Chapter 3.

f. A number of Acts of Parliament (Financial Services Act 1986, Building Societies Act 1986 and the Banking Act 1987) have changed the rules on the regulation of many financial services businesses. One change has been the imposition of a duty on auditors in certain circumstances to report improprieties directly to a regulatory body. This is a very interesting and controversial new idea which remains to be worked out in practice.

Guidance on this matter is now given to auditors in the Statement of Auditing Standards SAS 620 *The Auditors' Right and Duty to Report to Regulators in the Financial Sector*. This is a very sensitive matter but it does allow the auditor to report serious misconduct or incompetence to the regulatory body in order to protect the investing public.

Case study 1

Kwizeene Products Ltd, are wholesalers of household improvement goods with a network of twenty depots in England and Wales. The auditors, Watchhound & Co., are conducting the final audit of the financial statements for the year ending 31 December 20-6 in March 20-7.

The accounts include the following figures (in £'000).

	20-6	20-5
Turnover	10,500	10,100
Gross Profit	2,415	2,223
Net Profit	256	388
Stock	1,245	1,031
Debtors	1,472	1,211
Creditors	861	998

The auditor discovers the following:

a. The company is owned by the Gull family and controlled by Hugo Buzzard, a very dominating character who married the younger daughter of the company founder.

b. Hugo is negotiating for a renewal of overdraft facilities and for a loan to expand turnover.

c. In the interim audit, the wages area (with 95 employees) was found to have very weak controls. Limited tests at that time showed no major errors.

d. A routine test on the 21 representatives' expenses has just revealed that 13 of the 34 items were not supported by vouchers and appeared to be of expenses not actually incurred. The accountant responsible for payment of them referred Watchhound & Co. to Hugo who told them to mind their own business but that all such expenses were properly paid.

e. The auditors have discovered that certain stock lines were sold but were not purchased. They suspect that the items were stolen goods. The amount of the sales of these goods is not determinable without an analysis of the thousands of sales invoices.

Discussion

Discuss the implications of the figures in the accounts and all the other data for the auditors and for the audit of the 20-6 accounts of the company.

Case study 2

Offa Builders Merchants PLC have many branches in the Midlands and a total turnover of £20 million a year. Profits are £2 million and net assets £8 million. In the financial year ending 31.12.-8 the audit clerk on a routine visit to the large branch at Darlafield accidently overheard the accountant at the branch being given cash by a customer for some goods. Her suspicions were aroused and further investigations and questioning revealed that the accountant and the general manager had systematically defrauded the company of some £300,000 over the previous 3 years by selling goods for cash at a discount or by misappropriating cheques. In both cases, no invoices were raised or if they were then they were suppressed.

The main board were informed and the two miscreants dismissed but not prosecuted. Some £30,000 of the missing money was eventually recovered.

Discussion

Consider this case from the point of view of:

a. Materiality.
b. Internal control and the audit.
c. Previous years.
d. The Annual Accounts.
e. Accounting Records.
f. The auditor's report.
g. Reports to outsiders (e.g. the police)
h. Reports to management.

Student self testing questions *Questions with answers apparent from the text*

1. a. Define errors, irregularities, frauds, illegal acts. (4, 6)
   b. What are the auditors duties towards errors? (5)
   c. What are the auditors duties towards the detection of irregularities? (7)
   d. What is the relevance of materiality to these matters? (8)
   e. Who is responsible for internal control in a company? (10)
   f. What factors may indicate a risk of irregularities? (14)
   g. Explain the dictum 'an auditor is a watchdog not a bloodhound'. (23)
   h. What should an auditor do if he discovers an irregularity? (24)
   i. To whom should an auditor report irregularities? (25)
   j. Explain the relevance of the Companies Act 1985, Section 237 (1–4) to all this. (25)
   k. Summarise the requirements of SAS 110. (26)

Examination questions

1. The audit of Brentwood Ltd for the year ended 31 December 1998 on which you were engaged as audit senior was completed on 2 February 1999. Materiality was judged to be £150,000. As all tests yielded satisfactory results, you issued a clean opinion. In accordance with the quality control procedures operating in your practising firm, your partner reviewed your file in March and concluded that the audit complied with all auditing standards and that sufficient, appropriate and reliable audit evidence was on file to support the opinion issued.

On Friday 14 May 1999 you received a letter from Mr Nicholas Mare, the Managing Director of Brentwood Ltd, informing you that he had just received a postcard from the company's Financial Controller in Paraguay where he had absconded with the Marketing Assistant and £450,000 of the company's cash. Preliminary investigations carried out by the Managing Director indicated that the sum had been misappropriated over a period of 5 years. The Managing Director concluded his letter by asking how was it possible for you to miss such a large fraud for such a long period of time and how you could justify the clean audit opinion issued a few months previously.

Requirement:

Prepare a draft memorandum to the audit partner addressing the concerns of the Managing Director of Brentwood Ltd with specific reference to:

a. the respective responsibilities of the auditor and the directors with regard to the company's financial statements; and

(10 marks)

b. the auditor's responsibilities in relation to fraud.

(10 marks)

(ICAS)

2. The presence of fraud in any corporate collapse often results in far more media coverage of the event than there would otherwise be, and often results in litigation against the auditors involved. This was again illustrated earlier this year when the report on the Maxwell affair was released.

Required:

a. Discuss the respective responsibilities of directors and auditors with respect to fraud.

(6 marks)

b. Outline the main guidance available to auditors as regards fraud.

(13 marks)

c. Describe the work that the profession could carry out to improve the auditor's chances of detecting fraud.

(6 marks)

(ICAS)

Asset and liability verification

1. A large part of the final audit stage will be taken up with the verification of the assets and liabilities appearing in the balance sheet. There are well established techniques for verifying specific assets and liabilities. All auditing examinations contain one or more questions on this subject.

2. Chapter 20 sets out the methods of verification which are applicable to assets generally and also considers the detailed methods of verifying specific fixed assets and investments. Chapter 21 describes the verification of current assets other than stock. Chapter 22 is concerned with stock and Chapter 23 concerns liability verification and contains some of the matters which are currently worrying the profession.

20 Asset verification

Introduction

1. The auditor has a duty to verify all the assets appearing on the balance sheet and also a duty to verify that there are *no other* assets which ought to appear on the balance sheet.

Aspects to be verified

2. The following aspects of each asset must be verified:
    a. Cost.
    b. Authorisation.
    c. Value.
    d. Existence.
    e. Beneficial ownership.
    f. Presentation in the Accounts.

    These aspects can be remembered by the mnemonic CAVEBOP.

    Most examination questions in this area can be answered adequately by running through each of these and devising means of verifying each aspect.

    You will also appreciate that the amount of evidence required will depend partly on the risk of misstatement.

3. Older text books tended to stress *existence, ownership* and *value* only. The addition of presentation reflects the relatively greater importance attached now to the *fair* as well as the *true* view given by accounts and the importance of an appropriate selection and disclosure of *accounting policies*.

4. When verifying assets at a balance sheet data it is possible to divide the assets into two classes:
    a. Those *acquired* during the year under review.
    b. Those *held* at the date of the *previous* balance sheet.

For a. type assets it will be necessary to *vouch* their acquisition. This is why the terms *cost* and *authorisation* have been included in Para. 2.

For b. type assets, the acquisition will have been dealt with in a previous year. The presentation will, of course, need to be *consistent* with the presentation adopted in previous years. Most examination questions state whether or not the assets concerned were purchased in the year under review. You will appreciate that the distinction does not arise with current assets.

Verification methods

5. a. Make or request from client's staff a *schedule* of each asset. This schedule will show the following and suggest the associated verification procedures:

    i. **Opening balance**
        - Verify by reference to *previous year's* balance sheet and audit files.

    ii. **Acquisitions**
        - Vouch the *cost* with documentary evidence e.g. invoices.
        - Vouch the *authority* for the acquisition with minutes or with authorised delegated authority.

    iii. **Disposals**
        - Vouch the *authority* – minutes or company procedures.
        - Examine *documentation*.
        - Verify *reasonableness* of the proceeds.
        - Pay special attention to *scrappings*.
        - Note *accounting* treatment.

    iv. **Depreciation, amortisation** and other *write downs*
        - Vouch *authorisation* of policy with minutes.
        - Examine adequacy and appropriateness of policy.
        - Investigate *revaluations*.
        - Check *calculations*.

    v. The above should *reconcile* both as to physical quantity and sterling value of the closing balance.

    vi. The use of plant or other asset *registers* can be of great use to the auditor.

    vii. **Internal control** procedures for the purchase, disposal, accounting and maintenance of assets are very relevant.

    b. **Existence and ownership.** These are treated together but note that existence does not imply ownership. For example, my television set *exists* and is in my house, but is in fact owned by the Co-op from whom I rent it!

        Verification procedures include:

    i. **Physical inspection.** Auditors should not sit in offices but should get about seeing things. Of course, sitting in a client's office goes to confirm the existence of that office!

    ii. Inspection *of title deeds and certificates of ownership* e.g., share certificates. This is a technique that confirms together existence and ownership. Problems arise if the deeds are held by third parties (a certificate from the third party is needed) possibly as security for a loan.

iii. External verification. This applies primarily to current assets like bank accounts, debtors, loans etc. A letter of acknowledgement is sought from the bank, debtor etc.

iv. Ancillary evidence. Examples are:

The confirmation of the existence of property by examination of rate demands, repair bills and other outgoings. Ownership is not necessarily implied.

Investment ownership and existence tend to be confirmed by the receipt of dividends and interest.

c. Presentation and value

i. **Appropriate accounting policies** must be adopted, consistently applied, and adequately disclosed.

ii. **Accounting standards** must be followed.

iii. **Materiality** must be considered. For example, in a balance sheet of a large company it would be misleading to show an asset such as patents in a class by itself if its total value was negligible in relation to other assets.

iv. The *classification* of assets can be difficult. Certain industrial structures can be considered as buildings or as plant with consequent major differences in depreciation, profit, and asset and equity values. A number of interesting examples have cropped up in tax cases. A dry dock including the cost of excavation has been held to be plant (Barclay Curle 1969), as has a swimming pool for use on a caravan site (Beach Station Caravans 1974). The auditor may take a contrary view to the tax courts and of course to the board of the company he is auditing.

v. The choice of *disclosure* of an asset as a separate item or as part of a single figure representing a class of asset is important for a true and fair view. Also important is the choice of words used in the description. In some cases, assets could be classed as fixed or as current e.g., investments.

vi. The distinction between *revenue* and *capital* is important. Sometimes this is a matter of accounting policy e.g. research and development. Sometimes it is a matter of opinion; for example repair expenditure is revenue but may include an element of improvement which is capital.

d. **Other matters relevant to verification**

i. The *letter of representation*. This is dealt with in Chapter 32.

ii. **Reasonableness** and being *'put upon enquiry'* In all audit assignments, the auditor investigates thoroughly and seeks adequate assurances on the truth and fairness of all the items in the Accounts. However, he does not do so with a suspicious mind. He should not assume that there is something wrong, but if he comes across something which seems to him unlikely, unreasonable, suspicious he is said to be *'put upon enquiry'*. In such circumstances he is required to *probe the matter to the bottom* to adequately assure himself there exists nothing untoward or to unearth the whole matter. (Part of the judgement in re the Kingston Cotton Mill Co. Ltd, as long ago as 1896.)

iii. Some assets are pledged or mortgaged as securities for loans. This may involve deposit of title deeds etc., with a lender, or in some cases the asset itself. This creates problems for the auditor who must also see that the *liability* is properly described as *secured*.

iv. **Taxation.** Tax and capital allowance computations should be in accordance with asset accounts. Clearly the auditor will be *put upon enquiry* if claims for capital allowances are made for items of plant which do not appear in the plant register.

v. **Insurance.** The auditor would be *put upon enquiry* if there were no correspondence between the assets in the balance sheet and the assets insured, and if there were differences between the balance sheet figures and the insured values.

vi. **Other than balance sheet date verification**. Some assets can be verified at dates other than the balance sheet date. The techniques are discussed later but in sum they are:

Verify at an earlier date and reconcile with acquisitions and disposals to balance sheet date.

Verify at an earlier date and then parcel them up and seal the parcels. At balance sheet date examine acquisitions, vouch proceeds of disposals, and see all other items are still sealed.

vii. Third parties. Auditors must take special care to satisfy themselves that all assets held by third parties are included in the balance sheet and verified. Likewise, no assets owned by third parties may be included in the balance sheet.

Fixed assets

6. It is not possible to discuss in detail the verification of all possible types of fixed asset. We shall discuss in detail only freehold land and buildings. These two assets are obviously inseparable in ordinary circumstances, but accountants are increasingly seeing them as separate assets.

a. *Land*. Consider always for *all* assets if sub-division into separate types is possible. In this case there is:

i. Registered land.

ii. Unregistered land, or

Land bought in the year

Land owned at the end of the previous year.

Existence of all land is best verified by inspection.

Ownership of land is verified by a certificate from the land registry for registered land and by inspection of the deeds for unregistered land. This inspection is carried out by an auditor who is not normally an expert on conveyancing. However, it is enough for him to verify that the deeds are prima facie in order with, for example, the last conveyance being into the name of the client. Land bought in the year will be vouched by reference to the solicitor's completion statement and bill of costs (usual name for a solicitor's fee invoice) and correspondence.

The value of the land will be at

– cost

– below cost

– above cost.

Land at cost will be the norm and creates no problems. Land below cost will be unusual and the auditor will need to:

Examine the reason for the write down.

Examine the director's minute authorising it.

Appraise the adequacy of the write down.

Ensure adequate disclosure of the facts.

b. Buildings. Buildings can be:

i. Bought in the year.

ii. Owned at the beginning of the year.

iii. Under construction at the end of the year.

If under construction or bought in the year they can be:

Manufactured internally by the client.

Constructed by a builder.

Bought secondhand.

Buildings can be valued at:

– cost

– below cost

– above cost.

In the past, buildings have usually been valued at cost or above cost when periodic revaluations occur. The question of property revaluations is dealt with in a later chapter. FRS 15 recommends that buildings be depreciated over their useful life. Whatever depreciation policy is adopted the auditor must see that adequate disclosure is made and that the policy is consistently applied.

Investments

7. It is very important to distinguish the categories into which investments can be divided. These include:

a. Variability

i. Fixed sum deposits.

ii. Investments of varying value.

b. Quotation

i. Quoted investments.

ii. Unquoted investments.

c. Ownership proportion

i. Investments giving minority interests (i.e. less than 20%).

ii. Investments in associated companies (i.e. 20–50%).

iii. Investments in subsidiary companies (usually but not necessarily greater than 50%).

   d. Period of ownership
      i. Short-term investments.
      ii. Long-term investments.
   e. Treatment in Balance Sheet
      i. Investments which are current assets.
      ii. Investments which are not current assets.

8. Some special points to note on the verification of investments are:

   a. Internal control is very important. Note particularly the separation of duties of authorisation, custody and recording.

   b. Transaction documents. Students should try to see examples. Look at Extel and Moodie cards and read the Financial Times.

   c. Physical inspection is very desirable; *all* the certificates should be examined *together*.

   d. Sometimes the certificates are examined *before* the year end and parcelled up and sealed. Only unsealed parcels and new certificates need be checked at the year end.

   e. The Companies Act has much to say on the subject.

Summary

9. a Verification of assets always appears in auditing examinations.

   b. The verification is of assertions about each asset. A useful mnemonic is CAVEBOP.

   c. Assets can be:
      i. Acquired in the year.
      ii. Held at the end of the previous year.

   d. Verification methods vary according to the asset but many students have found the following list of points useful in examinations:

i.	Schedule of each asset.		xvi.	Materiality.
ii.	Cost verification.		xvii.	Put upon enquiry.
iii.	Registers of assets.		xviii.	Insurance.
iv.	Internal control.		xix.	Lessening in value – depreciation.
v.	Physical inspection.		xx.	Events after balance sheet date.
vi.	Title deeds.		xxi.	Disposal.
vii.	SSAPs and FRSs.		xxii.	Companies Act.
viii.	Classification.		xxiii.	Held by others.
ix.	Representation letter.		xxiv.	Ancillary evidence.
x.	External verification.		xxv.	Revaluation.
xi.	Authority.		xxvi.	Taxation.
xii.	Minutes and *correspondence*.		xxvii.	Auditing guidelines.
xiii.	Security for obligations.		xxviii.	Proper accounting records.
xiv.	Capital or Revenue.		xxix.	Risk of misstatement.
xv.	Other than balance sheet date.			

The initial letters form useful mnemonics!

Points to note

10. a. All auditing examinations contain questions on asset and/or liability verification.

   b. Students fail to answer adequately by making too few points. This chapter will provide enough ideas for students to make enough points in their answers.

   c. Questions on asset verification are sometimes on existence, ownership, value and presentation. Some are specifically on one or two aspects only. It is clearly vital to answer the question asked!

   d. It is not possible in this manual to give detailed verification procedures for all possible assets. To answer specific questions, remember CAVEBOP and the 29 points and apply them as required.

   e. Note that many syllabuses require students to have an appreciation of the accounting requirements of the Companies Act 1985 on disclosure of fixed assets and depreciation.

   f. Some companies transfer assets from current assets to fixed assets. Examples are:
   – a vehicle dealer transferring a stock item to fixed assets as the vehicle is to be used as a fixed asset e.g. as a rep's car or as a delivery van
   – a speculative builder may transfer unsold houses to fixed assets as the houses will be let as investment properties.

   There may be a tendency in times of trade recession for this to be done to avoid having a stock item valued at below cost i.e. at net realisable value. UITF Abstract 5 requires that where an asset is so transferred the transfer should be made at the lower of cost and net realisable value at the date of transfer. Thus the difference between carrying value pre transfer and the NRV at transfer date is a loss in the profit and loss account. Depreciation or other fixed asset valuation procedures start at the date of transfer.

   g. The extent and manner of verification of an asset depends on the degree of risk of misstatement possible with the asset. Inherent risk depends on many factors including the degree of estimation (e.g. provision for warranties), the complexity of the assets (e.g. work in progress), the judgement involved (e.g. stock at net realisable value) and the susceptibility to loss or misappropriation (e.g. cash), transactions not subject to ordinary processing (e.g. the acquisition of subsidiary companies). The extent of reliance on internal control in reducing substantive tests depends on the auditors' perception of control risk.

Case study 1

Pinocchio Robots PLC are manufacturers of industrial robots. They own a large amount of plant and machinery which is used in the manufacture of their products and is valued at some £14 million. The company maintain good records and internal control systems. There is a plant register based on a micro-computer. Each item of plant is recorded with fields as:

Description	Estimated life
Location	Estimated residual value
Supplier	Insured value
Manufacturer	Depreciation policy
Serial number/identifying number	Depreciation applied
Cost of purchase	Major repairs

Cost of installation	Capital allowances claimed
Date of purchase	Use in factory
Date of first use	Machine hour rate applicable
Guarantee/warranty expiry	Responsible officer
Grant received (if any)	Internal audit inspection dates
Manufacturers invoice number	Statutory inspection/report/certificate
Internally generated invoice number	

There are some 250 separate items.

Discussion

    a.   What facts about the plant need verification by the auditor?

    b.   What audit procedures will be applied?

    c.   How should plant appear in the annual accounts and notes attached to them?

    d.   What Accounting Standards are relevant?

Student self testing questions *Questions with answers apparent from the text*

1.   a.   What are the six aspects to be covered in verifying an asset? (2)

    b.   List the points that could be covered in verifying an asset. (9)

    c.   How is land and buildings verified? (6)

Exercises

1.   Outline an audit programme for the verification of the following assets:

    a.   Vehicles in a major haulage contractor.

    b.   Farm machinery and equipment in a 10,000 acre mixed farm.

    c.   Stock of land of a large speculative builder.

    d.   A new factory building on existing land of a major manufacturer.

    e.   Aircraft in a small airline.

    f.   The investment portfolio of Hopp Breweries PLC who make a point of having small-holdings in a range of competitor brewers and suppliers.

    g.   Holiday homes owned in the UK and overseas by Holiday Flats PLC.

    h.   Plant and machinery of Duv PLC a company which has been in the foundry industry but which is rapidly developing into new hi-tec metal bashing while running down its foundry activities.

   Assess the inherent and control risks in each one.

Examination question

1.   As a technician employed on the audit of Thames Engineers PLC, a large industrial company you have the task of auditing plant and machinery.

   Required:

    a.   Draft an audit programme which you would expect to follow. (9 marks)

    b.   The client has suggested that they wish to change the basis of depreciation from straight line to reducing balance over the same estimated life as the greatest loss in value of the plant occurs in the early years of its life. At the same time it is proposed to revalue certain old items of plant which have been completely written off but which still have a useful life. Draft a memorandum to the partner responsible for the audit suggesting the lines of a letter which he should write to the client indicating the principles involved and the effects of the changes. (8 marks)

c. What information has to be included in accounts with respect to future capital expenditure and how would you verify the figure? (5 marks)

d. What information might have to be included in accounts with respect to land and buildings where they are not regularly independently revalued and what is the auditor's responsibility for this information? (3 marks)

(AAT)

2. It is fundamental to an audit that the auditor should obtain reliable, relevant and sufficient evidence as to the ownership, valuation and existence of the client's assets.

You are required to explain the audit procedures necessary for the auditor to be satisfied on these points for:

a. freehold land and buildings (8 marks)
b. trade debtors (8 marks)
c. bank balances. (4 marks)

(ICA) (Total 20 marks)

21 Current asset verification

Introduction

1. This chapter considers some standard verification techniques for three types of current assets, debtors, cash at bank and loans. The asset verification techniques described in the previous chapter apply to these as to all assets, but as they are common examination subjects and some special techniques are commonly applied it is necessary to describe these particular techniques.

2. There is a Practice Note 16 Bank Reports for Audit Purposes.

Debtors

3. Debtors form a large item among the assets of most companies and their verification is essential. The general method of verifying debtors is:

a. Determine the system of internal control over sales and debtors. The system for debtors should ensure that:

i. Only bona fide sales bring debtors into being.

ii. All such sales are to approved customers.

iii. All such sales are recorded.

iv. Once recorded the debts are only eliminated by receipt of cash or on the authority of a responsible official.

v. Debts are collected promptly.

vi. Balances are regularly reviewed and aged, a proper system for follow up exists, and, if necessary, adequate provision for bad and doubtful debts is made.

b. Test the effectiveness of the system.

c. Obtain a schedule of debtors.

d. Test balances on ledger accounts to the schedule and *vice versa*.

e. Test casts of the schedule.

f. Examine make up of balances. They should be composed of specific items.

g. Ensure each account is settled from time to time.

h. Examine and check control accounts.

i. Enquire into credit balances.

j. Consider the valuation of the debtors. This is dealt with in the next paragraph.

Provision for bad and doubtful debts

4. The valuation of debtors is really a consideration of the adequacy of the provision for bad and doubtful debts. The auditor should consider the following matters:

a. The adequacy of the system of internal control relating to the approval of credit and following up of poor payers.

b. The period of credit allowed and taken.

c. Whether balances have been settled by the date of the audit.

d. Whether an account is made up of specific items or not.

e. Whether an account is within the maximum credit approved.

f. Reports on each debtor from collectors, trade associations, etc.

g. Present value and realisability of securities, if any, lodged as collateral.

h. Questions of set-off.

i. The state of legal proceedings and the legal status of the debtor e.g. in liquidation or bankruptcy.

j. Effect, if any, of the Statute of Limitations.

k. Comparison of debtors to sales with comparison of the ratio with those of previous periods and those achieved by other companies.

l. Evidence of any debt in dispute e.g. for non delivery, breakages, poor quality etc.

5. Note that:

a. Debts which are considered irrecoverable should be written off to the profit and loss account.

b. Provisions for doubtful debts should be set up against debts which are considered doubtful.

c. Some companies make round-sum or percentage provisions against doubtful debts. This practice is generally unacceptable to an auditor unless based on good statistical evidence which may come from past experience or may come from data about other similar undertakings which is obtainable from trade associations or which is publicly available.

Debtors circularisation

6. A practice that is becoming very common in the verification of debtors is to circularise the debtors or some of them for *direct confirmation*.

7. The advantages of this technique are:
   a. **Direct external evidence** is available for the existence and ownership of an asset.
   b. It provides confirmation of the effectiveness of the system of *internal control*.
   c. It assists in the auditor's evaluation of *cut-off* procedures.
   d. It provides evidence of items in dispute.
8. There are two methods, which can also be used together:
   a. **Negative** – the customer is asked to communicate only if he does *not* agree the balance. This method is mostly where internal control is very strong.
   b. **Positive** – customer is asked to reply whether he agrees the balance or not or is asked to supply the balance himself. This method is used where there is:
      i. Weak internal control.
      ii. Suspicion of irregularities.
      iii. Numerous bookkeeping errors.
9. The approach is as follows:
   a. Obtain the co-operation of the client – only he can ask third parties to divulge information.
   b. **Select method** – positive, negative, or a combination of the two.
   c. **Select** a sample. All customers can be circularised but this is unusual.
      i. Do not omit – nil balances

         credit balances

         accounts written off in the period.
      ii. Give weight to overdue or disputed balances.
      iii. Use stratified samples, e.g. all large balances and only some small ones.
   d. The letter should be from the *client*.
   e. It should request a reply *direct to the auditor*.
   f. It *may* contain a stamped, addressed, envelope or a pre-paid reply envelope.
   g. It must be *despatched by the auditor*.
   h. Receive and evaluate replies.
   i. *Follow up* when replies are not received. This is the major problem.
10. Circularisation is sometimes carried out at dates other than the year end. This will occur only when internal control is very strong.

Example of debtors circularisation letter (positive method)

FROM   3 April 20-6
HEDONITE MANUFACTURING LTD
CLOGHAMPTON

Dear Sir

As part of their normal audit procedures, we have been requested by our auditors Quibble Query & Co. to ask you to confirm direct to them your indebtedness to us as shown on the enclosed statement as at 31 December 20-5.

If the statement is in agreement with your records, please sign in the space provided below and return this letter directly to our auditors.

If the statement is not in agreement with your records please notify our auditors directly of the amount shown by your records and if possible send them full particulars of the difference.

It will be of assistance to us if you will give this request your early attention. We enclose a reply-paid envelope for your convenience.

Remittance should not be sent to our auditors.

Yours faithfully,

J. Brown, Company Secretary

....

Please do not detach

Name of Debtor

The balance shown on the statement at 31.12.-5 of £1,432.00 due from us is in agreement with our records at 31.12.-5.

.... Signature

.... Position

.... Company Stamp

To: Ecstatic Mining Ltd
Newcastle on Tyne

Bank balances

11. Verification of bank balances is effected by:

   a. Appraisal of the internal control system.

   b. Examination and investigation of the bank reconciliation, noting particularly:

      i. That all uncleared cheques have been cleared after date.

      ii. Lodgements credited after date, but actually paid in before date.

   c. Title should be verified by the direct confirmation from the bank. The bank must have the permission of the client to do this. The *bank letter* is usually on a standard form and opportunity is usually taken to ask the bank a number of questions at the same time.

   d. Value is not usually an issue with bank accounts particularly as banks are now highly regulated. However the Bank of Credit and Commerce International matter has shown that value must not be taken for granted. The auditor must always consider if a bank is in good standing.

12. Practice Note 16 *Bank Reports for Audit Purposes* makes a number of points:

   a. SAS 400 *Audit Evidence* requires auditors to seek appropriate audit evidence for all material items in the financial statements and the bank balances and other bank transactions are usually material.

   b. Excellent external confirmation of these matters can be obtained by direct confirmation from the bank.

13. The auditor should adopt the following procedures:

   a. Arrange for the client to give authorisation to the bank to reveal the information.

   b. Write directly, on headed notepaper, to the bank, at least two weeks before the relevant date, requesting one of three possible levels of information:

      i. *Standard* – used in most cases.

      ii *Supplementary* – used where the client has a more complex relationship with the bank such as trade finance and /or derivatives or commodity trading.

      iii. Additional information – to be specified.

The bank will have explicit instructions from the British Bankers' Association on how to respond.

The statement information will be Account and balance details, facilities (details of loans, overdrafts), securities charged, set-off arrangements and any additional banking relationships.

Supplementary information will be as standard but with information on trade finance (e.g. letters of credit etc.), derivatives and commodity trading

Loans

14. Loans are not usually material assets of companies other than those whose business it is to make loans. We shall consider two types of loans:

   a. Loans other than to directors.

      Verification will be:

      i. Examine and evaluate internal control. Authority is particularly important.

      ii. Obtain a schedule and test its accuracy.

      iii. Obtain certificates direct from debtors.

      iv. Examine agreements and ensure terms are being adhered to.

      v. If a loan is secured, examine the security and consider its value and realisability.

      vi. If a loan is guaranteed, examine the status of the guarantor.

      vii. Review the adequacy of provisions for bad debts. Bad debts often occur when a loan to an employee is made and the employee leaves before repayment is complete.

   b. Loans to directors and connected persons.

      This subject is the subject of extensive inclusions in the Companies Act.

      The auditor's duties are as follows:

      i. Review all loans to directors which were outstanding *at any time* during the year. *Materiality does not apply;* all loans must be reviewed.

      ii. Obtain a certificate of confirmation from the directors concerned.

iii. Ensure that all such loans are subject to board minute.

iv. Ensure that the law has been complied with.

v. Ensure that full disclosure is made as required.

vi. If the requisite information is not given in the accounts, the auditor is required to give the *requisite information* in his report. (Section 237 Companies Act 1985.)

Summary

15. a. The verification of current assets is a common examination subject.

b. Current assets are verified using the techniques discussed in the previous chapter.

c. Detailed verification techniques for debtors are explained.

d. The valuation of debtors is especially notable.

e. A common technique included in the verification process for debtors is direct circularisation which can be positive or negative or a mixture of both.

f. A part of the verification process for bank balances is the bank letter.

g. Loans to directors are subject to company law restrictions which you should know.

Points to note

16. a. The valuation of *all* current assets is the *lower of cost and net realisable value*. It is a common error to assume this method applies only to stock and work progress. Cost is perhaps a peculiar title for sums due to the company and means of course the amount which is due. This amount may differ from the amount collectable and it is the amount which will be collected which is the net realisable value.

b. Note all the detail in the debtors circularisation process.

c. Note in all these verification processes the importance of a proper evaluation and test of the internal control procedures.

d. Events after the accounting date (*post balance sheet events*) and before the date of the final audit are very useful in providing evidence to the auditor of existence, ownership and, particularly, value at the balance sheet date.

e. Presentation of assets in the balance sheet is always important and this is particularly so in the case of loans to directors.

f. Students should have an appreciation of the accounting requirements of the Companies Act 1985 on the disclosure of:
- debtors (long and short term) and related interest receivable
- cash and bank balances and related interest payable.

g. The make up of figures for debtors and bank balances must be considered to determine if:
- any items should be separately disclosed
- bank balances and overdrafts should properly not be set-off.

h. UITF Abstract 4 notes that debtors in current assets may include some items which are receivable after more than one year (examples are the trade debtors of lessors or deferred consideration in respect of a sale of an investment). Usually it is acceptable to disclose the long-term nature of these items in a note but where the items are so material in the context of total net current assets that readers may misinterpret the balance sheet then the amount should be shown on the face of the balance sheet.

Case study 1

John Dunn Locks Ltd are manufacturers of locks with some 6,000 customers in the UK. The auditors Key & Partners, are engaged on the audit of the debtors at 31.7.-6.

Discussion

What factors should the auditors take into account in considering the type and extent of debtors circularisation?

The auditors decide to negatively circularise 300 customers. There were 30 replies. Of these, 26 were timing differences which were easily resolved. The remaining four were:

1. Artichoke Builders Merchants
   - the goods invoiced in June never arrived.
2. Broccoli Construction
   - payment was made in April. We have the returned cheque.
3. Cabbage Hardware
   - the goods invoiced in July were damaged. We are waiting for a credit note.
4. Dill Building
   - the balance is incorrect. We have been unable to reconcile the balance for some months. We enclose a copy of our purchase ledger account.

What are the implications of these replies for the auditors?

Case study 2

Rectory Trading PLC have some 50 subsidiaries in various parts of the world. The group trades on credit both between group members and with thousands of other companies. The group have been plagued with bad debts and the provision for doubtful debts is a major issue.

Discussion

Devise an audit programme for the debtors and associated provision.

Student self testing questions *Questions with answers apparent from the text*

1. a. Outline the procedures for verifying debtors. (3)
   b. What matters should be considered in reviewing the provision for bad and doubtful debts? (4)
   c. Outline the procedures for both negative and positive circularisation. (6)
   d. What balances/accounts should not be overlooked? (9)
   e. What audit evidence accrues from the bank letter? (12)
   f. Summarise the contents of the standard bank letter? (13)
   g. When should it be sent? (13)
   h. How should loans be audited? (14)
   i. What are the Companies Act rules on loans to directors and connected persons?
   j. What are the auditor's duties on such loans? (14)

Exercises

1. Outline an audit programme for the following:
   a. Debtors for Spare parts plc who sell to a wide range of commercial and industrial customers in the UK and overseas.
   b. The Hire Purchases Debtors of Scrooge Finance Ltd, a finance company.
   c. A material amount of loans to employees by Libbod plc a baby clothing manufacturer.
   d. The bank balances of Pong plc. The company have large cash surpluses and make a point of switching these between banks both in the UK and overseas to get the best possible interest.
   e. Bills of exchange, both inland and foreign, of Esa Ltd who buy and sell commodities world wide.

Examination questions

1. a In conducting the audit of a mail order company, your internal control question-naires show that the stated system of control on incoming orders with remittances are ineffective. What action will you now take? (10 marks)
   b. Indicate the main points to which you would give attention in arranging a circulari-sation of debtors to obtain confirmation of year end debtors. (10 marks)

   (ICA) (Total 20 marks)

2. Audit evidence can be created by processes largely under the control of third parties. This type of evidence can be that which is part of the basic accounting records such as invoices and statements or it can be created by third parties at the request of the auditor. This latter technique is normally referred to as direct confirmation.

   Required:
   a. Discuss the quality of audit evidence generated by direct confirmation techniques, giving three examples other than debtors confirmation of when the technique might be used. (6 marks)
   b. List the sequence of steps involved when directly confirming debtors. (7 marks)
   c. Explain the circumstances when negative confirmation requests may be used. (4 marks)
   d. Explain what evidence may or may not be provided by a positive request for confir-mation from debtors. (3 marks)

   (ACCA) (20 marks)

3. You are the auditor of Trent Ltd, a china manufacturer, which exports 40% of sales to the US. You plan to commence the audit of the accounts for the year ended 30 April 2001 on 1 July 2001.

   Trade debtors are included in the balance sheet at the year end, net of a £150,000 debt provision (5%), at £2,850,000. In previous years there has been an extremely poor response to the debtors circularisation and a decision has been taken not to circularise debtors this year. In an attempt to reduce the exposure to the US dollar, Trent Ltd sells 50% of dollar receivables forward.

   Requirement:
   You are required to:

a. explain what substantive audit tests you would carry out in order to verify trade debtors; (12 marks)

b. state the audit tests you would carry out in order to form an opinion on the bad debts provision and the action you would take, if you concluded that it was misstated; and

(6 marks)

c. state what adjustment, if any, you would make to US dollar debtors on the basis that they have all been recorded at the actual exchange rate ruling on the date of sale.

(2 marks)

(ICAI) (Total 20 marks)

4. Cricket PLC is an expanding company specialising in the developing and marketing of computer software. The net profit for the year ended 31 March 1990 was £763,000 and the net asset value of the company at that date was £6,925,000.

Required:

State how you would verify the following items appearing in the company's financial statements:

a. Patents £500,000 (6 marks)

b. Bad and doubtful debts £25,000 (5 marks)

c. Interest on bank overdraft £15,000 (4 marks)

(AAT) (Total 15 marks)

22 Stock and work in progress

Introduction

1. The verification of stock and work in progress has a chapter to itself. It is often the *key* item in accounts.

As a fairly typical example consider Boots 2000 Accounts. Group profit before tax was £561 million and sales were £5,189 million. Stock was £689 million and the impact of a variation in the stock figure can easily be seen. The problem of stock is that the quantity and value are not derived from the double entry system but:

a. Quantity is usually ascertained at the year end by counting. Mistakes are extremely easy to make.

b. Condition is assessed at the same time and is a matter of opinion.

c. Valuation methods are many and various.

It will be seen that the figure attributed to stock is very important, it is difficult to compute accurately and causes more headaches to auditors than any other problem.

2. It cannot be stressed too much that it is the *directors'* responsibility to ensure that:

a. Stock and work in progress are correctly identified.

b. Physical quantities are correctly ascertained and recorded and condition assessed.

c. Valuation on proper bases is correctly made.

3. There is an auditing guideline: *Attendance at Stocktaking* issued in November 1983. Students are also reminded of SSAP 9 and IAS 2 *Inventories.*

4. This chapter considers stock under the following heading:

    a. Categories of stock
    b. Stocktaking procedures
    c. Auditors duties re the physical count
    d. Continuous stock records
    e. Stocktakes other than at year end
    f. Work in progress
    g. Overall tests
    h. Valuation
    i. Cut off
    j. Independent stocktakers
    k. A historical note.

Categories of stock

5. In answering any examination question and indeed in considering most problems in life, a first approach is to break the problem down into parts.

    Stock is not different from other matters and a primary division is into:

    a. Goods purchased for resale.
    b. Consumable stores (oils, fuels, spare parts etc.).
    c. Raw materials and components purchased for incorporation into products for sale.
    d. Products and services in intermediate stages of completion.
    e. Finished goods.
    f. Returnable containers.

    Cadbury Schweppes have c., e. and f. only. A shop is likely to have only a. and an engineering group all six.

6. A secondary division is:

    a. Stocks assessed by physical count at year end only.
    b. Stocks assessed near the year end and the year end total obtained by adjustment by sales and purchases.
    c. Stocks recorded on a *continuous inventory* system.

Stocktaking procedures

7. Although stocktaking may occur on only one day a year, it is essentially a part of the internal control system. A good set of procedures will have the following characteristics:

    a. **Where stock is based on records:**

        i.   Adequate stock records must be kept. They must be kept up to date.
        ii. All categories of stock (i.e. every item in stock) are checked physically at least once during the year and the amount found compared with the book record.
        iii. This checking is organised and systematic.
        iv. Differences found lead to correction of the records and a *proper investigation of the cause of the difference.*

b. **When stock is based on a year-end count:**

   i. Good planning so that the work is carried out carefully and systematically – early issue of stocktaking instructions with consideration of feedback from staff.

   ii. Division of the stocktake into manageable areas for control purposes.

   iii. Proper instructions for counting, weighing, measuring and checking.

   iv. Proper *cut-off* arrangements.

   v. Identification of defective, damaged, obsolete, and slow moving stock.

   vi. Identification of stock on the premises owned by third parties and of client's stock held by outside parties.

   vii. Proper control over the issue of blank stock sheets and the return of completed and unused stock sheets.

   viii. Identification of stocks held subject to reservation of title.

   ix. Identification of stocks and especially of high value items.

   x. Control of stock movement during the count.

   xi. Controls to ensure all stock is counted and, at that, once only.

   xii. Nomination of people responsible for each aspect of the count.

   xiii. Appropriate treatment for sealed containers, dangerous goods, and goods with special problems.

   Items iv., v., and viii. are important also for stock based on records.

Stocktaking – the auditor's duties

8. The auditor must satisfy himself as to the validity of the amount attributed to stock and work in progress in the balance sheet. He does this by first considering the client's system of internal control. This applies to stocktaking as it does to all areas of audit enquiry. It is essential for students to realise that stocktaking procedures are part of the system and the auditor examines the system by finding out what the system is, evaluating its effectiveness, and testing it.

9. The auditor's duties are usually divided into three parts – before, during and after the stocktake.

   a. Before the stocktake:

   i. Review previous year's working papers and discuss with management any significant changes from previous year.

   ii. Discuss stocktaking arrangements with management.

   iii. Familiarise himself with the nature and volume of stocks and especially with high value items.

   iv. Consider the location of stocks (e.g. at branches) and the problems thus caused for the client and the auditor.

   v. Consider likely points of difficulty e.g. cut off.

   vi. Consider internal audit involvement and if reliance can be placed upon it.

   vii. Arranging to obtain from third parties confirmation of stock held by them.

   viii. Establishing whether expert help may be needed (e.g. precious stones, antiques).

ix. Evaluate the effectiveness of the instructions, especially that they cover all items, meet potential difficulties, are discussed with, and adequately communicated to stocktaking staff. If necessary suggest improvements.

x. Review surrounding systems of internal control to identify areas of potential difficulty.

xi. Plan usage of audit staff as to availability to cover all required locations etc.

b. **During the stocktake**:

Audit practice now is for the auditor to *attend the stocktake*. The purpose of the attendance is not to take stock or to supervise the stocktake but to *observe* (another word here might be *witness*) the client's internal control system in action.

The actual work to be done is:

i. Observe the stocktake to ascertain that the client's employees are carrying out their instructions.

ii. Check the count of a selected number of lines. This must be done by selecting some items found to be present *and* some items recorded on the stock sheets.

iii. Note for follow up
   - Details of items selected by the auditors to compare with final stock sheets.
   - List of items counted in the auditor's presence.
   - Details of defective, damaged, obsolete or slow moving items.
   - Instances of stocktaking instructions not being followed.
   - Details of items for cut-off purposes.

iv. Enquiry into, observe and discuss with store-keeping staff the procedures for identifying damaged, obsolete and slow moving stock.

v. Enquire into and test the cut-off procedures.

vi. Form an impression of the magnitude of stock held for comparison with the Accounts.

vii. Record fully the work done and impressions of the stocktake in the working papers.

ix. If any aspects prove unsatisfactory, inform the management and request a recount.

x. High value items should be given special attention.

xi. Photocopies of rough stock sheets should be taken.

xii. Details of the sequence of stock sheets should be verified.

c. After the stocktake:

i. Check the cut-off with details of the last numbers of stock movement forms and goods inward and goods outwards notes during the year and after the year end.

ii. Test that the final stock sheets have been properly prepared from the count records. In particular the record of stocktake forms issued and returned must be checked.

iii. Follow up notes made at the attendance.

iv. Check final stock sheets for pricing, extensions, casting, summarising, and officials' signatures.

    v.   Inform management of any problems encountered in the stocktake for action in subsequent counts.

10. Non-attendance at the stocktake may occur through the auditor having numerous clients all with the same accounting date or the client may have stock at remote or overseas locations. The auditor must still satisfy himself on the stocktake. This can be done by:

    a.   Arranging for the stocktake to be at an earlier date.

    b.   Appointing agents, e.g. for overseas locations.

    c.   Examining continuous stocktake records more thoroughly.

    d.   Intensifying other stocktaking verification methods.

    e.   Using *rotational* methods.

None of these solutions is wholly satisfactory and the auditor must make very extensive enquiries before he gives a clean report.

Continuous stock records

11. Some companies which keep continuous stock records may wish to determine the quantity of stock at the year end by extracting the balances from the stock records without physically counting the stock on the year-end date. This *may* be acceptable to the auditor if:

    a.   The auditor is satisfied that the records are very reliable, accurate, and up to date, and *either*

    b. i.   The whole stock is physically compared with the records on at least one day in the year and reasonable correspondence is found, or

      ii.   Every item of stock is checked to the records at least once in the year in a systematic and orderly manner. The records of such checking should demonstrate reasonable concurrence between the actual stock and the records.

Stocktakes other than at the year end

12. The auditing guidelines state that stocktaking carried out before or after the year end may be acceptable for audit purposes provided records of stock movements in the intervening period are such that the movements can be examined and substantiated. The greater the interval the more difficult this will be. Acceptability depends also on there being a good system of internal control and satisfactory stock records.

Work in progress

13. All that has been said about stock applies equally to work in progress but this item presents even greater problems of ascertainment and valuation to the *directors* and to the auditors.

14. The auditor's investigations will include:

    a.   Inquiry into the costing system from which work in progress is ascertained.

    b.   Inquiry into the reliability of the costing system. In particular a costing system integrated with the financial accounting system will prima facie be more reliable because of the discipline of double entry and the inherent checks imposed by external data such as creditors' statements.

    c.   Inquiry into the checks made as part of the system on statistical data concerning inputs of materials and outputs of products and expectations.

d. Inquiry into the system of inspection and reporting thereon to enable due allowance to be made for scrapping and rectification work.

e. Inquiry into the basis on which overheads are included in costs. This should be based on SSAP 9.

f. Inquiry into the basis on which any element of profit is dealt with. Profit should be eliminated from work in progress. However it is legitimate to include an element of profit in long term contract work in progress in accordance with SSAP 9.

g. Where items such as buildings and plant are constructed internally, it is important for the auditor to make sure that if such items are under construction at the year end they are not included twice, i.e. in fixed assets and work in progress.

Overall tests

15. While detail work on the stocks and work in progress is imperative in an audit, there are a number of overall tests which are very important. These include:

a. **Reconciliation of changes** in stocks at successive year ends with records of movements, e.g. purchases and sales.

b. Comparison of *quantities* of each kind of stock held at year end with those held at previous year ends and with purchases and sales.

c. Consideration of *gross profit* ratio with that of previous years, other companies, and budgeted expectation.

d. Consideration of *rate of stockturn* with previous years etc.

e. Comparison of stock figures with budgets for stock, sales and purchases.

f. Consideration of standard costing records and the application of variances in the valuation of stock and work in progress.

Valuation of stock in trade and work in progress

16. Two problems in relation to stock which are really very fundamental to reporting profits have existed for many years. They are:

a. **Valuation** methods are many and various.

b. **Disclosure** of the methods of valuation used is not made.

The first problem has been partly solved by SSAP 9. This standard has met with much opposition and is in parts imprecise but it has certainly gone a long way towards solving the problem of variety of method.

The second problem is still with us and companies have a tendency to be vague on valuation methods. An example from the accounting policies of a major public company:

'Stocks:

Stocks are valued at the lower of cost and net realisable value. In respect of work in progress and finished goods cost includes all direct costs of production and the appropriate proportion of production overheads. '

One can comment that this statement is unnecessary as this is what is required by SSAP 9. What we do not know is how direct costs, production overheads and appropriate proportion are defined.

17. This manual is not going to summarise SSAP 9 but students must be familiar with it.

18. The auditor's duty is to:

   a. Ascertain accounting policies adopted for valuing stock.

   b. Consider the acceptability of the policies selected.

   c. Test the stock sheets or continuous stock records with relevant documents such as invoices and costing records to determine if 'cost' has been correctly arrived at.

   d. Examine and test the treatment of overheads.

   e. Test the treatment and examine evidence for items valued at net realisable value.

   f. Test the arithmetical accuracy of all calculations.

   g. Test the consistency with which the amounts have been computed.

   h. Consider the adequacy of the description used in the accounts and disclosure of the accounting policies adopted.

19. Note that the Companies Act 1985 codifies in the law many requirements of SSAP 9. Valuation of fungible assets may be FIFO, LIFO, weighted average price or any similar method.

Cut-off

20. This subject has been mentioned already. It is extremely important. Consider a trading account:

Opening Stock	100	Sales	1000
Purchases	750	Closing Stock	150
Gross Profit	300		
	1150		1150

Supposing goods valued at £50 were:

   a. Dispatched and invoiced by the supplier before balance sheet date, and

   b. Received after balance sheet date owing to delays in transit by rail, then they would be included in purchases as a consequence of a. and they would be excluded from closing stock as a consequence of b. This would mean an incorrect computation of the profit.

Avoiding this possibility is a vital part of the system of internal control as applied to stock and consequently of prime concern to the auditor.

21. A famous case on the subject of cut-off was:

   re Thomas Gerrard & Son Ltd, 1967. This was cotton company. The manager and principal shareholder:

   a. Post-dated purchases invoices received before the year end.

   b. Ante-dated sales invoice copies in the new year to dates prior to the year end.

   He did this quite openly for five half year periods for bigger sums each time thus turning losses into profits and causing the company to pay tax and dividends. The auditors discovered the alterations, asked questions and were put off by answers such as 'these were year end adjustments' or 'it is more convenient'.

   The judge awarded damages against the auditors on the grounds that:

   i. Once their suspicions were aroused they had a duty to probe the matter to the bottom.

ii. Auditors now have a duty to satisfy themselves as to the validity of stock in trade. This satisfaction cannot arise solely out of the assurances of one official however trustworthy in appearance.

Independent stocktakers

22. In some trades it is found that the stock is counted and valued by an independent firm of stocktakers. Examples include the jewellery, licensed and retail pharmacy trades.

The question arises as to whether this influences the extent of the auditor's examination. The answer is that the auditor has a duty to form an opinion on the amount at which stock is stated. He cannot simply accept an outside stocktaker's valuation but it is usual to do so if:

a. He is satisfied of the stocktaker's independence and standing (i.e. integrity and competence).

b. He has made enquiries and is satisfied:

i.   On the basis of valuation used.

ii. Proper cut-off procedures were employed.

Historical note

23. A study of the history of a subject will often illuminate its present condition. This is true of the audit of stock, and the three cases mentioned below are so well known in the profession as to form part of its folklore or mythology.

a. **re the Kingston Cotton Mill Co. Ltd, 1896.** The auditors failed to detect overstatements of the amounts of stock. They accepted a certificate of the manager on the amount of stock after comparing it with the stock journal which contained accounts for each item or class of items purporting to be in stock and a summary. The summary was determined by the auditors to be in agreement with the detailed accounts. In fact the entries were falsified to show more stock than was actually in existence. The auditors were exonerated on the grounds that it is no part of the auditor's duty to take stock and that he is entitled to rely upon other people for the details of stock in trade. The judge's remarks contained the famous phrase *'He is a watchdog, not a bloodhound'.* This means that if he discovers something which is suspicious he should probe it to the bottom but in the absence of suspicious circumstances he is only bound to be reasonably cautious and careful.

Today the judgement in this case would undoubtedly be against the auditor but the comfortable words of the judge have caused auditors for many generations to accept stock sheets without actually attending or enquiring too closely into the stocktake.

b. **McKesson and Robbins Inc., USA 1939.** In this almost unbelievable (except perhaps in America) case, the directors of the company created fictitious records of trading, sales, purchases, bank accounts, debtors, and stock so that the assets were overstated by over 20 million dollars. This extraordinary state of affairs was not detected by the auditors. In particular they did not attend the stocktake. Had they done so they would have rapidly realised that no stock existed!

c. **Allied Crude Vegetable Oil Refining Corporation of New Jersey 1963.** In this scandal, methods were used to fool auditors who were present at the stocktaking. Three methods, at least, were used:

i.   the quantity of vegetable oil in a tank was checked and before the quantity was checked in the second tank, the contents of the first tank were pumped through to the second tank.

ii. Using a dip stick to measure the quantity of oil in a tank. In reality the tank was empty and oil was contained only in a thin drainpipe down which the dipstick was dropped.

iii. Filling the tanks with water instead of oil.

Summary

24. a. Stock on a balance sheet is subject to a correct count, a correct assessment of condition, and appropriate selection of valuation bases.

b. Stock can be considered under a number of separate categories.

c. Some firms have stock records (continuous inventory) and some have not. The latter must have a stocktake at the year end.

d. Stocktaking procedures are a part of the internal control system.

e. Since Auditing Statement U9 issued in 1968 by the ICAEW, all audit firms must recognise that attendance at stocktaking to observe the incidence of internal control is *normal* audit practice.

f. Valuation of stock in trade is now governed by SSAP 9. Its contents must be known.

g. Detailed audit tests must be supplemented by overall tests.

h. Independent stocktakers can be used by clients and within limitations be relied upon by the auditor.

i. Cut-off is the most likely source of error and fraud in final accounts.

Points to note

25. a. Internal control assessment is a first consideration in all audit enquiry. Stocktaking methods are part of the internal control system.

b. This part of the internal control system only applies on one day a year and the auditor needs to witness the procedures being carried out to assess their effectiveness.

c. The valuation of stock has been done in numerous different ways in the past but SSAP 9 has reduced the number of acceptable methods.

d. Nonetheless firms still have some latitude in selecting accounting policies and the auditor must see that these are appropriate, consistent with previous periods, apply to all like items in the same period, and are adequately disclosed.

e. Cut-off procedures are most important.

f. The auditor's assessment of stock in trade will cover:

i.   existence – stocktaking procedures

ii. ownership – note goods in transit, goods at other premises, goods owned by others, reservation of title

iii. value – note problem of net realisable value.

g. The Companies Act requires companies to keep proper accounting records. Such proper accounting records include statements of stocktakings. Auditors must not only seek audit evidence that a true and fair view is shown by the stock figures in the

Accounts but also must investigate to determine that proper accounting records in the form of statements of stocktaking have been kept.

h. Work in progress can be very difficult to evaluate. Management generally rely on controls to ensure the completeness and accuracy of records of work in progress. Nonetheless inspection of work in progress by the auditor is desirable in that it gives evidence that work in progress exists and helps with determining the state of completion especially of large contracts.

i. Note that most syllabuses require an appreciation of the accounting requirements of the Companies Act 1985 re disclosure of stocks and work in progress.

j. Stocks and work in progress are an interesting example of the problem of risk. In most companies stocks are likely to be a material asset and the inherent risk of misstatement is high. Stocktaking is usually accompanied by control procedures designed to minimise misstatements but nonetheless the control risk is often high. Auditors are usually obliged to rely to a large extent on tests of control but if internal controls are weak, alternative substantive tests are often less than persuasive.

Case study 1

Aelfric Alchemist Supplies Ltd have a large warehouse in Wapping from which they supply their customers with over 3,000 different chemicals and chemical apparatus purchased from numerous suppliers both in the UK and overseas. They do not maintain a continuous inventory of their stocks. At the year end Thursday 31 July 20-6 they wish to assess the stock physically.

Discussion

a. Draw up full stocktaking instructions for the stocktake.

b. How should the stock be valued according to:

    i. SSAP 9

    ii. the Companies Act 1985?

c. How should the auditor seek evidence for the physical stock at 31.7.-6?

Case study 2

Osocheep Supermarkets Ltd have a main depot and five large supermarkets. Their financial year end is Thursday 31 March 20-8 and stock is to be evaluated as at the close of business on that date. The next day is an exceptionally busy one and much business in terms of deliveries from supplier, movements of stock, and sales. The sales margins are narrow and it is very important to obtain an accurate figure for stock. Goods in stock in the warehouse are kept on a continuous inventory system (quantities only) on a micro computer with a printout of the previous day's stock available at noon each day. The stock at branches is not recorded continuously. The bulk of the stock is carried in the back rooms and moved onto the supermarket shelves continuously during the day.

Discussion

What are the problems in this case re:

cut-off

stock identification and quantity determination

valuation?

Case study 3

Bizant Construction PLC are civil engineers specialising in large public buildings. At their year end (31.5.-9) the following contracts were in progress:

(All figures in £'000)

	A	B	C	D	E
Value of work done	300	700	800	420	70
Cumulative payments on account	220	730	850	300	65
Total costs incurred	240	600	830	440	95
Transferable to cost of sales	240	580	760	430	67
Provision for foreseeable losses				60	24

Discussion

    a. How should these figures be incorporated in the accounts?

    b. Outline an audit programme for these items.

Student self testing questions *Questions with answers apparent from the text*

1. a. What are the directors' responsibilities for stocktaking? (2)
    b. What categories of stock are there? (5, 6)
    c. List the characteristics of good stocktaking procedures. (7)
    d. What are the auditor's duties toward stocktaking:
      i. Before the stocktake?
      ii. During the stocktake?
      iii. After the stocktake? (9)
    e. What are the auditor's tasks in connection with work in progress? (14)
    f. What overall tests can be applied in respect of stock? (15)
    g. Summarise SSAP 9 requirements re the valuation of:
      i. stock
      ii. work in progress
      iii. long-term contracts.
    h. Summarise the famous cases:
      i. re Kingston Cotton Mill 1896
      ii. re McKesson and Robbins Inc. 1939
      iii. re Thomas Gerrard & Son Ltd 1967. (23)

Exercises

1. Draft an outline audit programme for the following:
    a. The sites under development of Jerry Ltd a speculative builder.
    b. The stock in Cheepy PLC a supermarket chain. No perpetual inventory is kept and the count is at the year end.
    c. The work in progress of Robotto PLC a manufacturer of complex machine tools partly to order and partly for stock. The company have a standard costing system.
    d. Stock of coal of Birnwell Ltd a private colliery. The stock at the surface was counted at the year end.

e. The stocks of Drinkie Ltd a chain of public houses and licensed restaurants. All the stocks are counted and valued by independent valuers.

f. The stock of Nicnac Ltd a wholesaler of components who have 2,000 separate lines. The company maintain a computerised stock control system (using average cost) and do not count at the year end.

g. The finished goods stocks of Babby Ltd a manufacturer of childrens' wear. The stock was counted five days before the year end.

h. The stocks of Feinwein Ltd wine merchants. The company keep most of the stocks at the premises of customers. Customers are invoiced for wines taken from the stocks kept on their premises.

i. The stocks of Olde Ltd an antique dealer specialising in small but very valuable items.

Examination question

1. Stocks and work in progress take many different forms, depending on the nature of the business. Many companies undertake contracts for work which last for more than one accounting period. The audit objectives concerning these long-term contracts do not differ greatly from those concerning normal stock and work in progress, except in so far as long-term contracts require the estimation of future revenues and costs in order to identify the profit to be recognised in the profit and loss account.

   Required:

   a. Explain why the audit of stocks and work in progress is often the most complex and time-consuming part of the audit. (6 marks)

   b. Describe the factors which are likely to affect the auditor's assessment of the inherent risk attached to long-term contract work in progress. (6 marks)

   c. Describe the audit work which would be performed in order to verify the value of long-term contract work in progress. (8 marks)

   (ACCA) (20 marks)

2. Rubella Yarns PLC manufacturers cotton yarn for sale to the textile industry. The stock of the company is valued on a standard cost basis and you are about to commence the final audit, having attended the physical stock count.

   You are required to:

   a. State under what circumstances standard cost would be a suitable method of pricing stocks for financial accounting purposes. (6 marks)

   b. Describe how you would satisfy yourself as auditor of Rubella Yarns PLC that the standard costs had been properly determined. (7 marks)

   c. Discuss briefly what action you would take if you discover that there are significant variances between actual and standard prices for stock. (7 marks)

   (ACCA) (Total 20 marks)

3. Gourmet PLC operates six food warehouses throughout Great Britain. The company makes bulk purchases from manufacturers and suppliers based within the United Kingdom and abroad. It distributes these goods to supermarkets and cash and carry wholesalers. Each warehouse maintains its own stock records from goods inwards and despatch notes. Head Office maintains a financial control over the stocks based on the daily value of sales and a value of daily purchases (based on selling price).

195

The company's year end is 30 November, which in 1991 falls on a Saturday. The Financial Director has arranged for a stocktake to be held on the preceding Wednesday and the warehouses will be closed on that day. The stock sheets are to be priced at selling price.

You are required to

a. State the audit procedures you would undertake in respect of the physical stocktake.

(10 marks)

b. State the matters to which you would give attention to ensure that the correct quantities and values of stock items are included in the Financial Statements.

(5 marks)

(AAT) (Total 15 marks)

4. Your client is an electrical wholesaler with a Head Office and four branches. The client has total annual sales of £10 million and total stocks of £2 million. The stocks are located as follows:

Head Office £100,000, Branch A £200,000, Branch B £500,000, Branch C £300,000, Branch D £900,000.

Your client is planning their year-end stocktaking.

a. List five things which your client should do to ensure an accurate stocktaking.

(10 marks)

b. List four things which you would do in planning your audit attendance at the stock-taking.

(8 marks)

(LCCI)

23 Liability verification

Introduction

1. A balance sheet will contain many liabilities grouped under various headings. The headings may include:

a. Share capital.

b. Reserves.

c. Creditors: amounts falling due after more than one year:

   i. debenture loans

   ii. bank loans and overdrafts

   iii. payments received on account

   iv. trade creditors

   v. bills of exchange payable

   vi. amounts owed to group companies

   vii. amounts owed to related companies

   viii. other creditors including taxation and social security

   ix. accruals and deferred income.

    d. Provisions for liabilities and charges
        i. pensions and similar obligations
        ii. taxation, including deferred taxation
        iii. other provisions.
    e. Creditors: amounts falling due within one year as in c. i. to ix.
    f. Contingent liabilities – incorporated by note only.

2. The auditors' duty is fourfold viz:
    a. To verify the *existence* of liabilities shown in the balance sheet.
    b. To verify the correctness of the *money amount* of such liabilities.
    c. To verify the appropriateness of the *description* given in the accounts and the adequacy of *disclosure*.
    d. To verify that *all* existing liabilities *are actually included* in the accounts.

The last of these causes the most difficulty.

Verification procedures

3. It is not possible to detail the procedures for verifying all possible liabilities. However, some general principles can be discerned, and these should be applied according to the particular set of circumstances met with in practice or in an examination. These are:
    a. **Schedule.** Request or make a *schedule* for each liability or class of liabilities. This should show the make-up of the liability with the opening balance, if any, all changes, and the closing balance.
    b. **Cut-off.** Verify *cut-off*. For example a trade creditor should not be included unless the goods were acquired before the year end.
    c. **Reasonableness.** Consider the *reasonableness* of the liability. Are there circumstances which ought to excite suspicion?
    d. **Internal control.** Determine, evaluate and test *internal control* procedures. This is particularly important for trade creditors.
    e. **Previous date clearance.** Consider the *liabilities at the previous accounting date*. Have they all been cleared?
    f. **Terms and conditions.** this applies principally to loans. The auditor should determine that all terms and conditions agreed when accepting a loan have been complied with. In recent years many loan deeds have contained undertakings by the company borrowing the money that it will keep a minimum proportion of equity (ordinary share capital and reserves) in its total capital (equity and loans). Breach of this agreement which has occurred frequently in property companies can lead to the appointment of a receiver.
    g. **Authority.** The authority for all liabilities should be sought. This will be found in the company minutes or directors' minutes and for some items the authority of the Memorandum and Articles may be needed.
    h. **Description**. The auditor must see that the description in the accounts of each liability is adequate.
    i. **Documents**. The auditor must examine all relevant documents. These will include invoices, correspondence, debenture deeds etc., according to the type of liability.

j. **Security**. Some liabilities are secured in various ways, usually by fixed or floating charges. The auditor must enquire into these and ensure that they have been registered. The Companies Act requires, for secured liabilities, that an indication of the general nature of the security be given and also the aggregate amount of debts included under the item covered by the security.

k. **Vouching.** The creation of each liability should be vouched, for example the receipt of a loan.

l. **Accounting policies.** The auditor must satisfy himself that appropriated accounting policies have been adopted and applied consistently.

m. **Letter of representation**. This is discussed further in the chapter on letters of representation.

n. **Interest and other ancillary evidence.** The evidence of loans tends to be evidenced by interest payments and other activities which stem from the existence of the loan.

o. **Disclosure.** All matters which need to be known to receive a *true and fair view* from the accounts must be disclosed. The Companies Acts provisions must be complied with.

p. **External verification.** With many liabilities it is possible to verify the liability directly with the creditor. This action will be taken with short-term loan creditors, bank overdrafts and, by a similar technique to that used with debtors, the trade creditors.

q. **Materiality.** Materiality comes into all accounting and auditing decisions.

r. **Post-balance sheet events**. These are probably more important in this area than in any other. There is a chapter on this subject later in the manual.

s. **Accounting Standards.** Liabilities must be accounted for in accordance with the accounting standards and UITF abstracts where relevant. Accounting standards that may be relevant to liabilities include FRSs 4, 5, 8, 12, 13, 16, 17, 19, 18 and SSAPs 17, 20, 24.

t. **Risk**. Assess the risk of misstatement.

4. Students may well remember these mnemonically. For any given liability all of them will not be required, but mentally going through them should be an excellent guide to what needs to be done.

Inclusion of all liabilities

5. It is not enough for the auditor to be satisfied that all the liabilities recorded in the books are correct and are incorporated in the final accounts. He must also be satisfied that no other liabilities exist which are not, for various reasons, in the books and the accounts. Examples of such unrecorded liabilities are:

a. Claims by employees for injury. Note that these should be covered by insurance under the Employers Liability (Compulsory Insurance) Act 1969.

b. Claims by ex employees for unfair dismissal.

c. Contributions to superannuation schemes.

d. Unfunded pension liabilities. A company may have a liability to pay past or present employees a pension in respect of past service and have no funds separated out for this purpose.

e. Liability to 'top-up' pension schemes. When money has been put into separate trusts to pay pensions, inflation has often meant that the amount is insufficient and the company may have to implement clauses in the scheme whereby they have to put in extra money which could run into millions of pounds.

f. Bonuses under profit sharing arrangements.

g. Returnable packages and containers.

h. Value added and other tax liabilities. The auditor's special knowledge of tax may lead him to suspect a liability of which the directors are blissfully ignorant.

i. Claims under warranties and guarantees.

j. Liabilities on debts which have been factored with recourse. To explain: A owes B £50. B sells (factors) the debt to C for £45. Thus B has no debt any more but £45 in the bank. A fails to pay C. C can claim £50 from B (he has recourse).

k. Bills receivable discounted (a special case of j.).

l. Pending law suits.

m. Losses on forward contracts. A Ltd makes a contract to sell a million tons of hedonite, which it does not have, at £50 a ton in six months' time. No entry will appear in the books or accounts, but when the time comes hedonite has risen on the commodity market to £70 a ton and A Ltd, buys in at that price in order to make the sale for which it has contracted.

6. It is important that the auditor appreciates that such liabilities can exist. He also has a positive obligation to take reasonable steps to unearth them.

The actions he would take would include:

a. Enquiry of the directors and other officers.

b. Obtain a letter of representation – see later in the chapter.

c. Examination of post balance sheet events. This will include an inspection of the purchase invoices and the cash book after date.

d. Examination of minutes where the existence of unrecorded liabilities may be mentioned.

e. A review of the working papers and previous years' working papers.

f. An awareness of the possibilities at all times when conducting the audit. For example, discovery during the audit that the client deals in 'futures' (5m.) will alert the auditor to the possibility of outstanding commitments.

Provisions

7. Students tend to confuse two words in common use. The correct use of these two words are:

a. **Provision** – any amount retained as reasonably necessary for the purpose of providing for any liability or loss which is either likely to be incurred, or certain to be incurred but uncertain as to amount or as to the date on which it will arise. (CA 1985 4th Sch. 89)

Thus a provision:

i. is a debit to profit and loss account (reducing profit and therefore dividends; hence retained)

ii. is for a likely or certain future payment

     iii. where the *amount* or the *date* of payment is uncertain.

  b. **Reserve** – that part of shareholders funds not accounted for by the nominal value of issued share capital or by the share premium account.

The need for the creation of provisions is an important consideration for directors who are responsible for Accounts and consequently for the auditors. Post balance sheet events can often cast light on the amount of provision required. The auditor has a duty to see that any provisions set up are used for the purpose for which they were set up and that any provisions which are no longer needed are transferred back to profit and loss account.

8. The rules in FRS 12 *Provisions, Liabilities and Assets* must be followed. Briefly, a provision should be recognised when an entity has a present obligation (legal or constructive) as a result of a past event, and it is *probable* that a transfer of economic benefits will be required to settle the obligation and a *reliable estimate* can be made of the obligation. Otherwise no provision should be made. A constructive obligation is one where the other party has a valid expectation of payment even though no legal obligation exists. Contingent liabilities should be disclosed by note unless the possibility of payment is remote.

Share capital

9. Share capital is effectively a special sort of liability of a company. When share capital has been issued in a year its verification is as follows:

  a. Ensure the issue is within the limits authorised by Memorandum and Articles.

  b. Ensure the issue was subject to a directors' minute.

  c. Ascertain and evaluate the system for the control of issue.

  d. Verify that the system has been properly operated. This will involve examining the prospectus (if there is one), applications, application and allotment sheets, the share register, cash received records, share certificate counterfoils, and repayment to unsuccessful applicants.

  e. When the issue was one which was contingent upon permission to deal being received from the Stock Exchange then:

     i. Ensure that permission has been obtained. If it has not been given all the money subscribed is returnable.

     ii. Ensure that all the money was contained in a separate bank account until all conditions were satisfied.

     iii. Ensure that the minimum subscription has been received. If there are not enough subscribers then the whole is returnable.

  f. When the issue is not for cash but for other consideration, e.g. the goodwill and other assets of a business, vouch the agreement and ensure that all entries are properly made.

  g. Vouch the payment of underwriting and other fees.

10. When no new issue of shares has been made the audit work will *include*:

  a. Determine the total of shares of each class as stated in the balance sheet and obtain a list of shareholdings which in total should agree with the balance sheet total.

  b. Test the balances in the share register with the list and *vice versa*.

c. If this is not possible at the balance sheet date, it may be permissible to do it earlier provided that the auditor is satisfied with the system of control over transfers.

d. When the share register is maintained by an independent firm of registrars (which is common with public companies) the auditor should obtain a certificate that the work outlined in a. and b. has been done. The certificate should state that the balances on the share registers agree with the issued capital at the balance sheet date.

Pending legal matters

11. This is a specially difficult area in practice because of the inherent uncertainty involved in estimating the outcome of legal actions. There are some audit actions which will lead to the verification of the existence but not necessarily the amount of liabilities arising out of legal actions. These include:

a. Reviewing the client's system for recording claims and disputes and the procedures for bringing these to the attention of the Board.

b. Reviewing the arrangements for instructing solicitors.

c. Examining the minutes of the Board or other responsible committee for references to or indications of possible claims.

d. Examine bills rendered by solicitors. As solicitors are often late in sending in bills they should be requested by the client to send in bills or estimates up to date or to confirm they have no charges unbilled.

e. Obtain a list of matters referred to solicitors from a director or other responsible official with an estimate of the possible ultimate liabilities.

f. Obtain a written assurance from the appropriate director or official that he is not aware of any matters referred to solicitors other than those disclosed.

12. If the auditor is at all in doubt he should obtain a direct confirmation of 11 e. from the company's legal adviser. The request must be sent by the client requesting the reply or that a copy of the reply be sent direct to the auditor. The letter to the solicitor should include a request for details of cases referred to the solicitor not mentioned in 11 e.

Letter to a client's legal adviser to confirm contingent liabilities arising out of pending legal matters

Messrs Scrooge & Co.
New St
Oldcastle
                                                                    26th September 20-6
Dear Sirs,

Joy Manufacturing Ltd

In connection with the preparation and audit of the accounts for the year ending 31 December 20-5 the directors have made estimates of the amounts of the ultimate liabilities (including costs) which might be incurred, and are regarded as material, in relation to the following matters on which you have been consulted. We should be glad if you would confirm that in your opinion these estimates are reasonable.

Matter	Estimated liability including costs
1. Claim by James Brown for wrongful dismissal	£2,000
2. Claim by Hedonite Manufacturing Ltd for damages in respect of faulty goods	£8,000
3. Action by Sultan of Difur for damages caused by late delivery of equipment	£nil
4. Action by Joyful Mfg PLC for breach of copyright in our Catalogue	£4,000

Yours faithfully,

Fussy & Co.

Chartered Accountants

Note that solicitor's opinion letters often do not satisfactorily resolve the auditor's uncertainties. Solicitors often say that the outcome of an action is 'unpredictable' or say that the company has 'meritorious defences'.

Debentures

13. Long-term loans are often evidenced by a piece of paper called a debenture. For this reason long-term loans are often called debentures. Such loans can be unsecured, secured by a fixed charge over a specific asset, or secured by a floating charge on all the assets. Secured liabilities are sometimes called mortgage debentures.

14. The verification procedures are:

   a. Obtain a schedule detailing the sums due at the beginning of the year, additions and redemptions(= repayments) and the sum due at the year end.

   b. Note, or photocopy, for the permanent file the terms and conditions of the loans as evidenced in the debenture deed.

   c. Agree opening balances with last year's papers.

   d. Vouch receipt of new loans with prospectus, board minutes, memorandum and articles, register of debenture holders etc.

   e. Vouch repayments with debenture deeds (terms are correctly interpreted, cash book, register of debenture holders etc.).

   f. Vouch interest payments with debenture deed, cash book and see amount paid is correctly n% of amount outstanding.

   g. Agree total amount outstanding with register of debenture holders.

h. If loans are secured, verify charge is registered at Companies House.

i. Verify disclosure is in accordance with Companies Act requirements. Note that long-term loans which are repayable within twelve months of the accounting date must be shown as such.

Accounting estimates

15. In this chapter we have considered many liabilities which are uncertain as to existence or amount. Liabilities are sometimes certain (e.g. most trade creditors) but some need to be estimated. There are many other areas of accounting where estimates need to be made including stock at net realisable value, depreciation and others. Some of these have been dealt with in the appropriate chapter of this book. However it seems a good idea to summarise at this point the auditing processes attached to accounting for estimates in general. There is a Statement of Auditing Standards SAS 420 *Audit of Accounting Estimates* and ISA 540 *Audit of Accounting Estimates*.

The following remarks can be made:

a. Accounting estimates have to be made in all areas where precise means of measurement cannot be applied. We have seen several examples in this book already (depreciation, stocks at NRV, lawsuits, warranty claims etc.).

b. The responsibility for these estimates lies with the directors or other governing body and may involve special knowledge and judgement. Some are routine, e.g. depreciation, and some are one-off e.g. the outcome of a lawsuit. Many are capable of reasonable estimation but some might not be. In the latter cases and if the matters are material, the auditor might consider that the uncertainty and /or the lack of objective data is so great that there are implications for the audit report – see Chapter 36.

c. Auditors should obtain sufficient appropriate audit evidence on all material accounting estimates. The evidence should give assurance that the estimates are *reasonable in the circumstances* and, when required, *appropriately disclosed.*

d. Possible audit procedures include:

    i. Review procedures and methods adopted by management to make accounting estimates. These may include internal audit. In some cases a formula will be used (e.g. in estimating warranty claims or in setting depreciation rates). There should be systems for continually reviewing these formulae. The fact that directors do actually consider the formulae or other methods of calculating estimates on a continuing basis is itself reassuring to the auditor!

    ii. Test these processes in connection with each estimate.

    iii. Evaluate the data and consider the assumptions on which the estimates have been made. For example in looking at depreciation, what assumptions on obsolescence have been made?

    iv. Check any calculations or applications of formulae.

    v.   Make an independent estimate on each estimate and compare it with that of the directors. Investigate any difference.

    vi. Compare estimates made in previous years with actual outcomes where known. Do the same for the independent estimates of the auditors.

    vii. Review subsequent events.

e.   At the final review stage of the audit, the auditor should make a review of the estimates (as with all the accounting data in the financial statements) and assess them in the light of:

    – her knowledge of the business

    – consistency with other evidence obtained during the audit.

f.   If the auditor considers that a material estimate is unreasonable, he should ask the directors to adjust the financial statements and if this is not done then he should consider there is a misstatement and ponder the implications for his auditor's report.

Summary

16. a.   The capital and liabilities side of the balance sheet is divided into a number of subheadings.

    b.   the auditor must verify the existence, amount, and adequate disclosure of all liabilities. He must also be satisfied that *all* liabilities are included.

    c.   Each liability is verified from whatever evidence is available but some general procedures common to most liabilities can be discerned.

    d.   Provisions are a difficult area. The auditor must take special care in considering the adequacy of provisions.

    e.   Share capital is verified like other liabilities but special procedures apply to new issues.

    f.   Pending legal matters can be verified by direct confirmation from the company's legal advisers.

    g.   There are some general points which can be made on the audit of all accounting estimates.

Points to note

17. a.   The liabilities side of the balance sheet is subject to numerous *Companies Act rules* on disclosure. These must be known.

    b.   Be very careful to use the words *provision* and *reserve* correctly. They are *not* synonymous for accruals and prepayments.

    c.   Two important matters in connection with liabilities are contingencies and post balance sheet events. They are discussed in Chapter 37.

d. The letter of representation may be evidence in this area, especially in the problem of inclusion of all liabilities. This is discussed in Chapter 32.

e. Some companies may have enormous potential liabilities arising out of environmental factors. Claims may be made against companies that supplied products, which at the time of supply were considered acceptable, but which are now seen as damaging. Vulnerable companies include tobacco, pharmaceutical and chemical companies. To some extent claims against such companies may be covered by insurance but that may also be a subject for endless litigation.

Case study 1

Horsebox, Postillion & Co. are a city firm of Chartered Certified Accountants. The firm's accounts are produced by the administration partner but are subject to audit by Blanket, Mange, another firm of Chartered Certified Accountants. In June 20-6, a partner in Horsebox who was suffering from overwork failed to realised that an error had occurred in the preparation and audit of the Accounts of International Maize Ltd. Stocks of maize in transit had been inadvertently included in the company's stocks in both the producing country and the receiving country. The company had been acquired by Universal Porage Inc. who have now discovered the mistake. They have given notice that they intend to bring an action to recover damages from Horsebox on the grounds that they relied on the audited accounts for the year ending 30.4.-6 and that they would not have purchased IM had they known of the error.

The stock of IM was overstated by £2.4 million as a consequence of the error. The profit of IM was reported as £4.3 million and UP paid £21 million cash for IM.

Horsebox carry professional indemnity insurance in the sum of £1 million.

The partners of Horsebox dislike each other and rely heavily on Blanket, Mange. No one at Horsebox has informed Blanket, Mange of the pending legal action.

Discussion

a. What auditing procedures might allow Blanket, Mange to discover the existence of the action?

b. How might the amount of the ultimate award and costs be determined by Blanket, Mange?

c. What other hidden liabilities might Horsebox have at their year end – 31.12.-6?

Student self testing questions *Questions with answers apparent from the text*

1. a. Reproduce the Companies Act Format 1 listing of capital, reserves and liabilities. (1)
   b. List the general procedures for verifying liabilities. (3)
   c. List some liabilities that may be omitted. (5)
   d. How can the auditor determine if all liabilities are included? (6)

e. Define provision and reserve. (7)

f. What factors about a liability must be verified by an auditor? (2)

g. How might audit evidence of the truth and fairness of the item 'share capital' be obtained? (9)

h. How might pending legal matters be dealt with by an auditor? (11, 12)

i. How can debentures be audited? (14)

j. List audit procedures in connection with accounting estimates (15)

Exercises

1. Draft an outline audit programme for the following:

    a. The trade creditors of Hurric Ltd a manufacturer of aircraft parts.

    b. The accruals and prepayments of Spit Ltd, a manufacturer of anoraks and similar clothing.

    c. The 16% convertible debentures of Beetroot PLC. The redemption date is 2012 and conversion is possible in any August. 4% of the debentures were converted in the year under review. The debentures are quoted.

    d. The overdraft of Turnip PLC which is secured.

    e. Taxation liabilities of Rich PLC, an international property company.

    f. A provision by Mangle Ltd against warranty liabilities in connection with a faulty product.

    g. A note to the accounts re a contingent liability for 'futures' by Pees Ltd a dealer in non-ferrous metals.

Examination question

1. Your audit supervisor has asked you to audit the liabilities of Glassware Ltd ('Glassware'), a small manufacturing company which makes paperweights and other glass ornaments. Included in its draft Balance Sheet are the following liabilities:

	£
Trade creditors	150,343
Obligations under finance leases	50,673
Corporation tax payable	15,404
Accruals	10,023
Bank overdraft	73,920
Other sundry creditors	5,980

Your supervisor has stressed that one of the major audit objectives in the audit of liabilities is that of 'completeness' and that you should ensure your audit work adequately covers this objective.

Required:

1. Explain why 'completeness' is a major objective in the audit of liabilities.

2. State the audit tests you would carry out to verify the completeness of Glassware's liabilities.

(ICAS)

2. Santa Teresa PLC is engaged in importing and exporting goods. As a result, the company has at any one time large balances on its Bills of Exchange Receivable and Bills of Exchange Payable Accounts.

Required:

Outline your audit method in connection with Bills of Exchange.

(LCCI) (15 marks)

3. The draft financial statements of your client company, which is a manufacturer of processed food, include the following items in the Balance Sheet:

(a) freehold land and buildings £4,200,000

(b) trade creditors £2,500,000

(c) bank loan £550,000

Required:

List, for each of the three items, five audit procedures which can be used to verify them.

(LCCI)(15 marks)

Audit evidence

1. Auditing is concerned with the verification of accounting data and with determining the *accuracy* and *reliability* of accounting statements and reports.

2. Verification does not mean seeking proof or absolute certainty in connection with the data and reports being audited. It means looking for sufficient *evidence* to satisfy oneself as auditor that the accounts show a true and fair view. What is sufficient evidence depends on what experience and knowledge of contemporary auditing standards tells one is satisfactory.

3. Chapter 24 deals with the theory of audit evidence and Chapters 25 and 26 deal with risk. Chapter 27 discusses statistical and other sampling methods, Chapter 28 reliance on other specialists and Chapter 29 service organisations and outsourcing.

24 Audit evidence

Introduction

1. This chapter may seem somewhat theoretical but in fact the material does make possible an approach to audit problems which can be useful in practice and also in examination.

   There is a Statement of Auditing Standards SAS 400 *Audit Evidence* and ISA 500 *Audit Evidence*.

Financial statements and assertions

2. Directors produce or cause to be produced financial statements. In doing so they are *asserting* that:

   a. The individual items are:
      i. Correctly described.
      ii. Show figures which are mathematically correct or fairly estimated.
   b. The accounts as a whole show a true and fair view.

3. The idea to grasp is that the *producer* of a set of accounts is making *assertions* about items in the accounts when he puts them in the accounts.

   The sort of assertions he is making are these:

   a. **Existence**: an asset or liability exists at the Balance Sheet date. This is an obvious assertion with such items as land and buildings, stocks and others.

   b. **Rights and obligations**: an asset or liability pertains to the entity at the Balance Sheet date. This means that the enterprise has for example ownership of an asset. Ownership as an idea is not simple and there may be all sorts of rights and obligations connected with a given asset or liability.

   c. **Occurrence**: a transaction or event took place which pertains to the enterprise during the relevant period. It may be possible for false transactions (e.g. sales or purchases) to be recorded. The assertion is that all recorded transactions actually took place.

d. **Completeness**: there are no unrecorded assets, liabilities, transactions or events or undisclosed items. This is important for all accounts items but is especially important for liabilities.

e. **Valuation**: an asset or liability is recorded at an appropriate carrying value. Appropriate may mean in accordance with generally accepted accounting principles, the Companies Act rules, Accounting Standards requirements and consistent with statements of accounting policies consistently applied.

f. **Measurement**: a transaction or event is recorded at the proper amount and revenue or expense allocated to the proper period.

g. **Presentation and disclosure**: an item is disclosed, classified and described in accordance with applicable reporting framework. For example fixed assets are subject to the Companies Act rules and to FRS 15 and other requirements. Exceptional items are subject to FRS 3.

4. As an example, we will look at an item in a balance sheet 'bank overdraft £10,250'. In including this item in the balance sheet, the directors are making these assertions:

a. That there is a liability to the company's bankers.

b. That at the balance sheet date this liability was £10,250.

c. That this amount is agreed by the bank.

d. That the overdraft was repayable on demand. If this were not so, it would not appear amongst the current liabilities and terms would be stated.

e. That the overdraft was not secured. If it were secured this fact would need to be stated.

f. That the company has the authority to borrow from its Memorandum and Articles.

g. That a bank reconciliation statement can be prepared.

h. That the bank is willing to let the overdraft continue.

5. If no item 'bank overdraft' appeared in the balance sheet, it would represent an assertion by the directors that no overdraft liability existed at the balance sheet date.

Audit evidence

6. The auditor's attitude to each item in the accounts will be as follows:

a. Identify the express and implied *assertions* made by the directors in including (or excluding) the item in the accounts.

b. Evaluate each assertion for relative importance to assess the quality and quantity of evidence required.

c. Collect information and evidence.

d. Assess the evidence for:

i. appropriateness. Appropriateness subsumes the ideas of quality and reliability of a particular piece of audit evidence and its relevance to a particular assertion.

ii. sufficiency. More of this in a later paragraph.

Note that audit evidence tends to be persuasive rather than absolute and that auditors tend to seek evidence from *different sources* or of a *different nature* to support the same assertion. Note also that auditors seek to provide *reasonable* but not *absolute* assurance that the financial statements are *free from misstatement*. Auditors do not normally examine all the information available but reach their conclusions about financial statement assertions using a variety of means including sampling.

7. Having formulated judgement on *each individual item* in (or omitted from) the accounts, the auditor must formulate a judgement on the truth and fairness of accounts *as a whole*. To do this he will need other evidence in addition to the judgements he has made on the individual items. As an extreme example, he may need evidence of the directors' implied assertion that the accounts should be drawn up on the going concern principle.

Limitations

8. The quality and quantity of evidence needs is constrained by the following:
   a. Absolute proof is impossible.
   b. Some assertions are not material.
   c. Time is limited. Accounts must be produced within a time scale and the auditor may have to make do with less than perfection to comply with the time scale.
   d. Money is limited. The ideal evidence may be too expensive to obtain.
   e. Sensitivity. Some items are of greater importance than others (valuation of property in property companies, for example) or capable of greater variations (stock and work in progress).

Varieties of evidence

9. The evidence an auditor collects can be divided into categories like this:
   a. **Observation.**
      i. Examination of physical assets.
      ii. Witnessing the internal control and bookkeeping procedures.
      iii. Observation of the records to ensure that book keeping and internal control procedures have been carried out.
   b. **Testimony from independent third parties.** e.g. bank letters, debtors circularisation.
   c. **Authoritative documents** prepared *outside* the firm e.g. title deeds, share and loan certificates, leases, contracts, franchises, invoices.
   d. **Authoritative documents** prepared *inside* the firm, e.g. minutes, copy invoices.
   e. **Testimony** from directors and officers *of the company*. This may be formal, for example the letter of representation, or informal, for example in replies to ICQ questions.
   f. **Satisfactory internal control**. For many items this is the most useful evidence.
   g. **Calculations performed by the auditor.** Evidence of the correctness of many figures can be obtained this way.
   h. **Subsequent events.** The audit is usually performed well after the year end and many assertions can be verified by reference to subsequent events.
   i. **Relationship evidence.** Evidence confirming the truth about one item may tend to confirm the truth about another. For example, evidence confirming the correctness of investment income also confirms some aspects of the item 'investments'.
   j. **Agreement with expectations.** Verification can be assisted by the computation and comparison of ratios and absolute magnitudes with those achieved (a) in the past; (b)

by other companies; and (c) budgeted. Conversely, inconsistencies and unusual or unexpected items will alert the auditor.

k. **External events.** The client is not isolated from the world, and the auditor should use his knowledge of current events in assessing a company's accounts. For example, consider revolutions and the value of overseas subsidiaries.

Basic techniques for collecting evidence

10. There are nine:
    a. **Physical examination and count.**
    b. **Confirmation.** This should be in writing, external sources being preferable to internal sources.
    c. **Examination of original documents.** Original documents should be compared with the entries in the books. The usual wording is vouching.
    d. **Re-computation.** Additions, calculations, balance extractions etc.
    e. **Retracing bookkeeping procedures.** Checking postings.
    f. **Scanning.** This is somewhat indefinite but is widely used, especially in seeking the unusual or the unlikely.
    g. **Inquiry.** Asking questions. This is a necessary and valid technique. However, auditors acquire a habit of always seeking confirmation of oral answers.
    h. **Correlation.** Seeking internal consistency in records and accounts.
    i. **Observation.** Seeing for oneself is the best possible confirmation especially in connection with internal control systems.

Test checking

11. This subject is explored further in the next chapter but needs some consideration here. It is not always necessary to obtain evidence about each individual transaction. The modern approach is to obtain evidence about each *type of transaction* by examining a representative *sample* of each type. This is called test checking and is applied as much to assets and liabilities as to routine transactions. The size of the sample to be tested depends on:
    a. the strength of the internal control system
    b. the materiality of the items
    c. the number of items involved
    d. the nature of the item
    e. the audit risk attached.

Sources

12. Sources of audit evidence include from within: systems, books, documents, assets, management and staff and from without: customers, suppliers, lenders, professional advisers etc.

13. The sources and amount of evidence required will depend on, materiality, relevance, and reliability of the evidence available from a source, and the cost and time involved.

14. Relevance of audit evidence depends upon whether it assists the auditor in forming an opinion on some aspect of the financial statements. For example evidence that indicates that a recorded asset exists is relevant to audit objectives.

Reliability

15. The reliability of audit evidence can be assessed to some extent on the following presumptions:

   a. Documentary evidence is more reliable than oral evidence.

   b. Evidence from outside the enterprise (e.g. bank letter) is more reliable than that secured solely from within the enterprise.

   c. Evidence originated by the auditor by such means as analysis and physical inspection is more reliable than evidence obtained from others (auditors always say 'show me' not 'tell me').

   d. Evidence for a figure in the Accounts is usually obtained from several sources (e.g. for debtors – a good system with internal controls, debtors circularisation, ratio analysis, payment after date etc.). The cumulative effect of several evidential sources which give a consistent view is greater than that from a single source (i.e. $2 + 2 = 5$).

   e. Original docments are more reliable than photocopies or facsimiles.

Sufficiency

16. Sufficiency is the great problem. The auditor's judgement will be influenced by:

   a. His knowledge of the business and its industry.

   b. The degree of audit risk. Assessment of this is helped by considering:

      i. Nature and materiality of items of account (e.g. stock is material and difficult to measure).

      ii. The auditor's experience of the reliability of the management and staff and the records.

      iii. The financial position of the enterprise (in a failing enterprise, directors may wish to bolster profits by over-valuing assets or suppressing liabilities).

      iv. Possible management bias (as iii.) but also the management may wish to 'even out' profits for stock market image or taxation reasons.

   c. The persuasiveness of the evidence.

   d. The nature of the accounting and internal control systems and the control environment.

17. The procedures for collecting evidence include:

   a. Systems and controls testing (with compliance tests).

   b. Substantive testing.

   c. Analytical review.

Summary

18. a. When the directors prepare accounts they are making *assertions* about the items in the accounts, items omitted from the accounts, and the accounts as a whole.

   b. The auditor conducts an audit by:

    i.   Identifying the assertions made.

    ii.   Considering the information and evidence he needs.

    iii.   Collecting the evidence and information.

    iv.   Evaluating the evidence.

    v.   Formulating a judgement.

c. There are some limitations to the ideal approach to the collection of evidence.

d. There are many different varieties of evidence. Some varieties are of more value than others.

e. There are nine techniques for collecting evidence.

f. An established method of collecting evidence is sampling.

g. Some legal decisions have appeared to guide the auditor in assessing what evidence he needs.

h. SAS 400 on audit evidence discusses relevance, reliability and sufficiency and gives some criteria for assessing these qualities in audit evidence.

Points to note

19. a. It is a very good idea both in practice and in examinations to identify what express and implied assertions are being made when an item appears in accounts or does not appear. You should get into the habit of doing this as often as possible.

b. A mental review of the varieties of evidence in Para. 9 and the techniques of evidence collection in Para. 10 will often suggest a comprehensive answer to practical and examination problems of verification.

c. Note particularly the value of strong internal control as evidence.

d. There is a distinction made in the more theoretical books on auditing between evidential matter and audit evidence. The auditor gathers immense quantities of evidential matter from the business records and management and staff and from third parties. This evidential matter is evaluated by the auditor. If it is relevant to the audit objectives (e.g. ownership of an asset or completeness of a revenue total) and it is reliable to any extent, it becomes audit evidence.

Case study 1

Down Market Department Stores PLC sell a high proportion of their merchandise on hire purchase. The system for dealing with HP sales is highly organised and well controlled. The HP debtors ledger is kept on a specially designed micro computer system. The HP debtors of the company at 30.9.-6 appear in the accounts at £4.6 million out of gross assets of £19.3 million.

Discussion

a. What assertions are the directors implying in stating the HP debtors at £4.6 million?

b. What possible misstatements could occur?

c. What varieties of evidence may be collected re this current asset?

d. What basic techniques for collecting evidence can be applied to the item?

Case study 2

Archaic Manufacturing PLC have a freehold factory which has been used to make the company's heavy metal products for generations. The factory was revalued ten years ago and is being depreciated over 50 years from that value. The company made a product for many years which has now been shown to be toxic and legal actions against the company have been expected. No mention occurs in the financial statements for these possible actions.

Discussion

a. What assertions are the directors' assertions re these matters?
b. What FRSs and/or International Accounting Standards are relevant here?
c. What kind of evidence might be collected?

Student self testing questions *Questions with answers apparent from the text*

1. a. What sort of assertions about items in accounts are directors making? (3)
   b. What varieties of audit evidence are there?(9)
   c. What basic techniques for obtaining audit evidence are there? (10)
   d. What criteria are there for determining the size of a sample to be used in test checking? (11)
   e. What criteria are there for assessing reliability? (15)
   f. What criteria are there for assessing sufficiency? (16)
   g. Distinguish audit evidence from evidential matter. (21)
   h List sources of audit evidence. (12)
   i. What might influence an auditor's judgement on sufficiency of audit evidence? (16)

Exercises

1. What assertions are being made by the directors including the following items in the accounts of Dahlia PLC a manufacturer of building materials and how might they be verified:
   a. A newly completed finished goods warehouse.
   b. Goodwill of a private business purchased in the year. The goodwill is being written off over 5 years.
   c. Debtors less a general provision for doubtful debts.
   d. Purchases.
   e. Directors' remuneration.
   f. Accrued interest on loans to customers.
   g. Stock of spare parts for plant and machinery.
   h. Plant and machinery.
2. Welth PLC is an investment trust company. List and give details of the varieties of evidence available to an auditor (Para. 9) for the item 'Investments' in the balance sheet. The company have both quoted and unquoted securities.
3. Crisant Ltd are a licensed maker of secured and unsecured loans to members of the public. The principal items in the accounts are interest receivable in the profit and loss account and loans in the balance sheet. Outline how the basic techniques for collecting evidence (Para. 10) can be applied to the audit of these items.

4. Aster Ltd manufacture and install process plant for customers in the food processing industry.

    a. Consider the evidence to be collected re the item debtors. Rank this in order of reliability (Para. 15).

    b. The auditors seek assurance that all liabilities have been included in the accounts. Certainty on this matter is not possible. Discuss the matters to be taken into account in considering the sufficiency of evidence that might be collected.

Examination question

1. 'The auditor should obtain relevant and reliable evidence to enable him to draw reasonable conclusions therefrom.'

    Required:

    a. List the various kinds of evidence which might be available to an auditor, giving an illustration of each kind. (10 marks)

    b. What general procedures should be gone through to obtain third party evidence? (5 marks)

    c. To what extent do you consider that a certificate from a trade debtor confirming agreement to a year-end balance provides relevant, reliable and sufficient evidence of the outstanding debt? What other work might be necessary to verify the debt? (10 marks)

    (AAT)

2. An auditor must ensure that statements made in the accounts for publication bearing the audit report give full information to the readers of those accounts.

    In the accounts for publication of Trimble PLC, there is an entry under creditors, amounts falling due within one year:

    'Bank overdraft £1,234,567'

    If the auditor makes no comment upon this entry, what may he expect it to tell the readers of the accounts? (12 marks)

    (LCC)

3. Legislation requires all companies to maintain statutory books and registers.

    Required:

    State the matters to which you would direct your attention when reviewing:

    a. The share register.

    b. The register of directors and secretaries and the register of directors' shareholdings.

    c. The minute books.

    d. The register of charges.

    (AAT)

25 Business risk

Introduction

1. In recent years, the larger firms have extended the concepts of risk analysis as an approach to auditing. The new more embracing concept is that of business risk.

    A definition of business risk is 'The threat that an event or action will adversely affect a business's ability to achieve its ongoing objectives, and can be split between external and internal factors'. We will consider possible factors later.

    The idea is that businesses face risks and an understanding of these risks gives the auditor a thorough understanding of the client's business and also suggests where misstatements may occur in the financial statements.

External risks

2. Risks arising from outside the company include:
    a. Changing legislation (e.g. the use of genetically modified foods).
    b. Changing interest rates (especially with highly geared companies).
    c. Changing exchange rates (e.g. the strong pound and the high price of British exports).
    d. Public opinion, attitudes, fashions (e.g. Marks & Spencer and other middle of the road retailers losing out to cheap shops and chic designer-wear fashions).
    e. Price wars initiated by competitors (e.g. supermarkets).
    f. Import competition (e.g. steel and electronics).
    g. Untried technologies and ideas (e.g. dot.com traders).
    h. Natural hazards (e.g. fire or flood or effects of global warming).
    i. Bad debts.
    j. Litigation (we live in an increasingly litigious society).
    k. Environmental matters.

    See how an understanding of the risks facing a client adds to an auditor's understanding of the client. See also how some of these may affect the financial statements. Some may affect the value of assets and some may affect the going concern concept for all or part of the enterprise.

Internal risks

3. Risks arising from inside the company include:
    a. Failure to modernise products, processes, labour relations, marketing.
    b. Employees.
    c. Board members.
    d. Failure to modernise e.g. failure to achieve ISOs or to use e-commerce.
    e. The process of dealing with suppliers or customers.
    f. Excessive reliance on a dominant chief executive.
    g. Cash flow including overtrading.

h. Gearing.

i. Related parties.

j. Inappropriate acquisitions.

k. Excessive reliance on one of a few products, customers, suppliers.

l. Internal controls.

m. Lack of research and development.

n. Computer systems failures.

o. Fraud.

Any of these risks can damage a company and may impact on the financial statements. Consider for yourself how this may happen! An example might be a company that manufactures goods that are subject to very strong import competition. Financial statements might be affected by the value of plant that may need to be replaced, staff may need to be made redundant and the going concern basis of parts of the business may need to be questioned.

Why use a business risk approach?

4. There are many reasons. These include:

a. Research showed that processing errors were rarely a cause of audit problems.

b. Major audit problems (e.g. companies failing shortly after a clear audit report) arise out of issues such as going concern, major fraud by top management, larger-scale systems breakdown, failure to modernise products, lack of response to market forces etc.

c. Investigation of business risk enables the auditor to have a profound knowledge of the business (as required by SAS 210 and ISA 310).

d. The approach *focuses* the audit on to the high risk areas.

e. The approach adds value to the audit and enables the auditor to offer some commercial benefits to the audit.

f. Auditors needs to be aware of such changes.

g. The previous emphasis on transactions and systems was expensive and uneconomic.

h. The pace of change in business and in computing and communications means that companies are much more at risk of failure than ever before. The global economy is more competitive and more unforgiving than national economies.

i. Audit firms wish to be in the van of innovation to attract clients.

j. The business risk review may show up areas where the audit firm can suggest that its highly paid services can be offered to the client.

k. Audit firms are anxious to show product differentiation to potential clients.

l. The business, environmental, corporate governance issues and the nature of management control are all now more significant for businesses. They also translate more quickly into the financial statements.

m. The approach tends to involve partners and senior managers much more in the planning stages of an audit.

5. There are some disadvantages to counter all these benefits.

a. More highly qualified and competent staff are required and that negates some of the efficiency gains.

b. The added value idea does tend to oppose the notion of independence which is very important currently.

Understanding the business risk approach

6. The business risk approach is radically new, and its implications are not fully worked out, but some general points can be made about it:

a. The direction of the audit is from the risks to the financial statements. Earlier approaches to auditing tended to start with the financial statements.

b. There is still a lack of clarity in the articulation between business risk and audit risk. However the ideas of inherent risk and control risk have tended to merge into the larger idea of business risk.

c. The ideas of inherent risk and control risk can be called residual risk which has to be minimised by audit action. And audit action carries with it detection risk

d. The approach is very much a high level approach. Much less of the 'can wages be paid to non-employees?' and much more of 'could the client close its Bristol factory and manufacture in China and what are the possible consequences for the company and its financial statements?'.

e. Because of the better understanding of the client's business it is possible to use analytical review more frequently as a verification of assertions procedure.

f. It is an aid to the client acceptance and continuation procedures ('Do we want this client?').

g. Going concern considerations are a natural by-product of business risk investigation and separate consideration of going concern may be unnecessary.

h. The audit needs to be tailor-made and a generalised approach to audits is neither productive nor economical. However this needs better trained and higher level staff.

i. Auditors need more understanding of business and to that end the larger firms set up large databases of information about the economy and the business world.

j. The concept implies a continuing relationship with the client rather than a one off, each year separate, view.

The client's approach to risk

7. The client can be helped to appreciate the risks facing it. (This is not a part of the audit but a useful, and lucrative for the auditor, aid to the client.) The potential effect of the risks on the financial statements depends on how the client deals with risk. Possible actions are:

a. Do nothing and hope for the best.

b. Develop internal controls. There is much emphasis on internal controls in the corporate governance literature and management of risk is a large part of it.

c. Develop quality controls over production of goods, production of services, staff recruitment.

d. Join in government schemes like Investors in People.

e. Diversify – acquisition, new products, multiple sourcing, adding to customer base perhaps by exporting.

f. Train staff.

g. Risk reduction – raising staff awareness of risk, tighter discipline in all areas, physical measures such as sprinklers, diversified computer systems instead of one complex one, active development of new products and markets. Simply not being complacent.

h. Transfer of risk – by insurance, sub-contracting, outsourcing.

i. Avoidance – e.g. manufacturing in countries where the market is, instead of exporting, and thus avoiding exchange rate risks and government import restrictions.

The implications of business risk for the audit

8. The auditor needs to plan the audit (SAS 200 and ISA 300) and needs to have an understanding of the business (SAS 210 and ISA 310). The study of business risk is a good way of understanding the business. The effects on planning may include:

a. A consideration of the control environment. The expression *control environment* crops up in numerous SASs and ISAs?

b. Does the management manage risk effectively?

c. Is the accounting system adequate both in Companies Act terms but also considering the complexities of modern business?

d. Do any risks threaten the going concern status of the company?

e. Do any of the risks have implications for cash flow?

f. Is there a high risk of fraud – e.g. poor controls, management override, egotistical ambition and arrogance in the chief executive?

g. Are there related parties with different agendas?

h. Is the business under threat of being taken over with the risk of management misstating financial statements?

i. Is there a risk of litigation against the company?

j. Is there any risk of withdrawal of support by loan or trade creditors?

9. In the end many of the audit risks come down to:

a. Possible misstatements due to lack of controls. Recent company failures (often shortly after clear audit reports) have been caused by overvaluation of stocks or underprovision for bad debts).

b. Working capital shortage leading to cash flow difficulties and technical insolvency (inability to pay debts as they fall due), often due to too rapid expansion.

c. Inappropriate accounting policies. These can often lead to overstatement of assets or understatement of liabilities.

d. Suppression or concealment of liabilities.

e. Fraud by management.

f. Related parties.

g. Going concern appropriateness.

h. Computer failures.

Business risk and audit risk

10. Audit risk in SAS 300 and ISA 400 is considered from two aspects – inherent risk and audit risk. Audit risk is divided into control risk and detection risk. In a sense business risk encompasses all of these. The arguments are:

a. The business faces numerous external and internal risks.

b. The auditor faces the risk of giving an audit opinion that is wrong in some particular.

c. The effect of the business risks is that the financial statements may contain a misstatement.

d. The audit risk arises out of the possibility of undetected misstatements in the financial statements.

e. A major risk facing most companies is the failure of internal controls to prevent or detect material errors or frauds leading to misstatements in the financial statements.

f. A major risk to auditors is their tests may fail to detect errors and frauds which lead to misstatements in the financial statements.

Designing the audit

11. The approach using business risk may be to:

a. Agree the assignment in a letter of engagement.

b. Discuss and review the business risks with the directors/management.

c. Plan the audit accordingly.

d. Carry out the audit.

e. At the final review stage of the audit, consider the business risks and any possible impact on misstatements in the financial statements.

f. Report.

Summary

12. a. A new approach to auditing is the investigation of business risk.

b. Business risk is the threat that an event or action will adversely affect a business's ability to achieve its ongoing objectives.

c. Business risk can arise from factors external to the client and factors within the client's business.

d. There are arguments in favour of this approach including the fact that processing errors are rarely the cause of audit problems.

e. Clients have different approaches to dealing with risk and the auditor needs an understanding of these, especially of the client's control environment.

f. Business risk has many implications including the possibility of misstatement in the financial statements.

Case study 1

You are the manager responsible for prospective new clients and you have visited Sheinton Publishing PLC which publishes a small range of fiction paperbacks. The chief executive and majority shareholder is Jamie and he has asked your firm to make a proposal for the company's audit and other services.

During the initial meeting you have ascertained the following:

The company's turnover has increased by about 20% a year for the last three years.

Jamie is a dominating personality who is very ambitious.

The company has recently paid very large sums to two relatively unknown authors for new books which Jamie thinks will be highly successful.

Sheinton has borrowed heavily from its bank and a major repayment of the loan is due shortly. The company is already on its overdraft limit as a result of the advances to the new authors. Jamie is in negotiation with a foreign bank for further finance.

Many of the company's books are printed in a country with an exchange rate which is very favourable to the UK. The financial press have lately suggested that this rate may change in the near future.

The company recently purchased a very large and very complex computer system to control all its affairs. Jamie confesses that he does not understand it and the IT manager has just left and gone to Australia.

The company have agreed to sponsor a sailor who is racing round the world single-handedly and the cost of this is not yet clear. The company has a racing yacht which Jamie sails.

The company have received a writ from a person who alleges he has been wronged by a book published by the company. The company has large stocks of this book and are contesting the issue.

The company have no formal management accounting system but the new IT system, when it is working will supply this.

Jamie wishes to maintain the company's high share price so that he can use the shares to take-over a competitor.

The company recently took over an ailing printing firm. Jamie reckons he can turn it round.

Discussion

a. Identify and describe the principal business risks relating to Sheinton.
b. Justify an appropriate audit strategy for the first audit of Sheinton.
c. Suggest some procedures that Sheinton could implement immediately to improve its accounting procedures and financial controls.

Student self testing questions

a. Define business risk. (1)
b. List some external risk facing companies. (2)
c. List some internal risks facing companies. (3)
d. Why do auditors use a business risk approach? (4)

e. What are the consequences of the approach? (6)

f. What can a company do about risk? (7)

g. The implications of business risk for the audit? (8)

26 Audit risk

Introduction

1. In recent years, the phrase audit risk has entered the vocabulary of auditing.

   Audit risk means the chance of damage to the audit firm as a result of giving an audit opinion that is wrong in some particular. Damage to the audit firm may be in the form of monetary damages paid to a client or third party as compensation for loss caused by the conduct (for example negligence) of the audit firm or simply loss of reputation with the client (and perhaps also the audit) or the business community.

   A wrong audit opinion means for example saying that the Accounts show a true and fair view when in fact they do not.

2. This chapter considers:

   a. i. normal audit risk
      ii. higher than normal risk
      iii. audit work risk.

   b. Audit firm organisation and audit risk.

   c. Particular audits and audit risk.

   d. The risk based audit approach.

   There is a Statement of Auditing Standards SAS 300 *Accounting and Control Systems and Audit Risk Assessments* and an ISA 400 *Risk Assessments and Internal Control*.

Normal audit risk

3. All audits involve risk. However strong the audit evidence and however careful the auditor, there is always a possibility of an error or fraud being undetected.

4. In general, if there are indications that audit risk is normal and there are no indications of higher than normal risk then the auditor who:

   a. organises his office and staff in a competent manner

   b. follows the auditing standards and guidelines

   is unlikely to be found negligent and to have to pay damages as a consequence of fraud or error not discovered by him.

5. Indications that risk is normal may include:

   a. Past experience indicates risk is normal.

   b. The management and staff of the client are competent and have integrity.

c. The accounting system is well designed, works and is subject to strong internal controls.

e. The client is old established and is not subject to rapid change.

f. The board of directors are actively engaged in the company and control and leadership is of good quality.

g. The board of directors has competent non-executive directors and better still, an audit committee.

6. Where audit risk is normal, then the auditor may approach his audit by relying on:

a. Key controls.

b. Substantive tests.

c. Analytical review.

Higher than normal risk

7. Some audit assignments involve high audit risk. The majority of audits contain at least one area of high risk.

8. Indications of higher than normal audit risk include:

a. Previous experience.

b. Future plans of the enterprise include sale or flotation on the Stock Exchange of the company.

c. High gearing.

d. Liquidity problems.

e. Poor management.

f. Lack of controls and/or poor bookkeeping.

g. Recent changes of ownership/control.

h. Dominance by a single person.

i. Rapid staff turnover.

j. In small companies, non-involvement of the proprietor or conversely over reliance on management for control.

k. Changes of accounting procedures or policies.

l. Evidence from background research.

m. Over reliance on one or a few products, customers, suppliers.

n. Recent high investment in new ventures or products.

o. Problems inherent in the nature of the business e.g. stock counting or valuing difficulties, difficulty in determining the extent of liabilities, warranty claims, cut-off.

p. The existence of 'put upon enquiry' situations.

9. The audit approach in high risk situations must be:

a. Sceptical.

b. To use high calibre audit staff.

c. Collection of a wide range of audit evidence in each area.

d. Meticulous preparation of audit working papers.

e. Probing of all high risk areas to the bottom.

f. Extreme care in drafting the audit report.

Audit work risk

10. All audit work involves normal risk and some audit work involves higher than normal risk. This is because there is always a possibility of the Accounts containing a mis-statement due to error or fraud.

   In addition to the audit risk arising from client activity there is also a risk that the audit work may be of an inadequate standard.

11. The risk arising from audit work may include:

   a. Failure to recognise put upon enquiry situations.

   b. Failure to draw the correct inferences from audit evidence and the analytical review.

   c. Use of the wrong procedures in a particular situation.

   d. Failure to perform necessary audit work because of time or cost considerations.

   e. Failure to detect error or fraud because of poor sampling method or inadequate sample sizes.

Audit firm organisation and audit risk

12. It is essential that an audit firm should organise its affairs in such a way as to minimise the risk of paying damages to clients or others arising out of negligent work.

13. Features of organisation which may minimise risk include:

   a. Proper recruitment and training of all personnel.

   b. Allocation of staff with appropriate ability to particular audits.

   c. Planning of the work of the firm in such a way that each audit can be approached in a relaxed but disciplined way and timing problems can be accommodated.

   d. Two way communication with staff on matters of general concern and in connection with specific audits.

   e. Use of audit manuals which conform to the audit standards and guidelines.

   f. Use of audit documentation which is comprehensive and yet which allows for special situations.

   g. Use of budgeting and other techniques to ensure that audits are remunerative and yet risk-minimising.

   h. Use of precise and frequently updated letters of engagement.

   i. Use of review techniques for all audits.

   j. Existence of a technical section so that all new developments (accounting, law, audit procedures) are rapidly incorporated into the firm's actions.

Particular audits and audit risk

14. Risks arising from a particular audit can be minimised by:

   a. Techniques for recognising the existence of audit risk.

   b. Segregating normal risk areas from high risk areas.

   c. Allocating staff who are competent to do the work especially in high risk areas.

d. Extensive background research into the client and its industry.

e. Careful planning with emphasis on high risk areas.

f. Comprehensive documentation.

g. Good briefing of audit staff.

h. Emphasis to staff on the need for recognition of high risk situations and good communication when high risk or put upon enquiry situations are discovered.

i. Particular attention to the conclusions reached from audit evidence.

j. Special emphasis on the analytical review.

k. Review of the audit work by a senior auditor unconnected with the particular audit.

l. Emphasis on materiality considerations and sample sizes.

The risk based audit methodology

15. Audit costs have been rising steadily in the last few years due to higher salaries (accountants are among the highest paid people), high office costs (accountants like to be in plush city centre offices) and higher professional indemnity premiums (accountants, it seems, make lots of mistakes).

At the same time audit fee resistance has risen due to competition, low growth in the market (except for the public sector) and the growth of competitive tendering for audits.

Consequently, audit firms are continually trying to reduce audit costs while at the same time reducing audit risk. This has led to the idea of risk based auditing being in some sense a distinct approach to auditing. Historically, auditing has progressed from being a largely *substantive testing* process, through a largely *systems* based process into a risk based method which uses a range of audit techniques including: substantive testing, internal control compliance, analytical review and the use of *inherent factors*.

Inherent factors include background knowledge of the client and past audit record indicating no special difficulties. According to Mautz and Sharaf, in their seminal work *The Philosophy of Auditing*, it is a valid auditing postulate that 'in the absence of evidence to the contrary what has held true for the client in the past will hold true in the future'.

Essentially auditing is the gathering of evidence about each part of the accounts but as absolute assurance is impossible, there is always some element of residual risk which has to be accepted. The extent of that acceptable risk is a matter of judgement. It can be seen as the product of the separate risks accepted in each type of evidence gathering. Thus:

Overall risk = Inherent risk × Control Risk × Analytical review risk × Substantive risk.

Thus if, for example, an audit situation was examined, found to be material and the risk factors assessed, the following set of figures might be assembled:

(the area may be debtors)

Overall acceptable risk 5% (= 5 chances in 100 of giving a wrong opinion).

Inherent risk (client is old established, well managed and no problems have been encountered in the area previously) 50%.

Control risk (internal control is strong, unchanged from last year, little possibility of management override) 20%.

Analytical control risk (figures tie up with credit sales, with previous years and with budgets subject to small changes stemming from different external conditions) 50%.

Thus substantive risk $= $ OR/IR $\times$ CR $\times$ AR $= 0.05/0.5*0.2*0.5$

$$= 1$$

This means the audit assurance required from substantive testing is 100% – 100% i.e. no assurance is required. Assurance from the other sources of evidence are sufficient to support an audit opinion with 5% risk. Most auditors would find this a bit strong but if you change the risk factor from control to 30% then the substantive risk becomes 67% and the level of assurance required from the evidence source substantive testing is only 100% – 67% = 33%. In effect, in designing statistical sampling tests for substantive testing the level of confidence required is only 33%. The sample sizes corresponding to this are likely to be very small.

Using the risk based audit strategy

16. a. The risk based equation outlined above is one of several possible. Others include:

$$AR = IR \times CR \times DR$$

$$AR = IR \times DR \times SR$$

where: AR is overall audit risk – the risk that the auditor will draw an invalid conclusion and wrongly qualify or not qualify his/her report.

IR is inherent risk – risk which derives from the nature of the entity and of its environment prior to the establishment of internal controls. Some enterprises are inherently more risky than others e.g. new v old established, high tech (computer manufacture) v low tech (hand-made up-market furniture).

DR = detection risk – the risk that the auditor's substantive procedures and his review of the financial statements will not detect material errors.

SR = sampling risk – detection risk arising out of sample based substantive tests.

Some of these are sub-sets of others (e.g. sampling risk of detection risk).

b. Care must be taken to weigh the risk from each source of evidence as it is gathered and then to avoid over auditing in the remaining evidence gathering. For example, if adequate weight is given to inherent factors and analytical review it may be that minimal internal control evaluation and/or substantive testing will be required.

c. It may be undesirable to carry out detailed ICQ and compliance testing techniques if:

i. a high level of assurance can be gained from inherent factors and analytical review

ii. a preliminary review indicates that controls appear to be very strong

iii. a high level of assurance was obtained in the previous year and the system has not changed

iv. the area is not material

v. a preliminary review indicates that controls are not strong and a high level of assurance will have to come from substantive testing.

d. Use computer aided auditing techniques wherever possible.

e. Use the same sample as far as possible for several tests both compliance and substantive. This takes us back to the old idea of block and depth tests. However care must be taken to think through each sample and clearly record what evidence is being obtained whether it be compliance (if so on what controls) or substantive. In any event random samples never include blocks of transactions.

f. In using sampling, always look for rational sampling methods including stratification.

g. Increase the role of internal audit. Smaller and smaller firms are turning to internal audit and audit firms should make maximum use of this resource.

h. Increase the use of accounting technicians for the actual sampling and employ high level staff for the thought behind the audit work. As a matter of comment, the use of clever recent graduates for audit work seems to be expensive (high salaries, low output as learners and with time off for study) and a turn off from auditing.

Summary

17. a. Audit risk is a term which has grown in importance in recent years.

b. Audit risk may be defined in two stages:

    i. The possibility that the financial statements contain material misstatements which have escaped detection by both, any internal controls on which the auditor has relied and on the auditor's own substantive tests and other work.

    ii. The possibility that the auditor may be required to pay damages to the client or other persons as a consequence of:

        1. the financial statements containing a misstatement, and

        2. the complaining party suffering loss as a direct consequence of relying on the financial statements, and

        3. negligence by the auditor in not detecting and reporting on the misstatement can be demonstrated.

c. Audit risk can be seen as normal or higher than normal.

d. Normal audit risk exists in all auditing situations.

e. Higher than normal audit risk can be associated with particular clients or with particular areas of a client's affairs.

f. Audit risk can arise from a client which is high risk as a whole, for particular areas of a client's affairs, or, from inadequacies in audit work.

g. Audit risk can be minimised by appropriate audit firm organisation and appropriate audit work on a particular client.

h. Many modern writers consider the use of risk based auditing as a new direction in auditing, contrasting with the older substantive testing and systems based auditing. Risk based auditing takes account of substantive test risk, internal control risk, detection risk, analytical control risk, sampling risk and inherent risk.

Points to note

18. a. Risk is a useful concept in planning all audit work. It is also a useful buzz word in examination answers.

b. Modern audit firms are increasingly adopting a *risk based* audit approach. This means that audits are divided into normal and high risk audits and individual audits are divided into normal risk areas and high risk areas. The normal risk areas are covered with emphasis on key controls and analytical review and the larger part of the audit effort is placed on the high risk areas.

c. This approach of focusing the audit on the high risk areas both minimises the auditor's risk and also makes economic sense from the auditor's, the client's and the public's points of view.

d. Spotting high risk areas is the important skill. Ideas which assist in this, include:

Identifying large or high value (material) items.

Recognising error prone conditions e.g. capital/revenue coding, stock and work in progress.

Briefing staff on the importance of put upon enquiry situations, the investigation of related parties, and the interpretation of new legislation and accounting standards.

e. One way to reduce audit risk is to acquire the quality standard ISO 9000 either on its own or as part of Total Quality Management. This subject is reviewed in more detail in Chapter 34 on quality control.

Case study 1

Stoke, Poges & Co., chartered certified accountants are planning their workload for the three months ending 31 March 20-7: their busy time. They have two partners, one highly skilled senior clerk and several trainees and semi-seniors in the firm. Audits to be done include:

Burke & Hare Ltd, an old established firm of funeral directors.
Growbig Construction Ltd, a newly established firm of speculative builders.
Safe and Sound Supermarket Ltd.
The Heartbreak Hotel Chain Ltd, whose aged proprietor lives in Jamaica.
Smart, Alick & Partners, estate agents.
Halley Electronics Ltd, who are looking for a listing on the Stock Exchange. They manufacture computer peripherals.
Giles Farm Products Ltd, whose major problem is excessive cash resources.
AHM Construction Ltd, a fast expanding firm of civil engineering contractors.
Cultural Video Shops Ltd.
Farcical Funnies Ltd, who run a series of scandal magazines and who recently changed management.

Discussion

a. Distinguish the normal risk companies from the higher than normal risk companies.

b. Who would you put in charge of these audits?

c. Does this case say anything about 'work risk'?

d. Identify possible high risk areas in each of these clients.

Case study 2

In the audit of Wodenfield Windows Ltd, a three-year-old replacement window company, the following data has to be considered:

The company's first two years have been successful but internal controls have been minimal and the control is in the hands of the founders Bill and Ben who are strong characters.

The director/shareholders seem determined to take all profits out of the company as directors' remuneration, leaving a minimum of capital for everyday use and expansion. The company are heavily financed by the bank.

In the year under review turnover and profit are up 50% while stock and debtors are up 65%, creditors are up 50% also.

Discussion

Assess this company from the risk point of view, considering likely risks from the perspectives of inherent risk, control risk, analytical review risk, detection risk, sampling risk, substantive risk.

Student self testing questions *Questions with answers apparent from the text*

1. a. What is audit risk? (1)
   b. What factors might indicate that risk is normal? (5)
   c. What factors might indicate higher than normal audit risk? (8)
   d. What is the audit approach in areas of high risk? (9)
   e. What is audit work risk? (10)
   f. How might audit work risk arise? (11)
   g. What audit firm organisation features might minimise audit risk? (13)
   h. How can risk in particular areas be minimised? (14)
   i. What is a risk based audit? (16)
   j. How can high risk areas be spotted? (16)
   k. Define overall audit risk, inherent risk, control risk, analytical review risk, detection risk, sampling risk, substantive risk. Put these risks into sets or categories.

Examination questions without answers

1. Some areas of an audit have a higher risk element than others.
   a. How may an external auditor identify such areas?
   b. What action should the auditor take upon discovery of such areas?   (15 marks)
   (LCCI)

2. It is important for an auditor to consider risk when planning, carrying out and coming to an opinion on the financial statements of a company. Audit risk has been categorised into:
   a. inherent risk
   b. control risk, and
   c. detection risk.

   The following equation is often used in determining audit risk:

   $AR = IR \times CR \times DR$

   where:

   AR = audit risk
   IR = inherent risk
   CR = control risk
   DR = detection risk.

You are required:

a. To define the following terms:

   i.   audit risk

   ii. inherent risk

   iii. control risk

   iv. detection risk.   (4 marks)

b. To explain the factors which affect inherent risk in an audit.   (7 marks)

c. To describe the work you will carry out to quantify the control risk in a purchases system.   (7 marks)

d. In relation to detection risk:

   i.   to consider the effect on the detection risk of the inherent risk and control risk, if the auditor requires a particular value of audit risk.

   ii. to briefly describe the audit checks you will perform in verifying trade creditors and accruals, and how these tests are affected by the value of the detection risk.   (7 marks)

                  (ACCA)

27 Statistical and other sampling methods

Introduction

1. A complete check of all the transactions and balances of a business is no longer required of an auditor. The reasons for this are:

   a. Economic – the cost in terms of expensive audit resources would be prohibitive.

   b. Time – the complete check would take so long that accounts would be ancient history before users saw them.

   c. Practical – users of accounts do not expect or require 100% accuracy. Materiality is very important in accounting as well as auditing.

   d. Psychological – a complete check would so bore the audit staff that their work would become ineffective and errors would be missed.

   e. Fruitfulness – a complete check would not add much to the worth of figures if, as would be normal, few errors were discovered. The emphasis in auditing should be on the *completeness* of record and the true and *fair* view.

2. In some cases a 100% check is still necessary. Some of these are:

   a. Categories which are few in number but of great importance e.g. land and buildings.

   b. Categories with special importance where materiality does not apply e.g. directors' emoluments and loans.

   c. Unusual, one-off, or exceptional items.

   d. Any area where the auditor is put upon enquiry.

   e. High risk areas.

3. In most areas a 100% check is not necessary and a test check is made, or, to put in audit terminology – evidence about a whole class of transactions or balances is obtained by examination of a sample of items taken from that class.

4. There are two approaches to sampling in auditing:
   a. judgement sampling
   b. statistical sampling.

   We will deal with each in turn and then review statistical sampling in more detail.

5. Note that the objective in all sampling is to *draw conclusions* about a large group of data, e.g. all the credit sales made in a period, or all the PAYE calculations or all the debtors, from an examination of a sample taken from the group.

6. There is a Statement of Auditing Standards SAS 430 *Statistical Sampling* and IAS 530 *Audit Sampling and Other Selective Testing Procedures.*

Objectives of audit sampling

7. SAS 100 requires that auditors should carry out procedures designed to obtain sufficient appropriate audit evidence to determine with reasonable confidence whether the financial statements are free of material misstatement.

   Two words in the last sentence are relevant here – reasonable and material. It is not necessary that auditors should ensure that financial statements are absolutely 100% accurate. Sampling does not provide absolute proof of 100% accuracy but it can provide reasonable assurance that some elements of the financial statements are free from material misstatement.

   Audit sampling means drawing conclusions about an entire set of data by testing a *representative* sample of items. The set of data which may be a set of account balances (e.g. debtors, creditors, fixed assets) or transactions (e.g. all wage payments, all advice notes) is called the *population*. The individual items making up the population are called *sampling units*.

Materiality and risk

8. a. An auditor is not required to have evidence that all items in a set of Accounts are 100% correct. His duty is to give an opinion on the truth and fairness of the Accounts. Errors can exist in the Accounts and yet the Accounts can still give a true and fair view. The maximum error that any particular magnitude can contain without marring the true and fair view is the *tolerable* error. Tolerable error is auditing materiality.

   In his audit planning, the auditor needs to determine the amount of tolerable error in any given population and to carry out tests to provide evidence that the actual errors in the population are less than the tolerable error. For example, stock can be a large amount in a set of accounts. Stock is computed by counting and weighing, by multiplying quantity by price and by summing individual values. Errors can occur at any of these stages. Applied prices may be incorrect. The effect of incorrect prices may be to compute a stock figures that is above or below the correct stock figure by an amount that is above the tolerable error.

b. *Audit risk*. This term applies to the risk that the auditor will draw an invalid conclusion from his audit procedures. Audit risk has several components:

    i. *Inherent risk* is the risk attached to any particular population because of factors like:

        The type of industry – a new manufacturing hi-tech industry is more prone to errors of all sorts than a stable business like a brewery.

        Previous experience indicates that significant errors have occurred.

        Some populations are always prone to error, e.g. stock calculations, work in progress.

    ii. *Control risk*. This is the risk that internal controls will not detect and prevent material errors. If this risk is large the auditor may eschew compliance tests altogether and apply only substantive tests.

    iii. *Detection risk*. This is the risk that the auditor's substantive procedures and analytical review will not detect material errors.

The assurance that an auditor seeks from sampling procedures is related to the audit risk that he perceives. The sample sizes required will be related to the audit risk that he perceives. The sample sizes required will be related to materiality and to audit risk.

To sample or not?

9. The auditor, in considering a particular population, has to consider how to obtain assurance about it. Sampling may be the solution. Factors which may be taken into account in considering whether or not to sample include:

a. Materiality. Petty cash expenditure may be so small that no conceivable error may affect the true and fair view of the accounts as a whole.

b. The number of items in the population. If these are few (e.g. land and buildings), a hundred per cent check may be economic.

c. Reliability of other forms of evidence – analytical review (e.g. wages relate closely to number of employees, budgets, previous years, etc.) – proof in total (VAT calculations). If other evidence is very strong, then a detailed check of a population (100% or a sample) may be unnecessary.

d. Cost and time considerations can be relevant in choosing between evidence seeking methods.

e. A combination of evidence seeking methods is often the optimal solution.

Stages of audit sampling

10. The stages of audit sampling are:

a. Planning the sample.

    – *Audit objectives*. Why is this test being carried out? What contribution does it make to the overall assessment of true and fair view?

    – *The population*. The population has to be defined precisely. This may be all sales rather than all sales invoices. (Can you see the difference?)

- *The sampling unit.* Note that in compliance testing it is the operation of the control on a transaction not the transaction which is the sampling unit.
- *The definition of error in substantive tests.* In stock calculations, an error of greater than £1 only may constitute an error for this purpose.
- *The definition of deviation in compliance tests.* The deviation may be any failure to carry out a control procedure or it may be a partial failure.
- *The assurance required.* This is a function of the other sources of evidence available.
- *The tolerable error or deviation rate.* This is related to materiality.
- *The expected error/deviation rate.* This is a factor which is not intuitively expected by students. In fact, errors increase the impreciseness of conclusions drawn from sampling and larger sample sizes are required if there are many errors.
- *Stratification.* It may be desirable to stratify the population into sub-populations and sample them separately or in some cases, such as high value items, do a hundred per cent check.

b. Selection of the items to be tested. This is dealt with in detail later in the chapter.
c. Testing the items.
d. Evaluating the results. This should also be done in stages:
  - Analyse the errors/deviations detected in relation to the planning definitions.
  - Use the errors/deviations detected to estimate the total error in the population. This is called *projection* of the errors from the sample to the population.
  - Assess the risk of an incorrect solution. This will be related to the amount of *projection* of error compared with the tolerable error and the availability of alternative evidence.

Judgement sampling

11. This means selecting a sample of appropriate size on the basis of the auditor's judgement of what is desirable. You could call it the 'seat of pants' approach.

   This approach has some advantages:
   a. The approach has been used for many years. It is well understood and refined by experience.
   b. The auditor can bring his judgement and expertise into play. Some auditors seem to have a sixth sense.
   c. No special knowledge of statistics is required.
   d. No time is spent on playing with mathematics. All the audit time is spent on auditing.

12. There are some disadvantages:
   a. It is unscientific.
   b. It is wasteful – usually sample sizes are too large.
   c. No quantitative results are obtained.
   d. Personal bias in the selection of samples is unavoidable.
   e. There is no real logic to the selection of the sample or its size.

f. The sample selection can be slanted to the auditors needs e.g. selection of items near the year end to help with cut-off evaluation.

g. The conclusions reached on the evidence from samples is usually vague – a feeling of 'it seems OK' or of vague disquiet.

13. Overall, judgement sampling is still the preferred method by a majority of auditors. Partly this can be defended on the grounds that the auditor is weighing several strands of evidence (internal control, business background, conversations with employees, subjective feelings, past experience, etc.) and is usually investigating several things at once (e.g. more than one control evidenced on an invoice, proper books, internal control compliance and substantive testing of totals) so that the whole process is too complex to reduce to the simple formulations of the statistician. On the other hand, the statistician can reply that judgement sampling in the past worked well because very large samples were always taken. Today, the small samples required by economic logic require careful measuring of the risks attached and this can only be done by the use of statistical techniques.

Statistical sampling

14. Drawing *inferences* about a large volume of data by an examination of a sample is a highly developed part of the discipline of *statistics*. It seems only common sense for the auditor to draw upon this body of knowledge in his own work. In practice, a high level of mathematical competence is required if valid conclusions are to be drawn from sample evidence. However most firms that use statistical sampling have drawn up complex plans which can be operated by staff without statistical training. These involve the use of tables, graphs or computer methods.

15. The advantages of using statistical sampling are:
   a. It is scientific.
   b. It is defensible.
   c. It provides precise mathematical statements about probabilities of being correct.
   d. It is efficient – overlarge sample sizes are not taken.
   e. It tends to cause uniform standards among different audit firms.
   f. It can be used by lower grade staff who would be unable to apply the judgement needed by judgement sampling.

   There are some disadvantages:
   a. As a technique it is not always fully understood so that false conclusions may be drawn from the results.
   b. Time is spent playing with mathematics which might better be spent on auditing.
   c. Audit judgement takes second place to precise mathematics.
   d. It is inflexible.
   e. Often several attributes of transactions or documents are tested at the same time. Statistics does not easily incorporate this.

   The rest of this chapter describes some of the facts and considerations that auditing students should digest.

Sample selection – characteristics

16. In auditing, a sample should be:

   a. Random – a random sample is one where each item of the population has an equal (or specified) chance of being selected. Statistical inferences may not be valid unless the sample is random.

   b. Representative – the sample should be representative of the differing items in the whole population. For example, it should contain a similar proportion of high and low value items to the population (e.g. all the debtors).

   c. Protective – protective, that is, of the auditor. More intensive auditing should occur on high value items known to be high risk.

   d. Unpredictable – client should not be able to know or guess which items will be examined.

17. There are several methods available to an auditor for selecting items. These include:

   a. **Haphazard** simply choosing items subjectively but avoiding bias. Bias might come in by tendency to favour items in a particular location or in an accessible file or conversely in picking items because they appear unusual. This method is acceptable for non-statistical sampling but is insufficiently rigorous for statistical sampling.

   b. **Simple random** all items in the population have (or are given) a number. Numbers are selected by a means which gives every number an equal chance of being selected. This is done using random number tables or computer or calculator generated random numbers.

   c. **Stratified** this means dividing the population into sub populations (strata = layers) and is useful when parts of the population have higher than normal risk (e.g. high value items, overseas debtors). Frequently high value items form a small part of the population and are 100% checked and the remainder are sampled.

   d. **Cluster sampling** this is useful when data is maintained in clusters (= groups or bunches) as wage records are kept in weeks or sales invoices in months. The idea is to select a cluster randomly and then to examine all the items in the cluster chosen. The problem with this method is that this sample may not be representative.

   e. **Random systematic** this method involves making a random start and then taking every nth item thereafter. This is a commonly use method which saves the work of computing random numbers. However the sample may not be representative as the population may have some serial properties.

   f. **Multi stage sampling** this method is appropriate when data is stored in two or more levels. For example stock in a retail chain of shops. The first stage is to randomly select a sample of shops and the second stage is to randomly select stock items from the chosen shops.

   g. **Block sampling** simply choosing at random one block of items eg all June invoices. This common sampling method has none of the desired characteristics and is not recommended.

   h. **Value weighted selection** this method uses the currency unit value rather than the items as the sampling population. It is now very popular and is described more fully later in the chapter, under *Monetary unit sampling*.

Sample sizes

18. There are several factors which must be considered when deciding upon the sample size. These include:

   a. **Population size** – surprisingly, in most instances this is not important and is only relevant in very small populations.

   b. **Level of confidence** – even a 100% sample (for human concentration reasons) will not give complete assurance. Auditors work to levels of confidence which can be expressed precisely. For example, a 5% confidence level means that there are 19 chances out of 20 that the sample is representative of the population as a whole. Of course, the converse view is that there is one chance in twenty that the sample, on which the auditor draws conclusions, is non-representative of the population as a whole.

   c. **Precision** – from a sample, it is not possible to say that I am 95% certain that, for example, the error rate in a population of stock calculations is x% but only that the error rate is x% $\pm y$% where $\pm y$ is the precision interval. Clearly the level of confidence and the precision interval are related, in that for a given sample size higher confidence can be expressed in a wider precision interval and vice versa.

   d. **Risk** – risk is a highly important concept in modern auditing and in high risk areas (e.g. coding of expense invoices into capital and revenue) a large sample will be desirable, because high confidence levels and narrow precision intervals are required.

   In statistical sampling, risk can be quantified and a particular level chosen.

   There are two types of risk:

   i. α risk – the risk of rejecting a population (e.g. all the stock calculations) when it is in fact right

   ii. β risk – the risk of accepting a population (e.g. debtors) when it in fact contains an unacceptable proportion of errors.

   The alpha and beta risks are related, in that reducing the alpha risk involves an increase in the beta risk and vice versa. If an auditor rejects a population (e.g. stock calculations) he must put his client to more work and also give himself more work. Thus the consequences of alpha risk are only more work and thus economic loss to the auditor. The consequences of beta risk are greater in that Accounts may be approved by the auditor but contain serious error. The costs to the client, the business community and others may be serious. If the errors are subsequently discovered the auditor may lose reputation and may suffer an action for negligence.

   Fortunately, the scientific nature of the auditor's use of statistical theory may well indicate that despite the actual erroneous opinion given by the auditor, his work was satisfactory and he was not negligent.

   e. **Materiality** – this is really a subset of risk. Materiality is fundamental to modern auditing and with all populations being sampled, materiality should be considered in fixing the sample size because:

   i. Populations that are material to the overall audit opinion (e.g. stock in most clients) must be sampled with smaller precision intervals and higher confidence levels.

   ii. Within a population, a materiality factor can be subjectively estimated (e.g. 5% either way on debtors) and precision intervals fixed accordingly.

f. **Subjective factors** – this is a most important and yet difficult area of consideration. The auditor expects to gain audit evidence about a population from a sample. However other audit evidence is available in addition to the evidence from the sample:

The existence of internal controls.

The auditors knowledge of the company, its staff and its environment.

Correlation evidence from other areas subject to audit.

Previous years' experience.

Analytical review.

Gut feeling.

Thus if the only evidence about a population is from the sample then a large sample is required. If the sampling evidence is merely topping up other evidence, then the sample need not be so large.

Most sampling plans used in practice explicitly build in these subjective factors.

g. **Expected error/deviation rate** – the theory requires that the sample size required is a function of the error/deviation rate. This is only known after the results have been evaluated. However, an estimate based on previous experience and knowledge of other factors may give a good indication. If the results indicate that the level of error/deviation was higher than expected, a larger sample may have to be taken.

The level of confidence and precision interval are statistical terms. The level of confidence is a function of the risk that the auditor is willing to accept. It is related to the subjective factors considered. The precision interval is equivalent to the materiality factor or tolerable error.

Tolerable error

19. Tolerable error is the maximum error in the population that auditors are willing to accept and still conclude that audit objectives have been achieved. The tolerable error in a population is usually determined in the planning stage. It is related to and affected by:

– materiality considerations

– assessment of control risk

– results of other audit procedures.

The essential procedure is to set a tolerable error rate and then to *project* the error rate in the population implied by the sampling results and then to compare the two. If the projected error is larger than the tolerable error then further auditing procedures will be necessary in the area.

Statistical sampling audit uses

20. Statistical sampling plans can be used in all auditing situations when evidence about a population is obtained by sampling.

21. Some popular uses include:

Compliance testing – the issue of sales credit notes is controlled by the requirement that all such should be approved by a departmental manager and this approval evidenced by a signature. The auditor would wish to confirm that this control was complied with by sampling the sales credit notes.

Substantive testing – in a client with very unreliable internal controls, the auditor may wish to verify that all despatches in a year have resulted in invoices in that year. The correspondence between despatch note and invoice can be sampled.

- stock calculations can be sampled.
- a sample of debtors only need be circularised.

Sampling methods

22. These include:
    a. Estimation sampling for variables – this method seeks to estimate (with a chosen level of confidence and precision interval) the total value of some population. For example the total value of debtors, stock or loose tools. The procedure is to extrapolate from a sample to an estimate of the total value. This estimate can be compared with the book value and if any difference is within the materiality limits pre-established, the auditor has evidence for the book value of the item.
    b. Estimation sampling for attributes – this method seeks to estimate the proportion of a population having a particular characteristic (= attribute), for example overdue debts or damaged stock or errors in coding invoices.

       Attribute sampling has the disadvantage that it only measures deviations from some norm but does not measure the monetary affect of that deviation. It is generally used in compliance testing where the extent of application of a control is to be determined.
    c. Acceptance sampling – this method seeks to discover the error rate in a population to determine whether the population is acceptable. It involves pre-determining a maximum error rate. Its uses are legion, including:
       i. Whether a control can be relied upon – if non compliance is greater than an acceptable rate, the control will not be relied upon and other audit tests will have to be applied.
       ii. Whether stock calculations can be relied on.

       If the error rate is greater than some acceptable proportion then the auditor will have to request the client to do the calculations again.
    d. Discovery sampling – this method extends acceptance sampling to an acceptance level of nil. For example, a system, with controls, exists in an investment trust company to ensure that all bonus issues are accepted and recorded. If even one bonus issue has not been recorded, the auditor will be unable to accept the controls and will have to seek other evidence. This method has been compared with seeking a needle in a haystack. It requires large samples.

Monetary unit sampling

23. This is a relatively new variant of discovery sampling which is thought to have wide application in auditing. This is because:
    a. Its application is appropriate with large variance populations. Large variance populations are those like debtors or stocks where the members of the population are of widely different sizes.

b. The method is suited to populations where errors are not expected.

c. It implicitly takes into account the auditor's concept of materiality.

24. Procedures are:

a. determine sample size. This will take into account:

    i. the size of the population

    ii. the minimum unacceptable error rate (related to materiality)

    iii. the beta risk desired.

b. List the items in the population (we will use debtors) e.g.

Debtor name	Amount of balance £	Cumulative £
Jones	620	620
Brown & Co.	4	624
XY Co. Ltd	1,320	1,944
JB PLC	220	2,164
RS Acne	4,197	6,361
. . .	. . .	. . .
. . .	. . .	. . .
	384,200	384,200

c. If the sample size were 100 items then take a random start say 1,402 and every 3,842th item thereafter; that is using systematic sampling with a random start.

The idea is that:

    i. the population of debtors is not the 1,250 debtors but 384,200 single £s

    ii. if the particular pound is chosen then the whole balance of which that £1 is a part will be investigated and any error quantified.

In our example, XY Co. Ltd, would be selected since 1,402 lies in their balance and RS Acne would also be chosen as 1,402 and 3,842 lies in their balance.

Note that the larger balances have a greater chance of being selected. This is protective for the auditor but it has been pointed out that balances that contain errors of understatement will have reduced chance of detection.

d. At the end of the process, evaluate the result which might be a conclusion that the auditor is 95% confident that the debtors are not overstated by more than £x. £x is the materiality factor chosen. If the conclusion is that the auditor finds that the debtors appear to be overstated by more than £x then he may take a larger sample and/or investigate the debtors more fully.

25. MUS (monetry unit sampling) has some disadvantages:

a. It does not cope easily with errors of understatement. A debtor balance which is underestimated will have a smaller chance of being selected than if it was correctly valued. Hence there is a reduced chance of selecting that balance and discovering the error.

b. It can be difficult to select samples if a computer cannot be used as manual selection will involve adding cumulatively through the population.

c. It is not possible to extend a sample if the error rate turns out to be higher than expected. In such cases an entirely new sample must be selected and evaluated.

26. MUS is especially useful in testing for overstatement where significant understatements are not expected. Examples of applications include debtors, fixed assets and stock. It is clearly not suitable for testing creditors where understatement is the primary characteristic to be tested.

Working papers

27. As in all audit work, the work done in audit sampling situations should be fully documented in the working papers. In particular the documentation in the working papers should show:

Planning the sample

a. Stating the audit objectives.

b. Definition of error or deviation.

c. The means of determining the sample size.

d. The tolerable error rate.

Selecting the items to be tested

e. The selection method used.

f. details of the items selected.

Testing the items

g. The tests carried out.

h. The errors or deviations noted.

Evaluating the results of the tests

i. Explanations of the causes of the errors or deviations.

j. The projection of errors or deviations.

k. The auditor's assessment of the assurance obtained as to the possible size of actual error or deviation rate.

l. The nature and details of the conclusions drawn from the sample results.

m. Details of further action taken where required (e.g. a larger sample or other forms of evidence gathering).

Summary

28. a. Traditionally, auditors have relied upon test checks or samples in forming conclusions about populations of data.

b. The size and composition of samples can be determined by the judgement of the auditor.

c. Alternatively statistical methods can be used. These have the advantage of enabling the auditor to draw conclusions like 'I am 95% certain that the error rate in the wage calculations is 1.4% ± .3%'.

d. Samples should be random, representative, protective and unpredictable.

e. Sample selection methods include haphazard, random, stratified, cluster, random systematic, multistage, block, and value weighted.

f.   Sample sizes are a function of:

population size, confidence levels and precision limits.

g.   Confidence levels and precision limits are a function of risk assessment, materiality and other subjective factors relating to other forms of audit evidence (internal control, analytical review, knowledge of the business, correlative factors).

h.   Statistical sampling can be used in all areas of an audit and with both compliance and substantive tests.

i.   Sampling methods include estimation sampling for variables, estimation sampling for attributes, acceptance and discovery sampling.

j.   A newly developed method of interest is monetary unit sampling (MUS).

Points to note

29. a.   The design of the sampling plans used by firms of accountants is a technical matter best done by the statistically trained.

b.   A manual of this kind is not the right place to teach the mechanics of sampling. There are several excellent works available on statistical sampling for accountants and auditors.

c.   Professional auditing examiners do not require a knowledge of the technical aspects of sampling beyond that given in this chapter.

d.   Materiality is very important in auditing. In sampling, materiality manifests itself in the term 'tolerable error' which is related to the statistical term precision interval.

e.   Risk is also a very important concept in auditing. The degree of risk determines the degree of assurance an auditor requires in an audit area. In statistical sampling this is related to the level of confidence required.

f.   Statistical sampling as an audit tool, like risk analysis, promises much but in practice delivers little. The problem presents itself to an auditor as 'What is an acceptable risk?' or 'What is the probability that these accounts or that figure contain an inaccuracy?'. These problems are incapable of quantification although most auditors could make a subjective assessment as to the risk being low, medium or high.

All auditors take a risk when they express a clean opinion on a set of accounts. However the risk may seem less acceptable in some circumstances. For examples:

–   when external users are sure to use the accounts (e.g. the bank in renewing a loan or a potential buyer of the company)

–   when the company is in facing financial problems if say it is possible that the company may go into receivership.

Case study 1

Hoopoe PLC are an old established large food processing company mainly buying poultry from local farmers, freezing them and selling them to retailers on credit terms. Assets employed total £6 million, turnover £15 million, profits are £1.8 million and debtors are £3 million. The company have excellent internal controls which the auditor has evaluated at the interim audit. The auditor is examining the debtors schedule. He finds that there are 3,900 items upon it. Four balances are over £100,000, being to large supermarket chains. 162 balances totalling £114,000 are for customers overseas.

Discussion

a. Discuss the tolerable error that might be acceptable in the case of debtors.

b. What audit risk factors are relevant? What substantive tests and analytical review techniques will enable the audit to reduce the detection risk?

c. What stratification will be required?

d. Outline the stages of a suitable audit sampling approach to the debtors in this case, determining the audit objectives, the population, the sampling unit, the definition of error, the sample selection method, and the sampling method. In each area, discuss the difficulties which might be encountered.

Case study 2

Sheek Clothing PLC is a retailer with 200 branches throughout the UK. Most of the branches are small. The stock and cut-off is a very significant item in the financial statements. Stock is counted physically at all branches on the nearest Sunday to March 31 and that Sunday becomes the year end. Each branch buys some stock on its own initiative and some from the company's central buying department in Birmingham.

Discussion

The auditors, Tick & Co., are planning the audit of stock in March 20-5. How might they use statistical or other sampling methods?

Student self testing questions *Questions with answers apparent from the text*

1. a. Why is a 100% check no longer usual in auditing? (1)
   b. Where is 100% check still applied? (2)
   c. What is meant by: representative, population; sampling units? (7)
   d. What is 'tolerable error' and how is it related to materiality? (8, 19)
   e. What is inherent risk, control risk, detection risk? (8)
      Give examples of each.
   f. What factors are relevant in considering whether to sample? (9)
   g. List the stages in sampling. (10)
   h. An auditor is looking at purchases. Should he see the population to be sampled as all goods entered in the goods received book or all purchase invoices? (10)
   i. An auditor is sampling (statistically) purchase invoices to ensure that all are checked against goods inwards notes. Such checks are evidenced by the signature of a clerk in a grid. Given the population size (25,000), the sample size (500) and that 24 items carried no signature, what should the auditor do? What conclusions can be drawn? Do this mathematically if you can or give the type of statement that can be made. Relate this statement to the audit objectives. (10)
   j. When is stratification desirable? (10)
   k. List the sampling methods available. (22)
   l. List the advantages and disadvantages of judgement sampling and of statistical sampling. (11, 12, 15)
   m. List some sample selection methods. (17)
   n. Distinguish level of confidence from precision interval. (18)
   o. Distinguish α (alpha) risk from β (beta) risk. (18)

p. List some statistical sampling techniques. (22)
q. Explain monetary unit sampling. (23)
r. Why is MUS not good for testing understatement? (25)
s. What is tolerable error? (19)

Examination questions

1. As a recently qualified accountant you joined the staff of a small professional firm a short time ago. Your first responsibility was to conduct the audit of the firm's major client, Western Chemicals PLC. You followed the traditionally audit programme which has been used by your employer for many years and relies extensively on traditional judgement sampling.

    During the audit a number of ideas occurred to you which you feel would be of benefit to your employer for future audits of his client.

    Required:

    Draft a memorandum to the partner responsible for the audit in which you:

    a. briefly state the advantages and disadvantages of following audit programmes which rely on traditional judgement sampling;   (10 marks)
    b. describe the statistical sampling techniques of random sampling and stratified sampling;   (3 marks)
    c. outline the advantages and disadvantages of statistical sampling techniques as opposed to traditional judgement sampling.   (7 marks)
                                                                                                   (ACCA)

2. It is important to recognise that audit sampling may be constructed on a non-statistical basis. If the auditor uses statistical sampling, probability theory will be used to determine sample size and random selection methods to ensure each item or £1 in value of the population has the same chance of selection. Non-statistical sampling, is more subjective than statistical sampling, typically using haphazard selection methods and placing no reliance upon probability theory. However, in certain circumstances statistical sampling techniques may be difficult to use. The auditor will review the circumstances of each audit before deciding whether to use statistical or non-statistical sampling.

    Required:

    a. List three situations where the auditor would be unlikely to use audit sampling techniques.   (3 marks)
    b. Explain what you understand by the following terms:
        i.   attribute sampling
        ii. monetary unit sampling.   (6 marks)
    c. Describe the factors which the auditor should consider when determining the size of a sample.   (6 marks)
    d. Describe to what extent statistical sampling enhances the quality of the audit evidence.   (5 marks)
                                                                                                   (ACCA)

28 Reliance on other specialists

Introduction

1. SAS 100 requires that an auditor should carry out procedures designed to obtain *sufficient appropriate audit evidence* to determine with reasonable confidence whether the financial statements are free of material misstatement.

2. In general the auditor's programme of work will provide him with sufficient reliable relevant evidence to enable him to give an unqualified opinion. However there can be circumstances where the auditor's knowledge is insufficient and he may then need to rely on the opinions of experts or specialists to help him form an opinion. This chapter is about reliance on other specialists.

3. There are Statements of Auditing Standards SAS 520 and ISA 620 *Using the Work of an Expert.*

Examples

4. Examples of specialists whose work may be relied upon by auditors include:

   a. Valuers – on the value of fixed assets such as freehold and leasehold property or more rarely plant and machinery and on the value of specialist stock in trade such as works of art, antiques, precious stones etc.

   b. Quantity surveyors – on the value of work done on long-term contracts.

   c. Actuaries – on the liability to be included for pension scheme liabilities.

   d. Geologists – on the quantity and quality of mineral reserves.

   e. Stockbrokers – on the value of stock exchanges securities.

   f. Lawyers – on the legal interpretation of contracts and agreements, or the outcome of disputes and litigation.

When will specialist opinions be relied on?

5. In certain kinds of businesses specialist opinions are a primary source of evidence. For example civil engineering businesses often employ independent quantity surveyors to value work in progress. Often an auditor has little other evidence on which to base his opinion on such values. Property companies incorporate values of properties in their accounts. The source of such valuations being specialist valuers. The auditor may have no other evidence except the specialist valuer's opinion.

6. Except in cases such as those in Paras. 4 and 5 the auditor does not need to seek specialist opinions because he has sufficient internal evidence or because the matter is not material. However there can be situations where an expert opinion may be essential evidence. For example the client, an entertainment management agency, has a contract which may or may not involve the payment of royalties to a former manager of an entertainer under contract. The matter has not yet gone to litigation and may well be settled amicably. If the amount payable is either nil or £50,000 depending on the interpretation of the contract then if the client's profit is £2 million then the matter is not material and the auditor will be content to accept either interpretation. If however the client is a small

one and £50,000 is very important to the view given by the Accounts, then the auditor may wish the client to seek specialist legal advice.

7. In general in deciding whether the auditor needs to have specialist opinions he will consider:

   a. The materiality of the item.

   b. The risk of significant error in an item. For example the amount of the value of some antiques valued at net realisable value may be material but any error in valuation may have only a small chance of being materially wrong. On the other hand, the risk of significant error in an assessment of the extractability of mineral from a mine may be very high.

   c. The complexity of the information and his own understanding of it and any specialism relating to it. The obligations of a client under a complex lease agreement involving a development property in Spain may require the opinion of a lawyer skilled in both English and Spanish Law.

   d. Other sources of audit evidence available on the matter.

The reliability of the specialist

8. Factors which may influence the auditor to rely upon or not to rely upon the work of a specialist include:

   a. **The competence of the specialist**. This may be indicated by technical qualifications, certification and licensing, membership of professional bodies, experience and reputation.

   b. **The independence of the specialist**. The degree of relationship with the client may be the key factor. Any specialist who is related to the directors or employees of the client or who has financial interest (other than his fee) with the client is clearly less than wholly independent. Apparent dependence may be mitigated by professional body disciplinary and ethical codes.

Agreement

9. If it is the intention of the auditor to place reliance on the work of a specialist, it is important to hold a consultation between auditor, client and specialist, at the time the specialist is appointed, to reach agreement on the work to be performed. The agreement should cover:

   a. Objectives, scope and subject matter of the specialist's work.

   b. Assumptions upon which the specialist's report depends and their compatibility with the Accounts. For example, are going concern or market values to be taken.

   c. A statement of the bases used in previous years and any change to be made.

   d. The use to be made of the specialist's findings. (He may need this for professional indemnity insurance purposes.)

   e. The form and content of the specialist's report or opinion.

   f. The sources of information to be provided to the specialist.

   g. The identification of any relationship which may affect the specialist's objectivity. An example of this may be the case of an architect who though in private practice obtains most of his commissions from the client who is subject to audit.

It is possible to use a specialist's opinion without this process but it is desirable to go through this procedure.

Evaluation of the specialist evidence

10. The sufficiency and reliability of such evidence will depend upon the nature of the evidence, the circumstances necessitating its preparation, the materiality of the matter and the auditor's assessment of the competence of the specialist and his independence from the client. In particular, the auditor should consider:

   a. Whether the opinion is given in accordance with an agreement such as that specified in Para. 9 above.

   b. Whether the data is compatible with the data used in preparing the financial statements.

   c. Whether the consistency convention has been followed.

   d. Whether the evidence appears to be reasonable. The auditor can often have an opinion on property values but the assessment of geological data may not be possible.

   e. Whether the specialist's findings have been incorporated correctly in the accounts.

   f. The effective date of the specialist's findings is acceptable. This relates to the importance of the date of the auditor's own report.

   g. Whether the specialist has qualified his/her opinion, or expressed any reservations.

   h. When the specialist has reported in previous years, whether the findings are compatible with those of earlier years.

   In any event, the auditor must apply his intellect to understanding at least the assumptions made and bases of valuation used.

   If the auditor is unable to reply upon the findings (e.g. if the specialist did not use data specified to him and also used in the accounts), then he may request the client to obtain an opinion from another specialist. This may seem extreme but in some cases it might avoid an audit report qualification.

The audit report

11. The auditor should not refer in his own report to any specialist opinion he has relied on because the auditor is solely responsible for his opinion and cannot share this responsibility.

12. The auditor may have to qualify his report when:

   a. The matter is material.

   b. There is no specialist evidence available and no satisfactory alternative evidence is available or when the auditor cannot rely on the specialist's evidence.

13. Qualification is only likely to be necessary:

   a. Where management are unable or unwilling to obtain necessary specialist evidence.

   b. Where the relevance or reliability of the specialist's evidence is uncertain.

   c. Where management refuses to accept or incorporate the evidence in the accounts.

   d. Where the management refuse to obtain a second opinion when the auditor deems it necessary.

Summary

14. a. In some cases, the opinion of a specialist would be essential evidence to an auditor.

   b. The specialist should have his terms of agreement drawn up after consultation with the auditor.

Points to note

15. a. An expert may be engaged by or employed by the entity or the auditor. When the expert is employed by the auditor then SAS 240 *Quality Control for Audit Work* will apply to the work.

   b. Auditors should never uncritically accept the opinion of a specialist.

   c. Corroborative evidence should always be sought.

   d. In all cases, the auditor has to consider whether he has relevant and reliable audit evidence which is sufficient to enable him to draw reasonable conclusions.

Case study 1

The Lonzim Co. Ltd, has invested 30% of its funds in a tract of land in Mambabwe. The company have spent the money on the land, mineral licences, prospecting and sundry works preparatory to extraction of the mineral Hedonite from which the rare metal Millenium can be obtained. The viability of the scheme is totally dependent on the quantity of ore in the mine and the quantity of Millenium in the ore. The company have taken a gamble on the matter following the findings of Clem Entyne, an employee of long standing, who has measured the size of the lode to his satisfaction with 'on site' borings and has sent to London samples which have been analysed and show a high proportion of Millenium. The auditor of the company John Orr is planning the audit of the year ending 31 December 20-7 in August 20-7.

Discussion

   a. How, in detail, might Orr obtain sufficient evidence for the appropriateness of the going concern basis for the assets in Mambabwe?

   b. How might the actual value of the assets there be verified?

Case study 2

Hermit Galleries PLC are international art dealers with a turnover of £30 million a year. They specialise in impressionist paintings and have a stock valued at £10 million. Recently it has been rumoured that some £4 million worth of their stock may be the work of a particularly brilliant forger.

Towards the end of the financial year the company have agreed with the auditor to commission a report on the authenticity of the stock from a well-known academic expert.

Discussion

Draw up the terms of reference for the expert.

Draft a check list to examine the expert's report as audit evidence.

The actual expert's opinion was certainty on the authenticity of 1.1 million pounds worth, certainty on the forged nature of 1.6 million pounds worth and doubt about the remainder.

What should the auditor do?

Student self testing questions *Questions with answers apparent from the text*

1. a. Give examples of reliance by auditors on the evidence supplied by specialists. (4)
    b. In what conditions may such reliance be required? (5)
    c. What factors indicate the reliability of the specialist? (8)
    d. What terms should appear in the agreement? (9)
    e. How should the auditor evaluate the evidence? (10)
    f. What might appear in the auditor's report on these matters? (11, 12)
    g. What should not appear in the report? (11)

Examination questions without answers

1. When verifying assets, the auditor will often have to rely on external confirmation of assets by third parties.

    Required:

    a. Indicate the major items which may need to be verified in this way. Who would be responsible for making the confirmation?   (6 marks)
    b. What points should the auditor consider when seeking to rely on third party verification?   (3 marks)
    c. What are the main items that should be included in the letter sent to a bank for audit purposes?   (6 marks)

    (AAT) (Total 15 marks)

2. Paragraph 4 of the Auditing Standard L101, *The Auditor's Operational Standard*, states that the auditor should obtain relevant and reliable audit evidence sufficient to enable him to draw reasonable conclusions therefrom.

    During the course of the audit, the auditor may need to consider audit evidence in the form of statistical data, reports, opinions, valuations or statements from specialists.

    Requirement:

    a. List 5 examples of situations where an auditor may wish to rely upon the report of a specialist.   (5 marks)
    b. Describe the principles that the auditor should follow when he wishes to place reliance on audit evidence provided by specialists.   (11 marks)

    (ICAI) (Total 16 marks)

29 Service organisations

Introduction

1. In the last 25 or so years there has been a substantial increase in the use of service organisations known as 'outsourcing'. This means using outside specialist organisations to perform functions which would otherwise be performed 'in house' or 'insourced'. Functions outsourced include:

   a. Information processing.

   b. Maintenance of accounting records.

   c. Facilities management.

   d. Maintenance of safe custody of assets, such as investments.

   e. Initiation or execution of transactions on behalf of the other entity.

   The use of service organisations can create considerable problems for auditors and this chapter considers the issues. There is SAS 480 *Service Organisations* and there is also an ISA 402 *'Audit Considerations Relating to Entities Using Service Organisations'*.

Why do firms outsource?

2. a. The problems of employing personnel (e.g. employment legislation, health and safety etc.) are passed on to others.

   b. It is often cheaper.

   c. Expertise is not available in house.

   d. Service organisations can keep up to date on equipment and expertise more easily than the user enterprise in a fast moving world.

   e. It reduces the time top management have to spend on housekeeping functions.

   f. Internal resources are freed for more productive activities.

Planning the audit

3. The auditor should, as always, obtain a knowledge of the client's business.

   The auditor, in planning the audit, should determine which activities are undertaken by service organisations and which are relevant to the audit.

   Likely areas for concern include:

   a. Accounting records.

   b. Other finance functions e.g. tax, payroll, debtor management, credit control.

   c. Management of assets.

   d. Undertaking or making arrangements for transactions as agent of the entity.

   The latter item may include firms selling on the Internet who outsource the collection of sales proceeds from service organisations which deal with credit card processing.

   Some outsourced function will have little relevance to the audit – for example office cleaning.

   Once the auditor has determined which outsourced functions are pertinent to the audit, she needs to assess the possible impact on the audit. Possible areas of concern include risk of misstatement in the financial statements and whether or not proper accounting records have been kept.

Having assessed the risks, the auditor can plan her actions in relation to each relevant outsourced function.

Contractual terms and obligations

4. The auditor should obtain and document an understanding of the contracted terms which apply to relevant activities and the way the user monitors those activities so as to ensure that it meets its fiduciary and other legal responsibilities.

Relevant points here include:

a. Right of access, by the user and /or the auditor to records held by the outsourcing company.

b. Whether the terms take proper account of statutory or regulatory body requirements. Of particular importance is the Companies Act requirement for proper accounting records.

c. Performance standards.

d. The extent of reliance on controls operated by the service organisation.

e. The indemnity offered to the user.

The first point is especially important as lack of access to records may mean that the auditor has to qualify his report on the grounds of limitation of scope.

Inherent risk

5. The auditor should determine the effect of relevant activities on her assessment of inherent risk and the user entity's control environment.

The first issue is the competence, integrity and going concern status of the outsourcing company. Items include:

a. The reputation of the service organisation for competence and integrity.

b. The existence of external supervision e.g. of investment management by regulatory authorities.

c. The extent to which indemnities offered by the outsourcer can be honoured.

The latter matter may be important if the accounting records were lost and the outsourcer could not honour its indemnity due to insolvency. This may then even affect the going concern status of the client.

Control risk

6. Issues here include:

a. The extent of controls operated by user personnel.

b. The extent of undertakings by the outsourcing company on controls.

c. User experience of errors and omissions.

d. The degree of monitoring by the user.

e. The extent of information on controls provided by the outsourcer.

f. The quality assurance in the outsourcer e.g. ISOs or internal audit.

Accounting records

7. When any or all of the accounting records are outsourced, the auditor faces special problems. These include:

    a. Whether the requirements of S 221 Companies Act have been met.

    b. Whether the requirements of any relevant regulatory bodies (e.g. IMRO) have been met.

    c. Whether all the information and explanations required by the auditor have been available.

    d. Whether all information required by The Corporate Governance Code (e.g. on directors' remuneration and internal controls) is available.

    e. Whether the records generally accord with relevant law and regulations.

    f. Whether all required audit evidence is available.

Audit evidence

8. Various approaches are available to satisfy the auditor's needs and these include:

    a. Inspecting records and documents held by the user.

    b. Establishing the effectiveness of controls in the user.

    c. Obtaining an undertaking by the outsourcer that its control systems do provide assurance as to the reliability of financial information.

    d. Obtaining representations to confirm balances and transactions from the service organisation.

    e. Analytical review of such records as are held by the audit client, and of returns and reports received by the client from the service organisation.

    f. Inspecting records and documents held by the service organisation.

    g. Reviewing information from the outsourcer and its auditors on the design and operation of internal controls operated by the outsourcer.

    h. Requesting the service organisation auditors or the user's internal audit function to perform specified procedures.

    The latter approach is perhaps very powerful but its application depends on the service agreement between the service organisation and the user.

Reports by service organisation's auditors

9. One possible piece of audit evidence is a report issued by the service organisation's auditors. These can be issued to user auditors and might cover such matters as:

    a. a description of the service organisation's accounting and internal control systems, ordinarily prepared by the management of the service organisation; and

    b. an opinion by the service organisation auditor that:

        i. the above description is accurate

        ii. the systems' controls have been placed in operation

        iii. the accounting and internal control systems are suitably designed to achieve their stated objectives; and

        iv. the accounting and internal control systems are operating effectively based on the results from the tests of control. In addition to the opinion on operating effectiveness the service organisation auditor would identify the tests of control performed and related results.

The user auditor then has to assess the report for sufficiency and reliability. She might do this by:

a. Assessing the standing and reputation of the service organisation's auditor.

b. Assessing the scope of the work performed.

c. Assess whether the report is sufficient and appropriate for its intended use.

A critical aspect of the report is the period covered. The user auditor must be content that the accounting records and the concomitant controls and systems were adequate for the whole period covered by the financial statements.

Summary

10. a. Outsourcing is a common way of dealing with many necessary functions.

b. This can present problems for an auditor, especially if accounting functions are outsourced.

c. Auditors need to obtain knowledge of all functions outsourced by the client.

d. The user auditor needs evidence that proper books of account have been kept and that the records form a reliable basis for the preparation of the financial statements.

e. Various approaches are possible in assessing the records including the records and controls operated by the user, assessing the competence, integrity and going concern status of the outsourcer, assessing the reports by the outsourcer and its auditor, inspecting the records at the outsourcer.

Points to note

11. a. Using service organisations or outsourcing is increasing but happily many outsourced functions pose few difficulties for the auditor. However the outsourcing of some or all of the accounting functions does pose real difficulties for the auditor.

b. The user's auditor should be wary of accepting the certificates of the outsourcing company or its auditor without considerable enquiry. Ultimately the user auditor needs to be satisfied that the records meet statutory and other requirements, form a reliable basis for the preparation of the financial statements and are adequately controlled. Enquiry should be made of the standing and competence of the outsourcer and its auditor and that the certificates cover all the relevant times and records and that testing was adequate.

Case study 1

Cuthbert Ltd outsources most of its accounting function to Sham Accounting Services Ltd. They have found the relationship with Sham very effective. However recently it has come to Cuthbert's attention that the statements of account sent by Cuthbert's main supplier have not been successfully reconciled for six months. The Chairman of Cuthbert has also heard a rumour that Sham are in financial difficulties.

Sham have sent a report by Ticketyboo & Co. their auditors, on the suitability of design and operating effectiveness of the system by which Cuthbert's records are maintained.

Magenta & Co., the auditors of Cuthbert, are engaged on the audit of Cuthbert for the year ended 31 December 200x.

Discussion

a. Why might Cuthbert Ltd outsource its accounting function?

b. What risks do Cuthbert Ltd run as a result of the outsourcing and how might these risks impinge on the financial statements?

c. What risks do Magenta run in the conduct of the audit?

d. Draw up a check list of matters that might concern Magenta on the issue.

e. Outline an audit programme for the audit.

Case study 2

Hippay PLC, a listed company, have outsourced their employee (including directors) remuneration to a service organisation. The company write bespoke and general application software for environmental recording.

Discussion

a. Discuss the business risks attached to this company both in general and in respect of the outsourcing.

b. Discuss the problems occasioned to the auditors by the outsourcing and how they might be overcome.

Student self testing questions

a. What SAS and IAS relate to service organisations? (1)

b. Why do firms outsource? (2)

c. What clauses in an outsourcing contract may be relevant to the auditor? (4)

d. List risks which arise to a firm as a result of outsourcing. (5)

e. What special risks arise form outsourcing accounting records? (7)

f. List actions that an audit can take to amass audit evidence in the presence of an outsourced function. (8) What might be covered in a report to users by an outsourcer's auditor? (9)

g. What actions should the user's auditor take in respect of such a report? (9)

Examination question

1. You are the auditor of Minexpo Ltd, a small company. In order to reduce the company's administrative costs the financial director proposes transferring all the electronic data processing for debtors and creditors to a computer bureau.

Requirement:

a. State two problems this may present to the auditor.

b. How may the auditor overcome the problems you have listed in (a) above?

(16 marks)

(LCCI)

Review of financial statements

1. The final stage of an audit is the analytical review by a senior member of the audit team of the financial statements. The objectives of this review are:

   a. to provide audit evidence by determining if the financial statements provide information which is both internally consistent and consistent with other information in the possession of the auditor (knowledge of the environment, the enterprise and of his detailed audit tests)

   b. to determine if the financial statements have been prepared using acceptable accounting policies, comply with Accounting Standards and other requirements and that there is adequate disclosure of relevant matters.

2. To conclude this section there are chapters on the true and fair view and on representations by management.

30 The final review stage of the audit

Introduction

1. At the end of the detailed work of the audit, auditors make an *overall review* of the financial statements before preparing their report. The review should be sufficiently detailed to enable the auditors, in conjunction with the conclusions drawn from the other audit evidence obtained, to give them a reasonable basis for their opinion on the financial statements.

2. There is a short Statement of Auditing Standards SAS 470 *Overall Review of Financial Statements*

The stages of an audit

3. The auditor next gathers audit *evidence* about *individual* items and *groups* of items which together make up the accounts.

4. The auditor is then in a position of knowing that he has sufficient evidence to substantiate the details of the accounts. He then needs to determine if the *accounts as a whole* have certain qualities. The final review assists in this determination.

The qualities required of final accounts

5. The final review is designed to elucidate the following qualities which hopefully are possessed by the final accounts.

   a. That they use acceptable accounting policies, which have been consistently applied and are appropriate to the business. Note that an acceptable policy (e.g. reducing balance depreciation) may be inappropriate for some assets (e.g. leaseholds or quarries).

   b. The results of operations (profit and loss account), state of affairs (balance sheet) and all other information included in the financial statements are *compatible* with each other and with the auditor's knowledge of the enterprise.

c. There is adequate *disclosure* of all appropriate matters and the information contained in the financial statements is suitably *classified* and *presented* (for example, a loan to a subsidiary should not be described as cash at bank).

d. There is compliance with statutory requirements (for example, the Companies Act).

e. There is compliance with other relevant regulations (for example stock exchange regulations).

f. There is compliance with accounting standards.

Auditor qualities

6. The auditor who performs a review needs certain qualities. These are:

a. An ability to distinguish between non-material, *material* and *fundamental* items.

b. An ability to assess the information gathered in the audit, for *accuracy* and *completeness*.

c. Skill, imagination and judgement.

d. An ability to recognise apparent *inconsistencies* which might indicate areas where errors, omissions, frauds or irregularities have occurred which might not have been revealed by the routine auditing procedures.

e. An ability to assess whether or not an audit opinion is possible at all.

Procedures

7. The following set of procedures should be adopted for the final review:

a. Accounting policies

Consider if they:

   i. are in accordance with *generally accepted accounting principles (GAAP)* and comply with the fundamental accounting concepts – going concern, accruals, consistency and prudence. They must also conform to the substance over form convention.

   ii. are acceptable to the particular circumstances

   iii. are commonly adopted in the particular industry

   iv. are consistently applied over the years

   v. are consistently applied throughout the enterprise

   vi. comply with all relevant accounting standards

   vii. are adequately disclosed in accordance with SSAP 2.

b. The circumstances of the enterprise

   i. Consider if the accounts are consistent with the auditor's knowledge of the underlying circumstances of the business and the information, explanations and conclusions reached on the audit.

   ii. Review the information in the accounts to determine if there are any abnormalities or inconsistencies. Background knowledge of the company is clearly essential for this.

c. Presentation and disclosure

   i. Consider if any conclusion that a reader might draw from his reading of the accounts would be justified and is consistent with the circumstances of the enterprise.

  ii. Consider if the substance of any transactions or activities is disclosed and not merely their form.

  iii. Consider if the presentation might have been unduly influenced by management's desire to present facts in a favourable light.

  iv. Consider if the review has indicated that there are new factors which might alter the policies used or the presentation of the accounts, and, special attention needs to be paid to going concern difficulties.

 d. Consider if all matters of importance have been disclosed by way of note if not in the financial statements.

Example

8. A final review by the auditor of Elspeth Carpet Manufacturing Ltd, using checklists revealed:

 a. Stocks of raw wool had been valued at replacement price. This was not equal to cost or net realisable value.

 b. Interest was shown in the profit and loss account as one sum notwithstanding that the company has both short and long-term loans.

 c. Debtors included a loan to a director of £7,500.

 d. The relationship between disclosed wages costs and disclosed social security costs had changed from the previous year.

 e. Trade creditors had changed from 38 days last year to 23 days this year.

 f. No depreciation had been charged on the company's new warehouse.

 g. The gain on the sale of an unwanted piece of land had been credited to administrative costs.

I will leave to the reader to work out the implications of these.

Summary

9. The final stages of an audit include a review of the financial statements, carried out by a suitably experienced senior or partner. The matter is covered by SAS 470.

Points to note

10. The final review is particularly important as current auditing opinion is moving more towards a consideration of the view given to users by financial statements. Of course, the detail is still important but emphasis must be on the view given by the accounts which must be true in detail and fair in totality.

11. The final review may reveal:

 a. That all is well.

 b. That further audit evidence may be required in some areas.

 c. That amendment to the accounts may be desirable. The client should be requested to make any such amendment.

 d. That a qualified audit report may be required.

12. An historical progression can be discerned in audit evidence gathering:

 a. Vouching of all transactions.

 b. Vouching of a sample of transactions – test checking.

c. Reliance on systems with compliance testing.

d. Analytical review techniques.

The emphasis in earlier times was on a. There is much more emphasis today on analytical review techniques. The final review stage of an audit is really a subset of the analytical review techniques spelt out in Chapter 16.

13. The Overall Review of Financial Statements is concerned with:

a. Accounting policies.

b. The results etc. are compatible with each other and with the auditor's knowledge of the enterprise.

c. Disclosure.

d. Statutory and other regulations.

e. What type of opinion, if any, can be given.

Case study

Angela is engaged on the 20-6 audit of Feloni Ltd who are printers and publishers of sheet music. She has noted the accounting policy disclosure statement which shows:

a. Stock is valued at the lower of cost and net realisable value. Cost includes production overheads based on a global labour hour rate based on output in 20-6. Unsold stocks of sheet music printed before 31.12.20-5 are written down to £1.

b. Advances to composers are written off as they are paid.

c. Plant is written off on the straight line basis over ten years.

d. The freehold property is amortised over 30 years.

She has also noted that:

a. The directors' report is optimistic about the current year and future year's success in selling old titles due to a revival of 70's music.

b. Stocks appear simply as stocks £120,000.

c. The company rents out a leasehold property it owns but has no use for. The notes to the accounts say Gross Rental Income £4,900.

d. No mention is made of the entry into liquidation on 13.3.-7 of a wholesale music warehouse who owed Feloni £142,000 on 13.3.-7 and £71,000 on 31.12.-6. Angela knows of the liquidation as her boss is the liquidator.

e. No mention is made of an action against a pop group for breach of copyright. The action was commenced on 31.3.-6 and already uncharged legal fees of about £10,000 have been incurred.

f. The list of directors shows 14 names and the remuneration breakdown only 13.

g. The directors' report shows that Joe Gigli, a director, has 1,000 shares in the company. She happened to note that the dividend paid to him indicated a shareholding substantially greater than that.

Discussion

What should Angela do about these matters?

Student self testing questions *Questions with answers apparent from the text*

1. a. What qualities are required of final accounts? (5)

b. What qualities are required of auditors? (6)

c. List the procedures required. (7)

d. What actions may be required as a result of a final review? (11)

e. Distinguish analytical review from overall review of financial statements. (12)

Exercises

1. The Harbridge Group PLC include in their annual report and accounts a statement of accounting policies. This statement includes the following:

   a. Government grants received in respect of capital expenditure on plant are being amortised to revenue over a period of five years.

   b. Stock has been valued at the lower of cost and net realisable value. Cost in the case of manufactured finished goods is standard total absorption cost.

   c. All plant and machinery is depreciated on a straight line basis over its estimated life which varies from seven to twelve years.

   d. Development expenditure on new products is included in stock in trade.

   e. Land and buildings including the investment properties in central London are depreciated on the straight line method over 50 years.

   f. Profits on sales to certain South American countries are taken to profit and loss account on receipt of the relevant cash which may be before or after the despatch of the goods.

   Required:

   Discuss these policies from the point of view of the true and fair view.

2. In conducting her final analytical review of the Accounts of San Serif Ltd a printing company, Geraldine the auditor discovers:

   – All plant is written off over five years but much of the plant is much older and works very well.

   – The company print a line of analysis paper which is sold by mail order to the accounting profession. Stocks of this paper are valued at paper cost only.

   – There is a 10% general provision for doubtful debts. Actual bad debts are few.

   The Managing Director is asked about these items and points out:

   – these policies have been used for many years;

   – surely it is OK to understate profits;

   – we do not want to pay lots of corporation tax or dividends.

   Required:

   Discuss this matter from the point of view of the true and fair view. (Hint – you may find it useful to consider expectation.)

Examination questions

1. You are the auditor of M Ltd, a company which manufactures three basic products, all of which are components for the electronics industry. The company sells to three major customers who account for 90% of the company's turnover, the remaining 10% of sales being to overseas customers. The company's year end is 31 December and for stock valuation purposes all completed components in stock at that date are valued using their standard costs.

(Note: There is no work in progress and no production takes place on the last day of the year.)

The standard costs are revised quarterly and those set at 1 October are used for year-end stock valuation purposes. Details of stock for the year ended 31 December 1984 are as follows:

		Component		Total Value of Stock at 31 Dec 1984
	A	B	C	
Number in stock at 31 December 1984	25,200	8,150	17,700	
Standard cost at 1 October 1984	£0.73	£2.16	£1.85	
Value at 31 December 1984 (using 1 Oct standard costs)	£18,396	£17,604	£32,745	£68,745
Number of components sold in year	55,420	48,900	92,400	
Standard cost of components sold in year	£39,600	£100,245	£166,320	
Actual cost of components sold in year	£40,350	£140,345	£150,850	
Revised standards for the quarter commencing 1 Jan 85 are as follows	£0.74	£2.20	£1.55	

Required:

a. Explain under what conditions standard costs may be used for year-end stock valuation purposes. (2 marks)

b. Using the figures given above carry out a review to determine the areas that do not appear to make sense and thus the areas on which the auditor would concentrate when substantiating the stock valued at £68,745 in the financial statement as at 31 December 1984. (12 marks)

c. State the TWO critical matters to be considered when auditing the standard labour cost and describe TWO audit tests that you would perform in substantiating such cost. (6 marks)

(ACCA) (20 marks)

2. You have gathered sufficient audit evidence to allow your review of the final accounts for publication of Frog PLC.

What matters would you look for in the final accounts for publication? (15 marks)

(LCC)

31 The true and fair view

Introduction

1. The expression 'true and fair view' is central to auditing and yet it is an abstraction whose meaning is far from clear.

2. a. The Companies Act states that every company balance sheet and profit and loss account must give a true and fair view of the state of affairs and of the profit or loss respectively (CA 1985 S.226). This requirement overrides the requirement to use a format.

   b. The auditor must report to the members on whether the financial statements show a true and fair view (CA 1985 S.235).

   c. SAS 600 *Auditors' Reports on Financial Statements* applies mainly to those financial statements intended to give a true and fair view.

   d. This chapter reviews the concept under a number of headings:

   historical, legal requirements, truth and fair view.

Accounting Standards

3. Schedule 4 requires that:

   a. Accounting policies shall be stated (original Para. 36 of 4th Schedule).

   b. 'It shall be stated whether the Accounts have been prepared in accordance with applicable accounting standards and particulars of any material departure from those standards and the reasons for it shall be given'.

   In effect this gives statutory recognition to the idea that to give a true and fair view, Accounts must comply with accounting standards.

Legal requirements

4. The true and fair view is a Companies Act concept and is therefore a legal notion. However neither the Companies Acts nor the courts have ever attempted to define it. The legal considerations have been discussed in a counsel's opinion published in *Accountancy* in November 1983.

5. The idea of 'true and fair view' is at a high level of *abstraction*. Similarly abstract words and phrases include 'reasonable care'. The idea must be applied to an infinite variety of different concrete facts. Clearly there will always be a *penumbral* area (neither completely in the sun nor completely in shadow) where opinions can differ as to whether a financial statement gives a true and fair view, or not, of a particular set of facts. For example valuing stock, sold after date at a profit, at cost gives a true and fair view, valuing damaged stock, which can only be sold at a loss, at cost would not give a true and fair view. But what precise value of net realisable value would give a true and fair view is subject to several opinions.

6. The *meaning* of true and fair view is constant in law and has not changed since 1947. However the *content* of the concept is subject to change and development. As an analogy consider the phrase 'poverty line'. The meaning of the word may be commonly under-

stood in the same way but the content will be differently perceived in India and England, in 1900 and 2000 and between individuals at any one time or in any particular country.

7. The courts have rarely given a view in any particular set of circumstances as to the content of a true and fair view. However the law appears to require that Accounts follow the *correct principles of commercial accountancy*. What are correct principles of commercial accountancy can be established by determining what accountants actually do. The courts will consider the evidence of expert witnesses. Today what accountants actually do is to conform to the Accounting Standards and to this extent the requirements of the Accounting Standards and the true and fair view coincide.

8. The idea to grasp is that of *expectation*. Users (investors etc.) of financial statements expect that Accounts will conform to the Accounting Standards and to other generally accepted accounting principles. For example, a true and fair view will be given by a set of Accounts in which freehold properties are valued at cost because anyone familiar with accounting, would *not expect* valuation at market value.

9. The Companies Act now gives substantial detailed disclosure requirements but spells out also the principles underlying the preparation of Accounts (CA 1985 4th schedule).

Truth

10. Investigation and discovery of anything is assisted by breaking down or classifying the thing into parts. We therefore will breakdown true and fair view into parts, beginning with true.

11. In practice the word 'true' is difficult to pin down as it also incorporates a high level of abstraction. However in accounting terms we can consider synonyms like – in accordance with fact or reality; not false or erroneous; representing the thing as it is.

12. Numerous Accounts items can be seen in this light. For example 'Freehold land … at cost £2,000,000'.

    It is either true or false that:

    a. Freehold land exists.

    b. The freehold land is the property of the company who hold a good title.

    c. The freehold land did cost the company £2,000,000.

    d. All the freehold land belonging to the company is included.

    On the other hand, the matter may not be as simple as it seems. For example:

    i. Good title may be a matter of opinion.

    ii. Historical cost may be a matter of opinion – are legal costs included? Subsequent costs (drainage, fencing) may be considered capital or revenue.

13. A dictionary definition of true also includes 'in accordance with reason or correct principles or received standard' which brings us back to generally accepted accounting principles and the Accounting Standards.

Fair view

14. The word 'view' is important in that Accounts cannot give a view in an abstract way. The view given cannot be divorced from the perceptions of a reader/user of the Accounts.

15. The idea of fairness involves a number of thoughts including:

a. **Expectation**. Any user has certain expectations from a set of Accounts. He/she presumes that the Accounts will conform to generally accepted accounting principles and the Accounting Standards. This had already been discussed under the legal considerations above.

b. **Relevance**. The fair view from the point of view of a user must mean that the view given by the Accounts will be relevant to the informational *needs* of the user. This needs some qualifying. It is assumed that Accounts show:

   – the resources (assets) employed in the enterprise

   – the claims (capital and liabilities) against the resources

   – the changes in resources and claims over a period (profit and loss account, cash flow statement).

   That is: the Accounts *report* on historical events. They are not intended for decision making even though they may be used for this purpose.

c. **Objectivity** – consisting of externally verifiable facts, rather than subjectively considered opinions. In practice, as we have seen under 'truth', most accounting figures are subjective or contain a substantial subjective element. As SSAP 2 puts it '... many business transactions have financial effects spreading over a number of years. Decisions have to be made on the extent to which expenditure incurred in one year can reasonably be expected to produce benefits in the form of revenue in other years ...'

d. **Freedom from bias** – the producer of Accounts (directors, managers) should not allow personal preferences to enter into their Accounts preparation work. For example, a desire to show a favourable profit should not influence a manager's assessment of the expected life of fixed assets, or the saleability of stock. In practice, all human activities are influenced by personal experience and prejudice. The important thing is to be aware of this and for an auditor to be aware of the tendency to bias in all financial reporting.

e. **Beyond simple conformity** – users of Accounts expect Accounts to conform to generally accepted accounting principles and the Accounting Standards. However simple rigid conformity can lead to a misleading view. For examples inclusion of profits from overseas branches may mislead shareholders when those profits are not available to shareholders because of exchange control restrictions.

f. **Least as good** – at one time, the prudence convention was so highly esteemed, that shareholders and auditors' expectations went no further than making sure that the true position was at least as good as that shown by the balance sheet. This extremely cautious and conservative view would be of little comfort to an investor who sold his shares for £1 each when if all the facts had been known, the shares would have fetched £5 each. Despite modern insistence on fairness up *and* down, the least-as-good syndrome lurks in every accountant's subconscious.

g. **Accounting principles** – the accounting *principles* and *policies* used should be:

   – in conformity with Accounting Standards (mostly!)

   – generally accepted

   – widely recognised and supported

   – appropriate and applicable in the particular circumstances.

In most areas, more than one policy will satisfy these criteria. For example, there are several different acceptable methods for depreciation and therefore several different measures of profit, all of which may give a true and fair view.

h. **Disclosure** – accounting is an aggregating and summarising process. A million transactions in a year can be summarised in a relatively few lines in a set of Accounts. The overall results and final position can only be appreciated by aggregating transactions and balances into suitable classes or categories. For an investor, a list of 10,000 sales ledger balances has little informational value but debtors £3.6 million is useful as it can be compared with previous years, sales, other figures on the Accounts etc. Too much disaggregation causes confusion between the wood and the trees and a general indigestibility. On the other hand too much aggregation can hide individual figures or sub-classes that ought properly to be disclosed. As an example, in 20-4 The Lemon Drop Trading Co. Ltd suffered a major bad debt of £300,000 and this was included in 'administrative expenses £720,000' in the profit and loss account. The net profit was £240,000 against £510,000 in 1983. Would not failure to disclose that administrative expenses included bad debts £300,000 (20-3 £6,500) mislead shareholders as to the *trend* of profits?

i. **Materiality** – the elusive accounting principle of materiality is intimately bound up with the true and fair view. An item is material if its disclosure or non-disclosure would make any difference to the view received by the user of the Accounts. Fairness is therefore a function of materiality. For example, a clerk in a company embezzled £50,000 and this sum proved irrecoverable. The company did not wish to disclose this loss separately as it was not material as the profit was over £2 million. The auditor might argue that disclosure would change the view given by the Accounts as shareholders might then have doubts about the directors' ability to control the company's affairs and shareholders might also wish to know company policy on prosecuting offenders of this sort.

Summary

16. a. The expression 'true and fair view' is an *abstract* idea of immense importance and difficulty.

b. The idea has a long history in company law but first came into its modern form in the Companies Act 1947.

c. The *meaning* of the phrase in company law is fairly clear but its content is both unclear and capable of development.

d. The meaning is closely bound up with the *expectations* of Accounts users. In particular they expect generally accepted accounting principles and policies and the Accounting Standards to be followed.

e. The phrase can be broken down into parts viz *true* and *fair view*. True can mean in accordance with the facts.

f. Fair view has many elements – accordance with expectations, relevance, informational needs, concordance with accounting purposes (reporting not decision making), objectivity, freedom from bias, disclosure and materiality.

g. Least-as-good ideas have to be avoided.

Points to note

17. a. Most people expect Accounts today to be accurate and comprehensive and to give a reasonable man a right understanding of the underlying results and position of the enterprise. This sounds reasonable but a closer inspection will reveal that most of these words are abstractions which are very difficult to interpret into the precise words and figures of financial statements.

   b. Accounts are apparently very precise. The profit was £141.3 million for example. This is very misleading. Accounting is not deterministic but probabilistic. There are many estimates and guesses in Accounts (e.g. depreciation) and different policies (e.g. FIFO or weighted average cost for stock valuation) that it has been suggested that a statement that the profit was in the range of £50–£300 million might be more realistic.

   c. Note the precise requirements of the Companies Act on format, accounting principles and disclosure are submerged in an overriding requirement that Accounts give a true and fair view.

Case study

Trumpton Foundries PLC manufacturing cast iron plaques for all purposes have, just published their accounts for the year ending 31.12.-6. Chigley, a shareholder, is thinking of selling his shares and is reading through the accounts to help him in his decision on selling or retaining his holding.

Some of the items in the accounts are:

	all in £'000	
	20-5	20-6
Turnover	2,369	2,576
Cost of sales	1,500	1,620
Net profit	215	220
Fixed assets	1,456	1,367
Stocks	245	289
Overdraft	167	260

Unrevealed by the accounts are the following items:

a. The company has substantial amounts of plant which have been fully depreciated.

b. In 20-6, the company accepted, at marginal cost + 10%, an order from America. The invoiced amount was £370,000. This was the company's first export order.

c. Cost of sales includes £213,000 being the cost of a research and development project carried on jointly with the local university. The project has led to significantly better and cheaper products.

d. In December 20-6 the company bought a very large consignment of fuel oil for £35,000 to take advantage of low prices.

Discussion

a. From the point of view of Chigley can these accounts be said to give a true and fair view?

b. Do the accounts conform to a legal view of truth and fairness?

c. Do accountants prepare accounts with a view of reporting wholly past activities to shareholders?

d. Consider the bank overdraft. To what extent can this be seen as being composed of matters which can be regarded as objectively 'true'? Are there also matters which are matters of opinion?

e. Should accounts offer 'point' figures of profits? Should they perhaps offer a range of profit figures or probabilistic estimates? Should a commentary be offered on matters with significance to understanding or the future of the enterprise? Where does this idea leave the auditor?

Student self testing questions *Questions with answers apparent from the text*

1. a. Relate true and fair to the Accounting Standards. (3)
    b. Summarise the legal view of true and fair. (4–8)
    c. What does true mean in the context of accounts? (10–13)
    d. What ideas are involved in the idea of fair? (14)
    e. Do accounts need to be relevant to the needs of users to show a true and fair view? (15)
    f. Can accounts be both objective and true? (15)
    g. Why should an auditor be aware of the problem of bias in accounts? (15)
    h. Contrast 'least as good' with 'true and fair'. (15)
    i. What qualities will accounting principles and policies used in accounts conform to? (15)
    j. Contrast disclosure with materiality. (15)

Examination question

1. One of the fundamental concepts in auditing is 'true and fair'. Despite this being a cornerstone of UK financial reporting and auditing for the last half century, the phrase has never been defined in company law.

Required:

Discuss the concept of true and fair, outlining the factors that should be considered by an auditor when forming a conclusion as to the truth and fairness of a set of accounts.

(25 marks)

(ICAS)

32 Representations by management

Introduction

1. It is now normal audit practice for the auditor to obtain a letter *from the management* addressed *to the auditor* confirming any representations given by the management to the auditor. This letter is known as the management letter or the letter of representation.

   Representations in this context can be defined as 'a statement made to convey an opinion'.

2. This chapter outlines the reasons why auditors obtain this letter, the procedures for so doing and finally the contents. We also consider audit action if management decline to sign such a lettter.

3. There is a Statement of Auditing Standards SAS 440 *Management Representations* and an ISA 580 *Management Representations*.

Reasons why the letter of representation is obtained

4. *The Companies Act 1985 Section 389A* entitles the auditor to require from the officers of the company such information and explanation as he thinks necessary for the performance of the duties of the auditors. Further Section 237 (3) gives a duty to the auditor to include in his report, any failure to obtain all the information and explanations which he deems necessary for the purposes of the audit.

5. *The Companies Act 1985 Section 389A (2)* strengthened CA85.S 389A (1) by making it a criminal offence, punishable by fine and/or imprisonment to make any statement (orally or in writing) which conveys, or purports to convey, any false or misleading information or explanation to the auditors.

6. Auditors are required to carry out procedures designed to obtain sufficient appropriate audit evidence to determine with reasonable confidence whether the financial statements are free of material misstatement. Representations from management are a source of evidence.

Management representations as audit evidence

7. In the course of an audit, numerous questions are asked of the client's management and staff. Replies are usually verbal. Most of the queries are:

   a. *Not material* to the financial statements. Examples are queries re missing documents or errors in bookkeeping, or

   b. Capable of being *corroborated* by other evidence. For example, provisions in respect of litigation can be confirmed by the client's solicitors or the life of plant can be confirmed by examining technical literature.

8. However, in some cases:

   a. Where knowledge of the facts is *confined to management*, for example, the management's intentions to close or keep open a material loss-making branch. This would have an affect on the value of the assets at the branch.

   b. Where the matter is principally one of *judgement* and *opinion*, for example, the realisability of old stock. Then:

  i.   the auditor should ensure that there is no *conflicting* evidence

  ii. the auditor may be unable to obtain *corroborating* evidence

  iii. the auditor should obtain *written confirmation* of any representations made.

9. The auditor must decide for himself whether the total of other evidence and management's written representations are sufficient for him to form an unqualified opinion.

Procedures

10. The following procedures should be adopted:

  a. The auditor should summarise in his *working papers* all matters that are material and also subject to uncorroborated oral representations by management.

  b. In addition these matters should be *either*:

    i. formally minuted as approved by the Board of Directors at a meeting ideally attended by the auditor

    ii. included in the signed letter of representation.

  c. Standard letters should not be used as:

    i.   each audit is different

    ii. the letter is important and should receive very careful attention

    iii. the management should participate in its production. There should be much drafting, review and discussion.

  d. The letter should be:

    i. signed at a high level – e.g. chief executive, financial director. SAS 440 suggests the chairman and secretary;

    ii. approved and minuted at a board meeting at which, ideally, the auditor would be present.

  e. The preparation of the letter should begin at an early stage, e.g. at the beginning of the final audit in order to avoid the possibility of the auditor being faced with a refusal to sign by the management. If there is a refusal by management to cooperate then the auditor should:

    i.   do all he can to persuade management to cooperate

    ii. prepare a statement setting out his understanding of the principal representations made, with a request that management confirm it

    iii. if management disagree with this statement, discuss and negotiate until a correct understanding has been reached

    iv. if management refuse altogether to cooperate, either on principle or because they are themselves uncertain about a particular matter, consider if he has obtained all the information and explanations he requires and consequently may need to qualify his report on grounds of limitation of scope.

  f. The representation letter or board resolution making representations should be approved as late as possible in the audit, after the analytical review, but, as it is audit evidence, before the audit report is prepared. If there is a long delay between the approval of the representation and the audit report, the auditor may need to do other audit work/or obtain a supplementary letter of representation. SAS 440 suggests dating the letter on the day the financial statements are approved.

Contents

11. The contents of the letter of representation should *not* include *routine* matters, for example, that all fixed assets exist and are the property of the company or that stock is valued at the lower of cost and net realisable value.

12. The letter should include *only* matters which:

    a. are material to the financial statements, and

    b. the auditors cannot obtain independent corroborative evidence.

13. SAS 440 *requires* that the auditors should obtain evidence that the directors acknowledge their collective responsibility for the presentation of the financial statements and have approved the financial statements. The place for this is the letter of representation. It also *requires* that auditors obtain written confirmation of representations from management on matters material to the financial statements when those representations are critical to obtaining sufficient appropriate audit evidence. This will include matters on which directors' intentions are vital or where knowledge of the facts are confined to management. Examples might be intentions on capital investment so that deferred tax does not become payable or the continuation of a project which might have little value if abandoned.

14.

Example of a letter of representation

To Puce, Watermelon & Co.
Chartered Accountants.

Gentlemen,

We confirm that to the best of our knowledge and belief, and, having made appropriate enquiries of other directors and officials of the company, the following representations given to you in connection with your audit of the company's financial statements for the year ending 31 December 20-3:

1. We acknowledge as directors our responsibility for the financial statements, which you have prepared for the company. All the accounting records have been made available to you for the purpose of your audit and all the transactions undertaken by the company have been properly reflected and recorded in the accounting records. All other records and related information, including minutes of all management and shareholders' meetings, have been made available to you.

2. The provision for warranty claims has been estimated at 2% of annual turnover as in previous years. This amount is in accordance with our opinion of the probable extent of warranty claims. We know of no events which would materially effect the amount of these claims.

3. As stated in Note 12 to the Accounts there exists a contingent liability in respect of the company's guarantee of the bank overdraft of NBG Ltd, an associated company now in receivership. In our opinion the assets of NBG Ltd will realise sufficient to satisfy the bank and no actual liability will arise.

4. It is the intention of the Board of Directors to continue production at our Trumpton plant for at least the next three years so that valuation of the assets and liabilities of that plant should appropriately be on the going concern basis.

Yours faithfully,

NJ Brown, Company Secretary

Signed on behalf of the Board of JBS Ltd.

14 April 20-4

Summary

15. a. A letter of representation is a letter from the management to the auditor confirming in writing opinions conveyed to the auditor orally.

b. It is obtained on the occasion of each audit.

c. The Companies Act 1985 Section 389A entitles the auditor to such information and explanation as he may require. In giving such information and explanation management should remember that the same section makes it a criminal offence to give false or misleading information to an auditor.

d. SAS 440 and ISA 580 govern this subject.

e. The letter should contain only matters which are material and for which the auditor cannot obtain corroborating evidence.

f. The principal items will be matters of which management alone have knowledge and matters of judgement and opinion.

g. The letter should also contain the directors' acknowledgement for their responsibilities under CA 1985 for preparing financial statements which give a true and fair view and a statement that all accounting records have been made available to the auditor and that all the transactions undertaken by the company have been properly reflected and recorded in the accounting records. It should also say that all other records and related information including minutes of all management and shareholders' meetings have been made available to the auditors.

h. Ideally the representation letter should be dated the same day as the directors formally approve the accounts.

Points to note

16. a. The letter of representation is a form of audit evidence but not of course the only form. Thus the auditor cannot rely on the letter of representation to save doing the audit.

b. The letter is used only on the restricted number of matters discussed in this chapter. This is a departure from previous practice when a wide range of routine matters were included.

c. The inclusion of only a limited range of matters tends to sharpen the focus on those matters included.

d. Special problems exist in this area for auditors of groups.

e. It is advisable for the auditors to ascertain that the persons responsible for the letter should understand what it is that they are being asked to confirm!

Case study

Bouncy, Gamine & Co. are auditors of the Zombrit Group. The accounts for the year ending 31.12.-6 are being subjected to the final review. The following matters have been noted by Maureen, the manager in charge:

a. The company has engaged in a number of long term contracts in Africa. During the last few years a minority of these have sustained losses. Work in progress at 31.12.-6 includes a substantial amount of African contracts. Some are valued at cost and some include attributable profit in accordance with SSAP 9. One contract has been valued with a provision for ultimate loss.

b. The group has set up a subsidiary in Zombaland to manufacture motor parts for sale in Central Africa. The group have lent this subsidiary material amounts but so far production difficulties, political problems and difficulties in finding adequate markets have plagued the project. All assets acquired by the subsidiary have been valued at cost.

c. The group have a property in Milton Keynes which they used as the regional head-quarters. This office has been closed and the staff transferred, with considerable opposition, to London. The property has been let to another company on a two year lease and has been treated in the accounts as an investment property in accordance with SSAP 19.

d. The company have a project to manufacture and sell a range of televideo kits so that executives can see each other whilst talking on the telephone. Production should commence in 20-7. All expenditure so far has been deferred in accordance with SSAP 13.

Discussion

a. Identify the matters connected with these items which the auditor may include in a letter of representation.

b. Draft such a letter.

Student self testing questions *Questions with answers apparent from the text*

1. a. Why should a letter of representation be obtained? (4–6)
   b. What kind of matter should be included in a letter of representation? (8)
   c. What procedures should be used? (10)

Examination questions

1. i. What are 'representations made by managements to the auditor'? (3 marks)
   ii. How far is the auditor justified in accepting management representations as audit evidence? (6 marks)
   ii. If the auditor is not satisfied with such representations, what action should be taken? (6 marks)

   (LCC) (Total 15 marks)

2. You are the audit senior in charge of the audit of Dorlcote Mill Ltd for the year ended 31 July 2002. The Managing Director, Dr Turnbull, has given you a draft of the letter of representation he proposes to issue, and has asked for your comments. The text of the letter is as follows:

   'Dear Sirs,

   I confirm the following representations given to you to assist you in preparing your accounts and conducting your audit:

   a. You have been given all the information and explanations you need to form your opinions.

   b. You have been given access to all the books and records of the company.

   c. No material instances of fraud or irregularity have occurred.

d. The stock has been valued at £50,000, by the directors.
e. The freehold premises are valued at £300,000, by the directors.
f. No material event has taken place since the Balance Sheet date of which you are unaware.

Yours faithfully

J. Turnbull'

Required:

a. Comment on the content of the draft letter. (5 marks)
b. Redraft the letter making appropriate assumptions where necessary. (10 marks)

(AAT) (Total 15 marks)

Planning and control of audits

1. The next section is concerned with effectiveness of organisation in an accountant's office and with the effective planning and control of individual audits.
2. Chapter 33 is on planning and Chapter 34 on quality control in auditing.

33 Planning

Introdution

1. It is of great importance that an audit is planned in advance because:
   a. The intended means of achieving the audit objectives must be established.
   b. The audit can be controlled and directed.
   c. Attention can be focused on to critical and high risk areas.
   d. The work can then be completed economically and to time scale requirements.
2. There is a Statement of Auditing Standards SAS 200 *Planning* and ISA 300 *Planning*. In addition SAS 210 *Knowledge of the Business* is relevant.
3. This chapter looks at matters to be taken into account, and the preparation of an audit plan.

Matters to take into account

4. a. The work to be performed in addition to the audit.
   b. Reviewing last years working papers.
   c. Changes in legislation (e.g. Financial Services Act 1986) or auditing or accounting practice (a new SAS, a new FRS).
   d. Analytical review of management accounts, consulting with management.
   e. Changes in the business or its management or ownership.
   f. Changes in systems or accounting procedures.
   g. Timing requirements.
   h. Extent of preparation by the client of analyses and summaries.
   i. Use of internal audit.
   j. Degree of reliance on internal controls.
   k. Joint auditors if any.
   l. Rotational testing.
   m. Liaison with the audit committee.
5. As an example of audit planning, we will consider the case of Stubby Widgets Ltd, a manufacturer, importer and wholesaler of widgets and the auditors who are Fastwork and Co. The December 20-6 audit plan is to be prepared by Fiona who is a new member

of staff. She has to consider all the matters mentioned in Para. 4 and finds the following data requires attention:

a. A special report has to be prepared for the Widget Manufacturers' Association on the cost structures in the company.

b. As Fiona is new to the audit she needs to read previous years' papers especially carefully as her predecessor has left Fastwork and the audit partner, to whom she reports, has also changed as old Mr Tick has retired and gone to live in the Bahamas. The 20-5 audit was completed in May 20-6 and the time is now July 20-6.

c. There are several new FRSs and SASs and some new relevant legislation. Happily all these are summarised in Fastwork's internal updating and Fiona is sent on courses regularly.

d. The client produces monthly accounts internally and Fiona finds that turnover increased substantially after March as a new branch was opened in Paris and two major new products began manufacture. These two products are new technology and the company have taken a risk in introducing them at this time. Substantial capital expenditure throughout the first part of the year has already led to liquidity problems and this has been added to by increases in stock and debtors.

e. A structural review of the company consequent on the items mentioned in d. has led to three senior directors and managers being retired early and new appointments made in June. There is a new financial manager.

f. A completely new networked computer system was installed in April and is working well.

g. The directors have expressed a wish for the audit to be completed by the end of March and they promise to have the accounts ready by mid February.

h. Every conceivable schedule is available from the computer system. Fiona feels she should think up analyses which will help her prepare her analytical review procedures.

i. The company have no internal audit.

j. The company rely heavily on internal controls. Fiona thinks that much audit reliance on internal controls may well be possible.

k. There are no joint auditors.

l. Fastwork and Co. do not generally engage in rotational testing as they see each audit as a single specific task.

m. There is no audit committee.

General strategy

6. SAS 200 suggests that there should be an *overall audit plan* which outlines the *general strategy* and a *detailed approach* specified in an *audit programme*. In simpler audits these two documents could be combined.

The general strategy will be directed toward the following matters:

a. **Terms of engagement** – work to be done – audit, precise accounting work to be done for client, tax etc., letters to be sent – letter of weakness etc., reports to third parties e.g. regulatory authorities.

b. **The client and its background** – history, products, locations, especially noting factors like a new managing director, a new computer, a new product.

c. **Important figures and ratios** – from previous years and, if available, from management and draft accounts.

d. **Audit risk areas** – these might include stock, work in progress, or dealings with a company under common ownership.

e. The effect of information technology on the audit.

f. **Extent of involvement of internal audit.**

g. **Requirement for involvement of specialists.** These may be from within the audit firm e.g. computer audit or rarely external specialists.

h. **Setting of materiality levels.**

i. **Client assistance.** Assistance from the client may be required in providing documents and analyses, providing computer time, arranging visits to branches.

j. **The audit approach.** The extent of reliance on internal control, the use of substantive tests and analytical review procedures.

k. **Timetable** – dates of interim, year end and final audits and of dead lines to meet e.g. AGM of company.

l. **Staffing requirement.**

m. **Budget and fee.**

n. The operating style (e.g. direction from the top or disseminated decision making) and **control consciousness** of directors and management.

o. Possibilities of **error or fraud.**

p. Involvement with **subsidiaries** and their auditors, branches, divisions and other components of the audit assignment.

q. **Regulatory** requirements (especially important in some types of company e.g. those in financial services.

r. **Going concern** issues.

7. The overall budget plan which Fiona needs to prepare includes:

a. An amendment of the Letter of Engagement to include the report to the Widget Manufacturers' Association and the visit to Paris where substantial stocks are held.

b. Need for a careful read of SSAP 20 as the Paris branch is the first item in a foreign currency.

c. Assessment of the impact of new managers and need for Fiona to meet all the relevant staff and tour the works.

d. Extra time needed to audit capital expenditure.

e. Identification of risk areas. These include going concern, capital/revenue identification on new plant, the branch in Paris, increased stocks and debtors, identification of all creditors especially as payment is likely to be slower, the new computer system even though this is apparently going well, the viability of the new products.

g. Need to plan year-end presence at stocktaking including Paris.

h. Need to spend time evaluating the new computer system and the internal controls which have been incorporated.

i.   Identification of areas which are not material and as far as possible setting materiality levels. Fiona finds that this is essentially very difficult and prefers to wait and see the detailed items as she audits them.

j.   The making of a list of all assets and liabilities, revenues and expenses so that detailed schedules of these can be requested from the client. For example she may request a breakdown of sales by product in order to examine the success/failure of the new products.

k.   Need to identify and test, at the interim audit, internal controls which she may wish to rely on.

l.   Need to audit assets and liabilities as much as possible before the year end in view of the short time available after the year end.

m.   Fiona will need staff for the interim (which is flexibly dated), at the year-end stock-take (including Paris) (an awkward time), and at the final which will be rapid and therefore may need extra staff.

n.   Extra work is required this year (capital expenditure, new computer system, faster audit, Paris, liquidity problems) and the fee will need to reflect this. Approach client early on this!

The audit programme

8.   The audit programme develops and documents the nature, timing and extent of planned audit procedures required to implement the overall audit plan. The audit programme essentially will consist of a very detailed list of things to be done and will show all assets, liabilities, revenues and expenses and such things as sample sizes, bases of selection of samples and when and where the programme is to be carried out. It is a set of instructions to staff.

It needs to take into account:

–   risks of error
–   amount of audit evidence required in each area
–   co-ordination of auditing with accounts preparation (if accounts are prepared by the audit team)
–   the co-ordination of any assistance from client staff e.g. on schedule preparation, availability of records, internal audit
–   involvement of other auditors (especially with groups) and experts if required.

Knowledge of the client's industry, business and organisation

9.   It is essential that all members of the audit team fully understand the client's industry, business and organisation. This is so because only that way can they judge the risks associated with the engagement. Also an economical and effective audit can only be carried out with a full knowledge of significant environmental, operational and organisational factors. Knowledge of such factors also helps in communication with client's staff, in assessing the reliability of management representations and in judging the appropriateness of accounting policies and disclosures. This knowledge can be gained from:

–   the client's annual report and accounts

- analytical review of the clients interim accounts, financial reports, variance analyses etc.
- internal audit reports
- visits to the client's premises and discussions with management and staff
- perusal of minutes of shareholders, directors, audit committee, budget committee etc.
- previous years audit files including the permanent file
- consideration of the state of the economy (audit staff are no doubt avid readers of the *Financial Times*)
- reports from within the audit firm which may be relevant to the client e.g. tax department and management consultancy
- perusal of relevant literature from credit rating agencies, stockbrokers, investment analysts
- perusal of relevant trade magazines and journals.

Note that there is a Statement of Auditing Standards SAS 210 *Knowledge of the Business*.

10. In the case of Stubby Widgets Ltd, background information would be obtained from a variety of sources including the monthly accounts, previous years' files and accounts, talking with the client's management and staff, reading minutes etc., review of trade magazines which may have a bearing on the viability of the company and its new products.

Summary

11. a. Planning is very important in auditing if the audit objectives are to be met economically, efficiently and to tight time and cost constraints.

   b. SAS 200 suggests that there should be, for each audit engagement, an overall audit plan and an audit programme.

   c. In planning an audit a thorough understanding of the client, its industry and surrounding matters needs to be gained by all audit staff. There are multiple ways of gaining this knowledge from reading the Financial Times to talking to client staff in the staff canteen. SAS 210 covers this topic.

Points to note

12. a. The plan should also emphasise the importance of:

   i. staffing requirements in terms of experience and special skills needed and of availability;

   ii. proper briefing of staff on the client and its industry, high risk areas, related party matters etc.

   b. A modern approach to audit planning is to assess the client for risk. A client which is felt to offer above average audit risk will need the most competent staff and this has to planned for. In addition identification of high risk areas in an audit enables the audit to be focused and the most resources put into the right areas.

   c. With modern audits resources are limited and costs high. The most effective and efficient audit can only be performed if it is well planned. Planning includes getting the right mix of evidence gathering in terms of analytical review, systems testing and substantive testing.

d. In the case of Stubby Widgets several new factors emerged for the 20-6 audit which necessitated forward planning in detail. These included the new computer system, the change of management, new capital investment, new products, liquidity problems, Paris, and a tight timetable for the final accounts. Without planning for these factors, the audit would be less efficient, less timely and more expensive.

e. However much an audit is planned, it is impossible to take into account every factor which will actually affect the audit. However identifying the probable factors will at least enable the audit firm to take them into account in formulating the plan and the staffing requirements.

f. SAS 200 requires that the audit work planned should be reviewed and, if necessary, revised during the audit. It advises that such changes should be documented.

Case study 1

Gnomic Garden Equipment PLC manufacture garden tools of all sorts from trowels to motor rotovators. They have three factories and some 800 employees. Turnover in 20-6 is expected to be £13 million about 2% up on 20-5. Exports take about 40% of turnover. Profit in 20-6 is expected to be about £400,000 against £1.2 million in previous years. During the year the company appointed a new dynamic young chief executive to halt the slide in profits. One of his first moves was to replace an old mainframe computer with a system of micros.

Spicy & Co. the auditors have been asked to complete the audit early as the new chief wants the annual general meeting to be in early April instead of early June. The company's year end is 31 December. The chief executive has also stated that the audit fee has always been far too high and he is looking for a much more efficient audit.

Spicy & Co's partner in charge of the 20-6 audit is considering the audit plan for the year ending 31.12-6 in June 20-6.

Discussion

a. Identify the areas of audit risk that may exist with this audit.
b. List the matters to be taken into account in formulating the audit plan.
c. Discuss ways in which the audit could be made more economical.
d. Draft an overall audit plan for the 20-6 audit.

Case Study 2

Nothingventure PLC is a property developer. The business is run by the highly entrepreneurial Creesus and consists of buying run down properties, redeveloping them and selling them on to investment companies. The business is highly speculative and highly geared. The company have several long-term loans with tight covenants. New properties are always taken on with borrowed bank money. Monique is planning the audit in 20-7 when she hears that Creesus has suffered a mild heart attack and will be away from work for three months at least. She conducts her audits by taking a business risk approach. The records are good but Creesus is well known to conduct business negotiations without reference to others. There is no internal audit but an audit committee of non-executive directors who are all close friends of Creesus.

Discussion

    a.   What business risks might confront this company?

    b.   What risks are faced by the auditor?

    c.   How might Monique balance the various approaches available to conduct this audit?

    d.   What might be the main elements of an audit plan?

Student self testing questions *Questions with answers apparent from the text*

1. a.   What matters must be taken into account in planning an audit? (4)

    b.   List matters which are relevant to the preparation of an overall audit plan. (6)

    c.   What is an audit programme and what must be taken into account in developing it? (8)

    d.   List ways in which knowledge of the business may be gained. (9)

Examination questions

1.   You are the audit manager of Goalatso PLC and at the initial planning meeting with the finance director you are advised that during the year the company acquired a 28 year lease over a piece of land on which it has erected a new office building. The cost of construction was £1.5 million, of which £100,000 related to the capitalisation of the company's own staff costs and overheads. The company had to borrow in order to finance the project and the final cost includes capitalised interest. The entire property is occupied by Goalatso PLC who vacated their existing short-term leased premises at the time of the move to the new premises. The old lease has still three years to run.

Required:

Draft paragraphs for inclusion in the audit planning memorandum highlighting:

    1.   the audit issues arising from the construction of the new premises; and

    2.   the audit work which you plan to carry out in relation to these matters

(ICAS)

2.   Your client, Communico Distributors Ltd, has for several years been a family owned company selling telephones and answering machines through its own dealer network in the South of England. In May 1990, the company was bought by two brothers, Peter and Charles Brown.

Shortly thereafter, the company acquired the exclusive United Kingdom distribution rights to a revolutionary car phone, manufactured in South Korea, which sells for about half the price of competitive products, and is fully compatible with all British mobile telephone networks.

During the year ending 31 August 1991, expansion has been rapid under the new management. Specifically:

    1)   The new car phone received extensive media acclaim during October and November 1990, which was accompanied by regional television advertising campaigns. Since then, monthly sales have increased from £500,000 to £1,600,000.

          Sales of the new car phone now account for 75% of the company's turnover.

    2)   The company has purchased dealer networks from three other companies and is negotiating to purchase two more which will then complete its national coverage.

    3)   Employee numbers have increased rapidly from 40 to 130, of which administration staff at head office have risen from 12 to 28.

4) In June 1991, the central distribution and servicing department moved from head office into larger premises in Milton Keynes.

This was necessary to handle not only the increased stocks and pre-delivery checks necessary, but also the rising level of after sales warranty work caused by manufacturing defects in the new car phone.

Requirement:

Prepare an outline planning memorandum for the audit of Communico Distributors Ltd for the year ending 31 August 1991, which identifies the potentially high risk areas of the audit and details how the audit effort will be directed to overcoming these problems.

(14 marks)

(ICEW)

34 Quality control

Introduction

1. It is of primary importance to the business world in general and to the auditing profession in particular that an audit should be a quality product. Audits should be extremely well done and yet be completed expeditiously and economically.

2. There is a Statement of Auditing Standards SAS 240 *Quality Control for Audit Work* (revised 2000) and ISA 220 *Quality Control for Audit Work.*

   SAS 240 requires that in all firms, quality control policies and procedures should be implemented both at the level of the **audit firm** and on **individual audits.**

3. This chapter deals with quality control under four heads:
   a. Audit firm organisation.
   b. Planning, controlling and recording individual audits.
   c. Reviews of audit firms procedures in general and of particular audits.
   d. The ISO 9000 series of Quality Management Systems.

Audit firm organisation

4. It is recognised that each firm has its own needs depending on size, geographical spread, special expertise etc., but all firms must organise quality control policy and procedures which ensure audits are performed:
   a. In accordance with approved auditing standards.
   b. In conformity with statutory (e.g. Companies Act) and contractual (letter of engagement) requirements.
   c. In conformity with personal (ethical) standards.
   d. In conformity with any professional standards set by the firm itself – many firms pride themselves on their professionalism.
   e. Economically and to time schedules.
   f. With minimum risk.

5. The procedures required are:

   a. Each firm should establish and monitor control policies and procedures and communicate these to all partners and staff. Larger firms employ printed manuals but smaller firms may have to rely on verbal instruction.

   b. *Acceptance and reappointments as auditor.* There should be a procedure for evaluating prospective clients with consideration of the firm's ability to meet the client's needs and for making the decision on acceptance which may be made by an individual partner, or by an individual partner, or by a committee.

   c. *Professional ethics.* Procedures to ensure all partners and staff are aware of and adhere to the principles of independence, objectivity, integrity and confidentiality. It is important to instruct staff who are not members of professional bodies and to monitor observance of ethical standards. For example, staff might not be aware on the prohibition on ownership of shares in client companies or may be unwilling to sell them if they are so aware. Consideration should be given to the auditor's independence and ability to serve the client properly and to the integrity of the client's management.

   d. *Skills and competence.* The object is to have a fully competent and skilled set of partners and staff. Procedures include:

      i. Recruitment only of suitably qualified and expert staff. Staffing needs should be planned ahead.

      ii. Technical training and updating. All partners and staff should be encouraged to learn, and to keep up-to-date with technical matters. The firm could provide literature, maintain a technical library, send people on courses and hold courses themselves. Some firms produce a special newsletter at intervals to update staff with technical developments.

      iii. On-the-job training and professional development. Planning, controlling and recording emphasises the importance of relating staff abilities to client need but opportunities should also be provided for staff to have adequate experience on a range of clients as on-the-job training. Performance of staff should be evaluated and discussed with staff concerned. This kind of assessment and feedback is now common practice in all walks of life.

   e. *Consultation.* Individual members of the firm should not take decisions on problem areas without consultation with others. Problem areas might be technical (e.g. computers where expert members of staff should be consulted) or matter of risk (e.g. to qualify or not to qualify). Sole practitioners are advised to consult with other firms or with professional advisory services.

   f. *Monitoring the firms quality control procedures.* Suitable procedures should be introduced to ensure that all procedures are working adequately. This is dealt with in the review section.

Individual audits

6. The control procedures to be applied to individual audits include:

   a. **Allocation of staff** – staff should have appropriate training, experience, proficiency and, if required, special skills (e.g. in computing).

   b. **Proper briefing of staff** – staff should be properly informed on:

    i.   objectives of the audit

    ii. timing required

    iii. the overall plan of the audit

    iv. significant accounting and auditing problems

    v. related parties

    vi. the need to bring problems and put upon enquiry situations to superiors.

c. **Audit completion checklist** – with sections for completion by staff and reporting partner. It is a common experience, that in the rush to complete an audit on time, matters of importance can be overlooked.

d. **Contentious matters** – all problems, special difficulties, and potential qualifications must be identified, recorded and discussed by, if necessary, the reporting partner with colleagues or even another practitioner.

e. **Documentation** – all audit work and conclusions reached must be fully recorded in the working papers.

f. **Reviews** – all audit work must be fully reviewed. This is dealt with in the next section.

g. **Acknowledgement** – all audit work and review action should be acknowledged in writing by the performer.

h. **Supervision** – personnel with supervisory responsibilities should monitor the progress of the audit to consider whether assistants have the necessary skills and competence to carry out their assigned tasks, assistants understand the audit directions and the work is carried out in accordance with the overall audit plan and the audit programme. I well remember carrying out audit work in the distant past without knowing what I was doing or why I was doing it! Times have, I hope, changed.

SAS 240

7. SAS 240 has some specific requirements:

a Firms should establish, and communicate to audit engagement partners and audit staff, quality control policy and processes. This will involve the establishment of an appropriate structure within the firm including the appointment of a senior audit partner to take responsibility for these matters. Such policy and processes should be fully documented.

b. Before accepting a new engagement or continuing with an existing one, firms should ensure they are competent to undertake the work, if there are any threats to their independence and objectivity and assess the integrity of the owners, directors and management of the entity.

c. Firms should have sufficient audit engagement partners and staff with the competencies necessary to meet their needs.

d. Firms should establish procedures to facilitate consultation in relation to difficult or contentious matters and document the consultations.

e. Audit engagement partners should ensure that audit work is directed, supervised and reviewed in a manner that provides reasonable assurance that the work has been performed competently.

Review

8. Firms should ensure that an independent review (by a partner who is not the engagement partner) is undertaken for all listed company audits. In addition, firms should establish policies setting out the circumstances in which an independent review should be performed for other audits, whether on the grounds of the public interest or audit risk. The independent review should take place before the issue of the audit report to provide an objective, independent assessment of the quality of the audit. The policies should set out in detail the manner in which the review is to be performed.

9. The independent review involves consideration of the following matters in order to assess the quality of the audit.

   a. the objectivity of the audit engagement partner and key audit staff and the independence of the firm

   b. the rigour of the planning process including the analysis of the key components of audit risk identified by the audit team and the adequacy of the planned responses to those risks

   c. the results of audit work and the appropriateness of the key judgements made, particularly in high risk areas

   d. the significance of any potential changes to the financial statements that the firm is aware of but which the management of the audited entity has declined to make

   e. whether all matters which may reasonably be judged by the auditors to be important and relevant to the directors, identified during the course of the audit, have been considered for reporting to the board of directors and/or the audit committee (or their equivalents); and

   f. the appropriateness of the draft auditors' report.

Monitoring

10. Firms should appoint a senior audit partner to take responsibility for monitoring the quality of audits carried out by the firm.

British standard ISO 9000 series

11. Some firms have considered it worthwhile to add quality control by being certified under the ISO 9000 series. This series is widely used by manufacturing firms but can also be used by service organisations.

Summary

12. a. Audit work must be controlled.

    b. This control is implicit in an audit firm's systems and procedures for carrying out audits.

    c. Audit work must be subject to review.

    d. Reviews are carried out in practice by a variety of categories of person from inside and outside the firm.

    e. It is possible for an audit firm to obtain ISO 9000 series certification.

Points to note

13. a. Auditors are under pressure to ensure that audit standards are high because:

i. Publicly aired failure is bad for business.

ii. Failure to live up to standards can lead to expensive litigation.

iii. Inefficiency is unprofitable.

b. Independent review by persons unconnected with the detail of an audit can lead to the discovery that:

i. The firm's procedures are not always followed.

ii. There are gaps in the procedures.

iii. There are technical matters of general interest which need investigation.

iv. Staff or partners are overworked.

v. Deadlines are too tight.

vi. There are deficiencies in the quality of the staff or in their training.

c. Quality control can be seen in several stages:

i. Proper organisation of the firm and its procedures.

ii. Planning for each audit.

iii. Control of each audit.

iv. Working papers.

v. Review of work done.

vi. Review of organisation and procedures.

d. It is important to distinguish between procedures designed to ensure the firm as a whole provide a high standard product in all professional engagements and procedures to ensure that each individual engagement is properly carried out. A review of an audit may be to sample the effectiveness of the overall procedures or may be to ensure that a particular audit was performed effectively.

e. In order to ensure that all that needed to be done on an audit was done, any review should be conducted on the basis of a checklist.

f. An important phrase is quality control policy and processes.

Drivers of quality include individual responsibilities, collective responsibilities, a quality culture, the collective wisdom of the audit team in resolving difficult or contentious matters, building quality into processes and monitoring the results.

Case study 1

George Hardprest is a sole practitioner with 12 unqualified staff and gross fees of £400,000.

Discussion

a. What training facilities should his firm provide?

b. George has been asked to take on the audit of a small company which has been criticised in the consumer column of the local paper. The proprietor has served a prison sentence for fraud. Should George accept the client?

c. George is the auditor of a company with cash flow difficulties. He is now inclined to 'include an explanatory paragraph' in his report – but the managing director has said that if he does George will lose the audit and that of another company under the same control. George is desperate to discuss the matter. With whom can he have discussions?

d. What ought to be included in George's technical library?

e. Would ISO 9000 help George?

Case study 2

Tickers are a largish firm and are concerned about quality control after a few near disastrous mistakes.

Discussion

What sort of mistakes might be meant?

Suggest a set of quality control policy processes which might improve matters.

Student self testing questions *Questions with answers apparent from the text*

1. a. In what ways should audits be performed? (4)
   b. What procedures might ensure audits are conducted in a quality manner? (5)
   c. What control procedures should be applied to individual audits? (6)

Examination questions

1. In your capacity as senior partner in charge of overseas audits in a large London firm of auditors, you are concerned with the effective maintenance of a high standard of work throughout the firm's overseas audits.

   State how you would seek to maintain the highest standard of work in all overseas audits. (12 marks)

   (LCC)

The auditors' report

1. The auditors' report is the end product of the audit. It has been traditionally very short but has been expanded considerably in Statement of Auditing Standards 600 – Auditors' Reports on Financial Statements.

2. Most auditors' reports are positive and end with a statement expressing the auditors' opinion that the financial statements show a true and fair view and comply with statutory requirements. Some, however, express this opinion with reservations or express a contrary opinion. These are *qualified* reports.

3. The chapters in this part of the book are:

   35. On the clear or unqualified opinion
   36. On qualified opinions
   37. On events after the Balance Sheet date which may have a bearing on the opinion
   38. On the vital subject of going concern
   39. On the special problems of amounts derived from preceding financial statements
   40. On the impact on audit opinions of accounting standards.

4. The principal authority on auditors' reports is the Statement of Auditing Standards 600 – *Auditors' Reports on Financial Statements*. SAS 600 is expanded by Practice Note PN 8 *Reports by Auditors Under Company Legislation in the UK*.

35 The auditors' reports

Introduction

1. The content of the auditors' report is governed by:

   a. statute – for companies this means the Companies Act 1985 (as amended by the Companies Act 1989) Sections 235–237.

   b. The Statement of Auditing Standards 600 – auditors' reports on financial statements. There is also ISA 700 *The Auditor's Report on Financial Statements*. Note also Bulletin 2001/2 Revisions to the wording of auditor's reports on financial statements and the interim review report.

The Companies Act 1985

2. The Companies Act 1985 Section 235 requires that the auditor's report shall state whether, in the auditor's opinion, the financial statements:

   a. have been properly prepared in accordance with the Act

   b. give a true and fair view.

   The auditor *must* state these matters in his report.

   Section 235 also requires that the auditor's report shall state the names of the auditors and be signed by them.

3.   In certain circumstances Sections 235 and 237 require the auditor to make further statements in the report. The circumstances are:

   a.   if, in the auditor's opinion, proper *accounting records* have not been kept

   b.   if, in the auditor's opinion, proper *returns* adequate for their audit have not been received from *branches* not visited by them

   c.   if, in the auditor's opinion, the company individual accounts are not in *agreement* with the accounting records and returns

   d.   if, in the auditor's opinion, they have failed to obtain all the *information and explanations* which to the best of their knowledge and belief, are necessary for the purpose of their audit

   e.   if, in the auditor's opinion, the information given in the *directors' report* is not consistent with the annual accounts.

   These matters are expanded upon in the next chapter.

4.   The Companies Act Section 237(4) gives the auditor a specific duty to include in his report certain information if that information is not given in the accounts. The information relates to Schedule 6 and concerns disclosure of information on emoluments and other benefits of directors and others.

Statement of Auditing Standards 600

5.   We will begin by reproducing an unqualified auditors' report in full:

Independent Auditors' report to the shareholders of Plonk PLC

We have audited the financial statements of Plonk PLC for the year ended 31 March 20-8 which comprise the Profit and Loss Account, the Balance Sheet, the Cash Flow Statement , the Statement of Total Recognised Gains and Losses and the Reconciliation of movements in shareholders' funds and the related notes. These financial statements have been prepared under the historical cost convention as modified by the revaluation of certain fixed assets and the accounting policies set out therein.

Respective responsibilities of directors and auditors

The directors' responsibilities for preparing the Annual Report and the financial statements in accordance with applicable law and United Kingdom Accounting Standards are set out in the Statement of Directors' Responsibilities.

Our responsibility is to audit the financial statements in accordance with relevant legal and regulatory requirements, United Kingdom Auditing Standards and the Listing Rules of the Financial Services Authority.

We report to you our opinion as to whether the financial statements give a true and fair a view and are properly prepared in accordance with the Companies Act 1985. We also report to you if, in our opinion, the Directors' Report is not consistent with the financial statements, if the company has not kept proper accounting records, if we have not received all the information and explanations we require for our audit, or if information specified by law or the Listing Rules regarding directors' remuneration and transactions with the company and other members of the group is not disclosed.

We review whether the Corporate Governance Statement reflects the company's compliance with the seven provisions of the Combined Code specified for our review by the Listing Rules,

---

and we report if it does not. We are not required to consider whether the board's statements on internal control cover all risks and controls, or form an opinion on the effectiveness of the group's corporate governance procedures or its risk end control procedures.

We read other information contained in the Annual Report and consider whether it is consistent with the audited financial statements. This other information comprises only the Directors' Report, the Chairman's Statement, the Operating and Financial Review and the Corporate Governance Statement. We consider the implications for our report if we become aware of any apparent misstatements or material inconsistencies with the financial statements. Our responsibilities do not extend to any other information.

Basis of audit opinion

We conducted our audit in accordance with United Kingdom Auditing Standards issued by the Auditing Practices Board. An audit includes examination, on a test basis, of evidence relevant to the amounts and disclosures in the financial statements. It also includes an assessment of the significant estimates and judgments made by the directors in the preparation of the financial statements, and of whether the accounting policies are appropriate to the company's circumstances, consistently applied and adequately disclosed.

We planned and performed our audit so as to obtain all the information and explanations, which we considered necessary in order to provide us with sufficient evidence to give reasonable assurance that the financial statements are free from material misstatement, whether caused by fraud or other irregularity or error. In forming our opinion we also evaluated the overall adequacy of the presentation of information in the financial statements.

Opinion

In our opinion the financial statements give a true and fair view of the state of the group's and the company's affairs as at 31 march 20-8 and of the group's profit for the year then ended and have been properly prepared in accordance with the Companies Act 1985

Sheinton & Co.	Albrighton
Registered auditors	24 June 20-8.

Note that the corporate governance statement is only required for listed companies.

6. Note the following characteristics of this report:
    a. A clear title – note the word 'independent'.
    b. It is addressed to the shareholders.
    c. Precise identification of what is and what is not being audited.
    d. The responsibility for the financial statements rests upon the directors.
    e. The UK listing authority is now the Financial Services Authority. It would be acceptable to say ' the UK listing authority'.
    f. The statement about the directors' remuneration is a consequence of the Companies Act and also the Corporate Governance rules (see the chapter on this later in the book).
    g. The Combined Code data will be dealt with in a later chapter.
    h. The reading of the other information is also dealt with later in the book.
    i. Mention of the rules governing UK audits.
    j. Mention of who the auditors are, and the date of the report.

Dating the report

7. The standard states that auditors should not express an opinion on financial statements until those statements and all other financial information contained in a a report of which the audited financial statements form a part (e.g. the Annual Report and Accounts) have been approved by the directors, and the auditors have considered all necessary available evidence.

8. Thus the auditors will sign only after:

    a. Receipt of the financial statements and accompanying documents in the form approved by the directors for release.

    b. Review of all documents which they should consider in addition to the financial statements (e.g. the directors' report, the Chairman's statement etc.).

    c. Completion of all procedures necessary to form an opinion including a review of post Balance Sheet events.

Summary financial statements

9. The Companies Act 1985 allows listed companies to send to shareholders a *summary* financial statement instead of the full annual report. This is governed by the Companies (Summary Financial Statement) Regulations 1995 and the auditor's response by Bulletin – the auditor's statement on the summary financial statement as modified by Bulletin 2001/2 (wording of auditors' reports).

10. The summary financial statement must be derived from the annual financial statements and directors' report and must explicitly follow the detailed requirements concerning the form and content, set out in the 1995 regulations. It is required to contain a statement by the company's auditors expressing their opinion as to whether these requirements have been met.

    The summary statement must also state whether the auditors' report on the full financial statements included a qualified opinion and if so must give the auditors' report in full.

11. A suitable report would be

Independent auditors' statement to the shareholders of Plonk PLC

We have examined the summary financial statement of Plonk PLC.

Respective responsibilities of directors and auditors

The directors are responsible for preparing the Summarised Annual Report with applicable law.

Our responsibility is to report to you our opinion on the consistency of the summary financial statement within the summarised Annual Report with the full annual accounts and Directors' Report, and its compliance with the relevant requirements of Section 251 of the Companies Act 1985 and the regulations made thereunder. We also read the other information contained in the summarised Annual Report and consider the implications for our report if we become aware of any apparent misstatements or material inconsistencies with the summary financial statement.

Basis of opinion

We conducted our work in accordance with Bulletin 1999/6 'The auditors' statement on the summary financial statement' issued by the Auditing Practices Board for use in the United Kingdom.

Opinion

In our opinion the summary financial statement is consistent with the full annual accounts and directors' report of Plonk PLC for the year ended 31 March 20-8 and complies with the applicable requirements of Section 251 of the Companies Act 1985 and the regulations made thereunder

Sheinton & Co.   Albrighton

Registered auditors

24 June 20-8.

The auditors' duties in respect of the summary financial statements may include:

a. Refer to the statement in the engagement letter.

b. Include the matter in the audit plan – it is desirable that work on the summary should be done at the same as the main audit.

c. Verify that the summary financial statement is consistent with the annual accounts and the directors' report. Inconsistencies may include:

   – simple mistakes

   – matters of opinion. An example of this may be in the summary of the directors' report where the summary may include all the optimistic matters and exclude all the more gloomy prognostications for the future

   – exclusion of matters which although not required by the regulations may be required (in the auditor's opinion) for a proper understanding of the accounts. An example may be the exclusion of a very large exceptional item or a non-adjusting post balance sheet event.

d. Verify that the statement complies with the requirements of S. 251 and the regulations.

e. While the auditors do not have to say that the summary statement gives a true and fair view (it cannot!) they should ensure that a statement is included in a prominent position like:

'This summary financial statement is only a summary of information in the group's financial statements and the directors' report. It does not contain sufficient information to allow for a full understanding of the results of the group or the state of affairs of the company or the group. For further information the full annual financial statements should be consulted. These can be obtained from the company's secretary.'

f. As the summary statement may be sent out as part of a newsletter or some other form of communication, the auditor should examine the whole communication and ensure that the summary financial statement forms an identifiable section and that the whole communication does not mislead.

g. If the auditor cannot give an unqualified report she should request the directors to make changes and if they do not she should issue a qualified report.

Statement of directors' responsibilities

12. Matters to be included in a description of the directors' responsibilities for the financial statements are:

a. Company law requires the directors to prepare financial statements for each year which give a true and fair view.

b. The directors are required to:
   - select suitable *accounting policies* and apply them *consistently*
   - make *judgments* and *estimates* that are reasonable and prudent
   - state whether applicable *accounting standards* have been followed (large companies only)
   - prepare the financial statements on a *going concern* basis unless it is inappropriate to presume that the company will continue in business.

c. The directors are responsible for keeping proper *accounting records*, for sa*feguarding the assets* and for taking reasonable steps for the prevention and detection of *fraud* and other irregularities.

Summary

13. a. The Companies Act 1985 requires inclusion in the auditors' report of an opinion on:
   - true and fair view
   - proper preparation in accordance with the Act.

b. The Statement of Auditing Standards 600 – *Auditors' Reports on Financial Statements* – has many requirements and suggestions including:
   - basic elements (title, addressees, financial statements identification, responsibilities of directors and auditors, basis of opinion, the opinion, signature of auditor, date)
   - a sample unqualified report.

c. Summary financial statements can be sent by listed companies and there are requirements for content , audit and auditor's report. Note that there are rules as to when a summary financial statement can be sent to a shareholder instead of a the full report and accounts.

d. The Companies Act 1985 requires in certain circumstances that the auditor report:
   - on proper accounting records not being kept
   - on proper returns from branches not visited by the auditor not being received
   - on the accounts not being in agreement with the accounting records
   - not receiving all the information and explanations he requires
   - certain items connected with directors if they are not included in the accounts as required by the Act
   - information in the directors' report is not consistent with that in the financial statements.

e. The date of the auditor's report is important.

f. The standard requires a statement of directors' responsibilities in the accounts or in the auditors' report.

Points to note

14. a. The standard unqualified report should be learned by heart.

   b. The purpose of the new requirements of Statement of Auditing Standards 600 is to aid communication between the auditors and the readers of the financial statements by tackling the *expectation gap*. The expectation gap exists because the public, including the investment community, generally are unclear about the role of the auditor. Many people think the auditor prepares the accounts and /or deals with tax and/or keeps the books but few realise precisely the restricted role the auditor actually plays. Essentially people expect more from an auditor than his actual role can supply, hence the expectation gap. The new and expanded report may help people to have a clearer view of what the auditor does and is responsible for.

   c. In Statement of Auditing Standards 600, material is defined so that a matter is *material* if its omission or misstatement would reasonably influence the decisions of a user of the financial statements. Materiality may be considered in the context of the financial statements as a whole, any individual primary statement within the financial statements or individual items included in them.

   d. The material in this chapter relates to companies but may be adapted to other kinds of entity. For examples a Committee of Management may be the responsible body instead of directors, The Code of Audit Practice for Local Authorities and the NHS in England and Wales may be the appropriate standards instead of the Auditing Standards, the Building Societies Act instead of the Companies Act etc.

   e. The auditor must not sign the report until the board have approved the accounts, the auditor has reviewed all documents that he/she is required to consider in addition to the financial statements, and, he/she has completed all procedures necessary to form an opinion including a review of post balance sheet events.

The dating of the auditor's report indicates that the auditor has completed these things. If the date is later than the directors' formal approval then the auditor must:
   - obtain assurance that the directors still approve the accounts
   - review subsequent events up to the date of signing the auditor's report.

Case study 1

Hall, Purpose and Co. Chartered Accountants are the auditors of General Trading PLC a company whose accounts are wholly based on the cost convention. The letter of engagement requires that the accounts and directors reports are in fact prepared as well as audited by Hall, Purpose. In the year ended 31 March 20-5, the company made a small loss and the board approved the accounts on 28 July 20-5. Due to holidays, the partner in charge at Hall, Purpose did not sign the accounts until August 29.

Discussion

a. Draft a full auditor's report assuming that there is no need for a qualified report.

b. What must Hall, Purpose do before signing their report on August 29?

c. The audit senior discovered that on August 19 the company announced that a contract it fully expected to get had in fact gone to another company and as a consequence the company would need to close its factory in Hartlepool which formed 10% of its fixed assets. What effect would this have on the auditor's report?

Case study 2

Stubby Lane Hockey and Social Club is an unincorporated club with a set of rules and a committee of management. They have 400 members and own their own ground and clubhouse. The freehold is registered in the names of trustees who are also members of the committee.

Discussion

Draft an unqualified auditor's report by the auditors (who are paid) Bully & Co.

Student self testing questions *Questions with answers apparent from the text*

1. a. State the principal authorities for a company auditor's report. (1)
   b. List the items the Companies Act requires in an auditor's report. (2, 3)
   c. What does CA 1985 S 237(4) say? (4)
   d. Write out a full unqualified auditors' report. (5)
   e. When can an auditors' report be dated? (14)
   f. Write out a full auditors' report on a summary financial statement. (11)
   g. List the auditors' duties in respect of a summary financial statement. (11)
   h. List the matters to be included in the description of directors' responsibilities. (12)
   i. What is the expectation gap? (14)
   j. Define material. (14)

Examination question

1. You are the senior in charge of the audit of Denham Ltd. On referencing the file, an audit junior realised that the audit report for the company had not been drafted and in the absence of any reference books he drafted an audit report which reads as follows:

   REPORT OF THE AUDITORS TO THE DIRECTORS

   The attached accounts have been audited by us.

   We certify that the accounts give a fair and reasonable view of the Directors' Report, Profit and Loss Account and Balance Sheet for the year ended 31 March 1990.

In our opinion, the Company has maintained proper books during the year and we believe that all the relevant sections of the Companies Act have been complied with.

ABC & ASSOCIATES

Accountants

Required:

Draft a memorandum to the audit junior pointing out the errors that have been made in drafting the report. Explain why the errors are significant and how they should be corrected. (15 marks)

Note: you are not required to redraft the audit report.

(AAT)

36 Qualified audit reports

Introduction

1. When auditors give a report like those in the previous chapter they are said to give a clean, clear or unqualified opinion. In some cases, the auditor is unable to give such an opinion for one or more of a large variety of reasons. In these cases an auditor is said to give a *qualified opinion*.

   The Companies Act 1995 Section 262 describes a qualified auditors' report as one where the auditor does not state the auditors' unqualified opinion that the accounts have been properly prepared in accordance with the Act.

   A qualified auditors' report is a disadvantage to a company for several reasons:

   a. it has legal consequences, notably in possibly restricting dividend payments – S.271

   b. it may lead to the Accounts being seen as less reliable by contact groups such as banks and other lenders and potential buyers of the business

   c. it reflects badly on the directors.

2. The principal source materials on qualified auditors' reports are:

   a. The Companies Act 1985

   b. The Statement of Auditing Standards 600 – *Auditors' Reports on Financial Statements* and ISA 700 *The Auditor's Report on Financial Statements.*

3. This chapter deals with the subject as:

   a. Qualifications in practice.

   b. Companies Act requirements.

   c. Types of qualification.

   d. Inherent uncertainty.

   e. Accounting standards.

   f. Examples of qualified reports.

   g. Example of an unqualified report with inherent uncertainty.

   h. Materiality.

Qualifications in practice

4. For many years, qualified reports were very rare. With the introduction of SSAPs, many of which were controversial, in the 1970s and 1980s qualified reports became commoner. However only a minority of reports were or are now qualified.

5. Private companies usually lack internal controls and many have cash dealings. For this reason it is very difficult for auditors to have adequate evidence of completeness of recording of transactions. As a result many auditors used what was called the type 6 qualified reports and a great number of auditors' reports were qualified in this very general way. SAS 600 requires that any qualification must be specific.

Companies Act requirements

6. The Companies Act 1985 Sections 235 and 237 requires a qualified report:

   a. if the financial statements have not been properly prepared in accordance with the Act

   b. if the financial statements do not give a true and fair view

   c. if proper accounting records have not been kept

   d. if proper returns adequate for their audit have not been received from branches not visited by the auditors

   e. if the company individual accounts are not in agreement with the accounting records and returns

   f. if the auditors have failed to obtain all the information and explanations which to the best of their knowledge and belief, are necessary for the purpose of their audit

   g. if the information given in the directors' report is not consistent with the annual accounts.

The Act does not state that non-compliance with an accounting standard is grounds for a qualified report but this may be so. We will discuss this later in the chapter.

These things may be matters of fact but may also be matters of opinion. Examples of matters that may lead to qualification under the above headings a. to g. are:

   a. Detailed disclosure as required by the Act is omitted in some area e.g. fixed assets.

   b. True and fair view is a difficult subject and is discussed in another chapter. However adoption of an inappropriate accounting policy, perhaps on depreciation, may be an example.

   c. See Chapter 4 on what is required by the Act. Any shortfall may lead to a qualification

   d. See Chapter 4 again.

   e. This seems unlikely but directors may deliberately produce financial statements which are not in agreement with the books.

   f. Insufficient audit evidence is a common form of qualification.

   g. The directors' report may say that the prospects for the company are poor and that steps will be taken to improve things by closing the company's factory in Tipton. However the balance sheet included the factory and its associated assets on a going concern basis.

Types of qualification

7. There are several types of qualification. These can be summarised as:

Nature of Circumstances	Very material and Pervasive	Less Material
Limitation of scope	Disclaimer	Possible adjustments
Disagreement	Adverse	Except for

To explain these terms:

Limitation of scope means a limitation of scope of the auditors' work that prevents them from obtaining sufficient evidence to express an unqualified opinion. Examples might be

a. a limitation imposed on the auditor as, for example, if he were not permitted to carry out an audit procedure considered necessary. Perhaps the directors may not permit a debtors' circularisation or may not allow the auditor to attend a stocktake.

b. a limitation outside the control of both auditors and directors. Perhaps necessary records existed but have been destroyed by fire or the auditor was prevented from attending a stocktake by a car breakdown.

Disagreement means that the auditors do not agree with the accounting treatment or disclosure of some item in the accounts. The financial statements may have an accounting policy (e.g. inclusion of overheads in finished goods stock on a global percentage of overheads to prime cost, when the auditor considers that a more complex apportionment is essential to the true and fair view).

Very material and pervasive. This term applies when the possible effect of the limitation of scope is so material or pervasive that the auditors are unable to express an opinion on the financial statements. Similarly when the matter giving rise to the disagreement is so material and pervasive that the financial statements are seriously misleading.

Less material means when the effect of the limitation is not so material or pervasive as to require a disclaimer. Similarly when the disagreement is not so material or pervasive as to require an adverse opinion.

Adverse opinion. An adverse opinion is one where the auditors state that the financial statements do not give a true and fair view.

A disclaimer of opinion occurs when the auditors conclude that they have not been able to obtain sufficient evidence to support, and accordingly are unable to express, an opinion on the financial statements.

Possible adjustments. The wording of the opinion should indicate that it is qualified as to the possible adjustments to the financial statements that might have been determined to be necessary had the limitation not existed.

Except for. The opinion is qualified by stating that the financial statements give a true and fair view except for the effects of any adjustments that might have been found necessary had the limitation not affected the evidence available to the auditors.

Inherent uncertainty

8. Inherent uncertainties are inevitable in accounting. Suppose that the company is engaged in litigation and the case will not be heard for many months and the verdict cannot be predicted. The only way to determine the uncertainty is to wait on the outcome of the trial but the financial statements must be produced to accord with Companies Act time limits and because shareholders need the accounts.

The directors should analyse the situation, obtain advice, make estimates, include them in the financial statements and disclose the situation in the notes to the financial statements in as clear a manner as possible.

The auditor should then form an opinion on the adequacy of the accounting treatment of this inherent uncertainty. This will involve consideration of:

- the appropriateness of any *accounting policies* dealing with the matter
- the *reasonableness* of the estimates included in the financial statements
- the adequacy of *disclosure*.

Some inherent uncertainties are *fundamental*. These are uncertainties where the degree of uncertainty and its potential impact on the view given by the financial statements may be very great. In determining whether an inherent uncertainty is fundamental, the auditors consider:

- the risk that the estimate included in the financial statements may be subject to change
- the range of possible outcomes
- the consequences of those outcomes on the view given by the financial statements.

Inherent uncertainties are regarded as fundamental when they involve a significant level of concern about the validity of the *going concern* basis or other matters whose potential effect on the financial statements is *unusually great*.

9. What to do about the auditors' report:

	Not Fundamental	**Fundamental**
Uncertainty is adequately accounted for and disclosed	Do nothing	Explanatory paragraph
Uncertainty is misstated or inadequately disclosed	'Except for' qualified opinion	Adverse qualified opinion

An *explanatory paragraph* is one which is included in the section of the auditors' report which sets out the basis of the opinion. It is not a qualification.

10. Students should appreciate that an inherent uncertainty is different from a limitation of scope. In this respect SAS 600 is different from the previous standard. An inherent uncertainty should be resolved by the passage of time when, say, the verdict of the court is given or when a vital loan is given (which was in doubt) or a business is sold at a satisfactory price (which was also in doubt). A limitation of scope occurs when evidence does or did exist (or reasonably could be expected to exist) but that evidence is not available to the auditors. In such cases a qualification or disclaimer of opinion is appropriate.

Accounting standards

11. The Companies Act 1985 requires financial statements to give a true and fair view. Financial statements that do not accord with applicable accounting standards will not in general give a true and fair view. Thus company financial statements should comply with applicable accounting standards. Further, large companies are required to state in their financial statements whether the financial statements have been prepared in accordance with accounting standards and to give particulars of any material departures from them and the reasons for the departures.

12. When an auditor concludes that there has been a departure that auditor should:

- assess whether there are sound reasons for the departure
- assess whether adequate disclosure has been made re the departure
- assess whether the departure is such that the financial statements do not give a true and fair view of the state of affairs or profit or loss.

Normally a departure from an accounting standard will result in the issue of a qualified or adverse opinion.

Examples of qualified reports

13. Here is an example of an *'except for'* opinion caused by *disagreement*:

Qualified opinion arising from disagreement about accounting treatment

Included in the stock shown on the balance sheet is an amount of £x valued at cost price. In our opinion as this stock is unsafe for consumption it is unlikely to be sold in the normal course of trade and it should be valued at scrap value of £y. This would reduce the profit after tax and net assets by £z.

Except for the incorrect valuation of stock, in our opinion the financial statements give a true and fair view of the state of the company's affairs as at 31 May 2006 and of its profit for the year then ended and have been properly prepared in accordance with the Companies Act 1985.

I have omitted the addressee etc., the names of the auditor and the standard parts.

You will note that most of this report is as usual apart from the *explanation* and the *qualified opinion*. It is important that the report contains a description of the *reasons* for the qualification and *quantified* effects on the financial statements. It is not sufficient to refer to notes attached to and forming part of the financial statements. The report itself must make the matter clear.

14. Here is an example of qualified opinion – *limitation on the work of an auditor*:

Basis of opinion

We conducted our audit in accordance with Auditing Standards issued by the Auditing Practices Board, except that the scope of our work was limited as explained below.

An audit includes examination, on a test basis, of evidence relevant to the amounts and disclosures in the financial statements. It also includes an assessment of the significant estimates and judgements made by the directors in the preparation of the financial statements, and of whether the accounting policies are appropriate to the company's circumstances, consistently applied and adequately disclosed.

We planned and performed our audit so as to obtain all the information and explanations which we considered necessary in order to provide us with sufficient evidence to give reasonable assurance that the financial statements are free from material misstatement, whether caused by fraud or other irregularity or error. However the evidence available to us was limited because £x of the company's purchases of metal scrap residues were paid for in cash from itinerant dealers. There was no system of control over these payments on which we could rely for the purpose of our audit. There were no other satisfactory audit procedures that we could adopt to confirm that these cash purchases were properly recorded.

In forming our opinion we also evaluated the overall adequacy of the presentation of information in the financial statements.

Qualified opinion arising from limitation of audit scope

Except for any adjustments that might have been found to be necessary had we been able to obtain sufficient evidence concerning cash purchases, in our opinion the financial statements give a true and fair view of the state of the company's affairs as at 31 May 2006 and of its profit for the year then ended and have been properly prepared in accordance with the Companies Act 1985.

In respect alone of the limitation on our work relating to cash purchases:

– we have not obtained all the information and explanations that we considered necessary for the purpose of our audit; and

– we were unable to determine whether proper accounting records had been maintained.

I have omitted the standard parts of the report. Note the reference at the end to *Companies Act requirements*.

15. Here is an example of a *disclaimer*:

> We planned and performed our audit so as to obtain all the information and explanations which we considered necessary in order to provide us with sufficient evidence to give reasonable assurance that the financial statements are free from material misstatement, whether caused by fraud or other irregularity or error. However, the evidence available to us was limited because we were prevented from travelling to Gomboland because of the state of war between that country and Ruritania. We were thus unable to obtain adequate evidence for the existence, ownership and value of the company's assets situated in Gomboland appearing in the Balance Sheet at £x. Any adjustment to this figure would have a consequential significant effect on the profit for the year.
>
> In forming our opinion we also evaluated the overall adequacy of the presentation of information in the financial statements.
>
> **Opinion: disclaimer on view given by the financial statements**
>
> Because of the possible effect of the limitation of evidence available to us, we were unable to form an opinion as to whether the financial statements give a true and fair view of the state of the company's affairs as at 31 March 20-9 or of its profit for the year then ended. In all other respects, in our opinion the financial statements have been properly prepared in accordance with the Companies Act 1985.
>
> In respect alone of the limitation on our work relating to the assets in Gomboland:
>
> – we have not obtained all the information and explanations that we considered necessary for the purpose of our audit; and
>
> – we were unable to determine whether proper accounting records had been maintained.

I have omitted the standard parts of the report. Note again the reference at the end to Companies Act requirements.

16. Here is an example of an *adverse* opinion:

> **Adverse opinion**
>
> As more fully explained in the note ... development expenditure on the Mark iv widget in the sum of £y has been deferred to future periods on the grounds that the Mark iv widget is technically feasible and is ultimately commercially viable. In our opinion the case for technical feasibility and commercial viability had not been made out at the date of our report and we consider that the expenditure should be written off in the current year.
>
> In view of the effect of the treatment of the development expenditure, in our opinion the financial statements do not give a true and fair view of the state of the company's affairs as at 31 May 20-8 and of its profit then ended. In all other respects, in our opinion the financial statements have been properly prepared in accordance with the Companies Act 1985.

Once again I have omitted the standard parts of the report.

Example of an unqualified opinion with an explanation of a fundamental uncertainty

17. Here is an example. Note that it is unqualified!

> … we also evaluated the overall adequacy of the presentation of information in the financial statements.
>
> **Fundamental uncertainty**
>
> In forming our opinion, we have considered the adequacy of the disclosures made in the financial statements concerning the possible outcomes of the litigation against the company in respect of alleged breach of a patent. The future settlement of this litigation could result in additional liabilities of unknown amount. Details of the circumstances relating to this fundamental uncertainty are described in note… Our opinion is not qualified in this respect.
>
> **Opinion**
>
> In our opinion the financial statements give a true and fair view of the state of the company's affairs as at 31 May 2006 and of its profit for the year then ended and have been properly prepared in accordance with the Companies Act 1985.

Materiality

18. Auditors are reluctant to qualify their reports and usually will not do so on trivial matters. It is important therefore to consider in all cases when a qualification is contemplated whether or not the matter is *material*.

Materiality is a particularly difficult matter in practice but is of great importance. It is always tempting to avoid the need to qualify a report by convincing oneself that the matter is not material. Great care should be taken before coming to a conclusion on matters of materiality.

The following considerations may be helpful in deciding matters of materiality:

a. **The Companies Acts** are full of of references to materiality. For example, there must be shown separately in the profit and loss account the amount, if material, charged to revenue in respect of sums payable for the hire of plant and machinery.

b. **Materiality is fundamental to accounting** which consists of aggregating, classifying, and presenting financial information. It is an area of professional judgement. It has been said that a good accountant is one who can competently judge matters of materiality.

c. **When materiality arises**. Suppose a company incurs a large bad debt. The question will rise as to whether the debt is material (= large) enough to require disclosure. If it is, should it be presented:

   i. as part of an omnibus figure (administrative expenses)

   ii. as a separate item (e.g. the note to the accounts might show a bad debt of £x caused by the collapse of Gone Broke Ltd.)

   iii. as a matter of special emphasis (e.g. show the profit before and after the bad debt)?

d. Supposing the bad debt was discovered after the accounts have gone to the printers, should the accounts be altered?

e. A further instance of materiality is whether a formula or accounting basis properly allows for special factors. For example, a company servicing cold stores may have a formula for evaluating future liabilities in respect of service contracts signed. Consistency requires that the accounts are always prepared on the same basis. However a special factor (e.g. inflation) may require a change of formula.

f. **How to assess an item's materiality**.

   i. Compare the magnitude of the item with the overall view presented by the accounts.

   ii. Compare the magnitude of the item with the magnitude of the same item in previous years.

   iii. Compare the magnitude of the item with the total of which it forms a part. (e.g. 'debtors' may include employee loans but if employee loans become large i.e. material, then ,the description 'debtors' may be inadequate.)

   iv. Consider the presentation and context of the item. Does it effect the true and fair view?

   v. Are there any statutory considerations?

   vi. Some items are *always* material e.g. directors' remuneration.

g. **Some overall considerations**.

   i. Whether or not an item is material may depend on the degree of approximation of the item of which it is a part. Depreciation errors are often not material because depreciation is itself subject to a great deal of approximation.

   ii. Small errors may seem large in years when profits are very small. In such cases materiality should be judged in the light of the normal dimensions of the business.

   iii. There can be critical points when materiality can be important, for example in turning a small profit into a small loss, or just making a company's assets exceed its liabilities, or in reversing a trend.

   iv. Some items have a significance disproportionate to their size, e.g. income from investments.

19. There is a Statement of Auditing Standards SAS 220 *Materiality and the Auditor* and *ISA 320 Audit Materiality*. The SAS requires that auditors consider materiality and its relationship with *audit risk*. It points out a number of issues:

   i. Materiality is a matter of professional judgement and it has both quantity (amount) and quality (nature) dimensions. Auditors should take it into account when considering the nature, timing and extent of audit procedures.

   ii. Materiality should be taken into account at the planning stage and re-considered if the outcome of tests, enquiries or examinations differs from expectation.

   iii. In evaluating whether the financial statements give a true and fair view, auditors should assess the materiality of the *aggregate of uncorrected statements*. These may be those identified during the audit and their best estimate of others which they have not quantified specifically. Examples might be numerous small errors in the sales ledger or in coding expense invoices. If the directors adjust the financial statements for these, all may be well but if not the *aggregate* misstatement may be material when each individual misstatement is not.

Divisible profits and dividends

20. The law allows companies to pay dividends only out of profits. Auditors should always seek evidence that any dividends paid or proposed by a client company are within the law. Special circumstances arise when the auditor issues a qualified report. Suppose York Widgets PLC have available profits of £100,000 and wish to pay a dividend of £50,000. The audit report was qualified for uncertainty because the stock at one location was not counted. If the stock at that location was included at £20,000, then the worst possible position could be that it was in fact nil. In that case the available profit would be measured at £80,000 and the dividend could be paid. In cases of qualified reports the auditor has to issue a statement as:

Auditors' statement to the members of XYZ Ltd pursuant to Section 271 (4) of The Companies Act 1985

We have audited the financial statements of XYZ Ltd for the year ended .... . in accordance with auditing standards issued by the Auditing Practices Board and have expressed a qualified opinion thereon in our report dated.....

Basis of opinion

We have carried out such procedures as we considered necessary to evaluate the effect of the qualified opinion for the determination of profits available for distribution.

Opinion

In our opinion the subject matter of that qualification is not material for determining, by reference to those financial statements, whether the distribution (dividend for the year ended …) of £ proposed by the company is permitted under Section 263 of the Companies Act 1985.

The work that the auditor needs to do to enable her to issue this report will depend on the qualification. In our York Widgets example, very little work will be required. Note that the difference between a qualification and an explanatory paragraph is very important. Only a qualification has a possible impact on the payment of dividends.

Summary

21. a. Some auditors' reports are qualified for one or more of several reasons.

b. The principal sources of material on qualified reports are the Companies Act 1985 and SAS 600 *Auditors' Report on Financial Statements* and ISA 320 *Audit Materiality*.

c. Qualified reports are relatively rare. Small companies with little control especially over cash transactions will often have qualified reports.

d. The Companies Act 1985 SS 235 and 237 specify several reasons for qualifications.

e. The main reasons given for qualified reports in SAS 600 are limitation in the scope of the work of the auditor and disagreement.

f. The effects of some limitations of scope are so material and pervasive that a disclaimer of opinion is required.

g. The effects of some disagreements can be so material and pervasive that the financial statements are seriously misleading. An adverse opinion is then required.

h. With other less material limitations of scope a qualified opinion should be given with the wording that the opinion is qualified as to the possible adjustments that might have been determined if the limitation had not existed.

i. With less material and pervasive disagreements an except for qualification is required.

j. Inherent uncertainty is endemic in accounting and inherent uncertainties do not lead to qualifications unless the matters are inadequately dealt with or disclosed.

k. Fundamental uncertainties will not lead to a qualification but to an explanatory paragraph.

l. In general departures from accounting standards lead to qualified reports.

m. SAS 600 gives some examples of qualified and other auditors' reports. This chapter includes some reports which conform to the wording in these examples.

n. Materiality is vital to accounting measurement and disclosure. Auditors' reports are only qualified for material matters.

o. Dividends can only be paid out of profits and qualified audit reports can impact on the payability of dividends.

Points to note

22. a. Auditors who feel a qualification is necessary for disagreement will normally request the directors to change the accounts. The directors will usually do this, so that no qualified report is necessary.

b. Because of the serious nature of a qualified report, auditors are always reluctant to qualify their report. However after XYZ Ltd has called in the receivers three months after the publication of financial statements showing a profit, everybody says 'surely something was wrong and the auditors should surely have qualified their report'.

c. Conversely, the auditors would be much criticised if they qualified their report, perhaps for going concern reasons, and this caused the company's collapse. The new unqualified report with a fundamental uncertainty explanation helps here because the auditors can comment on the uncertainty without actually qualifying their report.

d. Qualifications are only used for material matters. What is material is a matter of judgement but SAS 600 suggests that a matter is material if its omission or misstatement would reasonably influence the decisions of a user of the financial statements.

e. Note that many qualifications also imply that the auditors cannot say that proper accounting records have been kept in some area and also that all necessary information and explanations have not been received.

f. Qualifications should be well written:
- they should give information. They should not arouse suspicion or induce the reader to ask for more. They should not be like a newsvendors placard: 'world leader dead'. This statement is intended to induce the passer-by to ask for more
- they should be concise as is consistent with clarity. They should be long enough to be clear but not so long as to bore the reader

- they should be specific as to items and facts and as far as possible as to amounts
- the effect on the financial statements as a whole should be made clear
- the auditors' opinion should not be capable of being misinterpreted.

g. If a qualified audit report has been given on any company's accounts and the company wishes to pay a dividend then the auditor has certain additional duties.

h. SAS 600 requires that any limitation of scope imposed before an auditor has accepted an engagement, would require the auditor to decline the engagement. Similarly, if the directors impose a limitation of scope during the audit, the auditor should request the removal of the limitation. If this is not forthcoming, the auditor should consider resigning.

Case study 1

Althea Printing Machinery PLC have just had their accounts audited by Such, Loss, Chartered Certified Accountants. The manager and the partner in charge of the audit are considering the following matters which arose in the final review:

a. The accounting records did not adequately identify and separately record development expenditure on the project to create a new type of machine. £408,000 has been capitalised and is being amortised over three years including this year. The project is likely to be very successful and the capitalised expenditure was incurred.

b. The notes to the accounts state that:

'The company's assets in Southern Utopia have been nationalised and the amount to be paid as compensation is being negotiated. £100,000 has already been paid but the balance is totally uncertain.

Provision has been made (as an exceptional item) of half the remaining book values of £27,000'

c. The directors estimate the total net realisable value of four obsolete machines at one-half of cost i.e. £50,000. The manager knows of such a machine recently purchased by a client from another manufacturer at £5,000.

d. The directors refused permission for the auditors to circularise the creditors. The auditors wished to do this as some doubts ocurred over cut-off. Alternative tests have not proved totally convincing.

e. The new office block in the city which is partly used by the company and partly let out has not been depreciated. The directors expressed a view in the statement of accounting policies that the building is high quality and has suffered no diminution of value.

f. The company sold scrap metal from its operations for cash in the sum of £50,000. There is little audit evidence on the correctness of this sum.

g. The accounts show in the balance sheet:

'Preliminary expenses and discount on debentures £120,000.'

The manager has already discussed these items with the board who are determined to make no alteration to the accounts as they stand at present.

Student self testing questions *Questions with answers apparent from the text*

1. a. Why is a qualified report difficult for a company? (1)
   b. What are the main sources for information on qualified reports? (2)
   c. List the circumstances in which Sections 235 and 237 require qualification. (6)
   d. Reproduce the table in Para. 7. (7)
   e. Define limitation of scope. (7)
   f. When is an adverse opinion required? (7)
   g. When is a disclaimer of opinion required? (7)
   h. Define inherent uncertainty. (8)
   i. What should an auditor do about inherent uncertainties? (9)
   j. Define materiality. (18)
   k. What qualities are required of qualifications? (22)

Exercises

1. Write out in full audit reports in the following circumstances:
   a. The sales ledger of A Ltd is in a mess such that the debtors of £2,400,000 can be substantiated with a 95% probability only to within 10%.
   b. B PLC includes in its assets some properties valued at £3 million in a central American country which is undergoing civil war. The directors are happy to give a letter of representation that the properties exist, are owned by the company and are fairly valued. However the auditor is unable to visit the country or to verify the continued existence, ownership or value of the properties.
   c. C Ltd is engaged in litigation over some alleged copyright infringed by C Ltd. The alleged infringement took place over the previous year and the claim is for £4 million. The action is not expected to be heard for over a year and the outcome is anybody's guess. No provision has been made.
   d. D Ltd have included the goodwill arising on the acquisition of Joe's business (£500,000) in the balance sheet and are writing it off over 10 years. The auditor considers the life of the *purchased* goodwill as only two years.
   e. E Ltd failed to take stock at Branch 12 and included the stock at an estimated amount £400,000.
   f. F Ltd refused to disclose in the accounts:
      i. the loss of £300,000 caused by the defalcation of a director (now removed from office)
      ii. payments of an unfunded pension of £50,000 to a former director.
   g. G Ltd had income from gaming machines of an unknown amount and all this money was properly spent on legitimate cost of sales items. The balance sheet is fully acceptable to the auditor.
   h. The directors report states that the profit for the year of H PLC was £13 million. The profit and loss account shows a profit of £11 million + £2 million extraordinary item. Answer if:
      a. the auditor considers the item to be exceptional and not extraordinary
      b. the auditor thinks the item is extraordinary.
      All these items are material but not fundamental.

Examination question

1. During the course of your audit of the fixed assets of Eastern Engineering PLC at 31 March 1986 two problems have arisen.

   i. The calculations of the cost of direct labour incurred on assets in course of construction by the company's employees have been accidentally destroyed for the early part of the year. The direct labour cost involved is £10,000.

   ii. The company has received a government grant of £25,000 towards the cost of plant and equipment acquired during the year and expected to last for ten years. The grant has been credited in full to the profit and loss account as exceptional income.

   Required:

   a. List the general forms of qualification available to auditors in drafting their report and state the circumstances in which each is appropriate. (4 marks)

   b. State whether you feel that a qualified audit report would be necessary for each of the two circumstances outlined above, giving reasons in each case. (8 marks)

   c. On the assumption that you decide that a qualified audit report would be necessary with respect to the treatment of the government grant, draft the section of the report describing the matter (the whole report is not required). (4 marks)

   d. Outline the auditor's general responsibility with regard to the statement in the directors' report concerning the valuation of land and buildings. (2 marks)

   (ACCA) (Total 18 marks)

Examination question

1. During the course of their audit of the accounts for publication of Pilce PLC, Oldaud & Partners, the auditors, have observed a lack of consistency within the accounts.

Required:

   a. Give three examples of lack of consistency which would disturb the auditor.

   b. State what the auditor should do as a result.

   (LCCI)

37 Events after the balance sheet date

Introduction

1. This chapter deals with the auditor's consideration of events that occur after the balance sheet date by considering:

   a. the reason for the auditor's interest in such events

   b. SSAP 17 Accounting for post Balance Sheet events, IAS 10 Events after the Balance Sheet date and FRS 12 and IAS 37 Provisions, contingent liabilities and contingent assets

   c. the dating of the audit report

   d. some unusual but possible circumstances

e.   the auditor's procedures in this area.

2.   There is a Statement of Auditing Standards SAS 150 *Subsequent Events* and ISA 560 *Subsequent Events*.

The auditor's interest in post balance sheet events

3.   The preparation of a profit and loss account and Balance Sheet always involves the consideration of events which have or will occur after the date of the balance because at the year end there are numerous transactions in progress where the outcome is uncertain and post balance sheet events which have occurred or are expected to occur, must be examined to determine the appropriate values of assets and liabilities.

For example, the collectibility of debts, the net realisable value of old stock, the outcome of legal action are a function of future uncertain events. Almost all assets and liabilities are carried in the balance sheet at values which imply some judgement of future events. Even the value of fixed assets is a function of their expected future useful life.

4.   Since the preparer of a set of final accounts must use post balance sheet events in preparing Accounts, the auditor must seek evidence that:

a.   all post balance events have been considered and where appropriate used;

b.   balance sheet values correctly incorporate post balance sheet events.

Accounting standards

5.   In his review of post Balance Sheet events the auditor should seek evidence that the applicable accounting standards have been complied with.

Dating of audit reports

6.   The auditor should always date his audit report. The date should be as close as possible to the date of approval of the financial statements by the directors but must be *after* that date.

Period end to date of auditor's report

7.   SAS 150 requires that auditors should perform procedures designed to obtain sufficient appropriate audit evidence that:

a.   All material subsequent events up to the date of their report *which require adjustment of the financial statements* have been identified and incorporated in the accounts.

b.   All material subsequent events up to the date of their report *which require disclosure* (but not accounts alteration) have been identified and disclosed.

There are a number of possible procedures including:

i.   *Focusing* on matters, encountered in the audit, which are susceptible to change. These include cut-off, collection of debts, sales of stock at below cost etc.

ii.   Enquiring into management's procedures (if any) for dealing with subsequent events.

iii.   Reviewing accounting records.

iv.   Reviewing interim financial statements, budget reports, cash flow forecasts and other management information.

v.   Reading minutes and agendas of meetings of shareholders, directors and management committees.

v. Enquiring of management as to any events which may be relevant.

vi. Reading external documents such as stock exchange pronouncements and press reports which may affect the client's business. For example press discussion of the housing market may trigger enquiries as to the valuation of a house building company's stock of land.

Some specific enquiries may be made. The ones below are general but specific enquiries may occur to an auditor of a specific company. Some specific enquiries:

- current status of items involving subjective judgement e.g. litigation, sale of fixed assets or negotiation of new or renewable loans
- any new borrowings or similar commitments
- any sales of assets, actual or planned
- any disasters e.g. loss of assets or incurring of liabilities e.g. initiation of litigation against the client
- any intentions to merge, sell or to liquidate the undertaking (or part of it)
- any intention to make issues of shares or loans
- any intentions to take over another company
- any change in the risk profile of the company e.g. a major change in product or market extension
- any events which may change the going concern status of the company or any part of it.

Date of auditors' report to issue of financial statements

8. This may be a very short period but, in any event, SAS 150 advises that auditors have no obligation to perform procedures or make enquiries regarding the financial statements after the date of their report.

9. However auditors may become aware of subsequent events which may materially affect the financial statements. SAS 150 gives no examples but the settlement of major litigation may be a good example. In these cases the auditors should consider if the financial statements need amendment, discuss the matter with the directors and if necessary conduct further audit procedures and finally consider the implications for their report.

Issue of financial statements to annual general meeting

10. Similar remarks can be made as in the previous paragraph. However there are differences between events which occurred before the date of the audit report but of which the auditors only became aware after that date (this seems unlikely) and events which occurred after the date of the report. In the former case there are statutory provisions for amending the financial statements (Section 245). There are no such provisions in the latter case.

Summary

11. a. Post balance sheet events have an effect on the Accounts.

  b. Auditors must review these events.

  c. Authority for the treatment of post balance sheet events in Accounts is found in SSAP 17, FRS 12 and IAS 37.

d. Audit reports should be dated as soon as possible after the date of formal approval of the Accounts by the directors.

e. Subsequent events are dealt with in SAS 150 and ISA 560.

f. Auditors should apply procedures to discover the existence of relevant subsequent events which occur from the date of the financial statements to the date of signing the auditors' report.

g. There is no obligation on auditors to apply procedures to discover relevant subsequent events from the date of signing their report to the date of laying the financial statements before the company.

h. However, if the auditors become aware of such events they should discuss the matter with the directors, consider the implications for their report and take such actions as may seem necessary.

Points to note

12. a. The auditor should be aware of window dressing. For example:

Subsidiary A has some unsaleable widgets it has manufactured. On 31.12.-6 (the year end) it invoices these to Associate Company B. After the date the sale is reversed by a credit note. The objective of the 'sale' was to value the widgets at cost or above to remove the real loss in value in the widgets from the accounts. It is unlikely that the auditors of Subsidiary A or Associated Company B would realise the significance of the supposed transaction.

Case study 1

Claribel is conducting the final audit of Westwood PLC who are importers and dealers in timber and manufacturers of packing materials. The accounts show results which are comparable to those of the previous year. Claribel is puzzled by this as she knows that the company are having difficulties and that creditors are pressing and the bank is making difficulties over the overdraft. She is suspicious of the accounts and resolves to be especially vigilant in the audit of post balance sheet events. The company's year end is 31.3.-6 and she is doing the audit in mid June. Two specific items have come to her attention:

a. In the sales office she came across some promotional literature offering special very low prices for obsolete stock in July.

b. In conversation with the purchasing manager she discovers that the company has signed a barter deal with an exporter in Zombaland for the exchange of hard woods from Africa for some woodworking machinery of Westwood that is surplus to requirements. The contract was signed in February for completion in the winter of 20-6/7.

Discussion

List the procedures that Claribel should adopt re post balance sheet events.

What particular further facts should she elicit re a. and b.?

What might be the significance of these items for the accounts?

Case study 2

The auditor of Smokestack Manufacturing PLC is reviewing the financial statements of the company for the year ending 31 December 20-5. The following matters have come to light:

a. The company have given warranties on a new product that has had many sales in the year. Some of the products are faulty but the company have made no provision for them in the financial statements.

b. The company have an old factory site in Gomboland which has become polluted with heavy metals. There is no legal obligation to clear up the site (which they are trying to sell) but they have a prominent note in the annual report as to their commitment to environmental matters.

c. New legislation requires that the company fit smoke filters to their factory in Rotherham by 31 December 20-5. They have not done so.

Discussion

What should the auditor do about these matters?

Student self testing questions *Questions with answers apparent from the text*

1. a. Summarise SSAP 17 and its significance for the auditor. (6)
   b. Summarise SSAP 18 and its significance for the auditor. (7)
   c. Comment on the dating of audit reports. (8)
   d. List general and specific procedures to be adopted to identify relevant subsequent events. (9)
   e. Summarise an auditor's duties in respect of events occurring between the date of the auditors' report and the laying of the financial statements before the company. (10–12)

Examination question

1. An unqualified audit report normally states that the financial statements to which the report refers give a true and fair view of the state of the company's affairs at the balance sheet date and of its profits for the year ended on that date.

   Bearing in mind the above statement the directors of Midland Builders Ltd have drawn up accounts for the year ended 30 April 1987 which do not reflect certain events which have occurred since the year end. They justify their action on the grounds that the books and records correctly reflect what was known at the year end. The following are the events which are not reflected in the draft financial statements (in all cases the figures are material).

   i. At a meeting in May 1987 the local planning authority rejected the company's plans to develop one of its freehold sites. The site was included in the company's assets at its cost of £50,000 but it is likely that the site will have to be sold and will realise no more than £35,000 because of its reduced development potential.

   ii. Following the completion of a long-term contract in June 1987 it has been possible to calculate the final profit on the contract. It appears that the profit accrued at 30 April 1987 was underestimated by £20,000. This arose from a material error at 30 April 1987 in estimating the amount of work still to be completed.

iii. A public company in which Midland Builders Ltd held shares as a long-term trade investment announced in June 1987 that it was going into liquidation. The investment is shown in the balance sheet at its historical cost of £40,000 and a note of its stock market value at 30 April 1987 of £46,000 is included in the notes to the accounts. It now appears likely that the investment will prove worthless.

Required:

a. Discuss generally the effect which facts and events relating to a period but becoming known or occurring after the the end of an accounting period can have on the financial statements for the period in question. Comment on the directors' view that the books and records reflect what was known at the year end and that no further adjustments are required. (4 marks)

b. List FOUR detailed procedures which an auditor should adopt in order to detect post balance sheet events. (4 marks)

c. In respect of each of the three events described above, list the detailed work which the auditor should undertake and comment on the acceptability of the company's decision not to adjust its financial statements.

   i. Refusal of planning permission. (4 marks)
   ii. Completion of long-term contract. (5 marks)
   iii. Liquidation of trade investment.

(3 marks)
(ACCA)

38 Going concern

Introduction

1. In recent years, many companies and other enterprises have failed. That is: they have gone bust, into bankruptcy, into receivership or liquidation. The reasons for failure are many and varied but high gearing and high interest rates are often blamed. A fundamental accounting concept in FRS 18 and IASs 1 and 8 is going concern. This is defined as: an assumption that the enterprise will continue in operational existence for the foreseeable future. It means in particular that the Profit and Loss Account and Balance Sheet assume no intention or necessity to liquidate or curtail significantly the scale of operations. *Foreseeable future* is not defined further and we will consider it again later. the Companies Act 1985 Sch 4 (10) says that the company shall be presumed to be carrying on business as a going concern.

2. There have been many instances when a company have issued financial statements prepared on the going concern basis, have an unqualified auditors' report and then go bust shortly afterwards. The auditors are then much criticised. Surely, people say, they must have known the company was likely to fail! Hindsight is a valuable property as is an ability to see into the future! The modern view is that:

   a. the directors should consider the appropriateness of the going concern very carefully before preparing the financial statements

b. the auditors should form an opinion likewise.

3. There is a lengthy Statement of Auditing Standards SAS 130 *The Going Concern Basis in Financial Statements* and ISA 570 *Going Concerns.*

Consequences of going concern

4. The adoption of the going concern basis in financial statements means among other things:

a. Assets are recognised and measured on the basis that the enterprise expects to recover through use or realisation of the recorded amounts in the normal course of business. For example the plant and machinery is expected to be used for many years into the future and its net book value recovered through use. An abandonment of going concern basis would mean that the enterprise would immediately sell the plant and machinery when it may fetch only a small fraction of its book value.

b. Liabilities are recognised and measured on the basis that they will be discharged in the normal course of business. The Balance Sheet shows creditors due after 12 months and creditors due in less than 12 months. Abandonment of going concern basis would make them all payable immediately.

5. If financial statements are drawn up without the going concern basis then:

a. All assets would be valued at net realisable values. Most would have much lower values than going concern values.

b. All liabilities would be shown at the amount due. One notable change would be the inclusion of redundancy pay which is presumed not to be payable if the enterprise is continuing for ever or at least not until a long time into the future.

Directors' duties

6. The directors should consider carefully whether the going concern basis is appropriate. They do this by considering all available information. This does mean that they have to make a judgement about future events which are inherently uncertain. The question that arises is 'how far into the future do they need to look?'. The answer to that depends on a number of factors:

– the nature of the business. The future of a civil engineering contractor is inherently more uncertain than that of a firm of funeral directors

– the riskiness of the company or its industry. A one customer firm is more at risk than a firm with many customers. A highly geared company is more at risk than an all equity one

– external influences. A sudden increase in interest rates or a change in exchange rates can make some businesses unviable. Even a change in the weather from wet to dry can ruin an umbrella company.

7. So, how do directors review the going concern basis? Here are some procedures:

a. reflect on how long into the future to look by considering the matters in Para. 6 above

b. consider all the factors which are relevant: risk, known or expected changes in the economy and the circumstances of the company, ongoing transactions the outcome of which is uncertain

c. forecast financial statements

d. budgets and strategic plans

e. cash flow forecasts.

The auditors' procedures

8. SAS 130 requires that the auditor, when forming an opinion as to whether financial statements give a true and fair view, should consider the entity's ability to continue as a going concern, and any relevant disclosures in the financial statements.

The latter idea is relatively new. It suggests that when a reader of the financial statements might be expected to have doubts about the viability of the company and hence the appropriateness of the going concern basis, then some note or other disclosure should be made in the financial statements justifying the adoption of the going concern basis. More of this later.

Some possible procedures are:

a. assess the adequacy of the means by which the directors have satisfied themselves that the adoption of the going concern basis is appropriate

b. examine all appropriate evidence

c. assess the adequacy of the length of time into the future that the directors have looked

d. assess the systems or other means by which the directors have identified warnings of future risks and uncertainties.

e. examine budgets and other future plans and assess the reliability of such budgets by reference to past performance

f. examine management accounts and other reports of recent activities

g. consider the sensitivity of budgets and cash flow forecasts to variable factors both within the control of the directors (e.g. capital expenditure) and outside their control (e.g. interest rates or debt collection)

h. review any obligations, undertakings or guarantees arranged with other entities for the giving or receiving of support. Other entities may mean lenders, suppliers, customers or other companies in the same group. A UK company may be viable in itself but may have given guarantees to other members of the group and when, say, the holding company in Australia fails, the company goes down with it

i. survey the existence, adequacy and terms of borrowing facilities and supplier credit

j. appraise the key assumptions underlying the budgets, forecasts and other information used by the directors

k. assess the directors' plans for resolving any matters giving rise to concern (if any) about the appropriateness of the going concern basis. Such plans should be realistic, capable of resolving the doubts, and the directors should have firm intentions to put them into effect.

Finally the auditors should review all the information they have and all the audit evidence available and consider whether they can accept the going concern basis. They should always have all their evidence documented and their reasoning explained fully in the working papers.

Borrowing facilities

9. For many entities, survival is a matter of continuing to borrow, especially from the bank. Bank refusal to renew facilities is perhaps the most common precipitation of receivership and liquidation. Consequently the auditor, in cases where borrowing facilities are critical, needs to examine and review these facilities in detail. Procedures will include obtaining written confirmations of the existence and terms of borrowing facilities and assessing the intentions of the bank or other lenders.

Situations where these matters are of special importance include when the entity:

a. has had difficulty in negotiating or renewing finance

b. finds such facilities essential for survival

c. is expected to experience cash flow difficulties

d. finds that assets granted as security are declining in value

e. has breached the terms of borrowing or covenants made.

Auditors' reports

10. Several possibilities exists and the auditor needs to vary his action according to the situation. We discuss each in turn.

a. **The entity is clearly a going concern.** This will mainly arise when the *headroom* (as SAS 130 puts it) is large between the financial resources required in the foreseeable future and the financial resources available. The directors should still undertake an exercise to determine that this is so and the auditors should seek evidence that the directors have done so and that the going concern basis is appropriate.

b. **The entity is not, in the opinion of the auditors, a going concern.** There are two possibilities here. One is that the directors have prepared accounts on the going concern basis and the auditors disagree with that basis. In such cases the auditors should issue an *adverse* audit opinion. The second possibility is that the directors have prepared the accounts on a basis other than going concern. This will be rare. It can however arise if a company was formed with a specific purpose in mind (e.g. developing an estate or running a specific exhibition) and is to be wound up when the purpose has been achieved. In these cases the auditors need not qualify their report providing the financial statements contain the necessary disclosures so that readers of the accounts can understand the position. Annual financial statements are unlikely to be prepared at all if a company is about to go into insolvency and then the auditor's opinion does not really arise.

c. **The auditors may have concern about the appropriateness of the going concern basis.** In such cases they may be able to allay their concern by obtaining audit evidence that the directors have satisfied themselves that the going concern basis is appropriate by a thorough appraisal and taking specialist advice. Where the concern persists the auditor may feel that his fears will be allayed by some relevant disclosure in the financial statements. In this case the auditor should consider whether the disclosures are sufficient to give a true and fair view. If, in the auditor's opinion, they do not, then a qualification on grounds of disagreement is required. For example:

> **Qualified opinion arising from disagreements as to the adequacy of a disclosure in the financial statements**
>
> In our opinion, the financial statements should disclose the following matters. The company are required to repay a term loan on …… 20… They have been unable to obtain further long-term finance but their projections of trading and cash flow indicate that it will be possible to meet the repayment on the due date. The directors have informed us that their views are based upon their plans and their intentions to sell their American distribution company. Such a sale has not yet been agreed and, inherently, there can be no certainty that the company will be able to meet its obligation to repay its term loan.
>
> Except for the absence of the disclosure referred to above. In our opinion…

If the auditors consider that there is a considerable measure of concern but that it is adequately met by disclosures in the financial statements then they should not qualify their report but should include an explanatory paragraph in their report. For example:

Extract from the 'basis of opinion' section of the auditor's report:

> *Going concern*
>
> In forming our opinion, we have considered the adequacy of the disclosure made in note 4 of the financial statements concerning the uncertainty over the possible outcome of the litigation on the alleged infringement of a patent by the company. In view of this uncertainty we consider that it should be drawn to your attention, but our opinion is not qualified in this respect.

(Note 4 will have adequately explained that the company are alleged to have infringed a patent and if the allegation is proved the company will be unable to continue to make its main product. However the company vigorously deny the allegation and expect to win the action but there is still much doubt.)

The real world of small companies

11. In the past, very little attention was paid to going concern. It tended to be assumed except in circumstances where obvious worries existed. Now, it receives a great deal of attention and directors are expected to consider their position very carefully. For example the following considerations might be appropriate in a small retail company:

    – the company have prepared cash flow forecasts for the next six months including the five months after approval of the financial statements. These show adequate cash resources

    – the directors do not consider that forecasts for a longer period are necessary as they would be too uncertain to be useful and the current forecast shows a reasonable surplus

    – the directors have reviewed in detail the assumptions underlying the forecast including the level of turnover, the trend of expenses and capital expenditure and input pricing and found them acceptable

    – the company have recently renewed their overdraft facilities for the ensuing twelve months

    – the lease of the premises has three more years to run at the present rent

– further retail development in their precinct is likely to attract more customers without adding to competition, at least in the next year.

If the directors have undertaken this review, are prepared to represent this fact in writing to the auditor, the auditor has reviewed the directors' work and found evidence that the conclusions are reasonable, then the auditor can accept the going concern basis.

The new thing is that this work has to be done in all cases.

Corporate Governance reporting

12. The Combined Code on Corporate Governance requires directors to report on a number of aspects of corporate governance (see Chapter 52). You will usually find in modern reports and accounts a statement like:

'After making due enquiries, the directors have a reasonable expectation that the group has adequate resources to continue in operational existence for the foreseeable future. For this reason, they continue to adopt the going concern basis in preparing the accounts.'

The auditors should review and seek evidence to confirm this view. They do this by reviewing the directors' minute book, supporting documentary evidence on going concern basis, enquiring of the directors and obtaining written confirmations of the directors' oral representations on the subject.

Summary

13. a. Going concern is now a major issue.

b. SAS 130 and ISA 570 is relevant to this subject.

c. The definition of going concern should be learned.

d. Abandonment of the going concern basis means that assets will be valued at net realisable values and some liabilities will become payable including redundancy pay.

e. The directors have a duty to consider the going concern basis very carefully and make suitable enquiries.

f. The auditors have a duty also to consider the going concern basis and review and seek audit evidence on the directors own considerations and opinions.

g. A major issue in many going concern basis doubts is borrowing facilities. If in doubt the auditors need to confirm these directly with the bank and form an opinion on the bank's attitude toward supporting the company.

h. There are numerous situations where going concern basis is an issue. Some of these are financial, some operational, and some external to the entity.

i. The auditor will make no mention of going concern basis in his report if the company is clearly a going concern.

j. If it clearly is not then an adverse opinion is called for if the financial statements are prepared on a going concern basis.

k. If the financial statements are not prepared on a going concern basis, there are adequate explanations of the circumstances and the auditor concurs then an unqualified opinion is appropriate.

l. The grey area is when there are doubts about going concern but the auditor considers that the going concern basis gives a true and fair view. In such cases the notes to the accounts should give adequate explanations of the situation and the directors' assumptions. If they do then the auditor should include an explanatory paragraph in the opinion but not qualify his report. If the notes are inadequate then the auditor should qualify for disagreement.

m. The going concern basis is one of the issues requiring mention in the directors' report on compliance with the Combined Code on Corporate Governance.

Points to note

14. a. The going concern principle can be considered in relation to the enterprise as a whole or a part only. For example, if a branch were not a going concern, realisable value of assets would need to be substituted for book values and new liabilities may appear in respect of the branch.

b. The probability that a going concern qualification of an auditor's report may bring about a receivership or liquidation is a very real problem to auditors who have doubts about a client's future. The auditor should give his opinion without fear of the consequences to his client.

c. The Combined Code on Corporate Governance requires the directors of listed companies to make a statement on going concern in the annual report and accounts. The auditor is required to review the statement.

d. Note the definition of going concern and the paradox that efforts to continue a company (e.g. by closing factories) may lead to the going concern basis being inappropriate for part of a company.

e. SAS 130 has much to say on the time period which has to be reviewed for going concern basis. The length of the period clearly relates to the circumstances of the entity and the consequent risks. Directors should pay attention to a period of at least one year from the date of approval of the financial statements. If not they should disclose this fact. If they do not so disclose, then the auditor should do so in the basis of opinion section but need not qualify the report.

f. If the auditors consider that representations from the directors are critical to obtaining sufficient audit evidence on going concern basis and the directors decline to provide them, then they may feel a need to qualify their report on grounds of limitation of scope. This could be *except for* or a *disclaimer*.

Case study 1

Conglom PLC is a quoted company primarily in the home computer industry but with a wide range of divisions, many in other industries. It has expanded quickly by heavy borrowing from banks and the issue of loan stock.

Discussion

What indications might the auditor find that may cast doubts on the appropriateness of the going concern concept for the company?

What alternative strategies may Conglom adopt to survive and hence to allow the auditors to give an unqualified report?

Suppose that the survival of the company was wholly conditional on very large sales of the company's new home computer over the next six months in the so far untried market in continental Europe.

Draft a suitable set of alternative audit reports.

Case study 2

Pingo Manufacturing Ltd have traded successfully for many years and, in recent boom times, planned an extension to the factory to enable a doubling of turnover. The factory was completed in 20-3 with the aid of a very large bank loan. The company has always been short of working capital and also have a substantial overdraft which frequently exceeds the facility. The expected increase in turnover never occurred because of the recession. The auditor is John Jumpy FCCA.

Discussion

What evidence might the directors produce to justify their opinion that the company is a going concern and how might Jumpy validate the evidence?

Suppose the directors based their opinion on an assumption of an end to the recession and a large increase in turnover both in the UK and overseas. How would this affect Jumpy?

Student self testing questions *Questions with answers apparent from the text*

1. a. Define the going concern basis. (1)
    b. List the consequences of the going concern basis. (4, 5)
    c. List the directors' duties in respect of going concern basis. (6, 7)
    d. List the auditors' procedures. (8)
    e. List the possible auditors' reports. (10)
    f. State the Combined Code requirements on going concern basis. (12)

Examination questions

1. a. Explain the going concern concept. (3 marks)
    b. According to Auditing Guideline L410, The Auditor's Consideration in Respect of Going Concern:

    '…a company rarely ceases to carry on business without any prior indications, either of inability to meet debts as they fall due, or of problems that raise questions about the continuation of the business.'

    Requirement:

    You are required to identify any seven examples of such 'prior indications' and write a short explanatory note on each of the examples you have selected. (14 marks)

    (ICAI) (Total 17 marks)

    N. B. You are not required to comment on the relative significance of each example.

2. You are a senior with a firm of chartered accountants. You are about to commence working on the audit of Crusader Ltd, a family owned and managed limited company. You have been informed by a business contact that the company has not been trading very successfully and is having difficulties with its bankers. However, you are not aware of any of the specific details.

The manager in charge of the audit is also aware of this information and is concerned about the ability of Crusader Ltd to continue trading. He has asked you to visit the company in order to ascertain the current state of affairs.

Requirement:

a. Draw up a list of questions that you would wish to ask, and details of any information that you would wish to obtain from, the finance director of Crusader Ltd during your visit so as to enable you to assess the future viability of the company.

b. Explain briefly the audit opinion that you would give assuming you concluded, after carrying out appropriate audit procedures, that there was a fundamental uncertainty regarding the ability of the company to continue trading. The audit opinion should be in accordance with SAS 600, *Auditors' Reports on Financial Statements*.

You are *not* required to draft the audit report.

(ICAI)

39 Opening balances and comparatives

Introduction

1. This chapter is concerned with the Accounts of the business for the year *before* the Accounts being audited. The first part considers the Companies Act requirements, the second explains the auditor's interest, the third the auditor's procedures and the final part reviews some problems which may arise in practice.

2. There is a Statement of Auditing Standards SAS 450 *Opening Balances and Comparatives* and ISAs 510 *Initial Engagements – Opening Balances* and 710 *Comparatives*.

Companies Act requirements

3. The Companies Act (Schedule 4(4)) states that corresponding amounts are required to be disclosed in respect of every item in a company's balance sheet and profit and loss account for the financial year immediately preceding that to which the balance sheet and profit and loss account relates.

4. Corresponding amounts for the previous year are commonly known as the comparative figures and current practice is to print one narrative and two sets of figures as:

	20-6	20-5
	£'000	£'000
Fixed assets	£6,420	£6,180

Where the corresponding amount is not comparable (= able to be compared) with the amount shown in the previous years' Accounts then:

a. the previous year's figure should be adjusted, and

b. particulars of the adjustment and the reasons for it shown in the notes.

5. Note also the requirements of FRS 3 on acquisitions, discontinued operations, prior period adjustments and comparatives. In particular see Paras. 7, 29, 30 and 60–64.

The auditor's interest

6. The auditor is interested in the preceding year's figures because:

    a. These figures form the opening position from which the present year's figures are derived. For example, the opening stock is a component of the cost of sales figure. Thus the auditor must be assured that the opening figures have been properly brought forward.

    b. Accounting policies must be applied consistently from year to year.

    c. Corresponding amounts must be shown (see Para. 3 above) and the auditor must seek evidence that they are properly shown.

7. The auditor is *not* required to express any opinion on the corresponding figures as such but he is responsible for seeing that they:

    a. are the amounts which appeared in the preceding period's Accounts, or

    b. have been restated to achieve consistency or comparability, or

    c. have been restated due to a change in accounting policy or a correction of a fundamental error as required by FRS 3.

Audit procedures

8. If the auditor was the auditor of the preceding Accounts (a *continuing auditor*) *and* issued an unqualified report then he should:

    a. Consider whether his audit of the current period has revealed any matters casting doubt on the previous year's figures.

    b. Satisfy himself that the balances have been properly brought forward and incorporated in the books.

    c. Satisfy himself that the preceding period's figures have been properly and consistently classified and disclosed as comparative figures.

    d. Satisfy himself that consistent accounting policies have been applied.

Problem situations

9. When the preceding period's Accounts were *audited by another firm* (known as *predecessor auditors*). In order to be satisfied on the items in Para. 8 above, the auditor will have to perform additional work as:

    a. Consultations with the *client's* management.

    b. Review of the *client's* records, working papers and accounting and control procedures for the preceding period particularly as they affect the opening position.

    c. Consider whether work on the present year's Accounts provides also evidence regarding opening balances.

    d. *If* the above are insufficient then the auditor may have to perform some substantive tests on the opening balances.

    e. It may be that the auditor may wish to *consult with the previous auditor*. This is often done but is usually limited to seeking information on the previous auditor's audit of particular areas (usually high risk areas such as stock), or on matters not adequately dealt with in the client's records.

10. Normally, the actions outlined will enable the auditor to give an unqualified report at least in respect of use of the previous year's figures but it may be that some material matter cannot be adequately evidenced and then a report like the following may be required:

AUDITORS' REPORT TO THE MEMBERS OF XYZ LIMITED

As usual down to '… or other irregularity or error'.

However, the evidence available to us was limited because we were not appointed auditors of the company until … and in consequence did not report on the financial statements for the year ended …. There were no satisfactory audit procedures that we could adopt to confirm the amount of stock and work in progress included in the preceding period's financial statements at a value of £x.

In forming our opinion we also evaluated the overall adequacy of the presentation of information in the financial statements.

Qualified opinion arising from limitation in audit scope

Except for any adjustments that might have been found to be necessary had we been able to obtain sufficient evidence concerning opening stock and work in progress, in our opinion the financial statements give a true and fair view of the state of the company's affairs as at … and of its profit for the year then ended and have been properly prepared in accordance with the Companies Act 1985.

In respect alone of the limitation on our work relating to opening stock and work and progress:

– we have not obtained all the information and explanations that we considered necessary for the purpose of our audit and

– we were unable to determine whether proper accounting records had been maintained.

Laurel and Hardy	22 High Street
Registered Auditors	Boghampton
Dated …	

---

11. When the preceding period's audit report was qualified:

   a. If the matter has been resolved and no qualification is required in respect of the current Accounts then no qualification will be required.

   b. If the matter is still unresolved then the auditor should qualify his report as:

AUDITORS' REPORT TO THE MEMBERS OF …

as usual down to the complete Basis of Opinion paragraph then:

Qualified opinion arising from disagreement about accounting treatment

As indicated in note … to the financial statements debtors include an amount of £.. which is the subject of litigation but against which no provision has been made. We have not been able to satisfy ourselves that this amount will be recoverable in full. We qualified our audit report on the financial statements at … (date of preceding financial statements) with regard to the same matter.

Except for the absence of this provision, in our opinion the financial statements give a true and fair view of the state of the company's affairs as at 31 May 2006 and of its profit for the year then ended and have been properly prepared in accordance with the Companies Act 1985.

Stringent & Co. etc.

---

c. If the previous period's accounts contained:

   i. actual or possible mis-statement in the profit and loss account (not therefore affecting the opening figures)

   ii. misclassification of the preceding period's financial statements

   iii. a restatement of the previous figures with which the auditor disagrees or does not have a restatement that the auditor does want, then a qualified report is required.

12. When the previous period's accounts were not subject to audit. This may be because the exemption provisions of the Companies Act Section 249 applied to the previous year and the accounts were not audited. Points that may be made include:

   – the opening balances must be substantiated. This may be done by work on current year matters, special substantive tests on opening balances, consultations with management and review of records, working papers and accounting control procedures for the preceding period

   – much depends on the accounting policies followed (a complex one e.g. on the learning curve or deferment of development expenditure may need confirmation of calculations), the materiality of the opening balances and the nature and risk of misstatement of them

   – if sufficient evidence cannot be obtained then a report like that in Para. 10 may be required.

Summary

13. a. Preceding financial statements have a bearing on current year's statements because:

   i. they are the opening figures to the current year's Accounts;

   ii. consistency of accounting policy is required;

   iii. they are comparative figures.

   b. The Companies Acts have requirements for comparative figures to be shown.

   c. The auditor has a duty towards these figures.

   d. Problems arise if the previous year's audit was performed by another firm or if the previous year's audit report was qualified.

Points to note

14. a. If an uncertainty exists in the opening stock then the auditor cannot say the profit gives a true and fair view since the opening stock is part of the profit computation. However he can say the balance sheet gives a true and fair view since the opening stock is not part of the balance sheet.

   b. FRS 3 has also pronounced on prior year adjustments.

   c. FRS 3 also pronounces on comparative figures:

   'Comparative figures should be given for all primary statements and such notes as are required by FRS 3. The comparative figures in respect of the profit and loss account should include in the continuing category only the results of those operations included in the current period's continuing operations.' The auditor should verify that correct comparatives of continuing, discontinued and acquisition operations are shown.

d. To some extent SAS 450 is not specific but uses terms like 'the auditors should consider the implications for their report'. In essence the auditor will normally check only that the comparatives agree with previous year's accounts and consistent policies have been applied. The auditors must also bear in mind FRS 3 and acquisitions, prior year adjustments etc. Problems arise when there are report qualifications in the current or previous year's audit reports, when the previous year's accounts were audited by predecessor auditors or were not audited, when the auditor comes across material misstatements in the previous year's accounts or if the opening balances cannot be substantiated.

Case study 1

Lettice & Co. have been appointed auditors of Limp Ltd manufacturers of handkerchiefs in succession to Celery who retired due to ill health. Suresh is currently reviewing the final accounts and discovers the following:

(The audit is on the year ending 31.12.-6.)

a. An examination of the stock sheets at 31.12.-5 reveals that stock has been valued at prime cost £85,000 instead of £120,000 the full cost. Celery had not picked this up.

b. A freehold property had been purchased on 23.2.-5 for £800,000 (inc. land £200,000). No depreciation had been charged in 20-5. The building is old and Suresh estimated its useful economic life at 25 years.

c. The auditors' report on the 20-5 accounts was qualified. Celery had discovered that there was a cut-off uncertainty on creditors in the amount of £30,500. This will never now be resolved.

d. In view of the errors found in the 20-5 accounts Suresh is unhappy about all the figures in the 20-5 balance sheet.

Discussion

a. What work should Suresh do on the figures in the 20-5 balance sheet?

b. How should the items a., b., c., be treated in the accounts for 20-6 with their corresponding figures?

c. Draft the auditor's report on the 20-6 accounts. Assume no problems arose other than those stated.

Student self testing questions *Questions with answers apparent from the text*

1. a. What is the auditor's interest in corresponding figures? (3)
   b. What aspects of the corresponding figures is the auditor responsible for? (6)
   c. What should the auditor do re previous accounts if he audited them and gave a clean report? (8)
   d. What additional work should be performed if the previous accounts were audited by another firm? (9)
   e. What paragraphs would appear in an auditor's report if there was an uncertainty in the opening stock? (10)

Examination question without answers

1. You are the senior assigned to the audit of Paradox Ltd, a new audit client of the chartered accountancy firm for which you work.

At the pre audit meeting attended by Mr Grant, the company's financial director, you learn that the company has a significant debt collection problem arising mainly from the complete lack of internal controls over the sales and debtors transaction flows.

You have been advised that the lack of controls has given rise to incorrect invoicing, loss of customers and little or no formal debt follow-up procedures. From discussions with Mr Simms, the company's financial controller, you have also learned that the previous auditors were never successful in their attempts to secure replies to their debtor circularisation letters.

You have noted that the previous year's audit report was qualified with regard to the auditor's inability to substantiate the closing trade debtors balance as a result of inadequacies in the sales and debtors records.

The manager in charge of the audit has advised you that the standard client acceptance procedures have been completed, including professional clearance from the previous auditors and that the partner has accepted the company as a client of the firm.

Requirement:

a. Prepare a very brief plan for the audit of sales and debtors and outline the difficulties which you might encounter in the circumstances outlined above.

b. Set out the basic internal controls that you consider should be established in the areas of sales and debtors.

c. Draft a brief letter to Mr Grant, the company's financial director, advising him as to the type of audit report he may expect in the current year:

    i.   assuming that the current year's trade debtor balance *can* be substantiated and that there are no other unresolved audit issues; and

    ii. assuming that the current year's trade debtor balance *cannot* be substantiated and that there are no other unresolved audit issues.

In both circumstances, you are to assume that you will be unable to substantiate the prior year trade debtor balance from work carried out in the current year.

You should set out clearly the opinion that would be given in each of the circumstances in c. i. and c. ii. You are *not* required to draft the audit report.

(ICAI)

40 Auditing and accounting standards

Introduction

1. Accounting standards are authoritative statements of how particular types of transaction and other events should be reflected in financial statements and accordingly compliance with accounting standards will normally be necessary for financial statements to give a true and fair view.

2. The professional bodies expect their members (including auditors) who assume responsibilities in respect of financial accounts to *observe* accounting standards.

3. *Significant departures* from standards should occur rarely and only to preserve the true and fair view. The effect of such departures should be disclosed and explained. Auditors

should ensure that significant departures are disclosed and to the extent that their concurrence is stated or implied, justify them.

The Companies Act requires that such departures are disclosed, explained and the reasons for the departure given.If the auditor, after much thought, agrees with the departure he must ensure that the matter is properly disclosed and explained in the accounts but need not mention the matter in his report. If he does not approve the departure then he must qualify his report.

4.   The SSAPs and FRSs have some legal backing. The Companies Act has included some specific items included in SSAPs notably on accounting principles and stock. In *Lloyd Cheyham* v *Littlejohn* 1985, the judge stated that SSAP 2 was very strong evidence as to what is the proper standard and unjustified departure from it would be a breach of duty.

The Companies Act 1989 requires a statement concerning conformity with Accounting Standards in the statement of accounting policies.

FRS 18 Accounting policies

5.   This FRS appeared in 2000 and replaced SSAP 2. The salient points are:

  a.   The FRS does not apply to small entities.

  b.   Policies chosen should be consistent with accounting standards, UITF abstracts and legislation.

  c.   Where choice of policy is allowed the most appropriate should be chosen.

  d.   The going concern and accruals bases should be used.

  e.   Appropriateness should be judged on the criteria of relevance, reliability, comparability and understandability.

  f.   Benefits of appropriate policies may be balanced against the cost of applying the policies.

  g.   Policies should be reviewed regularly but comparability is important.

  h.   There is a distinction between policies and estimation techniques.

  i.   A change to an estimation technique should not be accounted for as a prior period adjustment unless it represents the correction of a fundamental error or a new accounting standard or UITF or new legislation has appeared.

  j.   A description of material policies should be disclosed.

  k.   A description of material estimation technique should be disclosed.

  l.   Any changes should be disclosed with explanations of why, the prior period effects and an estimate of the changes to current financial statements. Similarly with material changes to estimation techniques.

  m.   There should be a statement of compliance with any relevant SORPs.

  n.   In the going concern assessment, there should be disclosed any material uncertainties, the future period considered if less than one year and the fact, if it is so, that the financial statements are not prepared on the going concern basis with reasons.

Accounting policies and estimation techniques

6.   It is not always clear what is a change of accounting policy and what is a change of estimation technique. An example is a change of depreciation method from straight line to

reducing balance. This is a change of estimation technique and not a change of policy. The reason is that the same historical cost measurement basis is being used but the estimation technique used to measure the unexpired portion of each vehicle's economic benefits is different.

Summary

7. a. Auditors are expected to ensure Accounting Standards are observed.

    b. Departures from Accounting Standards may occur to preserve the true and fair view. Auditors must consider all departures and ensure they are disclosed and explained. If they disagree with the departure then they must qualify their report. If they agree they must justify but need make no mention in their report.

    c. There is a distinction between accounting policies and estimation techniques.

Points to note

8. Students are expected to know the SSAPs and FRSs when sitting auditing examinations.

Case study 1

Trying PLC are desperately trying to fight off a hostile take-over bid by Goth PLC. In the attempt, the company have turned to creative accounting to raise profits in the current year. The following are some things they have done:

    a. They have capitalised substantial research and development expenditure on a new product.

    b. They have reclassified certain office costs as selling costs instead of administration costs.

    c. They have ignored a warranty obligation in the financial statements on the grounds that they cannot easily estimate the amount.

    d. They have made no change to depreciation policy on an expensive machine which is not now usable as it is excessively polluting.

    e. They have purchased a company for its customer base. The goodwill arising on consolidation has been capitalised and not amortised on the grounds that the goodwill has not diminished in value.

    f. A grant from a foreign government to help the cost of building a factory in that country has been taken to profit and loss account.

Discussion

    a. What should the auditor do about these items?

    b. How might the auditor discover the items?

Student self testing questions *Questions with answers apparent from the text*

1. a. What do Accounting Standards try to do? (1)

    b. What responsibilities have qualified accountants towards the Accounting Standards? (2)

    c. What rules apply to departures and auditors? (3)

Exercises

1. Discuss the auditors' responsibilities in the following situations:

   a. Client A PLC has not included the group's share of an associated company's exceptional item in its consolidated profit and loss account.

   b. B Ltd, a department store, has not included stock in its statement of accounting policies.

   c. C PLC has calculated EPS as net profit after tax on continuing operations excluding exceptional items.

   d. D PLC has accounted for government grants by means of a deferred credit and has included the deferred credit in shareholders funds.

   e. E Ltd has included VAT on customers' accounts in debtors.

   f. F PLC has included the profit on sale of its factory in extraordinary items. It has built and is occupying a new factory. The move involved some redundancy costs which it has not disclosed.

   g. A lease which fits the requirements for a finance lease has not been capitalised.

   h. H PLC has some redundant stocks. These have been valued at realisable value without taking account of sales commission.

   i. I PLC, a civil engineering contractor, has included in turnover the estimated value of work done on a very large overseas contract. The contract was very keenly priced and some 8% of the contract has been completed.

   j. J PLC has omitted a statement of total recognised gains and losses from its accounts on the grounds that all gains and losses except the immediate write off goodwill arising on its acquisition of JJ PLC have gone through the Profit and Loss Account.

   k. K PLC is an engineering company with numerous items of plant. In the past, plant at the Willenhall factory has been depreciated by the reducing balance method although the other factories have used the sum of digits method. The Willenhall items have been brought into line with the rest of the factories this year but no disclosure of this fact has been made.

   l. L PLC, a consumer electronics company, have five major development projects on hand. All of these have been treated under the deferral method. The company is going through a thin time with regard to sales and has liquidity problems.

   m. M PLC has a large transfer to deferred tax this year.

   n. N PLC has sold a piece of surplus land adjacent to its factory after date for 30% more than its book value.

   o. O Ltd has guaranteed the overdraft of Oo Ltd, a customer, to ensure continuity of sales to that customer. No note to this effect appears in the accounts as the directors say that the possibility of payment is unlikely but not remote and disclosure would tell PP Ltd, another customer, about the relationship and cause PP Ltd to withdraw their custom.

Examination questions

1. Burghley Industries PLC is a company with divisions in several parts of the United Kingdom. For several years, it has received regional development grants in respect of some of its capital expenditure.

   Required:

a. State how these grants should be treated in the financial statements. (5 marks)

b. Tabulate the steps you would take in order to verify the receipt of these grants. (6 marks)

c. If the directors of Burghley Industries PLC decided to credit the whole of the grants to the profit and loss account in the current period, what action (if any), would you take? (4 marks)

(AAT) (Total 15 marks)

2. During the year under audit, Millhouse PLC decided to change its method of calculating depreciation on machinery from a reducing balance method to a revaluation method. This is fully reported by the company in the accounts for publication presented to you for audit.

As auditor, what would you do in connection with this change in the accounting method? *(LCC) (14 marks)*

3. In its annual accounts, a company states its 'accounting policies'.

Required:

a. What should an auditor look for in reviewing the client's accounting policies. (9 Marks)

b. How far might the results of the review of the client's accounting policies affect the audit and audit report? (6 Marks)

(LCCI)(Total 15 marks)

4. You are in charge of the audit of The Varden Lock Company Ltd for the year ended 30 September 1990. Recently you have been informed of the following occurrences by the managing director:

a. On 25 October 1990 a debtor who owed the company £50,000 at the year end was declared bankrupt. It is not expected that the receiver will pay a dividend to the unsecured creditors. The balance is part of the total debtor balance of £650,000.

b. A lease has been entered into during the year. It is a five-year lease of equipment at £75,000 per year. The total lease payments (less a finance charge) have been capitalised, the costs being written off on a straight line basis over six years:

c. An actuarial review of the company's occupational pension scheme has revealed that the scheme is overfunded. The directors have therefore decided to take a 'pension holiday', with no payments being made for the next three years and no charges being made to the profit and loss account for the same period.

Required:

Discuss each of these points and advise as to how they should be treated, referring where appropriate to the relevant legislation or Statement of Standard Accounting Practice. In addition state any other information that you might require before giving a definitive answer. (15 Marks)

(AAT)

Particular audits

1. This section considers the audit problems of particular audit clients. Chapter 41 describes the preliminaries required on a first audit, and concludes with a note on the effect of client size on the relative audit emphasis to be placed on vouching, systems reliance and analytical review.

2. Small companies present special problems which are discussed in Chapter 42 and the audits of different types of businesses are discussed in Chapter 43.

41 The first audit

Introduction

1. Usually when audit firms are appointed as auditors to an enterprise, they remain auditors for many years. In the first year after appointment they have to set up the permanent file and make themselves familiar with the client and its history. Subsequently, the audit will be easier as much of the information necessary as background to the audit will already be on file subject to review and updating.

   Hence, the first audit will be of particular importance and will take rather longer and use more experienced staff than later audits.

Stages in the first audit

2. These are as follows:

   a. Before accepting an audit engagement an accountant should first consider whether or not he can take on the work from an ethical, legal and practical point of view. The ethical considerations have been dealt with in Chapter 8. As an example, an accountancy firm whose senior partner has been a director of the proposed client for some years, could not accept the audit, even if the partner resigned as a director.

      The legal considerations have been dealt with in Chapter 3. As an example an unqualified accountant who was not recognised by the Department of Trade could not become auditor of a company.

      The practical considerations concern whether or not the auditor has the physical resources to carry out the audit satisfactorily. The problems that might arise here include the size of the client in relation to the audit firm. Ford Motors may be too much for a small firm in downtown Walsall. Other problems include geographical location and the need for special knowledge for example, of computers or the special nature of the client's trade, and bunching of client year ends.

   b. **Professional etiquette.** If the organisation has an auditor who is ceasing to act, i.e. one is replacing another accountant, then the professional bodies require the new auditor to communicate with the previous auditor. The detail of this procedure is dealt with in Para. 3.

c. **Confirmation of appointment**. The new auditor must confirm that he has been properly and legally appointed. He does this by examining the minute books of meetings at which he was appointed and placing a copy of the appropriate minute on his new permanent file. In companies the minutes will be of the company in general meeting or in some cases of the directors.

d. **Letter of engagement**. In companies, the auditor's work is laid down by the companies acts but even in these cases the auditor may be asked to perform additional work, perhaps in the areas of taxation, accountancy, systems, etc. In partnerships, the work to be performed by the auditor must be a matter of agreement between the partners and the auditor. The letter of engagement sets out the agreement between the auditor and his client. This matter has been dealt with in Chapter 9.

When and if the first four matters have been dealt with the auditor can commence work.

e. The *permanent file* should then be set up. This should contain the items detailed in Chapter 17 on working papers.

In addition, the following work should be done to complete the file:

i. Review the business, its industry, markets, customers, processes, personnel, etc.

ii. If the company is a member of a group, determine the group structure and the trading and financial arrangements between the client and other group members.

iii. If the company has related company relationships or is in common ownership with other companies, research the trading and financial arrangements.

iv. Obtain a copy of the company's file at Companies House. A complete copy can now be obtained on microfiche.

v. Determine the business interests, both past and present, of the client management. This information can be obtained by interview and by file searches of companies who have directors in common.

vi. Determine if there are any unusual clauses in the memorandum and articles, past qualified audit reports, unusual accounting policies, dependence on single suppliers or customers, important franchising or royalty agreements.

f. Tour the company's premises, noting the nature of the business and any special difficulties which might arise in accounting or valuation. The sort of difficulties which might occur which would be noted in the first visit would be assessing quantity and value of stock and work in progress in manufacturing or chemical process industries. On this tour opportunity can be taken of meeting the organisation's officers and senior staff.

g. Make a note of important dates, e.g. dates of directors, partners, and company meetings, date of interim accounts, final accounts, dividend payments, etc.

h. *Risk assessment*. SAS 300 requires the auditor to:

– obtain an understanding of the accounting and internal control systems sufficient to plan the audit and develop an effective audit approach

– use professional judgement to assess the components of audit risk and to design audit procedures to ensure it is reduced to an acceptably low level.

On the first audit, these requirements are particularly important.

If the audit approach requires a business risk assessment then carry out such an assessment.

i. Prepare an *audit* plan.

j. Prepare a *time budget* and *allocate staff*.

The first audit can now be commenced.

Professional etiquette

3. All professional bodies have codes of conduct governing the relationship between members of the profession and their brother and sister members and the relationship with their clients. Some of the ethical code is explicit and some is implicit but usually understood by members as a consequence of their professional training and experience.

One of the more well known aspects of the ethical code concerns changes in auditor. Organisations can change their auditors at will providing they follow the statutory rules and the particular rules governing the organisation. In the case of a company, this means the Companies Acts and the Company's Articles of Association. However, the professional bodies, e.g. the Institutes of Chartered Accountants and the Chartered Association of Certified Accountants have special rules which their members follow. These are:

a. A member (of an accounting body) on being asked to act as auditor should request the *client's permission* to communicate with the previous auditor (if there is one).

b. If this permission is refused, refuse the appointment as auditor.

c. If permission is given *request in writing*:

all the information which ought to be made available to him/her to enable him/her to decide whether or not he/she is prepared to accept the appointment.

d. A member receiving such a request should, in turn, request the *client's permission* to discuss the client's affairs with the proposed new auditor.

e. If this permission is *refused*, the old auditor will inform the new auditor who will then refuse the appointment.

f. If permission is given then the old auditor:

i. Discloses to the proposed auditor all information which he will need to decide whether or not to accept the appointment.

ii. Discuss freely with the new auditor all matters relevant to the appointment which the new auditor will need to know.

The reason for this rigmarole is:

i. It is a matter of courtesy between professional men.

ii. It enables the proposed auditor to know if it is proper for him to accept the appointment.

iii. It safeguards the position of the retiring auditor.

iv. It protects the shareholders and others interested in the final accounts.

Here is an example of a professional etiquette letter:

Letter to be sent to existing auditors on proposed change of professional appointment (professional etiquette)

Messrs Little, Small & Co.   24 June 20-9

Dear Sirs,

Going Places Limited

We have been invited to accept nomination as auditors to the above company and have been informed that your firm currently acts in that capacity.

We should be grateful if you would let us know whether there is any information of which we should be aware when deciding whether or not to accept this nomination.

Yours faithfully,

Bigg, Large & Co.

Preceding financial statements

4. The new auditor will obtain copies of at least the previous five years' financial statements. This will be important because:

    a. Analytical review includes absolute and ratio comparisons with previous Accounts.

    b. Previous year's figures form the opening position for a current year's Accounts.

    c. Comparative figures must be shown.

    d. Previous years' Accounts may have qualified auditor's reports.

    This matter is dealt with in Chapter 36 in that part of the book dealing with auditors' reports.

5. It is necessary to form an approach to an audit. Possible approaches include:

    a. Substantive testing.

    b. Balance sheet approach.

    c. Business risk approach.

    d. Audit risk approach.

    e. Systems based audits.

    f. Revenue, expenditure and other cycles.

    g. Directional testing.

    h. Analytical review.

    These are not mutually exclusive and some combination of them is usually adopted.

    a. Substantive testing. This has been described earlier in the book and involves tests of details of transactions and balances, review of minutes of directors' meetings and enquiry. It is used on smaller audits when internal controls are few and on items in financial statements which are high risk or particularly important. Substantive testing includes analytical review.

    b. The Balance Sheet approach is predicated on the idea that the Balance Sheet is the most important document of the financial statements. The theory is that if the Balance Sheet is free of misstatement and gives a true and fair view, the Profit and Loss Account and Cash Flow statement cannot be far behind. This approach is most suitable for small companies and larger companies where assets and liabilities are substantial in relation to throughput such as property companies and investment companies.

c. The business risk approach has been considered in a previous chapter. Its use is common amongst the larger firms and larger audit clients. However its use is rare among smaller firms of auditors. The basic idea is to identify material business risks and focus the audit upon areas possibly subject to misstatement because of these risks.

d. The audit risk approach is a subset of business risk and is a requirement for auditors because of SAS 300 and ISA 400. Risks include inherent risks and audit risk comprising compliance risk and detection risk. The idea is to focus the audit on those aspects of the financial statements most at risk of misstatement.

e. Systems based audits are predicated on the idea that it is uneconomic to audit every transaction and that would in any case be useless and there is no way of seeking evidence that all transactions are included. If the system of internal controls is strong and applied throughout the period under review then the routine transactions should be complete and correctly recorded and summarised. This approach is still widely used but is very expensive in practice.

f. Revenue, expenditure and other cycles involves viewing the client as having a series of cycles of activities – sales, purchases, cash and bank, wages and salaries, stocks, capital expenditure etc. Each cycle could be audited in turn. In practice this is simply the systems based audit and was the standard approach until recently.

g. Directional testing is an approach that considers each item in the financial statements for possible misstatements but in one of two possible directions overstatement or understatement. Directors and managers often have some motive for understating or overstating profits or net worth. The reasons for a desire for overstatement may be to meet expectations, requirements of lenders and shareholders or to fulfil previously made forecasts, to fight off a take-over bid or to boost management remuneration when this is based on profit. Conversely, some managements may wish to reduce the measurement of profit. This will particularly be true for private companies because management may wish to reduce tax liabilities or lower the value of the company for capital gains tax or inheritance tax purposes. It is important for an auditor to be aware of these tendencies in client companies and a legitimate audit methodology can be built upon this idea.

h. Analytical review has already been discussed in a previous chapter. It is now a requirement of SAS 410 and ISA 520. Analytical review is now widely used as an audit approach but needs to be supplemented by systems based approaches and other substantive tests.

Summary

6. a. The first audit of a new client is a specially important one as there is much work to be done which will not need to be repeated, but will require review and updating in later audits.

   b. The main work before commencing the detailed work of the audit is:

   i. Communicate with retiring auditor *if any*.

   ii. Confirm *appointment* is valid.

iii. Send and obtain acknowledgement of the *letter of engagement*.

iv. Set up the *permanent file* – in an examination give the headings of the contents.

v. Tour the enterprise and meet directors and staff.

vi. Note important dates.

viii. Examine accounting and control systems and make risk assessments.

vii. Prepare the audit programme.

ix. Prepare time budget and allocate staff.

c. The rules of professional conduct require proposed new auditors to communicate in writing with the previous or existing auditors.

d. The audit approach needs to be selected by some combination of the possible approaches in Para. 5.

Points to note

7. a. Much of the work set out in Para. 2e. is directed towards:

   i. determining if there are any related parties

   ii. identifying areas of audit risk.

   b. Professional etiquette. The communication process between existing and proposed auditors is rigidly adhered to in practice. Note that it is a rule of the professional bodies, not of statute.

Case study 1

Honest & Co. (gross fees £260,000) have been introduced to George Brash, director and principal shareholder in George Brash Ltd, manufacturers of kitchen units. The introduction has been arranged by the bank manager who wishes the company to appoint a qualified accountant and registered auditors instead of Cyril who is not qualified. George agrees to this and meets Honest. At the interview Brash talks the whole time as if the sole task of the auditor is to minimise his tax liabilities. He mentions casually that he had just received a letter from the Inspector of Taxes asking him if his tax return is complete in all particulars. George also states that the company have 30 employees, a turnover of £600,000 and an audit fee of £3,000 which he considers high but Cyril did save him a lot of tax.

It turns out that both George and Honest are members of the Stuffs Golf Club but have never met. George is also an uncle of Gladys, Honest's newly appointed junior typist.

The company's last accounts were for the year ending 31.3.-6 and the interview was on 28.5.-6.

It appears that the company keep excellent records using a commercial micro computer package.

Discussion

a. Go through Honest's routines for considering acceptance of new clients. Should George Brash be taken on?

b. Draft the letter to Cyril.

c. Assuming Honest & Co. accept the audit, outline the procedures to be gone through before starting the audit proper.

d. Prepare an outline audit plan emphasising the timing aspects.

Case study 2

George Rich Ltd is a company owning considerable commercial property (some of it mortgaged) in the UK. The company is largely owned by George Rich and his wife. They live in Portugal. The management of the company is conducted by Silas Sly who is chief executive but has no shares in the company. George is anxious to show low profits and assets on the financial statements to avoid taxation.

Discussion

Consider the business risks with this company and the also the audit risk.

Discuss possible audit approaches.

Student self testing questions *Questions with answers apparent from the text*

1. a. What work should be done before commencing the detail work on a new audit? (2)
   b. List the stages of a professional etiquette exchange of letters. (3)
   c. What work should be carried out on previous accounts? Explain the purposes of the work in each case. (4)
   d. List possible approaches to an audit. (5)

Examination question

1. The firm of Lee & Co. was re-appointed as auditor of Eastern Engineering PLC at the last annual general meeting. Subsequently, however, Eastern Engineering PLC has grown considerably as a result of acquiring other companies and Lee & Co. has decided that it does not have the resources to audit the enlarged group.

   Required:
   a. How can Lee & Co. resign its appointment before the next annual general meeting? What statement must accompany the resignation? (3 marks)
   b. What actions must the company take on receipt of the notice of resignation? (2 marks)
   c. How may the casual vacancy arising be filled and what procedures are necessary before the company's next annual general meeting at which the appointment will be confirmed? (3 marks)
   d. The new auditor will undoubtedly contact Lee & Co. to ascertain certain matters. Draft the letter which the new auditor should send to Lee & Co. (4 marks)
   e. What actions should Lee & Co. take on receipt of the letter from the proposed new auditor and what information should be given? What are the reasons for the various procedures involved? (6 marks)
   f. What do you understand by 'the auditor's lien'? Lee & Co's files relating to Eastern Engineering PLC contain many working papers including:
      i. schedules prepared for audit purposes
      ii. a fixed assets register maintained at the client's request; and
      iii. computations and correspondence relating to corporation tax.
      Discuss the extent to which in normal circumstances they are required to make these documents available to their former client and the new auditor. (7 marks)
      (AAT) (Total 25 marks)

42 Small companies

Introduction

1. Most UK companies are small. The law allows small businesses to trade with limited liability but then requires them to conform to the onerous requirements of the Companies Act. The price of limited liability is disclosure but also much bureaucracy. However there are many relaxations and exemptions from the requirements.

2. This chapter considers small and medium sized companies from several points of view:

   a. Dispensations from appointment of an auditor at the AGM.

   b. Small company audit exemption.

   c. Arguments for and against small and medium-sized company audits.

   d. Abbreviated accounts.

   e. Dormant companies.

   f. The FRRSE financial reporting standard for small companies.

   g. PN 13 The audit of small businesses and IAPS. The special considerations in the audit of small businesses.

   h. Independent professional review.

Dispensations from appointment of an auditor at the AGM

3. Under section 386 Companies Act 1985 a private company may elect (by elective resolution) to dispense with the obligation to appoint auditors annually. Such a company's auditors are deemed to be re-appointed each year.

Small company audit exemption

4. Under S. 249A Companies Act 1985 a small company is exempt from the requirement to have its accounts audited and consequently does not need an auditor. This is subject to certain conditions:

   a. Turnover not more than £1 million.

   b. Balance Sheet total not more than £1.4 million.

   c. It is not a public company or a banking or insurance company.

   d. It is not authorised person or an appointed representative under the Financial Services Act 1986.

   e. It was not a parent company or a subsidiary undertaking.

   However, members of the company, holding not less than 10% of the share capital can require an audit and an auditor.

   It is expected that the government will raise the above exemption limits at intervals initially to £4.8 million turnover. Watch the press on this!

Arguments for and against small and medium sized company audits

5. This subject is very much in the news at the time of writing. The arguments are:

Against an audit

a. Audits are expensive for small companies.

b. They employ highly qualified personnel but achieve little.

c. Alternative and cheaper procedures are just as effective.

d. Audits are merely compliance procedures and add no commercial benefit to the economy as a whole or to individual small companies.

e. Institutions such as banks have their own procedures for monitoring performance and have no need of an audit.

f. Abbreviated accounts ten months after the year end, even if audited, are not of much use.

g. There is often no split between ownership and control (the directors are the shareholders).

For an audit

a. Banking covenants may require audited accounts.

b. Growing companies may need audited accounts in the future (for flotation purposes perhaps).

c. Auditors give assurance to directors that statutory, FRS and SSAP and other requirements have been met.

d. Providers of debt, equity and credit often require audited accounts.

e. Many regulators require audited accounts.

f. Tax inspections can be disastrous and auditors can often uncover likely problems.

g. Audits often uncover frauds and errors and give assurance to directors in this area.

h. Auditors of SMEs generally give advice on all manner of issues.

i. Directors and shareholders often do not trust each other but are too polite to say so. A statutory audit gives them comfort.

j. Matters such as money laundering, environmental compliance and health and safety are often uncovered by an audit.

k. The larger banks have stated that they could not support a rise in the turnover limit above £1 million.

l. The accounting bodies have also stated that could not support a rise in the turnover limit above £1 million.

Abbreviated accounts

6. Small and medium sized companies are permitted to *file*, at Companies House, abbreviated financial statements. They must however produce a full set as normal. Briefly the abbreviated accounts for a small company will be omit the Profit and Loss Account and directors' report and there are some other relaxations. A medium sized company may omit some items in the Profit and Loss Account.

7. The exemption limits for small and medium sized companies are:

	Small sized company	Medium sized company
Turnover	Not more than £2.8 million	Not more than £11.2 million
Balance sheet total	Not more than £1.4 million	Not more than £5.6 million
Number of employees	Not more than 50	Not more than 250

8. The auditors' report need not be filed but the auditors have some duties where abbreviated accounts are delivered (filed). They have to attach a special report stating that in their opinion:

   a. The company is entitled to deliver abbreviated accounts.

   b. The abbreviated accounts to be delivered are properly prepared.

   If the auditors' report is qualified then the special report must include the full auditors' report together with any further material necessary to understand the qualification.

Dormant companies

9. Dormant companies do not need an auditor. Dormant means that the company has had no significant accounting transaction in the relevant period. It does not apply to public companies, banking or insurance companies or to an authorised person or an appointed representative under the Financial Services Act 1986. It does apply if either is a parent company or a subsidiary undertaking.

Financial Reporting Standard for Smaller Entities

10. The FRSs, SSAPs and UITF abstracts are onerous for large companies but much more so for small entities. As a result the ASB has issued this Accounting Standard. It sets out in 140 pages how the financial statements of small entities should be prepared. Small companies are exempt from the other Accounting Standards and the UITF Abstracts. However they may find the other Accounting Standards and the UITF Abstracts, not as mandatory, but as a means of establishing current practice.

11. Small companies are as defined in the Companies Act and exclude large or medium sized companies, banks, building societies, insurance companies, authorised persons under the Financial Services Act 1986 and members of groups that contain any of these types of entity.

PN 13 The audit of small businesses and IAPS – the special considerations in the audit of small businesses

12. This Practice Note has much to say on the audit of small businesses (46 pages) and reviews the application of individual SASs to small businesses. Some salient points are:

   a. Small businesses are special for auditing because of their intrinsic characteristics, the professional relationship nature between the auditor and small businesses and other factors including legal matters and the limitations of small firms of auditors.

   b. Small businesses are those which have:

    i. a concentration of ownership and management

    ii. few sources of income and uncomplicated activities

    iii. simple record keeping

    iv. limited internal controls with management over-ride.

c. It is usually possible for some internal controls to be instituted (pre-printed consecutively numbered invoices etc.).

d. Owner-managers generally have unlimited opportunities for over-ride of controls. As a result errors may be overlooked, assets may be misappropriated and fraudulent transactions take place. On the plus side, owner-managers can exercise much personal control over transactions. Auditors should neither assume that management is dishonest nor assume unquestioned honesty. The watchword is 'show me' not 'tell me'.

e. Smallness and uncomplicated activities, and the close personal relationship with an auditor, make a thorough knowledge of the business much easier.

f. Auditors of small businesses usually prepare the accounts and usually perform other tasks for the business (balancing the books, tax matters, advice etc.) and this close acquaintance with the business can constitute good audit evidence.

g. Auditors of small businesses must always stay objective and should not take over the role of management.

h. Occasionally the uncertainty surrounding small businesses can be *so pervasive* that the business is unauditable. In such cases it may be better to decline to accept or resign the post of auditor or to disclaim an opinion. Usually where uncertainty exists (e.g. on cash sales) an except for opinion is given.

i. Small businesses are subject to the plethora of laws, rules and regulations which afflict all businesses. Auditors need to be aware of these and the potential impact on possible misstatement in the financial statements.

j. Small businesses have more going concern uncertainty than larger businesses as they are often vulnerable to cash flow problems, one or just a few customers, bad debts, single products etc.

k. Completeness is a major problem for small business audits due to the lack of internal controls and a possible tendency of the owner manager to manipulate the business for his own purposes. There are often ways of confirming completeness by analytical review, consecutive numbering, physical reconciliations, and review of transactions after date etc.

l. Related parties can be a problem as owner-managers tend to confuse the business affairs with their own affairs.

As with all audits, a letter of representation is normally obtained from the management. This will include specific references and assurances on completeness of transaction recording especially where cash sales are concerned.

Independent professional review

13. The audit exemption limit has been raised to £1 million and will probably go up to £4.8 million. There are very large number of companies which may dispense with an audit but would like a lesser form of assurance on their financial statements. The government

propose that in the future there will an alternative available called an Independent Professional Review (IPR). This is a form of assurance which is something less than an audit. The differences between an audit and an IPR are:

Audit	Review
High assurance	Moderate assurance
Positive opinion	Negative opinion
Tests of detail	Analytical procedures and enquiry
Obtain and document evidence for all financial statements assertions	No evidence required
Report to members	Report to the Board or to the company

14. The procedures required for an IPR are:

a. Consider your suitability to accept the assignment.

b. Agree an engagement letter.

c. Plan the work to be done (including materiality level).

d. Document all work done.

e. Obtain or update knowledge of the business. It is arguable whether the level of knowledge required is the same as or rather less with an audit. If the reviewer prepared the financial statements, then he/she will probable have obtained sufficient knowledge in the process of preparation.

f. Seek satisfaction that the financial statements are likely to provide a sound accounting platform for the performance of the review. If the reviewer prepared the accounts, obviously they will! Otherwise inspect the quality of the bookkeeping and inspect control accounts, bank reconciliations etc.

g. Perform an in-depth analytical review of the Profit and Loss Account and Balance Sheet. It is not easy to determine the depth of this but it will include comparing ratios against previous years, budgets and industry averages. Other matters may include inspecting an aged list of debtors for anomalies, and reviewing items that required particular management judgement.

h. Make enquiries of the directors.

i. Review the financial statements to see that they comply with the FRSSE and the Companies Act.

j. Review the financial statements to see that they conform to properly explained GAAPs.

k. Consider subsequent events, i.e. events after the performance of the review up to the date the financial statements are approved.

l. Obtain management representations, i.e. written confirmation of oral representations.

m. Draw conclusions and report.

15. The enquiries that the auditor would make to the directors would be into:

    a. Any anomalous variances the review might have indicated (e.g. longer debtor payment period than last year or interest does not square with the liabilities).

    b. Any significant discussions at directors, or shareholders, meetings. It is desirable to read the minutes.

    c. Major matters affecting the company in the year (e.g. new share issues, acquisitions, major capital expenditure).

    d. Any need for impairment of assets, required provisions, disclosures, contingencies, commitments, post balance sheet events, related party transactions.

16. At the end of the review, a report will be prepared. An example of such a report might be:

Review report to the members of AB Limited

We have reviewed the accompanying Balance Sheet of AB Limited at 31 December 200–, and the related statements of income and cash flows for the year then ended. These financial statements are the responsibility of the company's management. Our responsibility is to issue a report on these financial statements based on our review.

We conducted our review in accordance with the International Standard of Auditing applicable to review engagements. This standard requires that we plan and perform the review to obtain moderate assurance as to whether the financial statements are free of material misstatement. A review is limited primarily to enquiries of company personnel and analytical procedures applied to financial data and thus provides less assurance than an audit. We have not performed an audit and, accordingly, we do not express an audit opinion.

Based on our review, nothing has come to our attention that causes us to believe that the accompanying financial statements do not give a true and fair view in accordance with International Accounting Standards.

Kaftan & Co.   10 March 200–

1 High Street

Anytown

This report is drawn up in accordance with International Auditing Standard 910 *'Engagements to Review Financial Statements'*. Consequently the last paragraph states the negative view that that there is no reason to believe that the financial statements do not give a true and fair view and accord with International Accounting Standards. Currently there is no UK standard on the IPR. It was expected that one would appear but the latest news is that the Institute of Chartered Accountants in England and Wales are opposed to the idea of an IPR. We wait and see!

17. It is possible to give a qualified report. The first two paragraphs would be the same and a third and fourth might be:

> 'Management has informed us that no provision has been made for a possible bad debt. We consider that a provision of £x should be made and net income and shareholders' equity reduced by that amount.
>
> Based on our review, except for the effects of the overstatement of debtors described in the previous paragraph, nothing has come to our attention that causes us to believe that the accompanying financial statements do not give a true and fair view in accordance with International Accounting Standards.'

In practice it is unlikely that the directors would issue or publish a review report with a qualification and normally the suggestions of the reviewer would be taken up in the financial statements.

Summary

18. a. Private companies may elect to appoint their auditor in perpetuity.

    b. Most small companies need not have an auditor.

    c. An important current issue is whether a small company's financial statements should be audited.

    d. Small and medium sized companies may file abbreviated accounts.

    e. Dormant companies do not need an auditor.

    f. The FRSSE and PN 13 have much to say.

    g. A new procedure is the Independent Professional Review.

Points to note

19. a The arguments for and against an audit are good exam subjects.

    b. The whole issue of excessive laws, rules, regulation and bureaucracy as they affect small and medium sized businesses is very much on the agenda. Changes need to be monitored.

    c. Audits of all companies and enterprises are governed by the same principles and need for evidence. The particular application of these principles and need for evidence is governed by the practice note.

    d. Small companies are often owned and run by entrepreneurs who are not interested in obeying the bureaucratic rules and see the company as extensions of themselves. This can make life difficult for the auditor. As a result audit risk can be higher in small companies. The need for evidence is still paramount but the type of evidence available may be different from that available in larger enterprises.

Case study 1

Winfred Metal Reclamation Ltd buy scrap metal residues from local companies and treat the residues to recover the metal which is then sold to other local companies. Some purchases are made from itinerant scrap merchants. No evidence is available for the purchase of this scrap which totalled £60,000 in the year ending 30 November 20-6. However there is no evidence that it is incorrect and a director is willing to give a letter of representation containing the usual assurances re completeness and validity. The auditors find all other matter to be satisfactory and records are good.

Figures in the year ending 30.11.-6 are:

	£
Purchases	376,000
Net Profit	24,000
Balance sheet total	121,000
Employees	5

Discussion

a. Is it possible for this company to dispense with an audit? Is this a good idea?

b. Can the company file abbreviated accounts? What should the auditor do if they do?

c. Draft the audit report on the alternative basis of an unqualified report, a report qualified on purchases, a report qualified on accounting records, a disclaimer. What would you do?

Case study 2

Fing Ltd run a garden centre and buy in all that they sell. In previous years they have had an audit from Brown & Co. In the year ending 31 December 20-5, they find themselves exempt from the need for an audit and have elected to dispense with the audit. Brown has been asked to perform an IPR. The financial statements are actually prepared by the owner-manager's brother who has a business studies degree and is the financial director. Brown accepts the appointment and finds on doing his analytical review that the profits are much as the previous year but that the creditors seem well down and the stock is higher than normal. Brown knows that the owner-manager George Fing is trying to sell the business.

Discussion

a. Should the company have had an audit?

b. Should Brown have accepted the IPR?

c. What work should Brown do?

d. Draft a report.

Student self testing questions

20. a   How are auditors appointed if a company elects not to appoint them annually? (3)

b. What companies are exempt from audit? (4)

c. Rehearse the arguments for and against small company audits. (5)

d. What companies can file abbreviated accounts? (6)

e. What abbreviations are allowed? (5)

f. What accounting standards apply to small companies? (9)

g. How does the audit of a small business differ from a large business? (11)

h. Describe an independent professional review. (12–15)

Examination questions

1. The audit of the accounts of small companies creates additional problems for the auditor, when compared with auditing the accounts of large companies. Also it has been suggested that the statutory audit requirement for small companies should be abolished. You are required to:

    a. Briefly discuss the problems of auditing the accounts of small companies. Your answer should describe the circumstances where it is possible to give an unqualified audit opinion on:

        i.   the Balance Sheet

        ii. the Profit and Loss Account.   (7 marks)

    b. Briefly consider the extent to which the statutory accounts of small companies and the statutory audit thereof satisfy the needs of the following users of accounts:

        i.   directors of the company

        ii. shareholders, who are not directors of the company

        iii. creditors including banks

        iv   the Inland Revenue and Customs & Excise (for VAT).   (6 marks)

    c. Discuss the arguments for and against the audit of the accounts of small companies, and give your view on whether the statutory audit of small companies should be abolished.   (12 marks)

    (ACCA) (Total 25 marks)

2. It is widely recognised that the way in which audits of small, owner-managed businesses are conducted will, of necessity, be different to those of larger businesses with formal and well developed systems of internal control on which the auditor can place reliance. It is also generally accepted that the most effective practical form of internal control for a small, owner-managed business is the close involvement of the owner-manager.

    Requirement:

    a. Describe and explain, with the use of appropriate examples, the ways in which an owner-manager can exercise control in such a business.

    b. Discuss briefly the issues that an auditor would need to consider before planning to place reliance on the 'control' provided by the close involvement of the owner-manager in the running of the business.

    c. Discuss the substantive evidence that an auditor may seek to rely upon in order to assure himself as to the completeness of income in a small, owner-managed business. You are to assume that there is no effective internal control upon which the auditor can rely.

    (ICAI)

344

43 Audits of different types of businesses

Introduction

1. There are innumerable types of business and all of them have Accounts, prepared and most of them have these accounts audited. Ideally students would meet every kind of business in their training but in practice only a few are encountered.

2. Every type of business has its audit problems but the sheer number of different types makes it impossible to discuss these problems in this manual in any other than a general way.

3. Some enterprises, for example Local Authorities or Building Societies, are subject to specific statutory requirements on conduct of affairs, Accounts preparation and audit.

4. Some enterprises should have their audits conducted in accordance with specific auditing Practice Notes. These include charities, banks, building societies, insurers, registered social landlords and investment businesses. These Practice Notes are very detailed and giving a detailed account of how to do an audit for all of them would require a manual of unacceptable length. It is unreasonable to expect students to have detailed knowledge of the audit of every type of enterprise and this is not really necessary. For exam purposes it is usually possible to apply a general approach to an audit which will conform to the specialised guidelines giving a general knowledge about enterprises and some imagination.

Common approaches

5. The approach to any particular audit will clearly require some modification to any general approach. However there are many ways in which a general pattern can be used in planning any audit.

   These ideas include setting up a permanent file with:

   a. A copy of any statutory material relating to the conduct of the enterprise, accounts or its audit. For companies this is unnecessary as all auditors know the Companies Act by heart.

   b. A copy of the rules and regulations, constitution or other document governing the specific enterprise. In the case of companies this means the memorandum and articles and in a partnership, the agreement.

   c. An engagement letter.

   d. A copy of the minute relating to the appointment of the auditor.

   e. Notes on the background to the enterprise, the industry it is part of, and its history and prospects.

   f. Notes on the internal structure of the enterprise, products, locations, production systems, personnel, management etc.

   g. Copies of all past accounts with notes on accounting policies and significant ratios. Include also any prospectuses.

6. The audit will need to be planned with audit risk in mind. The balance of audit approach between reliance on internal control, substantive testing and analytical review will need to be determined and documented. The audit should always be conducted in

accordance with ethical principles and especially the Fundamental Principles. The audit will also need to be conducted in accordance with the SASs.

Specific enterprises

7   The specific approach to a particular audit is a function of the type of business involved. A good approach might be:

a.   Revenues and expense. Consider the kinds of revenue and expense you would expect and the particular problems which might arise in controlling them and recording them.

b.   Assets and liabilities. Consider the kinds of assets and liabilities which are likely to be found and any particular problems which might arise in verifying their existence, ownership, valuation and presentation in the accounts.

c.   Internal control. Consider any special problems which might arise. A likely area is cash receipts.

d.   Accounting policies. Consider any problems of accounting measurement which affect the accounts.

e.   Audit risk. Consider any matters which might give rise to greater than normal audit risk. In some enterprises these might be cash receipts, in others the valuation of stock and work in progress.

f.   Consider any accounting or auditing rules required by statute. For example the audit of building societies is governed by the Building Societies Act 1986.

g.   Consider the requirement of any regulatory body, for example the Building Societies Commission or IMRO.

h.   Consider the requirements of any SORP.

i.   Consider any specific Practice Note or other official guidance on how to conduct the audit.

j.   Consider the form of report which should have the following sections:

   i.   addressee
   ii.   financial statements audited
   iii.   auditing standards followed
   iv.   respective responsibilities of management and auditors
   v.   the work done
   vi.   the basis of the auditor's opinion
   vii.   the audit opinion (which is usually in true and fair terms)
   viii. any other opinions prescribed by statute or other official requirements
   ix.   identity of the auditor
   x.   date of the report.

Summary

8.   a.   Audits can be conducted on the accounts of any enterprise. All are different and present different auditing problems.

   b.   All audits should be conducted in accordance with the Ethical Code, the Auditing Standards, any Practice Notes or Bulletins and with any relevant statute.

    c. A general approach to all audits can be determined.

    d. Each audit can present special features in revenues, expenses, assets and liabilities, internal control, accounting polices and audit risks.

Points to note

9. Examiners do not expect detailed knowledge of special sorts of enterprises but do expect imagination from the examinee. The tendency is to a case study approach so that the student can apply general auditing principles to specific cases.

As an example the auditing of a Housing Association may present special features but primarily it is just an audit. The rental income should be verified as in any rent receivable situation. Outgoings can be verified with vouchers and other evidence as in any business. Students with imagination will realise that outgoings should be authorised by the management committee and the authorisation evidenced by a minute. Outgoings must also be within the constitutional powers of the Association. Financial statements should conform to the SASs and the relevant SORP. The audit should be conducted in accordance with PN 14 .

Case study 1

Suburbelec Ltd is a private company owned and directed by Wyre. The company have a shop in the suburbs of Wentown and repair and sell televisions, videos and other electrical and electronic appliances and apparatus. They also sell records and tapes and run a video library. They also offer television and video rentals. The company is heavily indebted to the bank but is reasonably profitable. The company rent the premises on a seven year lease with three years to run.

Discussion

    a. Draw up a memorandum detailing: types of revenue, types of expense, types of asset and types of liability, internal control problems, business and audit risk areas.

    b. List the contents of a permanent audit file for this company.

Case study 2

Alan, Bruce, Cheryl and Donna are in a partnership as dental surgeons. Their accounts are prepared for years ending 31 March by Evan, a chartered certified accountant. The partners have requested that this year (year to 31 March 20-7) the accounts should be done as early as possible and should be subject to a full audit. The practice does both National Health Service and private work. A legally drawn partnership agreement exists. The partnership own the freehold of the building in which they carry on their practice. The building is subject to a mortgage. The partners employ four dental nurses, three receptionists, one of whom keeps the excellent accounting records.

Discussion

    a. Draw up an engagement letter. Evan has not previously agreed one with the partners.

    b. Draw up the audit plan in detail.

    c. Identify any accounting problems that may occur.

    d. Draft an auditor's report assuming all is well and no qualification is necessary.

e. What problems may arise if the audit is to be completed by 30 April 20-7?

Case study 3

The employees of Big PLC are all members of an occupational pension scheme run by trustees. Watchdog is the auditor and is approaching the audit for the calendar year 20-1.

Discussion

Without considering the specific detail of PN 15 and using your knowledge and imagination:

    a. List the documents and institutions that might be relevant to the audit and financial statements.

    b. Explain how the scheme might work.

    c. List the business and audit risks relating to the scheme.

    d. State who might you report to.

    e. Prepare an audit plan.

Student self testing questions

1. a. List the contents of the permanent file. (5)

    b. What general principles apply to all audits? (6)

    c. List the steps in a general audit approach. (7)

    d. What will be the contents of an audit report? (7)

Examination question

1. The Howdedo Charity derives income from the following sources

    a. Legacies from friends of the charity.

    b. Donations received in cash through the post from the public.

    c. Street collections and flag days.

    d. Grants from the government.

Required

Outline the internal control the auditor might expect the charity to use in respect of *each* of the above sources of income.

(LCCI)

The examination did not ask for this but you should also outline how you might audit these items.

Internal auditing

1. Auditing has been regarded, in this manual, as the activity carried on by the auditor when he verifies accounting data, determines the accuracy and reliability of accounting statements and reports, and then reports upon his efforts. It is essentially an activity carried on by an *independent person* with the aim of *reporting on the truth and fairness* of financial statements.

2. Another type of auditing – internal auditing – exists in business and this part of the manual deals with it.

3. This type of auditing is included in this manual because:

    a. Students of auditing should at least know what it is.

    b. External auditors often find their work overlaps that of the internal auditor and an understanding must be established between internal and external auditors.

    c. Examinations often include questions requiring some knowledge of internal auditing.

4. Chapter 44 deals with internal auditing. Chapter 45 deals with the reliance which an external auditor may place on the work of the internal auditor.

44 Internal auditing

Introduction

1. Very large organisations (and some small ones) have found a need for an internal audit in addition to an external audit. Internal auditors are employees of the organisation and work exclusively for the organisation. Their functions partly overlap those of the external auditors and in part are quite different.

2. The *precise* functions of external auditors are either laid down by statute or embodied in a letter of engagement. The functions (which are rarely *precisely* laid down) of internal auditors are determined by management and vary greatly from organisation to organisation.

3. The importance of internal audit has been recognised by the committee on corporate governance and the listing rules now have a section on it. See Points to note at the end of this chapter.

4. Internal audit can be defined as:

    'An independent appraisal function established by the management of an organisation for the review of the internal control system as a service to the organisation. It objectively examines, evaluates and reports on the adequacy of internal control as a contribution to the proper, economic, efficient and effective use of resources.'

5. Internal auditing is thus:

    a. Carried on by independent personnel. Internal auditors are employees of the firm and thus independence is not always easy to achieve. However it can be assisted by:

- having the scope to arrange its own priorities and activities
- having unrestricted access to records, assets and personnel
- freedom to report to higher management and where it exists to an audit committee
- IA personnel with an objective frame of mind
- IA personnel who have no conflicts of interest or any restrictions placed upon their work by management
- IA personnel having no responsibility for line work or for new systems. A person cannot be objective about something he/she has taken responsibility for. On the other hand the IA should be consulted on new or revised systems
- IA personnel who have no non-audit work.

Since internal auditors are employees it is difficult to ensure that they are truly independent in mind and attitude.

b. An appraisal function. The internal auditor's job is to appraise the activity of others, not to perform a specific part of data processing. For example, a person who spent his time checking employee expense claims is not performing an internal audit function. But an employee who spent some time reviewing the system for checking employee expense claims may well be performing an internal audit function.

c. As a service to the organisation.

The management requires that:

i. Its *policies* are fulfilled.

ii. The *information* it requires to manage effectively is reliable and complete. This information is *not only* that provided by the accounting system.

iii. The organisation's assets are safeguarded.

iv. The internal control system is well designed.

v. The internal control system works in practice.

The internal auditor's activities will be directed to ensuring that these requirements are met.

The internal auditor can be seen as the eye of the board within the enterprise.

d. Other duties may include:

i. Being concerned with the implementation of social responsibility policies adopted by top management. An example of this is in energy saving.

ii. Being concerned with the response of the internal control system to errors and required changes to prevent errors.

iii. Being concerned with the response of the internal control system to external stimuli. The world does not stand still and the internal control system must continually change.

iv. Acting as a training officer in internal control matters.

vi. Auditing the information given to management particularly interim accounts and management accounting reports.

vii. Taking a share of the external auditor's responsibility in relation to the figures in the annual accounts.

viii. Being concerned with compliance with external regulations such as those on the environment, money laundering, financial services, related parties etc.

Essential elements of internal audit

6.   The essential elements of internal audit are:

a.   Independence – see above.

b.   Staffing – the internal audit unit should be adequately staffed in terms of numbers, grades and experience.

c.   Training – all internal audit should be fully trained.

d.   Relationships – internal auditors should foster constructive working relationships and mutual understanding with management, with external auditors, with any review agencies (e.g. management consultants) and where appropriate with an audit committee. Mutual understanding is the goal.

e.   Due care – an internal auditor should behave much as an external auditor in terms of skill, care and judgement. He should be up to date technically and have personal standards of knowledge, honesty, probity and integrity much as an external auditor. It is desirable that an internal auditor be qualified as much because of the ethical as the technical standards implied by membership of a professional body.

f.   Specifically the stages of internal audit planning are:

i.   identify the objectives of the organisation (the organisation may have a mission statement)

ii.   define the IA objectives

iii.   take account of relevant changes in legislation and other external factors (e.g. new legislation)

iv.   obtain a comprehensive understanding of the organisation's systems, structures and operations

v.   identify, evaluate and rank risks to which the organisation is exposed (e.g. retail cash sales, potential stock losses)

vi.   take account of changes in structures or major systems in the organisation (e.g. a change in the computer system)

vii.   take account of known strengths and weaknesses in the internal control system

viii.   take account of management concerns and expectations

ix.   identify audit areas by service, functions and major systems

x.   determine the type of audit: e.g. systems (e.g. sales or stock control), verification (e.g. cash balances or vehicles), or value of money (e.g. the internal audit department or the old peoples homes in a Local Authority)

xi.   take account of the plans of external audit and other review agencies (e.g. the regulatory agencies in financial services, banking or insurance)

xii.   assess staff resources required and match with resources available (there never are enough!)

g.   Systems controls – the internal auditor must verify the operations of the system in much the same way as an external auditor i.e. by investigation, recording, identification of controls and compliance testing of the controls. However an internal auditor is also concerned with:

- the organisation's business being conducted in an orderly and *efficient* manner
- adherence to management *policies* and *directives*
- promoting the most *economic*, *efficient* and *effective* use of resources in achieving the management's policies
- ensuring compliance with statutory requirements
- securing as far as possible the completeness and accuracy of the records
- safeguarding the assets.

h. Evidence – the internal auditor has similar standards for evidence as an external auditor, he will evaluate audit evidence in terms of sufficiency, relevance and reliability.

i. Reporting – the internal auditor must produce timely, accurate and comprehensive reports to management on a regular basis. These should report on the matters outlines in g. above and with the accuracy of information given to management and give recommendations for change.

External and internal auditors compared and contrasted

7. **Common interests**

a. An effective system of internal control.

b. Continuous effective operation of such system.

c. Adequate management information flow.

d. Asset safeguarding.

e. Adequate accounting system (for example to comply with the Companies Act 1985).

f. Ensuring compliance with statutory and regulatory requirements.

8. **Differences**

a. **Scope** – the extent of the work undertaken. Internal audit work is determined by management but the external auditor's work is laid down by *statute*.

b. **Approach**. The internal auditor may have a number of aims in his work including an appraisal of the efficiency of the internal control system and the management information system. The external auditor is interested primarily in the truth and fairness of the accounts.

c. **Responsibility**. The internal auditor is answerable only to management. The external auditor is responsible to shareholders and arguably to an even wider public. Both are of course answerable to their consciences and the ethical conceptions of their professional bodies.

9. **Areas of work overlap**. This can apply in the following areas:

a. Examination of the system of *internal control*.

b. *Examination of the accounting records* and supporting documents.

c. Verification of assets and liabilities.

d. Observation, enquiry and the making of statistical and accounting ratio measurements.

Summary

10. a. Internal auditing is a fast growing and important activity.

b. Internal auditing has a definition.

c. The essential elements of an internal audit function are: independence, staffing, training, relationships, due care, planning, controlling, recording, systems controls, evidence and reporting.

d. There are differences between internal and external audits in terms of: scope, approach, responsibility and persons to report to.

Points to note

11. a. The work of internal auditors very often includes checking documents. An example of this is that local authority internal auditors often examine the documents and authorities supporting payments. This kind of work is not included in the definition in Para. 4. By this definition, the work of the internal auditor is directed towards the appraisal of the controls applied by other people in the organisation.

b. Internal auditing is now considered a major discipline and there are many textbooks on the subject. This manual is about external auditing and I have included internal auditing only in outline.

c. It is important that internal audit report to the highest level, preferably the board or an audit committee.

d. The Combined Code on Corporate Governance requires that *listed* companies, which do not have an internal audit function, should from time to time review the need for one. It also says that the directors should annually review the factors (e.g. increased risks) which might make an internal audit function desirable. Companies that do have an internal audit function should annually review the scope of work, authority and resources, having regard to any new factors such as increased business risk, reorganisations, systems changes, increased incidence of unexpected occurrences. If the company does not have an internal audit function and the board has not reviewed the need for one, the listing rules require the board to disclose these facts. If the auditor finds that the disclosure by the board is not in accordance with the work actually carried out by the directors, then a report like that of Para. 9 of Chapter 36 may be necessary.

e. A summary of the stages in a systems audit might be:

   i. Identify the system parameters (e.g. the details of a system for identifying bad credit risks before sales).

   ii. Determine the control objectives (e.g. to prevent sales to bad credit risks).

   iii. Identify expected controls to meet control objectives (e.g. inspection of sales ledger account before granting credit to existing customer).

   iv. Review the system against expected controls (e.g. is inspection of the sales ledger account included in the system?).

   v. Test the controls designed into the system against control objectives (e.g. are the sales ledger inspections and other controls adequate [or alternatively too stiff] to prevent sales to bad risks).

   vi. Test the actual controls for effectiveness against control objectives.

vii. Test the operation of controls in practice.

viii. Give an opinion based on audit objectives as to whether the system provides an adequate basis for effective control and whether it is properly operated in practice.

Note that the external auditor may have more restricted aims in examining internal controls. In our case she may only be interested in the controls because she wishes to place part reliance on the controls in assessing the adequacy of the bad debt provision.

f. Internal audit is very important in many entities as a contribution toward *value for money*. Value for money essentially has three aspects:

i. Economy – acquire inputs of the appropriate quality and quantity at *lowest possible cost*.

ii. Efficiency – maximum outputs for minimum inputs.

iii. Effectiveness – how well intended goals and effects are achieved.

Case study 1

Boggle Manufacturing PLC is a manufacturer of mechanical engineering products with six factories, twelve sales depots in the UK and six in Europe. They have 4,000 employees. The company have a good system of budgetary control and standard costing. The chairman of the company is also a vice chairman of an ecological pressure group. The company have come under financial pressure to reduce costs to restore profitability.

Discussion

Draw up a job specification for the appointment of an internal auditor.

Case study 2

Rapiddev PLC is a listed company in the food processing industry. They have 12 factory sites and 3,000 workers. They have grown very rapidly in recent years under the direction of Dev who is a very dynamic character. He tries to operate on the lowest possible costs and sees internal control as himself and his factory managers. The company have recently moved into the production of mass produced Indian meals and have gambled that they will grab a large market share. They have an audit committee (not liked by Dev) but no internal audit function.

Discussion

a. What advantages might accrue to the company if they set up an internal audit function?

b. What duties re internal audit are imposed on the company by the code?

c. How might the auditors approach the audit?

d. What specific duties are imposed on the auditor re internal control and internal audit?

Student self testing questions *Questions with answers apparent from the text*

1. a. Define internal auditing. (4)

b. List characteristics of independence for an internal auditor. (5a)

c. Should an internal audit prepare a bank reconciliation statement? (5b)

d. What may an organisation require from internal audit? (5c)

e. List some duties of an internal auditor. (5d)

f. List the essential elements of internal audit. (6)

g. List common interests of internal and external auditors. (7)

h. List the differences between them. (8)

i. List the stages in internal audit planning (6f)

j. List the stages in a systems audit of bank reconciliations (11e)

Examination questions

1. Grumbleweed PLC is appointing an internal auditor.

  a. Outline the nature of internal auditing. (3 marks)

  b. What qualities would you look for when appointing an internal auditor? (3 marks)

  c. Give two examples of the work done by an internal auditor. (6 marks)

  d. To whom should an internal auditor report? (3 Marks)

(LCCI) (Total 15 marks)

2. One of the roles of internal audit is the safeguarding of assets and one of the big risks to business assets is that of fraud. If the auditor is to be successful in ensuring that adequate controls exist to deter fraud and to detect it he/she should be aware of the circumstances in which fraud may be fostered.

  a. What are the main causes of, or circumstances which foster, fraud? (12 marks)

  b. What safeguards would the auditor look for to deter and detect fraud? (8 marks)

(ICA) (Total 20 Marks)

45 Reliance on internal audit

Introduction

1. Many larger organisations have an internal audit department. The personnel of this department will be employees of the organisation and their work will be directed by the management or to the Audit Committee if there is one. However, they often have a degree of independence and may report to the Board directly or, at least, to top management. The work they do may include work also done by the external auditor. Consequently, it is economic good sense for the external auditor to consider whether he can reduce his own work by placing reliance on the work of an internal auditor.

2. There is a Statement of Auditing Standards SAS 500 *Considering the Work of Internal Audit* and ISA 610 *Considering the Work of Internal Auditing.*

3. The previous chapter considers internal auditing as a separate but related discipline to external auditing.

Reasons for co-operation

4. Internal audit is an element of the internal control system established by management. Thus as external auditors are accustomed to place reliance on internal controls they will consider if reliance can be placed on this element.

5. Some of the objectives of internal audit are the same as those of the external auditor. For example, the internal auditor will perform work on the documentation and evaluation of accounting systems and internal controls and will carry out compliance and substantive tests. It makes economic sense to reduce the work of the external auditor by relying on work done by the internal auditor.

Basis of co-operation

6. The external auditor may utilise the work of the internal auditor in two ways:

    a. by taking into account the work done by the internal auditor

    b. by agreeing with management that internal audit will render direct assistance to the external auditor.

Nature of internal auditing

7. The scope and objectives of internal audit are set by management and vary widely. The areas of activity may include:

    a. reviewing accounting systems and internal control

    b. examining financial and operating information for management, including detailed testing of transactions and balances

    c. reviewing the economy, efficiency and effectiveness of operations and of the functioning of non financial controls

    d. review of the implementation of corporate policies, plans and procedures

    e. special investigations

    f. review of compliance with laws, regulations and other external requirements and with management and directives and other internal requirements.

8. Some of these functions are directly relevant to the objectives of the external auditor – seeking evidence of the truth and fairness etc., of items in the Accounts. Even special investigations may be relevant. For example, an investigation into the extent of slow moving stock is relevant to the value of stock or an investigation into the viability of a branch may be evidence as to the correctness of the using of going concern values for that branch's assets.

    A modern example of a relevant investigation may be into compliance with statute or regulatory body requirements. The internal audit department may be assigned to determine the detailed controls designed to ensure compliance with some environmental requirement. This may not seem to be of interest to the external auditor but the fact may be that non-compliance may lead to the closure of a factory and consequent losses and expenses and removal of going concern values to some part of the assets. Clearly the external auditor in such a case must have assurance that compliance is assured and the internal auditor may be able to provide that assurance.

9. Some of the functions are clearly not relevant to the external auditor's objectives. For example, the cost of a control is not relevant, only its effectiveness.

10. Some internal audit work is not audit work at all but is a part of internal control. For example, internal audit in Local Authorities may scrutinise and approve expense claims. Such work is an internal control but it is not auditing.

Assessment

11. Before placing any reliance on the work of an internal auditor, the external auditor must assess the internal auditor and his work in the following areas:

   a. *Independence*. The internal auditor may be an employee of the organisation, but he may be able to organise his own activities and report his findings to a high level in management. An internal auditor on whom the external auditor places reliance must be independent and be able to communicate freely with the external.

   b. The *scope* and *objectives* of the internal audit function areas such as 7.a. and b. are likely to be useful to the external auditor. But c., d. and e. may also. For example, an investigation into a fraud may supply evidence to the external auditor that the extent of the fraud is not material.

   c. *Due professional care*. To be useful to an external auditor the internal auditor's work must be done in a professional manner. That is, it must be properly planned, controlled, supervised, recorded and reviewed. The auditor who arrives in the morning and says to himself 'what shall I do today?', is not much use.

   d. *Technical competence*. Membership of a professional body with its competence and ethical implications is desirable. Ongoing training in specialist areas, such as computers, is useful.

   e. *Reporting standards*. A useful internal auditor will provide high standard reports which are acted upon by management.

   f. *Resource available*. An internal audit department that is starved of resources will not be very useful to the external auditor.

12. The assessment should be thorough and fully documented and included in the working papers. If the conclusion is that the internal audit department is weak or unreliable, then this fact should be communicated in the external auditor's 'report to management'.

Extent of reliance

13. The extent of reliance depends on many factors including:

   a. The *materiality* of the areas or items to be tested. Petty cash expenditure may probably be left to the internal auditor.

   b. The level of *audit* risk inherent in the areas or items. The value of work in progress in a civil engineering company or the provision for doubtful debts in a hire purchase company, are high risk areas which the external auditor must see to himself.

   c. The level of *judgement* required. The level of delayed repairs in a truck leasing company requires careful judgement.

   d. The sufficiency of *complementary* audit evidence. The internal audit may be relied upon to audit debtors accounting procedures if the external auditor has evidence in the form of a debtor's circularisation.

   e. *Specialist* skills possessed by internal audit staff. In a bank, the internal audit department will have specialist knowledge and skills in the appraisal of the bank's computer systems.

Detailed planning

14. Having decided that he *may* be able to place reliance on the work of the internal auditor, the external auditor should:

    a. agree with the chief of internal audit the timing, test levels, sample selection procedures and the form of documentation to be used

    b. record the fact of his intended reliance, its extent and the reason for the fact and extent, in his working papers

    c. confirm with top management that he is doing so.

Controlling

15. In order to be able to ultimately place reliance on the work of the internal auditor, the external auditor should:

    a. consider whether the work has been properly staffed, planned, supervised, reviewed and recorded

    b. compare the results with other evidence (e.g. debtors circularisation)

    c. satisfy himself that any unusual or 'put upon enquiry' items have been fully resolved

    d. examined the reports made and the management's response to the reports

    e. ensure the work is to be done in time.

    At the conclusion, the arrangements should be reviewed to make things even better next year.

Recording

16. The external auditor will have a high standard of recording in working papers. The internal auditor's work must be equally good if it is to be relied upon.

Evidence

17. The detailed material in this chapter is important for students, but you should not lose sight of the fact that an audit is about *audit evidence*. The work of the internal auditor is evidential material. Whether it is good evidence supplying a reasonable basis for conclusions to be reached, is a matter of judgement. It may be desirable for the external auditor to test the work of the internal auditor by supplementary procedures or by re-testing transactions or balances tested by the internal auditor.

Report to management

18. Whether or not any work of the internal auditor is relied upon, the internal auditor may uncover and report on weaknesses in internal controls. If the internal auditor reports to management and management responds, then the matter may rest there. If, however, weaknesses are material and the response by management inadequate, then it may be desirable to include the weaknesses in the external auditor's own *report to management*.

Summary

19. a. Internal and external auditors do similar work and economics dictates that they should co-operate.

b. Internal auditing has many objectives and some of these may be useful to an external auditor.

c. The external auditor must assess the internal auditor and his work.

d. The extent of reliance may depend on materiality, audit risks, level of judgement required, the level of complementary evidence and the specialist skills required.

e. The process of relying on the work of an internal auditor must be planned, controlled and recorded.

Points to note

20. a. With constant pressure on costs and fee levels, external auditors are increasingly tempted to rely on the work of the internal auditor.

b. Internal auditing is a growth field and the subject of this chapter will increase an importance.

c. In many large organisations, e.g. banks, the external auditor has no choice but to rely on the work of the internal auditor.

d. Increased computerisation with its concommitant increase in potential fraud, has led to an upgrading in the importance and quality of internal audit.

e. Internal auditing can be carried out by the enterprise's own staff, a third party or the external audit firm. Whoever carries it on, it is still a part of the enterprise's activities. It can never have the necessary degree of autonomy or objectivity as is required by the external auditor when expressing an opinion on the financial statements.

Case study 1

Shark Estate Agents Ltd is a company offering estate agency services to the public through a network of branches in the Midlands. The company has some 270 staff in all. The board consists of six people, a part-time chairman, a chief executive, two other full time executives and two representatives of the owners. The company is jointly owned by an American bank and a city property group. The company have an internal audit department consisting of Legge who is a young chartered certified accountant and Foot who is an accounting technician. They also have a secretary, Mavis. They report their activities monthly in detail to the board and to the audit committees of the American bank and the city property group.

Discussion

a. What work would the internal audit department do?

b. In what ways may the external auditors place reliance on their work?

c. Draw up a check list which the external auditor could use to assess the internal auditors as potentially being capable of producing work on which the external auditors may rely.

Student self testing questions *Questions with answers apparent from the text*

1. a. Why might an external audit rely on the work of an internal auditor? (1)

b. In what way may they co-operate? (6)

c. How may the external auditor assess the internal auditor and his work? (11)

d. What factors influence the extent of reliance in a particular area? (13)

e. How might the co-operation be planned and controlled? (14, 15)

f. What implications has all this for the external auditors' working papers? (16)

Examination question

1. The growing recognition by management of the benefits of good internal control, and the complexities of an adequate system of internal control have led to the development of internal auditing as a form of control over all other internal controls. The emergence of the internal auditor as a specialist in internal control is the result of an evolutionary process similar in many ways to the evolution of independent auditing.

   Required:

   a. Explain why the internal and independent auditors' review of internal control procedures differ in purpose. (4 marks)

   b. Explain the reasons why an internal auditor should or should not report his findings on internal control to the following selection of company officials:

   i. the chief accountant

   ii. the board of directors. (6 marks)

   c. Explain whether the independent auditor can place any reliance upon the internal auditor's work when the latter's main role is to be of service and assistance to management. (6 marks)

   d. List four internal control procedures which could be performed on a regular basis by the manager of a small company which does not have an internal audit department. (4 marks)

   (ACCA) (20 marks)

2. You are the external auditor of Stores PLC, a large company which operates a country-wide chain of department stores selling a variety of goods including foods, clothing and household items. The company has an internal audit department which visits branches on a rotational basis.

   You are required to explain:

   a. The audit steps you consider necessary to establish to your satisfaction the completeness, accuracy and validity of the branch accounting records, and

   b. the steps you would take if your audit procedures led you to conclude that there were serious weaknesses in the application of branch procedures at several branches.

   (IComA)

Auditors and the law

1. You will already have appreciated that the law has relevance for auditors. The companies acts and their effect on auditors have taken up a large part of the manual.

2. Other branches of the law have also affected auditors and this part considers some of them. Some of the points made are about controversial issues which have practical and examination importance at the present time.

3. Chapter 46 deals with an auditor's obligations and liabilities under the law and Chapter 47 deals with unlawful acts.

46 Auditors' liability

Introduction

1. Auditors perform audits and sign audit reports. These reports are the auditors' opinions on the truth and fairness etc. of financial statements. Auditors are known to be competent and honest. So if the auditors say financial statements show a true and fair view, readers of the financial statements will have faith in them because they have faith in the auditors.

2. As his work is relied upon by others the auditor clearly has a responsibility to do his work honestly and carefully. The judge in the London and General Bank case (1895) said:

   'He must be honest – that is, he must not certify what he does not believe to be true, and he must take reasonable care and skill before he believes that what he certifies is true.'

3. What is *reasonable care and skill* depends on the circumstances and is very difficult to assess in any given case. What is clear is that:

   a. An auditor may fail to exercise sufficient skill and care.

   b. As a consequence, some fraud or error may be undiscovered, or he may fail to discover that the accounts fail to show a true and fair view, or may contain a material misstatement.

   c. As a consequence somebody who relies on the work of the auditor may lose money.

   d. This loss of money flows from the failure of the auditor to do his job properly.

   For example, Hank PLC., may buy Rabbit Ltd because inter alia, they believed that the accounts of Rabbit Ltd, showed a true and fair view of the liabilities of that company. It turned out that there were several liabilities excluded from the accounts. Botch & Co., the auditors, had failed to discover this as they had not applied the standard tests. Hank PLC would have paid less for Rabbit Ltd, or not bought the company at all had they known about the error in the Accounts.

   e. This point is the vital one, the auditor *may* have to make good from his own resources the loss suffered by another person.

4. The auditor may (this mercifully rare) be dishonest or connive at the dishonesty of others.

5. The problems are:
   a. *What is reasonable care and skill?* We will discuss this later.
   b. To *whom does the auditor have a moral responsibility to do his work properly.* The answer is to his conscience and to any person who relies on his work.
   c. *To whom does the auditor have a legal responsibility?* By legal responsibility we mean an obligation to make good from his own pocket losses suffered by others, or to be more precise 'to pay damages which flow from his negligence'. This is a very difficult question which we shall review in due course.
   d. But first, we shall consider the *criminal law* and the auditor.

6. The criminal law applies to all citizens and auditors could find themselves in the dock if they committed any act which was against the law. Auditors acting as auditors generally do not break the law but it is not impossible to imagine an auditor conspiring with others to defraud the investing public by deliberately publishing a false prospectus. There are some specific crimes or misdemeanours which an auditor may commit. These include:

The Companies Act 1985:
– S.389 Person acting as a company auditor knowing himself to be disqualified.
– S.389A Subsidiary company auditor failing to give information to auditors of parent company.
– S.394A Person ceasing to hold office as auditor, failing to deposit statement as to circumstances.
– S.458 Being a party to carrying on company's business with intent to defraud creditors, or for any fraudulent purpose.

Insolvency Act 1986. Accountants who act as liquidators, receivers or trustees can easily commit technical offences but there are few offences to trap the auditor except perhaps S.208 where, as an officer, he misconducts himself in the course of winding up.

Financial Services Act 1986. There are a number of offences which an auditor can commit under this Act

Civil liability under the common law

7. What is negligence? One definition is: some act or omission which occurs because the person concerned (e.g. an auditor) failed to exercise that degree of reasonable skill and care which is reasonably to be expected in the circumstances of the case. What is reasonable is not what a super careful and expert auditor would do but what an ordinary skilled man (or woman) would do in the circumstances. In the circumstances is an interesting idea. Auditors are expected to carry out audits following the requirements and guidance of the Auditing Standards and using their professional judgement. For example an auditor must consider the going concern basis by following the precepts of SAS 130. However auditing is a sampling process and evidence can be gained by such methods as analytical review and internal control evaluation. Not everything is examined in minute detail for cost and timeliness reasons and because the benefits would hardly outweigh the costs. However routine tests may be inadequate if the auditor is:
   – put upon enquiry
   – encounters increased cause for suspicion
   – the bells start ringing.

In these circumstances the auditor needs to do more than routine testing and evidence gathering. In the words of the old case, he or she needs to probe the matter to the bottom. For example if the auditor comes across a small number of purchase invoices which seem to have dates altered from pre year end to post year end then he is alerted to a possible deliberate attempt to improve the profit as measured. The whole matter is likely to be material and must be probed fully.

A useful equation is that negligence occurs if:

$$\text{Probability of harm or error} \times \text{Gravity of harm or error} > \text{Probability of its discovery by the audit tests conducted}$$

Let us see some examples of this. Suppose in a small company the wages area is controlled by one clerk. In such cases, there is a probability that a fraud could be committed and remain undetected, so the probability of harm is high. On the other hand the gravity of harm done cannot be great as any undetectable fraud could only be a small fraction of the total costs of the enterprise. The auditor might judge that no more tests should be conducted than in cases where internal controls were stronger. In a speculative building company which has built a number of estates on reclaimed land, the probability that damage might occur to the houses is small as all the appropriate tests and certificates were obtained. However the gravity of harm could be very great if a whole estate proved worthless as a result of undiscovered pollution on the reclaimed land. Perhaps in this case the left-hand side of the equation would require extra audit procedures. A third example is that of a company which hedged its exposure to losses on its investment portfolio by dealing in derivatives. In such cases the probability of harm is high and the gravity of any harm could be very great (witness Barings Bank). The auditor needs to investigate and find evidence on the matter in very great detail.

8. The famous case of the *London Oil Storage Co. Ltd 1904* will illuminate the idea of negligence and of loss.

The petty cash was misappropriated over a period of years so that the balance per the petty cash book was £796 in 1902 whereas there was only £30 in the cash box. The auditor did not count the cash and therefore did not discover the embezzlement. It was established that:

a. The auditor was negligent in not counting the cash as he should have been *put upon enquiry* by the surprisingly large amount (in 1902) of the book balance.

b. The company suffered loss.

c. The loss was caused by:

   i. The *directors'* failure to exercise proper control as is their duty.

   ii. The auditors. Not because they failed to discover the loss *already made* (clearly a loss cannot be caused by failing to discover it) but because their failure to discover a loss in previous years led to *further* defalcation.

The auditors should have appreciated that the unusual size of the petty cash balance indicated a probability of harm or error and the gravity of possible harm was also large (in 1904) and so the audit tests conducted were insufficient.

d. The auditors were ordered to repay the loss caused by their negligence which was assessed at five guineas only.

The Hedley Byrne case

9. The next problem to consider follows from the modern concept that financial statements with auditors reports are relied upon not only by the persons with whom the auditors have contractual relations (the company, for example) but also many other people whom we can call *third parties.*

10. If the auditor is negligent and fails to discover that accounts do not show a true and fair view, then other people who rely on the accounts may suffer loss. Such people may include *lenders* or people who may want to *buy the business* or shareholders.

11. The question is 'Does the auditor have a *legal obligation* to recompense third parties who suffer loss as a consequence of his negligence?'. Such an obligation might arise under the *law of tort,* torts being civil wrongs done to people.

12. In the case of *Candler v Crane Christmas & Co. 1959* it was decided that the auditor has no legal obligation in the absence of a *contractual or fiduciary relationship.*

13. However, doubt was cast on this judgement in the case of Hedley, Byrne & Co. Ltd v Heller & Partners Ltd in 1963. The House of Lords decided that the Candler case was wrongly decided and that actions for professional negligence can arise if financial loss is suffered by third parties who rely on the professional skill and judgement of persons with whom they have no contractual or fiduciary relationship. The case concerned a bank and not an accountant but the principle could extend to accountants and auditors.

14. The law was substantially clarified in February 1990 by the decision of the House of Lords in the case of *Caparo Industries PLC v Dickman and Others.* The facts of this case were that Caparo Industries PLC purchased shares in Fidelity PLC from June 1984 and subsequently made a successful takeover bid for Fidelity. Caparo alleged that the purchase of most of the shares were made in reliance on Fidelity's accounts for the year to 31 March 1984 which had been audited by Touche Ross and that those accounts were inaccurate. Caparo alleged that if the true facts had been known they would not have made a bid. The decision was that in these circumstances the auditors owed no duty of care to the shareholders (actual or potential) in respect of investment decisions.

15. Their lordships reviewed the intended purpose of statutory accounts. Primarily the accounts were sent to shareholders in the company in order that they may exercise their proprietary functions that is for the protection of the company and its informed control by the body of shareholders. Clearly accounts can be used for all manner of investment and other decisions but that is not their purpose. If the auditor was negligent and inaccurate accounts were sent to shareholders then they were deprived of their rights to exercise their powers in general meeting. In such cases it is for the company to seek a remedy from the auditors not individual shareholders. To widen the scope of duty of an auditor to include loss caused by reliance on accounts for a purpose for which they were not supplied would be to extend the scope unreasonably.

16. After this decision the profession and insurers breathed a collective sigh of relief. However many commentators were disturbed by the idea that accounts could not be relied upon in making investment decisions. However I take the view that one can rely upon a set of accounts without having the power to sue the auditors if they were negligent. The auditors are not insurers and are not paid to accept a liability to outside parties but only to their clients.

17. However legal opinion is that this decision does not entirely let auditors off the hook. They may still be liable to third parties if at the time of the audit they were aware of the investment in contemplation, knew the investor would receive the accounts and knew the investor was likely to rely on the accounts in considering the investment. Effectively, in auditing a company which is underfunded or vulnerable to takeover the auditor must be careful in his relations with third parties who might be considering an investment so that he is fully aware of his obligations in undertaking the audit.

Minimising liabilities

18. Auditors and accountants can minimise their potential liability for professional negligence in several ways:

    a. by not being negligent

    b. by following the precepts of the auditing standards

    c. by agreeing the duties and responsibilities in an engagement letter. This should specify the specific tasks to be undertaken and exclude specifically those that are not to be undertaken. It should also define the responsibilities to be undertaken by the client and specify any limitations on the work to be undertaken

    d. by defining in their report the precise work undertaken, the work not undertaken, and any limitations to the work. This is so that any third party will have knowledge of the responsibility accepted by the auditor for the work done

    e. by stating in the engagement letter the purpose for which the report has been prepared and that the client may not use it for any other purpose

    f. by stating in any report the purpose of the report and that it may not be relied on for any other purpose

    g. by advising the client in the engagement letter of the need to obtain permission to use the name of the accountant and withholding permission in appropriate cases

    h. by identifying the authorised recipients of reports in the engagement letter and in the report

    i. by limiting or excluding liability by a term in the engagement letter or, to third parties, by a disclaimer in a report.

    j. by obtaining an indemnity from the client or third party

    k. by defining the scope of professional competence to include only matters within the accountants' competence. Do not take on work you are not proficient at.

You will appreciate that an auditor's report under the Companies Act cannot include disclaimers, etc. but it now does include the work done and the responsibilities of the auditors and the directors. However the advice holds good for special investigations and audits for special purposes.

You will also appreciate that auditors and accountants are now required to hold professional indemnity insurance.

The future

19. The problem of liability in tort, and also under contract law, of auditors to companies is currently a very hot potato. Interesting matters that are current include:

    a. a campaign for reform in the USA where awards against auditors have been very great

b. statutory capping (limiting) awards in New South Wales

c. proposals for proportionate liability in the UK and elsewhere. Where negligence can be proved against directors and auditors jointly the usual situation is that the directors have not the funds to pay (they are not insured) and the auditors (or their insurers) have to pay the lot

d. The Companies Act 1989 allowed auditors to be limited liability companies. KMPG partners have voted to turn part of the audit practice into a limited company. KMPG Audit PLC will still be liable for losses occasioned by the company's negligence but the risk of bankruptcy is taken away from the individual partners. Other firms are considering incorporating

e. potential claims against auditors of astronomical sums exist in a number of very public cases. These include BCCI (a claim of up to $3 billion has been mooted) and Lloyds

f. There have been cases where damages have been awarded againts firms of accountants in connection with the audited accounts of companies which have been taken over by other companies. Some damage awards are not fully covered by insurance and there can be a substantial personal loss by the partners.

g. A proposed law in Jersey in the Channel Islands to introduce limited liability partnerships. British firms of auditors should be able to register under this law in Jersey. The effect will be that the firms will have unlimited liability and could go bust. But the individual partners would have limited liability and thus be protected against catastrophic litigation. This is similiar to the situation in the US where firms register under similar legislation in Delaware. This idea is known as the Delaware option.

h. The Limited Liability Partnerships Act 2000 makes limited liability partnerships possible from 2001. Professional firms will be able to register under this Act. The effect of such registration will be:

   i.   An LLP is a new form of body corporate and has its own separate legal personality.

   ii. An LLP has unlimited liability under contracts made and in tort.

   iii. The individual partners have no liabilities to the clients or others (contrast this with ordinary partnerships where liability can extend to all the partners individually).

   iv. An LLP must register and file audited financial statements in true and fair terms.

We wait to see whether accounting firms will register under this new Act.

Should auditors' liabilities be extended?

20. There are some arguments in favour of extending the apparent legal duties of care by auditors to individual shareholders, purchasers of shares and possibly other third parties:

These include:

a. Third parties do rely on the integrity of audited accounts and would seem right that a legal liability should reflect that.

b. Professional men are paid and should therefore be accountable.

c. Where the company suffers loss (e.g. from fraud or theft) because of the auditors' negligence then the current existing legal remedy by the company against the auditor is appropriate. However if the directors overstate the assets and the auditor fails to discover this then the company does not suffer loss. However the shareholders or potential shareholders may suffer loss and it seems right that they should be able to recover this from the auditors.

d. If liability is not extended then the public may perceive that the auditor is liable to no-one, there is no need for the auditor to exercise skill and care and the accounts are not reliable and are of little benefit.

21. There are also many counter arguments including:

a. It is unreasonable and unrealistic to say auditors have a 'liability in an indeterminate amount for an indeterminate time to an indeterminate class' to use the words of Lord Justice Cardozo in 1931.

b. Practical difficulties in deciding whether accounts were relied upon or not – a goldmine for lawyers.

c. The current legal framework sees the purpose of preparing and auditing accounts as assisting shareholders in assessing the stewardship of the directors not in assisting investors in their investments.

d. Audit fees would be astronomic if full liability for investment decisions were taken on.

e. The legal responsibility for producing accounts rests with the directors and it would seem inequitable if the liability arising out of incorrect accounts were transferred to auditors.

f. The work required on an audit would need to be greatly extended at an enormous cost which, on a welfare economics standpoint, would be a misuse of scarce resources.

g. The company pays the auditor and consequently expects to recover damages if the company loses as a result of auditor negligence. However investors do not pay the auditor and so should not expect to recover.

h. Insurance cover for professional indemnity would be even more difficult and expensive to obtain.

Summary

22. a. The criminal law makes possible prosecutions against auditors who act dishonestly or recklessly or connive at dishonesty.

b. Civil liability can arise under the Companies Act and the Common Law.

c. In certain circumstances, civil liability can arise under the law of tort. This type of liability is currently a matter of discussion.

Points to note

23. a. Liability can *only* arise if

i. The auditor can be shown to be negligent.

ii. Loss has been suffered.

iii. The negligence is the *direct cause* of the loss.

    iv. The auditor has *legal* liability in the circumstances.,

b. The section on minimising liabilities is very important. All auditors now have to have insurance cover under professional indemnity policies.

c. Cases of professional negligence concerning auditors very rarely come before the courts as such cases are settled out of court. That such cases are numerous is evidenced by rocketing professional indemnity premiums. The author takes the view that if more cases were allowed to come to the courts the issues of:

    i. what is negligence

    ii. to whom does the auditor have a legal responsibility

would be come clearer.

However in individual cases, a court hearing would involve enormous costs in terms of legal fees, partner time, and adverse publicity.

d. Auditors are required to perform their work with reasonable skill and care. It now seems well established that this means that the auditor must apply the standards of reasonable competent modern auditor. The modern auditor applies all the auditing standards and guidelines. Essentially the defence to a negligence claim is that the auditor followed the auditing standards and guidelines, but see Para. 7.

e. Auditors are now required to carry professional indemnity insurance. There is a tendency to sue the auditor knowing that he will not have to pay but his insurer will. The effect of this is that the insurer will insist on reasonable skill and care on the part of his insured. In addition the professional bodies are required to act under the Companies Act 1989 as regulators of the conduct of their members. Professional accountants like lawyers, insurance brokers and others are finding themselves highly regulated. Perhaps this will lead to higher standards of care.

f. The tests of liability in court are *proximity, foreseeability and reasonableness.*

g. The Contracts (Rights of Third Parties) Act 1999 is now in force. It is too early to say if it will have any effect on auditors' liability.

Case study 1

Wing Prayer & Co. a small firm of Chartered Certified Accountants are the auditors to AHM Publishing Co. Ltd, publishers of text books. During the audit of the December 20-5 accounts the audit senior engaged on the audit fell ill with overwork and was replaced by Guy a third-year graduate trainee. Guy finished the audit and the partner signed a report. Shortly after the AGM which was on 23.6.-6 negotiations began for the sale of the company to Amalgamated Publishers PLC who acquired the company in November 20-6.

The audit of AHM's 20-6 accounts by Puce, Watermelon in March 20-7 revealed that a printing bill for two of AHM's titles dated 30.11.-5 had been disputed and thus not entered in the books. The matter was resolved in August 20-6 when AHM paid the £8,000 owing. The bill was not accrued in the 20-5 accounts.

Amalgamated paid £60,000 for AHM whose reported profits net of management remuneration were: 20-3 £16,000, 20-4 £13,000, 20-5 £17,000.

Amalgamated sued Wing Prayer & Co. for damages.

Discussion

    a. Discuss in detail all the issues raised by this case.

    b. How might Wing Prayer & Co. minimise the chances of a repetition of the case?

Case study 2

Niggle & Co., the auditors to Daffodil Widgets Ltd, gave an unqualified report on 14 December 20-7 on the accounts for the year ending 30 June 20-7. These accounts were seen by The Wednesfield Bank PLC in September 20-8 and the bank lent £50,000 to Daffodil on short-term overdraft on 19 September 20-8. In March 20-9 the company went into liquidation still owing the bank £50,000. The company was hopelessly insolvent and the bank recovered nothing. It turned out that the accounts of June 20-7 were defective in that several substantial creditors were omitted from the accounts. Had these creditors been included it would have been apparent that Daffodil was not a going concern in June 20-7.

Discussion

Can the bank recover from Niggle and Co.?

Student self testing questions *Questions with answers apparent from the text*

1. a. How can an auditor be criminally liable under the Companies Act? (6)

    b. How can an auditor be liable for damages under the Common Law? (7)

    c. Summarise the London Oil Storage case and its lessons. (8)

    d. How can an auditor be liable under the Law of Tort? (9–17)

    e. What conditions must be satisfied for an auditor to have to pay damages for a tort? (23)

    f. Summarise the Hedley Byrne case and its lessons. (13)

    g. How can an audit firm minimise its potential for paying damages? (18)

    h. Summarise the Caparo case. (14)

Examination questions

1. The accountancy profession is constantly concerned by the problem of auditors' liability. Required:

    a. To which parties might the auditor be liable?   (3 marks)

    b. Under what circumstances might the auditor be liable to third parties?   (5 marks)

    c. Your firm has been the auditor of Bonner Publishing for many years. It has recently been discovered that for the past few years, the managing director has consistently overvalued stock. Prepare a note for your audit partner advising him of the possible defences should a liability claim arise.   (7 marks)

(AAT) (Total 15 marks)

2. Audit risk is a combination of the risk that the financial statements being audited may contain material errors and that these errors may not be detected by the auditor's testing procedures. A failure to detect such errors may leave the auditor liable for losses suffered by other parties.

Required:

a. Briefly describe what you understand by the terms 'inherent risk', 'control risk' and 'detection risk'. (5 marks)

b. Explain, in the light of recent case law, what you understand to be the auditor's liability for losses suffered by other parties. (10 marks)

(AAT) (Total 15 marks)

47 Unlawful acts of clients and their staffs

Introduction

1. This subject is a fascinating one for students who may see themselves in the role of Sherlock Holmes. However, the reality of discovering or being involved in crimes committed by a client or members of the client's staff is usually unpleasant or a cause for anguished inner conflict.

2. In practice, an auditor must always act scrupulously and correctly and in accordance with the law.

   He should:

   a. Take legal advice if necessary.

   b. Read the guidance provided by the professional body and by the auditing standards. Current guidance is contained in:

      – *Requirements in Relations to Money Laundering* (this a technical release)

      – *Professional Conduct in Relation to Defaults or Unlawful Acts* (this is ICAEW guidance for members in practice)

      – *SAS 110 Fraud and Error* (see also Chapter 19)

      – *SAS 120 Consideration of Law and Regulations*

      – *SAS 620 The Auditor's Right and Duty to Report to Regulators in the Financial Sector.*

3. An accountant must not himself commit a criminal offence.

   He would do so if he:

   a. Advises a client to commit a criminal offence.

   b. Aids a client in devising or executing a crime.

   c. Agrees with a client to conceal or destroy evidence or mislead the police with untrue statements.

   d. Knows a client has committed an arrestable offence and acts with intent to impede his arrest and prosecution. Impede does not include refusing to answer questions or refusing to produce documents without the client's consent.

   e. Knows the client has committed an offence and agrees to accept consideration (e.g. an excessive audit fee) for withholding information.

f. Knows that the client has committed treason or terrorist offences and fails to report the offence to the proper authority.

g. Various activities in connection with money laundering – see later.

Discovery of unlawful acts

4. If an auditor discovers an unlawful act he will not usually disclose this to the police or other authority unless:

a. The client authorises disclosure.

b. The disclosure is compelled by process of law, e.g. a court order.

c. Disclosure is required in the auditor's own interest e.g. in defending himself against civil or criminal actions.

d. The circumstances are such that the auditor has a public duty to disclose. If he discovers an intention to commit a serious crime or tort for example.

e. Disclosure is required in the circumstances envisaged by advice given on money laundering and disclosure to regulators in the financial sector.

5. The auditor should not disclose unlawful acts (except as outlined in Para. 4) because a common practice of disclosure would impair the frankness with which client and auditor relationships are characterised. Similar frank relationships are common with professional people including doctors, priests, lawyers and bankers.

6. The auditor, on discovering an unlawful act, should consider:

a. That he must do nothing to assist in the offence or to prevent its disclosure.

b. That he must bring all offences of employees to the notice of his client.

c. Accounts must have an auditor's report. If the offence is such that its non-disclosure means that the accounts do not show a true and fair view, he must insist on disclosure or qualify his report.

d. Discovery of material defects in previous accounts should be pointed out to the client with a recommendation for disclosure. If the defect requires the treatment required under FRS 3 on prior year items, disclosure must be made or the auditor's report must be qualified.

e. Should he resign?

Remember that if an auditor resigns, he must make a Statement of Circumstances, detailing the circumstances surrounding his resignation.

Companies

7. Auditors have a statutory obligation to report on the accounts of their company clients. If a qualification is required, then the auditor's report must be qualified. Auditors appointed under statutes e.g. the Companies Acts should not avoid *qualifying their reports by resigning.*

8. If the auditor discovers that previous accounts were materially false then:

a. FRS 3 prior year items may apply.

b. If FRS 3 does not apply, nonetheless shareholders and others may need to be informed. This may put the auditor in a tricky position. He should take *legal advice* and possibly *consult his professional body* before doing anything.

c. In liquidation the auditor can disclose any matter he wishes to the liquidator who in fact becomes his client. Note that the ethical codes of the professional bodies prohibit an auditor from being appointed liquidator of the same company.

Illegal acts and the future

9. Currently all companies are subject to a wide range of regulations in the areas of employment, health and safety, planning, environment etc. Breach of such regulations either intentionally or inadvertently is common. Most of these matters are outside the current remit of the auditor and many are beyond an auditor's competence. However the auditor may come across breaches of regulations in his audit work and normally he will advise his client accordingly. Whether he should inform the proper authorities is a difficult matter although there could be seen to be a public duty to do so in certain very serious circumstances.

The Cadbury Committee took the view that it is the responsibility of the Board of directors to establish what their legal duties are and to ensure that they monitor compliance with them. The committee also took the view that this would be enhanced if the auditor's role were to check that Boards had established their legal requirements and that a working system for monitoring compliance was in place. The committee recognise that it would be difficult to ascribe a wider role than this to the auditor as the auditor would be unlikely to have the necessary expertise. The committee recommended that this subject should be further considered by the accountancy and legal professions and representatives of preparers of accounts.

SAS 120 Consideration of law and regulations

10. SAS 120 makes the following points:

a. Auditors should plan and perform their audit procedures, and evaluate and report on the results thereof, recognising that *non-compliance* by the entity with law or regulations may *materially* affect the *financial statements*. Some clients are in heavily regulated sectors such as banking or waste disposal and auditors must be particularly aware of the effect of non-compliance with such clients. However all businesses are now regulated generally in such areas as planning, health and safety, racial and sexual discrimination and many others. The effect of non-compliance can be fines or litigation which means that *actual or contingent liabilities* should be included in the financial statements. These may be non-material in amount but the auditor needs to be satisfied that this is so. The effect of non-compliance can be more serious including loss of licences or authorisation to continue in business. This may have implications for the financial statements in many ways including the assumption of *going concern* basis.

b. It is the responsibility of *directors* to take steps to ensure that their entity complies with laws and regulations, to establish arrangements for preventing and detecting any non-compliance and to prepare financial statements which comply with all laws and regulations.

c. Directors may fulfil their responsibilities by:
   - maintaining an up-to-date *register* of relevant laws and regulations and monitoring any changes to these
   - instituting and operating appropriate systems of *internal control*

- developing a *code of conduct* to inform employees and to ensure employees are trained and that sanctions exist against breaches
- engaging legal advisers to assist in this area
- maintaining a register of complaints and breaches
- in large companies, maintaining internal audit and compliance functions as separate departments.

d. Auditors plan their work with a reasonable expectation of detecting material misstatements in the financial statements that may arise through non-compliance. As a simple example, an auditor would need evidence that a new building constructed for a client had planning consent and complied with building regulations. Auditors however cannot be expected to find all breaches as many breaches have no material effect on the financial statements, audit procedures include sampling and audit evidence is persuasive rather than conclusive. There is also the points that auditors may rely on internal controls in many areas and these may not always reveal breaches and the auditor cannot be expected to detect non-compliance hidden by collusive behaviour, forgery, override of controls or intentional misrepresentations by management.

e. The auditors should obtain sufficient appropriate audit evidence about compliance with those laws and regulations which relate directly to the preparation of, or the inclusion or disclosure of specific items in, the financial statements. Examples are the Companies Act, other statutes and SORPs.

f. The auditors should perform procedures to help identify possible or actual instances of non-compliance with those laws and regulations which provide a legal framework within which the entity conducts its business and which are central to the entity's ability to conduct its business and hence to its financial statements. Examples of such laws and regulations may be pertinent in entities such as financial service companies, casinos, bus companies. Procedures may include obtaining a general understanding of the rules, inspection of licences and correspondence with authorities, enquiry of the directors on any non-compliance and obtaining written assurance from the directors that they have given the auditors all information on non-compliance.

g. On the audit, staff should be alert for instances of actual or possible breaches which might affect the financial statements.

h. When actual or possible breaches are encountered the auditors should gather all possible information and evidence, evaluate it and fully document their evidence, reasoning, findings and conclusions. The matters should be discussed with management and in rare cases, after due consideration and taking legal advice, reported to third parties.

i. Effects of non-compliance on the auditors' report. There are several possibilities (see Chapter 36):

- fundamental uncertainty about the consequences – include an explanatory paragraph in the report
- disagreement with the consequent accounting treatment or disclosure – adverse or qualified opinion

- inability to determine the existence of or consequences of a non-compliance – a disclaimer or a qualified opinion on grounds of limitation of scope.

Money laundering

11. There is much public disquiet about money laundering by drug traffickers, terrorist organisations and other criminal persons. The government added to the possibilities of preventing and detecting such activities in the Criminal Justice Act 1993 and The Money Laundering Regulations of 1994. The effect of this legislation on accountants and auditors is to add a risk of committing criminal offences. It is now a criminal offence to fail to maintain appropriate procedures for the prevention or reporting of money laundering, while carrying out relevant financial business. Possible professional activities here include banking, insurance and investment business but also advice and administrative services in the ordering of personal affairs, advice on setting up trusts, companies and other bodies, arranging loans and acting as a trustee. In engaging in any such activities accountants need to have procedures to recognise, prevent and report money laundering. Reporting of money laundering suspicions is specifically exempted from *all confidentiality* requirements. It is also notable that it is a criminal offence to disclose (e.g. to the directors) that a money laundering suspicion has been reported to the authorities. Clearly the guilty parties must not be given the tip off to run or cover up their misdoings.

It is also notable that the Money Laundering Regulations apply to all accounting firms authorised by the ICAEW or other body to carry out investment business. Most firms are so authorised. The consequence of this is that firms must have procedures in place:

- for identification of clients. This means they must know with whom they are dealing with when accepting a new client. Beware the possibility that your new client is a Mafioso in disguise

- for keeping records of all transactions for five years

- for internal reporting. This means that staff must have the identity of a person to whom they can report

- as may be necessary for the purposes of forestalling and preventing money laundering.

The ICAEW guidance finishes by saying that members providing services as *auditors*, directors, trustees or professional advisers are obliged to report money laundering suspicions through their own firm's procedures, independently of any procedures that their clients may have for reporting similar suspicions.

Summary

12. a. Auditors may uncover criminal offences committed by a client or an employee of the client.

b. This puts them in a difficult position. The auditor should act carefully and correctly and, if necessary, take legal advice.

c. Auditors must not themselves commit criminal offences and should know the circumstances in which a criminal offence may be committed by not doing something.

d. The auditor should not jeopardize a professional relationship by disclosing offences except in specified circumstances.

e. Auditors have a responsibility to give an opinion on company accounts which they should not avoid by resignation.

f. The Cadbury Committee recommend extending the regulations of the regulatory sector which enables auditors to report reasonable suspicion of fraud to the proper authorities to the generality of companies. They do not recommend however that statute establish an obligation to do so.

g. The Cadbury Committee recommend some extension of auditor's duties in respect of directors duties to establish their responsibilities under a wide range of legal requirements and monitor compliance.

h. Auditors must be aware of the possible impact of non-compliance with law and regulations on the financial statements in their audit planning and procedures.

i. Firms of accountants must have procedures in place to recognise and report suspicions of money laundering activities.

Points to note

13. a. The auditor's duty when he discovers an unlawful act or when he is made aware of an unlawful act while conducting his audit is not always clear.

b. In examinations any questions on the subject should be answered by scrupulously following the advice given in this chapter.

c. Many writers have criticised this advice on the grounds that an auditor has a public duty which overrides his inclination to protect himself and his client.

Recent Department of Trade and Industry enquiry reports have implied that the auditor should seek disclosure of matters which concern a wider range of people than himself and his client. The matter is currently subject to much debate.

d. An interesting ethical dilemma is when an auditor discovers a material fraud by a member of the client's staff against the client which had been continuing for some years. On looking into the matter the auditor discovers that if he reports the matter to his client, his client could sue him for recovery of the amount lost since the first occasion when the auditor should have discovered the fraud.

e. The general rules to be followed in the circumstances described in this chapter are:

    i.   take legal advice

    ii. resign but do not do so if you are the auditor of a company

    iii. advise the client to make full disclosure to the relevant authorities.

    iv. consider whether statutes (e.g. on money laundering or financial services) or the public interest require disclosure to the proper authorities.

f. Normally disclosure will be preceded by discussion with the directors but in some instances (e.g. money laundering or where the directors themselves are involved or the auditor has lost confidence in the integrity of the directors) disclosure may be without informing the directors.

g. Essentially the auditor has three duties:

    – confidentiality

    – to give an unbiased opinion on the financial statements

    – to report to the proper authorities in certain circumstances.

In the past the first duty tended to overrule the other two but the trend is now the other way.

h. The rules sometimes conflict and are not often clear-cut. Practising auditors need to be very wary.

i. The Financial Services Act requires the auditor to report some matters to the regulating bodies over the heads of his clients.

Case study 1

Alien Corn Ltd are dealers in agricultural produce. Data about the company include:

Turnover – £600,000

Profit before proprietoral remuneration – £40,000

Shareholders – 16, all related, of which four are directors. Forty percent of the shares are held by distant relatives.

The auditors are Wright, Pickle & Co.

The audit of the accounts for the year ending 31.10.– 6 is being conducted by Andrew, an unqualified senior. During the audit, he discovers:

a. the company have paid Christmas bonuses to staff amounting to £500 without deducting PAYE. A PAYE inspection is arranged for next week. He advises the company to destroy the petty cash book in which these payments are recorded together with the vouchers. Petty cash books last about 6 months and the payments concerned are in the one before the current one. Andrew has already given it an audit inspection.

b. Andrew discovered by accident that Miss Debra Meenor, who handles purchases invoices had been passing for payment invoices (about £5,000 a year) for goods which had not been purchased. The invoices were from a firm owned by Miss Meenor's father. The practice had been going on for several years.

c. Andrew compared the despatch notes with the sales invoices and discovered that some six despatches of goods had not resulted in invoices. All the despatches were to a firm in the Irish Republic. Quite by chance Andrew had noticed a bank statement in the managing director's in-tray from an Irish Bank and had wondered about it.

Discussion

a. Discuss the implications of these discoveries?

b. What should Andrew and his firm do about them?

Case study 2

Gunges Ltd are a chemical company in Wolverhampton making speciality chemicals for export to third world companies. The company is owned by the Gunge family but is run by Bismuth who was recruited because of his sales experience in Africa and South America. The Board consists of four Gunges and Bismuth but rarely meets. The auditor is Raymond and he has made a number of discoveries in the course of his audit:

a. The company are making material payments to a numbered Swiss bank account. Bismuth (who Raymond trusts not at all) tells Raymond that these are commissions to third world government officials who obtain business for the company.

b. Workers appear to be handling what look like dangerous chemicals without proper protective gear. Bismuth tells Raymond that the regulations are known to Gunge and are all followed.

c. A pipe seems to be discharging chemicals into the adjacent canal. Bismuth tells Raymond that he has a licence to do this but declines to show it to Raymond.

Discussion

Discuss the implications of these discoveries for Raymond.

Student self testing questions

a. When can an auditor disclose unlawful acts to the police? (4)

b. Why does an accountant have a professional duty of confidence? (5)

c. What should an auditor do if he discovers an unlawful act? (5, 6)

d. Outline the requirements of SAS 120. (10)

e. Outline the money laundering regulations. (11)

Examination question

Note: you can now answer this using the actual standards.

1. You are the auditor of Bistro Ltd, a company that operates five restaurants. During the course of your planning of the audit for the year ended 31 March 1990, the managing director has informed you that he is concerned about the margins achieved in one of the restaurants and he is particularly worried that cash or stock may have been misappropriated.

   You have established that there is one staff member responsible for all of the company's accounting functions, including bank reconciliations, and that accounting records are maintained for goods inwards, purchases, sales and cash. Stock is counted every three months.

   Requirement:

   You are required to:

   a. Detail the audit tests you would undertake in respect of cash sales and banking.
   (10 Marks)

   b. Indicate what other steps you might take in addition to those normally undertaken at the year end, in order to establish whether any misappropriation has taken place; and
   (5 Marks)

   c. State briefly your responsibilities in respect of the detection of fraud and irregularities.
   (5 Marks)
   (ICAI) (Total Marks 20)

2. You have been the auditor of Dennis Trading Ltd for many years. During this period you have never had occasion to qualify your audit report, nor have you had any reason to doubt the honesty of the management or the employees of the company.

   The following matters have come to your attention this year:

   a. Your audit manager informs you that she has heard from a member of the wages department that the head of the department has recently bought a villa in Barbados, a yacht, a four-seater aeroplane and a new Porsche motor car.

b. A junior carrying out sequence checks on sales invoices from one of the branches has discovered that invoices are missing; it appears that this only happens on one day a week and they always relate to cash sales.

c. During the whole of the period you have been auditor, the managing director has misappropriated substantial (and increasing) sums of money reported as 'Construction Costs'.

Required:

Describe the steps that you might take to attempt to resolve the situations outlined above. Indicate also how they may affect you personally as auditor.

(AAT) (15 Marks)

Chapter 48 Corporate governance

Introduction

1. The way in which companies are run and controlled has been a matter of concern to government, the Stock Exchange, the investing community, lawyers and auditors for many years. The matter is known as corporate governance and includes issues of accountability as well as management and organisation. In recent years several committees have met and reported on the issue and finally The Combined Code of the Committee on Corporate Governance was issued. It is now part of the listing agreement of the Stock Exchange and listed companies are required to conform to the code. Relevant documents include Bulletin 1999/5 *The Combined Code: requirements of auditors under the listing rules, The Combined Code and the Turnbull Report: internal control – guidance for directors.*

2. The code has many provisions and any annual report and accounts of a listed company contains sections which are a consequence of the code. Students are advised to read annual reports and note these sections. Some of the sections have consequences for the auditor and this chapter is about them.

Directors' duties

3. The table overleaf gives a summary of some of the requirements:

4. The seven specific issues are:

a. The Board should have a formal schedule of matters specifically reserved to it for decision.

b. There should be a procedure agreed by the board for directors in the furtherance of their duties to take independent professional advice if necessary, at the company's expense.

c. Non-executive directors should be appointed for specified terms subject to re-election and to Companies Act provisions relating to the removal of a director, and re-appointment should not be automatic.

d. All directors should be subject to election by shareholders, at the first opportunity after their appointment, and to re-election thereafter at intervals of no more than

Subject	Listing rule requirement	Auditor requirements
Principles of good governance	The directors have to disclose in a narrative statement in the annual report how they have applied the code principles	Read only
Code provisions	A statement by the directors in the annual report as to whether they have complied throughout the year with the code provisions	Review seven specific matters and read the rest
Directors' remuneration	Inclusion in the annual report of a statement of directors' remuneration	Audit and include in the audit report as if this was in the financial statements
Going concern	Inclusion in the annual report of a statement by the directors that the business is a going concern with supporting assumptions or qualifications as necessary	Review

three years. The names of directors submitted for election or re-election should be accompanied by sufficient biographical details to enable shareholders to take an informed decision on their election.

e. The directors should explain their responsibility for preparing the accounts and there should be a statement by the auditors about their reporting responsibilities.

f. The directors should, at least annually, conduct a review of the effectiveness of the group's system of internal controls and should report to shareholders that they have done so. The review should cover all controls, including financial, operational and compliance controls and risk management.

g. The board should establish an audit committee of at least three directors, all non-executive, with written terms of reference which deal clearly with its authority and duties. The members of the committee, a majority of whom should be independent non-executive directors, should be named in the report and accounts.

The auditor's duties

5. The auditor's duties are summarised in Para. 3 above. There are three levels:

a. Include the extension to the directors' remuneration matters in the normal auditing and reporting duties.

b. Review the directors' statement on Going Concern and the seven other items.

c. Read the rest of the information included on corporate governance in the annual report.

Directors' remuneration

6. The requirements of the listing agreement go well beyond the requirements of the Companies Act and include details of the remuneration, pension contributions and other matters of each named director. The auditor should include the requirements in the normal audit work and the auditor's report (the 'We have audited ... section) will include the directors' remuneration statement.

7. However the auditor may conclude that the company has not complied fully with the disclosure requirements. In such cases the auditor need not qualify his report unless the non-compliance includes also a non-compliance with the Companies Act requirements. Assuming only that the listing rules have not been complied with, the auditor will add, immediately after the opinion section.

Other matter

The Listing Rules of the London Stock Exchange require us to report any instances when the company has not complied with certain of the disclosure requirements set out in the Rules. In this connection we report that in our opinion, the company has not complied with the requirements of paragraph 12.43A(c)(ix)(b)(ii) of those Rules because the board's report on directors' remuneration does not disclose the right of John Doe to retire at age 35 on a full pension.

Items to be reviewed

8. The review should take the following form:

The auditor should obtain appropriate evidence to support the compliance statement made by the company. Appropriate evidence can be gained by the following procedures:

a. Reviewing the minutes of the meetings of the Board and of relevant board committees (audit, nomination, remuneration, risk management etc.).

b. Reviewing relevant supporting documents prepared for the board or board committees.

c. Making enquiries of the directors and the company secretary.

d. Attending meetings of the audit committee (or other committee) when the annual report and accounts and statements of compliance are considered and approved for submission to the board.

The auditor may ask for a letter of representation of written or oral representations made in the course of the review.

9. If the review reveals some non-compliance the auditor again does not qualify his report but includes a statement like:

> *Other matter*
>
> We have reviewed the board's description of its process for reviewing the effectiveness of internal control set out on page x of the annual report. In our opinion the board's comments concerning their review of typhoon risk management do not appropriately reflect our understanding of the process undertaken by the board because only 80% of the Pacific locations were included.

The read requirement

10. This is effectively covered by Chapter 47 and SAS 160 Other information in documents containing audited financial statements or ISA 720. Any apparent inconsistencies or any apparent misstatements in the corporate governance statements should be resolved and the directors should amend the material. If this does not happen then the auditor should:

    a. If the financial statements are incorrect, qualify her report.

    b. If the financial statements are correct and the other information is incorrect or inadequate, make a statement in the auditor's report. This statement is however not a qualification.

Summary

11. a. Corporate governance has become an important issue at the present time.

    b. The Combined Code of the Committee on Corporate Governance should be complied with.

    c. Directors of UK listed companies have duties both for procedures and for reporting actions.

    d. Auditors have some duties connected with the reports by the directors on their compliance with the requirements of the Code.

    e. These duties include reporting in true and fair terms re extensions to directors' remuneration disclosures, reviewing certain items and reading for consistency and misstatement all other corporate governance disclosures in the annual report.

    f. Auditors may need to report departures from the Code by a statement in the auditor's report.

Points to note

12. a. The provisions of the Code only apply to UK listed companies.

    b. It is advisable for students to read one or more complete annual reports of listed companies to see how these things work out in practice.

    c. The work to be done by the auditor must be spelt out clearly in the letter of engagement.

    d. In some circumstances there may be a departure from a code provision specified for auditor review but there is a proper disclosure of this fact and the reasons for it In such cases the auditor may not need to report the departure in her report.

Case study 1

Hugh is the auditor of Whacko PLC which has just completed its first year as a listed company. In the audit it came to Hugh's attention that:

a. The directors have reviewed the effectiveness of internal controls but have omitted risk management in their US subsidiary which is 10% of the group.

b. The directors' remuneration statement does not make mention of payments made to supplement the pension of a former director who resigned before the company became listed.

Discussion

a. Draft sections in the letter of engagement re the Combined Code matters.

b. Draft an outline audit programme for the Combined Code matters.

c. Draft the complete auditor's report.

49 Compilation reports and direct reporting engagements

Introduction

1. Accountants in practice perform many different assignments for their clients. This book is about auditing assignments but frequently accountants are also asked to prepare financial statements either in order to audit them or simply to prepare them without a subsequent audit. Preparation of financial statements can also be termed compilation of financial statements. There is an ISA 930 *Engagements to Compile Financial Information* and a technical release *Reports on Accounts Compiled by Accountants*.

2. We shall then consider other audit related services including attest functions, due diligence, direct reporting engagements, agreed upon procedures and assurance engagements.

Procedures for compiling financial statements

3. The following procedures should be adopted:

a. Act with integrity at all times and behave in accordance with the fundamental Principles.

b. Agree an engagement letter with the client making it clear that the engagement is not an audit and that management is responsible for the accuracy and completeness of the compiled financial statements.

c. Gain some limited understanding of the business.

d. Prepare the financial statements using generally accepted accounting principles. The financial statements should also comply with the accounting standards. Ideally the financial statements should include a statement of any significant accounting policies.

e. It is usual to perform limited other procedures including analytical review and enquiry of management. The accountant should then ascertain that the financial statements are in accordance with her understanding of the business.

f. Request a letter of representation from the management. This will cover estimates made by the management and an assurance that all necessary information has been given to the accountants and that the information is complete and reliable. Any relevant explanations given orally will also be included.

g. Ensure that, on the face of the financial statements, the sole trader/all the partners/ authorised representative of the Board/Trustees/Committee of management etc., have included and signed a statement such as: 'I/we approve these accounts and confirm that I/we have made available all relevant records and information for their compilation.'

h. Issue a report such as:

Accountants' report on the unaudited accounts of Mrs Sole Trader

As described on page … you have approved the accounts for the year ended 31 December 20-4 set out on pages … to … In accordance with your instructions, we have compiled these unaudited accounts from the accounting records and information and explanations supplied to us.

Blott & Co., Chartered Accountants   31 July 20-4
Donington

---

4. In the event of the accountant finding that the financial statements contain a misstatement or are otherwise misleading, he should discuss the matter and recommend amendment. If the management insist on no alteration then he should resign or include an explanatory paragraph in his report.

Assurance services

5. The objective of an assurance engagement is for a professional accountant to evaluate or measure a subject matter that is the responsibility of another party against identified suitable criteria, and to express a conclusion that provides the intended user with a level of assurance about that subject matter.

Assurance engagements performed by professional accountants are intended to enhance the credibility of information about a subject matter by evaluating whether the subject matter conforms in all material respects with suitable criteria, thereby improving the likelihood that the information will meet the needs of an intended user. In this regard, the level of assurance provided by the professional accountant's conclusion conveys the degree of confidence that the intended user may place in the credibility of the subject matter. There is a broad range of assurance engagements, which includes any combination of the following.

a. engagements to report on a broad range of subject matters covering financial and non-financial information

b. engagements intended to provide high or moderate levels of assurance

c. attest and direct reporting engagements

d. engagements to report internally and externally

e. engagements in the private and public sector.

Attest functions

6. To attest to something is to bear witness or affirm it. Thus the Association of Widget Makers requires that all its members must annually review the procedures they perform to secure compliance with the quality control requirements of the Association. The directors of A Ltd duly performed the review but the Association need to know that the review has been performed. To that end Tickers Chartered Certified Accountants are engaged to assure the Society that the review has been performed. Tickers might do this by:

a. enquiry of the directors to obtain an understanding of the process defined by the Board for its review and compare their understanding to the statement made by the Board to the Association

b. review of the documentation prepared by or for the directors to support their statement and assessing whether or not it provides sound support for that statement

c. reporting to the Association that the review has been carried out.

The accountants may well say that the review by the Board was conducted in accordance with the Association's recommendations but will not say anything about the processes to secure compliance with quality control requirements. Their work and their report is simply to attest to the fact that the Board carried out a review.

Due diligence

7. This term is normally associated with take-overs and mergers. When a company is taken over or merged all parties need to be assured that what is purported to be actually is. For example A PLC takes over B PLC and needs to be assured that the assets of B are as stated. An accounting firm will be engaged to investigate and report on this aspect of the purported information. Due diligence can be carried out by accountants but also actuaries, surveyors, lawyers and other professionals and sometimes by the staff of the taking over company. Usually the take-over or merger is not completed until due diligence is completed. Where a due diligence report involving an opinion is required, the investigation is a direct reporting engagement.

Direct reporting engagements

8. Direct reporting engagements are those where accountants are required to give a special report on some *aspects* of a client's affairs. It is not easy to define but a special report arises when, at the request of his client and in accordance with instructions received and any relevant statutory or contractual obligations, an accountant carries out an *independent examination* of financial or other information prepared by his client for use by a *third party*, and then *reports* his findings and conclusions by expressing an *opinion*, on the information

These do not include reports on audited financial statements, prospectuses or profit forecasts, comfort letters associated with published documents or circulars, valuations, and the preparation of financial statements or information on which no opinion is expressed.

9. The approach to a direct reporting engagement is:

a. Carry out the work in accordance with the ethical code.

b. Agree a precise letter of engagement. It is important to ensure that all parties (the audit firm, the persons requiring the special report, the person or enterprise who is responsible for the information being reported on) understand their responsibilities, their relationship and what is to be done.

c. Plan, control and record the work done.

d. Obtain evidence – from documents and records, enquiries of management and others, analytical review, enquiry of third parties.

e. Draw conclusions.

f. Report.

10. The report should contain the following parts:

a. Title – accountant's report to . . . On . . .

b. Addressee.

c. A description of the subject matter of the engagement and time period.

d. Responsibilities of all parties.

e. Restricted nature of the report – who the report may not be shown to.

f. Identification of standards used in the engagement e.g. The International Standard on Assurance Engagements.

g. The criteria against which the subject matter was evaluated.

h. The conclusion and any denial, reservations or qualifications to the conclusion.

i. The date.

j. The name, description and address of the reporting accountant.

Agreed-upon procedures

11. An agreed-upon procedures' engagement, in which the party engaging the professional accountant or the intended user determines the procedures to be performed and the professional accountant provides a report of factual findings as a result of undertaking those procedures, is not an assurance engagement.

You will note that in normal reporting engagements the accountant decides upon his own procedures and the engagement is about reporting not about what to do or how to do it i.e. ends not means.

Summary

12. a. Accountants are often called upon to prepare (compile) financial statements without necessarily being asked to audit them.

b. Accountants are also asked to undertake assurance engagements.

c. Accountants can also be asked to perform attest functions.

d. Accountants are also asked to undertake due diligence.

e. There are also direct reporting engagements and agreed–upon procedures engagements.

Points to note

13. a. Firms of accountants are commercial enterprises as well as professional practices. They continually seek new work and new areas of application of their expertise. Auditing is not seen as especially lucrative and consultancy has been the major earner. Several firms have now sold off their consultancy arms, mainly as a response to demands for more overt independence. The demand for various forms of assurance and attesting has increased and will probably be major activities for accountants in the future.

  b. The vocabulary of assurance and other engagements has been established by the International Auditing Practices Committee (IAPC) and a series of ISAs. The APB in the UK has yet to pronounce but there is a now rather out of date Audit Brief *Special Reports of Accountants* issued in 1984.

  c. Assurance engagements are governed internationally by the *International Standard on Assurance Engagements*. An assurance engagement is one where a professional accountant is engaged to evaluate or measure a subject matter that is the responsibility of another party against identified suitable criteria, and to express a conclusion that provides the intended user with a level of assurance about that subject matter. This includes attest and direct reporting engagements but excludes agreed-upon procedures and compilation engagements.

  d. Engagements to perform agreed-upon procedures are governed by ISA 920 *Engagements to Perform Agreed-upon Procedures Regarding Financial Information*.

  e. Engagements to compile financial information are governed by ISA 930 *Engagements to Compile Financial Information*.

  f. There is also ISA 800 *The Auditors' Report on Special Purpose Audit Engagements*. These include: financial statements prepared in accordance with a comprehensive basis of accounting other than IASs or National standards (e.g. UK FRSs), specified accounts or elements of accounts, compliance with contractual agreements and summarised financial statements.

Student self testing questions

  a. List the procedures that should be adopted in compiling financial statements. (3)
  b. What should an accountant do if the financial statements contain a misstatement or are otherwise misleading? (5)
  c. State the objective of an assurance engagement. (5)
  d. What is an attest function? (6)
  e. What is due diligence? (7)
  f. What is a direct reporting engagement? (8)
  g. How should a direct reporting engagement be carried out? (9)
  h. What should appear in a direct reporting engagement report? (10)
  i. What is an agreed-upon procedures engagement? (11)

Case study 1

Wessex is the auditor of Laudanum PLC and has been asked as a special purpose audit engagement to express an opinion on a schedule of debtors. The report is required by the Unlikely Bank PLC in connection with a loan.

Discussion

Produce a report on the schedule on the basis that:

a. It is correct.

b. It contains one debt which the company consider good but Wessex considers to be bad.

50 Computers and the auditor

Introduction

1. Virtually all enterprises now have at least their accounting records on a computer. As a result computing as a special subject in auditing is no longer pertinent. Computing or computer information systems are a component of almost all audits. However it is worth considering how computer systems have affected auditing and we do that in this chapter.

2. There is an ISA 401 *Auditing in a Computer Information Systems Environment* and there are three slightly out of date International Auditing Practice Statements.

Basic considerations

3. In planning the audit, the auditor should consider how the presence of a CIS (computer information system) may affect the client's accounting and internal control system and the conduct of the audit. The main considerations are likely to be:

a. How to obtain a sufficient understanding of what may be a very complex accounting and internal control system.

b. Inherent, control and detection risks and how to assess them.

c. The design and performance of substantive and compliance tests.

d. The need for specialist computer literate audit staff. Most firms now have the necessary expertise.

Complexity of systems

4. Auditing the output of complex computerised systems is difficult because:

a. The sheer volume of transactions processed means that detail is inaccessible.

b. The computer automatically generates material transactions (e.g. direct debits).

c. The computer performs complex calculations without demonstrating how it has done them (total of overdue debts, interest charged to customers).

d. Transactions are exchanged electronically (EDI) with other organisations (e.g. customers and suppliers) – for example orders can be generated automatically. This is a new idea which may well dominate commerce over the next few years.

e. Organisational aspects of CIS restrict segregation of duties and reduce manual review and supervision.

f. Data and balances may be difficult to access and may be short-lived.

Risk and CISs

5. There are many characteristics of CISs which create problems both for the client and for the auditor in his risk assessment. These characteristics include:

a. A control environment where management often feel they have no control over or understanding of transactions and records. Well has it been said that once engineers ran companies, then accountants ran them and nowadays the IT manager runs them!

b. A lack of transaction trail or audit trail. It can be hard or impossible to trace a transaction through from, say a sales order, to its inclusion in the trading account and as a debtor in the Balance Sheet.

c. Uniform and totally accurate processing eliminates clerical errors. This is a plus point.

d. Lack of segregation of duties. Commonly in the past every transaction would probably be reviewed and processed by several people. This no longer happens and frauds may proliferate as a result.

e. The potential for fraud and error as a result of system or programme faults. Once a fault is in a system, the system happily processes incorrectly for ever as no human intervention or review may be included in the controls or the fault may simply not be visible as processing is not transparent. Examples may include the use of the wrong price for the sale of a product or a wage rate wrongly entered. Then recipients of the output (customers and employees) will only inform the company if the error is to their detriment.

f. The initiation or execution of transactions may be automatic. The system may be fraudulently programmed to produce fraudulent transactions or transactions may be initiated or processed erroneously.

g. Output may not be complete. A computer generated total of overdue debts or a list of goods received unmatched with purchase invoices may be incomplete but the manager reviewing the list will have no way of knowing this.

h. Management may have the use of sophisticated search, selection, calculational and comparative analytical techniques which may enhance control. This is a plus point.

i. The auditor may be able to use computer aided auditing techniques (CAATs).

6. The auditor needs to assess the risks – business, inherent, control and audit which impinge on the audit. He must especially assess the risks in terms of possibility of misstatement in the financial statements and, as computer systems failure can cause the company to fail, the risk to the going concern applicability. The risks are particularly deficiencies in the pervasive CIS activities which may include a great potential for fraud and error.

Approaches to audits with computerised accounting systems

7. The approach taken by auditors to computerised records varies. Possible approaches include:

    Auditing round the computer. This means examining evidence for all items in the financial statements without getting immersed in the detail of the CIS. The benefits of this approach are that it saves much time. The justification is largely that the computer is 100% accurate in processing and material processing errors simply do not occur. The drawback to this is that once an application is programmed to process an item incorrectly (e.g. doubling the wages paid to the wages staff) then it processes exactly as it is programmed to do for ever. However major frauds and errors or systems failures should be picked up in the assets and liability verification. If the processing of sales is incorrect then the debtors audit will discover it. If the sales application uses the wrong prices, two things can happen. The pricing is too high then the customer will inform the firm and the error will be corrected. If the pricing is too low, then the gross profit ratio and other analytical review will discover it. This approach is suitable for small businesses but it can also be said that it is easier to understand a smaller system than the immense complexities of CISs in large-scale enterprises.

    Understanding the CIS. It is usually impossible for auditors to fully understand a system. Not even the client's IT manager can do this. Knowledge of a system is distributed among the client's computer staff. However knowledge of detailed programming in applications may be known by nobody. However it is possible for an auditor to understand the main features of a system and the control environment in which it operates.

8. The actual approach adopted by an auditor depends on the auditor's experience of the client, the control environment, the complexity of the system, the risk profile of the client and the risk of misstatement in the financial statements.

Internal control in CIS systems

9. Internal controls in computerised systems can be seen as two categories: general controls and applications controls.

    General controls include:

    a. Establishing a general attitude and environment in which all relevant personnel (computer and other) are aware of the need for control.

    b. Laid down procedures for setting up all systems and applications. These must involve full consultation on planning, writing and implementation.

    c. Full documentation and recording of all systems and applications.

    d. Fully documented and recorded testing.

    e. Procedures for formal approval and acceptance of all new and changed applications.

    f. Tight control over systems developers and programmers.

    g. Where outside contractors are used (e.g. software houses), there must be adequate definition of system objectives and full briefing of requirements, adequate testing and implementation procedures, full documentation and adequate continuing support.

    h. Proper segregation of duties both between computer personnel and other personnel and within computer departments.

i.   Access controls such as physical barriers and passwords.

j.   Backup and reconstruction facilities.

Applications controls include:

a.   Completeness controls.

b.   User created control totals for comparison with computer generated totals.

c.   Comparison with previously generated files e.g. sales order entries against sales invoices created.

d.   Sequential numbering.

e.   Batch registers.

f.   Establishing run to run controls.

g.   Integrity of files. Master files and standing data files are particularly important and print outs at intervals for manual investigation may be desirable.

h.   Validity of input.

i.   Control totals and prelists.

j.   Exception reports.

k.   Programmed controls such as the use of a PIN at cash points.

l.   Manual authorisation of input documents with evidence of authorisation.

m.   Controls over coding. This may be very important as errors can lead to misstatement in financial statements. If, for example, the code for capital expenditure was put on a purchase invoice instead of the code for repairs.

n.   Input validity checks such as:

o.   Format checks e.g. alphabetic or numerical, all fields input.

p.   Check digit verification.

q.   Master file compatibility e.g. does the customer exist on the master file of approved customers.

r.   Range checks e.g. is the input within acceptable limits such as hours worked by Joe this week not exceeding 60.

s.   Batch totals and prelists.

t.   Sequence checks – is any worker missing this week or entered twice.

u.   Logical inference – are the VAT and net and gross entered compatible.

Testing and computerised records

10. **Substantive testing** of computer records is possible and sometimes necessary. Its extent depends on the degree of reliance the auditor has placed on the internal controls. The degree of that reliance will depend on the results of his review and compliance testing of the internal controls over the accounting records.

11. Substantive testing includes two basic approaches both of which may be used.

Manual techniques. These include:

a   Review of exception reports. The auditor will attempt to confirm these with other data. An example is the comparison of an outstanding despatch note listing with actual despatch notes.

b. Totalling. Relevant totals, for example of debtors and creditors can be manually verified.

c. Reperformance. The auditor may reperform a sample of computer generated calculations, for example stock extensions, depreciation or interest.

d. Reconciliations. These will include reconciliations of computer listings with creditors' statements, bank statements, actual stock, personnel records etc.

Use of Computer assisted audit techniques (CAATs)

12 These consist of computer programs used by an auditor to:

a. Read magnetic files and to extract specified information from the files.

b. Carry out audit work on the contents of the file.

These programs are sometimes known as enquiry or interrogation programs. They are usually written in high level languages. They are usually written by or for an audit firm but clients' own interrogation programs can be used; such programs are available from software houses.

Staff unskilled in programming can be easily taught to put their search or operating requirements into a simple coded form which the computer audit program can interpret and apply to the files selected.

Uses of computer audit programs

13. a. Selection of representative or randomly chosen transactions or items for audit tests e.g. item number 36 and every 14th item thereafter.

b. Scrutiny of files and selection of exceptional items for examination e.g. all wages payments over £400, or all stock lines worth more than £1,000 in total.

c. Comparison of two files and printing out differences e.g. payrolls at two selected dates.

d. Preparation of exception reports, e.g. overdue debts.

e. Stratification of data e.g. stock lines or debtors, with a view to examination of only of material items. Carrying out detail tests and calculations.

f. Verifying data such as stock or fixed assets at the interim stage and comparing the examined file with the year end file so that only changed items need be examined at the final audit.

g. Comparison of files at succeeding year ends to identify changes in the composition of stock.

h. The use of test packs. These are the use of sample inputs (including faulty input) to test the response of programs to input. They test the rejection of erroneous items and unreasonable items. They also test that the program correctly processes data.

Summary

14. a. Almost all enterprises use computerised systems.

b. Auditors need to have some understanding of CISs and the problem is how much detailed understanding is necessary.

c. CISs present risks to enterprises and hence to the auditors. These risks include fraud, computer breakdown, accounting record inaccuracy and going concern.

d. The approaches to the audit include auditing round the computer, detailed investigation of the system and somewhere between these.

e. Computerised systems need general and application controls.

f. Computerised records can be tested by manual techniques but also by CAATs.

Points to note

15. a. Inadequate computer systems can be disastrous and lead to company failure. For example, a system accepted returned goods, issued credit notes but did not update the stock records led to the company assuming it had more stock than it had. This was not known by a consortium who purchased the company. When the stock shortfalls were discovered the company went into liquidation and the buyers lost their money.

b. Frauds can be perpetrated for a long time without discovery. This can lead to misstatements in the financial statements but also loss of going concern status.

c. Clerical errors are eliminated in computer systems once the data has been entered. Auditors can refocus the audit away from clerical errors to other sources of misstatement.

d. The degree of detail that an auditor needs to understand in CISs is a difficult decision.

e. CAATs can be very sophisticated. Programs can do much more than search files, re-perform calculations, extract data, make lists and compare data in different files. They can do statistical analyses and calculations like regression calculations.

f. The use of off the peg accounting software is now very common. However it does not always work well and auditors need to be aware of this.

g. Auditors should never forget the basic Companies Act requirement for proper accounting records.

Case study 1

Birds Nest Soups PLC have the following system for dealing with purchase invoices:

The purchasing department gather and approve all incoming purchase invoices.

After approval the invoices are batched and sent weekly to the computer department.

The computer department process them by updating the purchase ledger and the nominal ledger.

The company do not take settlement discounts.

Discussion

a. What applications controls would you expect to find at each stage of the processing? Controls can be manual or programmed.

b. What general controls would you hope to find to ensure the integrity of program and data files, to prevent or enable recovery from systems, hardware or program malfunction, fraud or sabotage?

c. What errors and frauds could exist in the purchase invoice area which might lead to material misstatement in the financial statements?

d. What issues could affect the auditor's approach to the audit of this area?

e. Discuss the relative emphasis to be place on internal control reliance, substantive testing and analytical review.

f. What items might be included in a test pack to test the program controls in the program to process purchase invoices?

g. How might a computer audit program be used in this area?

Case study 2

Bitco PLC are a large component manufacturer. They have some 4,000 employees and 5,000 customers. Among the files used on their computer are:

a. Weekly payroll. All employees are paid by bank transfer. The file is saved onto CD monthly and overwritten. A file is retained of employees with PAYE information.

b. A personnel record with details of all employees. Annually, left employees are divested onto a CD.

c. A file of loans to employees (these are extensive) and interest is added monthly. Loans that have been repaid are removed annually onto CD.

d. A file of unpaid sales invoices. Statements are printed out and cash and invoices are removed monthly after extraction of the monthly statements. The company have a bad debt problem.

e. A file which forms the plant register.

Discussion

a. Suggest a number of uses of computer audit programs on the audit of the company.

b. What audit evidence would emerge from these uses?

Student self testing questions

a. What special considerations apply to planning audits with CISs? (3)

b. List the problems implicit in complex CISs. (4)

c. List the risk characteristics of CISs. (5)

d. How might an auditor approach an audit with a CIS? (7)

e. List general controls that might be found with a CIS. (9)

f. List general applications controls that might be found with a CIS. (9)

g. List manual means of seeking audit evidence of computer output. (11)

h. List some uses of CAATs. (12)

Examination questions

1. Describe the controls you would expect a company with a fully computerised accounting system to adopt in order to reduce the possibility of errors in input.

   (LCCI)

2. You are currently engaged in planning the audit of the financial statements of E Ltd as at 30 June 1985. The company runs a wholesale electrical business buying directly from national and overseas suppliers and selling to both large and small retailers. This will be the first accounting period during which all transactions relating to the sales, purchases, wages and general ledger systems will be processed and recorded by computer. Your

firm of certified accountants has experience of auditing computerised accounting systems and has decided as a matter of policy that during this year's audit of the financial statements of E Ltd it will be essential to test all the controls over the computerised accounting systems and to use computer audit programs to test the accounting records.

Required:

a. Outline how an audit is affected by the accounting transactions and records being processed by computer and held on computer file.

b. Describe what is meant by:
   i. application controls
   ii. general controls.

c. Give two examples of specific application controls over data being processed through E Ltd's purchase system describing the purpose of each control.

d. Outline what you understand by the term computer assisted audit techniques

e. CAATs and the benefits that may be derived from using them and give two examples of how CAATs might effectively be used in the audit of E Ltd's year-end trade debtors.

(ACCA)

51 Group accounts

Introduction

1. Larger companies are generally arranged in groups so that there is a holding company and that company itself owns, either wholly or partly, other companies called subsidiaries. Most listed companies are groups but many private companies are also groups. English company legislation (and most other legal regimes) requires a Profit and Loss Account and Balance Sheet and other financial statements to be prepared for the group as a whole as well as for the individual companies comprising the group. Group accounts are difficult as all accounting students are well aware.

2. Accounting for groups in the UK is governed by the Companies Act and by FRS 2 *Accounting for Subsidiary Undertakings* and FRS 9 *Associates and Joint Ventures*. Internationally there is IAS 27 *Consolidated Financial Statements and Accounting for Investments in Subsidiaries* and IAS 28 *Accounting for Investments in Associates*.

3. Auditing documents include SAS 510 *The Relationship Between Principal Auditors and Other Auditors*.

4. This chapter covers the audit of holding companies, the audit of groups, and the special considerations pertaining when the group auditor is not the auditor of some or all of the subsidiaries.

The audit of holding companies

5. The published Accounts of a holding company will consist of a *Balance Sheet*. Among the assets of the holding company will be *investments in subsidiary companies.* There will not usually be a published profit and loss account as the Companies Acts allow a holding company to publish only a *consolidated profit and loss Account.*

    However, the notes to the company's individual Balance Sheet must show the company's profit or loss for the financial year.

6. The Companies Act has numerous and detailed requirements on the presentation of a holding company's own balance sheet. If you cannot remember these, you should revise them before continuing.

Audit considerations

7. The audit of the Accounts of a holding company follows the same lines as any company audit. However, special consideration must be given to the dealings with and presentation of the investments in subsidiary companies.

8. The verification of the investments in subsidiary companies will include the following work.

    a. **Audit schedule**

        The current file should contain a schedule with the following data:

        i.   All the data which the Companies Act require to be disclosed in the holding company's own accounts.

        ii. Companies of the Accounts of each subsidiary with a note of who are the auditors (the holding company auditor may audit all, some or none of the subsidiaries), and of any qualification in any of the auditors' reports.

        iii. A summary of all movements in investments in subsidiaries and on current and loan accounts with each subsidiary.

        iv. Reconciliation of inter-company balances.

        The last item creates much difficulty in practice.

    b. **Verification of existence and ownership of investments in subsidiaries**

        This is effected:

        i.   By examining share certificates. If the certificates are not in the name of the holding company, there should be blank signed transfers and declarations of trust by the persons who own the shares on behalf of the holding company.

        ii. If the certificates are held by third parties (e.g. bankers), by obtaining a certificate from the custodian stating that they are held free of any encumbrance (e.g. the shares are not held as security for a loan) or, if encumbered, the nature of the encumbrance. The auditor should satisfy himself that the share certificates are held by third parties in the *ordinary course of business* and that no circumstances *putting him upon enquiry* arise.

    c. **Verification of current and loan accounts with subsidiaries**

        i.   This is normally effected by obtaining a certificate from each subsidiary acknowledging the balances concerned.

ii.   If the auditor of the holding company is also the auditor of the subsidiary, he can reconcile the entries in both sets of books himself.

iii. The auditor should satisfy himself that dealings between group companies have not been used to cover material fraud.

d.   **Verification of value**

i.   If the shares were acquired in the year, vouch the acquisition in the usual way, considering *cost* and *authorisation*. Examine accounting treatment of the premium or discount on acquisition and of any dividends received out of pre-acquisition profits.

ii. The balance sheet date value of each subsidiary must be considered. The auditor should regard such investments as the same as other assets in his duty towards their value.

If ordinary investments are held as *fixed assets* and their value has fallen below book value, then there is *no need* for the book value to be reduced to market value *unless* the fall in value is regarded as permanent.

If ordinary investments are held as *current assets* and their value has fallen below *book value then the book value must be written down to net realisable value.*

Investments in subsidiary companies are *not* current assets but it is necessary for such investments to be written down if their value has fallen *below book value.* Hence the auditor must form an opinion of the value of each investment in a subsidiary company.

There are several points to note in assessing the value.

i.   whether the investments were purchased at a premium over net assets.

ii.   The present net assets of the subsidiary excluding goodwill.

iii. The profitability of the subsidiary.

iv.   Whether the subsidiary has made losses.

This latter point can cause confusion. If the subsidiary makes a loss then it is reasonable to suppose its value has fallen *but it does not follow that its value will fall below book value.* If, however, since acquisition, losses have exceeded profits then it is reasonable to suppose that the value has fallen *below* cost.

Special consideration must be given to the value of overseas subsidiaries which are located in politically unstable countries.

Group accounts

9.   Group accounts cause much difficulty to students but it is assumed that readers of this manual are totally familiar with both the companies act material in this area and with the methods commonly employed to prepare consolidated accounts. If you are uncertain of this subject please revise before continuing.

Note particularly when consolidated accounts are not required and the alternatives to consolidated accounts.

Students should also be familiar with the requirements of FRS 2, FRS 6 and FRS 7.

Small and medium size groups

10. Small and medium sized groups are exempt from the requirement to prepare group accounts providing no member of the group is a public company, an authorised institution under the Banking Act 1987, an insurance company or an authorised person under the Financial Services Act 1986.

The group must satisfy TWO of the following conditions:

	Small		Medium sized	
	Net	Gross	Net	Gross
Turnover	£2.8M	£3.36M	£11.2M	£13.44M
Balance Sheet Total	£1.4M	£1.68M	£5.6M	£6.72M
Number of employees	50		250	

Note: – M = Million

- net means with the set-offs and other adjustments required by Sch. 4A (e.g. reducing assets to values excluding intra-group profit margins)
- gross means before such adjustments
- either net or gross figures can be used.

Clearly, a small company also qualifies as a medium sized one and the difference between the two is as to whether the parent company qualifies to file abbreviated individual accounts.

To take advantage of this exemption, the directors need a report from the auditor stating whether, in the opinion of the auditor, the company is entitled to the exemption. The report has to be attached to the individual accounts of the company.

Auditors' duties

11. The auditors' duties are somewhat onerous. He is required to express an opinion on the truth and fairness and compliance with the Companies Act of the consolidated accounts. This involves two stages:

   a. Forming an opinion on the truth, fairness, and compliance with statute of Accounts of each material company in the group.

   b. Forming an opinion on the truth, fairness, and compliance with statute of the consolidated accounts as a whole which are, of course, prepared from the Accounts of the individual companies.

   This task is difficult in all cases but is especially so in cases where a material amount of the net assets and profits of the group arise in subsidiaries which are audited by *other auditors*. This subject is dealt with later.

12. The work required in considering consolidated accounts is as follows:

   a. **Current audit file data**

      1. A complete list of subsidiaries showing the share holdings of the holding company or of other group members where there are sub-subsidiaries (sometimes known as vertical groupings).

      2. Copies of the Accounts of each subsidiary noting.

         i. Qualified audit reports.

         ii. Agreement of inter-company balances.

      iii. The division between pre- and post-acquisition profits.

      iv. Accounting policies adopted.

      v. That each set of accounts is properly signed by directors and auditors.

3. Questionnaires used to determine the work undertaken by subsidiary company auditors (discussed later).

4. Letters of weakness sent by each subsidiary company auditor.

5. A check list showing companies act requirements.

6. A check list showing FRS 2, FRS 6 and FRS 7 requirements.

7. A note of whether or not the group is entitled to small or medium sized group filing exemptions.

b. **Accounting policies.** These should preferably be uniform throughout the group and proper disclosure of material policies should be made. If they are not uniform, the auditor should request that they should become so and if it is not possible (for overseas legislation reasons for example) then a full disclosure must be made.

c. **Consolidated adjustments** and the preparation of the consolidated accounts. The auditor must verify that the adjustments have been correctly carried out both conceptually and mathematically.

d. **Companies act requirements.** The auditor must verify that all required disclosures have been made in the form prescribed. Alternative presentation to consolidated accounts must be considered. Consolidation may give a misleading view, but this would be very rare.

e. **See that all material subsidiaries have been audited.** Otherwise an opinion cannot be formed.

f. **Investigate non co-terminous accounts.** This should apply only to overseas subsidiaries, who may have year ends different from the holding company for legal or for other reasons.

g. **Investigate for 'window dressing'.** H Ltd, a holding company has a subsidiary S Ltd. H has a cash at the bank and S has an overdraft. The group directors would prefer that the overdraft was not shown in the consolidated balance sheet. They arrange that H draws a cheque in favour of S to repay the overdraft immediately before year end. Immediately after year end a cheque for the same amount is sent by S to H. Neither cheque is cleared. This is a sample of window dressing or artificial creation of a situation which though true does not fairly represent the underlying reality.

h. **Consider foreign subsidiaries.** There are special problems such as blocked currencies and political issues which may make the consolidation misleading. Accounting policies on currency conversion should conform to SSAP 20.

i. As with all auditing assignments the inherent risks must be evaluated. The extent of auditing procedures in each area will depend on this assessment and also on the materiality of each area.

Subsidiaries with different auditor

13. The auditor of the Holding Company (the *principal auditor*) has to give an opinion on the consolidated accounts which may incorporate the Accounts of material subsidiaries audited by other firms (the *other auditors*).

14. The directors of the Holding Company have a duty to produce Consolidated Accounts which show a true and fair view and comply with statute. The principal auditor has a duty to express an opinion on the consolidated accounts as a whole *even though* he has not carried out an audit on some of the figures that are included in them.

15. The principal auditor, then, is responsible for Accounts which he did not audit. He must make sufficient enquiries to satisfy himself that all the figures are reliable.

16. The work that the principal auditor must do to satisfy himself of the reliability of the Accounts audited by a secondary auditor is:

   a. **Accounting policies.** The primary directors should have arranged for uniform accounting policies to be applied to all group company accounts. Where this is not so (perhaps for overseas legislative reasons) the principal auditors should ensure that full information is available for altering the Accounts, or if this is not possible that the differing policies are fully explained.

   b. **Availability of information.** The primary directors should have sufficient control over the subsidiaries to enable them to secure all the information that is needed about:

   i. Accounting policies.

   ii. Items needing disclosure.

   iii. Consolidated adjustments.

   If the primary directors lack sufficient information, then the principal auditor should seek *from the primary directors* permission to approach the subsidiaries or the secondary auditors direct.

   The Companies Act 1985 Section 389A gives:

   1. A subsidiary company and its auditor a duty to give a principal auditor any information or explanation that he needs.

   2. A holding company a duty to obtain data from a subsidiary if the principal auditor requires it.

   c. **Scope of the work of the other auditors.** The principal auditors will need to be satisfied that:

   1. All material aspects of the subsidiaries' Accounts have been audited.

   2. That the work of the secondary auditors can be relied on. The answer to the latter problem is clearly difficult in that it boils down to a professional man asking himself if he can rely on the work of a fellow professional man.

   Whether or not he can depends on:

   i. What does the principal auditor know of the other auditor? After some years this will be resolved.

   ii. What auditing 'standards' govern the work of the other auditor? Standards are higher for example in the United States than they are in Gombovia.

    iii. What are the legal auditing requirements in the country where the other auditor works?

    iv. Who appointed the other auditor and to whom does he report? There may not be an arms length relationship between the primary board and the other auditors.

    v. Has any limitation been placed on the work of the other auditor?

    vi. Are the other auditors independent in all respects?

    vii. Is the other auditors' examination adequate and reasonable *in the principal auditor's opinion?*

Having considered the above, the principal auditor will have to consider whether any of the answers to the point above will cause him to qualify his report. He will also have to consider if any *qualifications* in the other auditors' reports need to be carried through to the principal auditors' report.

  d. **Materiality.** Some subsidiaries will be so small in relation to the whole group that the problem of reliability of their Accounts can be ignored.

Note that a subsidiary can be not material in the context of the group but that several subsidiaries taken together can be material. In such cases each subsidiary has to be seen as material.

Consultations with secondary auditors

17. In all material cases it will be necessary for the primary auditor to consult with the other auditors.

The steps required are:

  a. Obtain authority to do so through the respective boards of directors.

  b. Request *written explanations* of the other auditors' *procedures* and *findings* with oral back up if necessary.

  c. Examine the other auditors' *files* and *working papers.*

18. In practice, the principal auditor will compile a questionnaire to be completed by the other auditors. It is important to discuss the questionnaire with the other auditors *before* they undertake their audit.

Audit reports and other auditors

19. In the past it was common to find audit reports with statements that certain subsidiaries were audited by other auditors. SAS 510 advises against this idea as readers should not be misled into thinking that the principal auditor was other than fully responsible for his opinion on the group accounts.

It is suggested that the notes to the accounts could give an indication of material subsidiaries not audited by the principal auditor.

Post balance sheet events

20. The auditors of a group must carry out a review to identify events after the balance sheet date which are of significance to the group. This review must identify events which are significant to the group as a whole and which may occur in subsidiary companies. Where subsidiaries are audited by other auditors, an additional burden is put upon the principal auditor to ensure that an adequate review is carried out by other auditors.

Representations by management

21. The directors of a holding company have responsibility for producing group accounts. It may be that the group auditor may require representations from the directors of the holding company in respect of group matters. It may also be that the group auditor may require representations on group matters from subsidiary company boards. The source of representations depends on the management structure of the group.

Associated companies

22. The rules relating to the incorporation of the results of associated companies in group accounts are not found in the Companies Acts but in FRS 9. If you cannot remember these rules, you should revise them before continuing.

23. All that has been said in this chapter about subsidiary companies applies equally to associated companies. The principal auditor is likely to have even more difficulty in forming an opinion on consolidated accounts when the results of associated companies are included. This is because:

   a. An associated company is less likely to have the principal auditor as its auditor.

   b. The holding company is likely to have less influence on an associated company than on a subsidiary.

   c. The Companies Act 1985 assigns no duties to directors and auditors of associated companies to disclose information to principal auditors. However, some associated companies may be required to be consolidated as they are 'subsidiary undertakings' and their boards must give information to the principal auditors.

   d. An associated company is likely to have a different year end from the holding company.

   e. An associated company may well have different accounting policies.

Summary

24. a. Holding (parent) companies have, as their principal asset, investments in and loan and current accounts with subsidiaries.

   b. The auditor has extensive duties in connection with the holding company Balance Sheet.

   c. Small and medium sized groups have some exemptions from compiling and filing group accounts.

   d. The group auditor is responsible for an opinion on the group accounts.

   e. SAS 510 has requirements when subsidiaries have auditors who are not the group auditor.

   f. The existence of associated companies involves some audit problems.

Points to note

25. a. The accounting rules of the Companies Act and the relevant FRSs are complex and difficult. Advanced students of auditing need to know them.

   b. Be careful to distinguish auditing questions on holding companies from those on groups and those on different auditors of subsidiaries.

   c. The value of subsidiaries on the holding company Balance Sheet is a difficult area.

d. Note carefully that the group auditor is responsible for the audit opinion on the group accounts even when she is not the auditor of some of the subsidiaries. The opinion should not make any reference to the fact that she did not audit all the subsidiaries.

e. SAS 510 is a popular exam topic.

f. The relationship between group (primary) and subsidiary (secondary) auditors can be a difficult one.

g. In evaluating the work of a secondary auditor, quality control can be very important.

Case study 1

Foss Chemicals Ltd make chemicals for the defence industry. They had no subsidiary companies but in mid 20-6, they acquired 60% of the share capital of an American company for £600,000 paid partly in cash and partly in shares in Foss. The net assets of the American company, Forrus Inc., were about £800,000 at the time of purchase. Since then the company has made a loss of £200,000, but is expected to break even next year and make a large profit after that.

Discussion

a. Draw up a list of audit procedures that Paul, the auditor of Foss, should carry out in connection with Forrus. The audit of Forrus is carried out by an American firm. Paul is engaged on the audit of Foss's 20-6 accounts.

b. How should the matters connected with Forrus appear in Foss's own accounts? Foss advanced £120,000 as a loan to Forrus and has a trading balance of Dr £60,000 at 31.12. -6.

Case study 2

Continued from Case Study 1. Foss Chemicals have gross assets of £14 million and profits of £700,000.

Discussion

a. Review FRS 2 in the light of the Foss–Forrus case.

b. What matters should Paul consider when reviewing the group accounts?

c. What actions should Paul take with regard to the audit by the American firm of the accounts of Forrus?

d. Identify the risks and the risk areas that Paul should worry about.

Student self testing questions

1. a. How should the value of investments on a holding company balance sheet be audited? (8)

b. What exemptions from compiling and filing group accounts are available? (10)

c. List the auditor's duties re group accounts. (12, 13)

d. How should a principal auditor evaluate the work of a secondary auditor? (16)

e. Why is it difficult to form an opinion when consolidated accounts include associated companies? (23)

Examination questions

1. You are employed in a practising firm of chartered accountants which has recently acquired a new client, Urbino Ltd, in which the principal shareholders are also directors. The directors are currently preparing the consolidated financial statements for the year ended 31 December 1994, and, as the final audit is due to begin quite shortly, you recently held a planning meeting with the audit partner.

   At that meeting, the partner noted that an audit approach had yet to be determined in respect of directors' remuneration and interests and their proper disclosure in the financial statements of Urbino Ltd. He is aware that these areas can be complex and is anxious that, in accordance with L203, *Audit Evidence*, the audit approach chosen should balance the relevance and reliability of evidence available from each source with the time and cost involved in obtaining it.

   You have assembled the following background information:

   (1) Urbino Ltd is a large privately owned holding company with a number of subsidiary and associated undertakings.

   (2) The board of directors of Urbino comprises both non-executive and executive directors. The boards of all subsidiary undertakings are made up from these same persons. Certain directors also sit on the boards of associated undertakings.

   (3) Non-executive directors receive fees for their services. Executive directors receive remuneration packages related solely to their executive appointments. These packages include salaries, bonuses, pension contributions and other benefits.

   (4) Each director holds shares in Urbino Ltd and in some of its subsidiary undertakings.

   You have completed your interim audit visit during which your compliance testing confirmed that the system of accounting and internal control within Urbino Ltd and its subsidiary undertakings had operated effectively during 1994.

   Requirement:

   Prepare a short memorandum to the audit partner in which you should:

   a. identify the principal audit procedures which might be adopted in order to verify that the disclosures included in the draft consolidated financial statements in relation to:

      i. directors' remuneration

      ii. directors' interests

      are complete and accurate in all material respects; and

   b. conclude as to the most appropriate audit approach to adopt in the light of the audit partner's wish to balance the relevance and reliability of available evidence with the time and cost involved in obtaining it.

   NB: your answer should *not* deal with directors' loans or transactions.

   (ICAI)

2. Ipanema PLC has one subsidiary company called Copacabana Ltd. In your capacity as auditor of Ipanema PLC and as group auditor, you have been investigating the inter-company current accounts and discover that they fail to agree.

   Required:

   a. What possible reasons might there be for the lack of agreement? (3 marks)

   b. What is the group auditor's responsibility in connection with the difference? (3 marks)

c. What audit method should you adopt? (6 marks)

(LCCI) (Total 12 marks)

3. You are the group auditor to Erewash PLC. During the year under audit review, the group acquired a majority shareholding in Trent Valley Ltd. You are not the auditor of Trent Valley Ltd, whose present auditors will continue in office.

State what specific audit methods you might undertake in connection with the acquisition of Trent Valley Ltd. (15 marks)

(LCCI)

52 Other statements and interim accounts

Introduction

1. The other statements we are concerned with are:
    a. The chairman's report.
    b. The directors' report.
    c. Group accounts.
    d. Cash flow statements.
    e. Notes to Accounts.
    f. Comparative figures.
    g. Statistical summaries.
    h. Lists of subsidiary and associated companies.
    i. Accounting policies.
    j. Any other information or statements in the annual report.
    k. Corporate governance.
    l. Statement of directors' responsibilities.
    m. Board's report on remuneration.

    There is SAS 160 *Other Information in Documents Containing Audited Financial Statements* and an ISA 720 with the same title.

2. The listing agreement requires that listed companies must issue an interim statement covering the first half of the financial year. The auditors may be asked to review the interim statement and make a report. The topic is covered in Bulletin 99/4 *Review of Interim Financial Information*.

Directors' report

3. The Companies Act requires that a directors' report shall be prepared each financial year.

4. The auditor is not responsible for the directors' report and does not audit it or give an opinion on it. However S.235(3) The Companies Act 1985 requires:

    'The auditors shall consider whether the information given in the directors' report for the financial year for which the annual accounts are prepared is consistent with those accounts; and if they are of the opinion that it is not they shall state that fact in their report.'

SAS 160 requires that the auditors should read the directors' report and if as a result they find any material inconsistencies with the audited financial statements, they should seek to resolve them. An example of an inconsistency is if the plant and machinery at the Birmingham plant was in the balance sheet at cost less depreciation but the directors' report said that this plant and machinery was to be scrapped and replaced with modern plant in the coming year.

If any inconsistencies come to light then the auditors should ask the directors to resolve the differences and make any necessary alterations to the accounts and/or to the directors' report. The directors will normally accede to this and the matter ends there.

If the directors decline to make any alteration then the position could be either or both of:

a. the financial statements are incorrect. In this case the auditors will possibly need to qualify their report

b. the directors' report is incorrect. In this case the precepts of S.253(3) apply and the auditor should include a reference in his report. As an example:

'Inconsistency between the financial statements and the directors' report

In our opinion, the information given in paragraph 8 of the directors' report is not consistent with these financial statements. That paragraph states without amplification that the company achieved a 10% growth in profitability in the year. The Profit and Loss Account shows that the operating profit declined by 5% and the growth in net profit after tax was experienced only because of the inclusion of an exceptional item of £3.1 million on gains on the disposal of a subsidiary company.'

Note: this form of report is not a qualified report as the opinion on the financial statements is unaffected.

If the auditors consider that there is a *material misstatement* in the directors' report but it does not require that the financial statements be amended and the directors decline to change the alleged misstatement then the auditors should take legal advice as to what to do or possibly resign the engagement. SAS 160 gives no example but an example might be if there were major misstatements on the identity of the directors' or their shareholdings. You will appreciate that such is a misstatement but is not an inconsistency.

Schedules and statements

5. Company auditors are required to express an opinion on the financial statements. These are not simply the Profit and Loss Account and Balance Sheet but may include a number of separate schedules and statements:

    -   the company accounts
    -   the group accounts
    -   notes, attached to and forming part of, the accounts
    -   comparative figures
    -   schedule of accounting policies
    -   lists of subsidiary and associated companies
    -   cash flow statement.

The auditor's responsibility for these is as for the profit and loss account and balance sheet. However see Chapter 39 for the comparative figures

Other documents

6. The annual report of a company may include other documents and material. For example, the chairman's statement, statistical summaries, a photograph of the board of directors and yet others.

   SAS 160 requires that all other statements, documents and information issued with audited financial statements should be reviewed by the auditors for inconsistencies with the financial statements and for misstatements within the other material. As with the directors' report any misstatement or inconsistency should be discussed with the directors and normally they make the necessary alterations and that is the end of the matter. However if the directors fail to make the required alterations then:

   a. if the financial statements are incorrect, qualify their report

   b. if the matter does not affect the financial statements but is an apparent misstatement or a material inconsistency then consider including an explanatory paragraph describing the apparent misstatement or a material inconsistency. This does not constitute a qualification.

   Auditors must distinguish a factual error from a matter of judgement. In matters of judgement auditors should not substitute their judgement for that of the directors but in severe cases they should take legal advice. Alternatives or additions to the explanatory paragraph include exercising their right to be heard at the AGM and resigning and making a statement under S 394 Companies Act 1985.

Interim accounts

7. The Stock Exchange listing agreement requires that listed companies publish a half-yearly report amounting to a summarised Profit and Loss Account and an explanatory statement relating to their activities for the first half year. In addition an ASB statement interim reports, adds a statement of total recognised gains and losses, a summarised Balance Sheet, a summarised cash flow statement and associated notes. There is often other information such as a chairman's statement. Auditors are required to review just the documents recommended by the ASB statement and to report on their review.

8. The object of a review is to enable the auditors to say that they are not aware of any material modifications that should be made to the financial information as presented. The basis of a review is the making enquiries of management and applying analytical procedures to the financial information and underlying financial data and based thereon, assessing whether the accounting policies and presentation have been consistently applied. A review *excludes* audit procedures such as tests of controls and verification of assets and liabilities and transactions. It is substantially *less in scope* than an audit. It provides only a *moderate level* of assurance.

9. The procedures that should be adopted for a review are suggested at length in the bulletin and consist in essence of:

   a. Agree an engagement letter.

   b. Plan the work including undertaking an update of the auditors' knowledge of the business and assessing the potential risk of material misstatement.

c.   Obtain evidence by a process of enquiry and analytical procedures.

d.   Review prior year matters including any points raised in management letters – consider the subsequent events review carried out on the previous audit.

e.   Enquiry about any changes, planned or actual, to ownership, systems, operations, controls, risks, control environment etc.

f.   Checking significant balances from the accounting records to the trial balance and to the accounts.

g.   Reviewing minutes etc.

h.   Reviewing accounting policies used.

i.   Enquiry about subsequent events up to the date of approval of the interim accounts.

j.   Reviewing the going concern basis.

k.   Obtaining written representations from the directors.

l.   Read any other information sent out with the interim statement.

m.   Discuss findings with the directors and the audit committee report.

10. An example of a report might be:

Independent review report to A PLC

Introduction

We have been instructed by the company to review the financial information set out on pages ...to ... and we have read the other information contained in the interim report and considered whether it contains any apparent misstatements or material inconsistencies with the financial information,

Directors' responsibilities

The interim report, including the financial information contained there in is the responsibility of, and has been approved by the directors. The Listing Rules of the London Stock Exchange require that the accounting policies and presentation applied to the interim figures should be consistent with those applied in preparing the preceding annual accounts except where any changes, and the reasons for them, are disclosed.

Review work performed

We conducted our review in accordance with guidance contained in Bulletin 1999/4 issued by the Auditing Practices Board. A review consists principally of making enquiries of group management and applying analytical procedures to the financial information and underlying financial data and based thereon, assessing whether the accounting policies and presentation have been consistently applied unless otherwise disclosed. A review excludes audit procedures such as tests of controls and verification of assets, liabilities and transactions. It is substantially less in scope than an audit performed in accordance with auditing standards and therefore provides a lower level of assurance than an audit. Accordingly we do not express an audit opinion on the financial information.

Review conclusion

On the basis of our review we are not aware of any material modifications that should be made to the financial information as presented for the six months ended 30 June 20-6.

Tickers	Donington
Chartered Certified Accountants	30 July 20-6

---

11. It is possible to issue a modified report if there is any change (or no change when one is required) in accounting policies or if there is an apparent misstatement or material inconsistency. If a modified report is required the report will be the same but with an extra paragraph in the conclusion:

> Included in the stock shown on the Balance Sheet is an amount of £x valued at cost. In our view this stock is unlikely to be sold at this amount and should be valued at net realisable value, reducing profit before tax by £y and net assets by £z.
>
> On the basis of our review, with the exception of the matter described in the preceding paragraph, we are not aware of any material modifications that should be made to the financial information as presented for the six months ended 30 June 20-6.

Summary

12 a. A directors' report is a requirement of The Companies Act.

b. The auditor is not responsible for the directors' report and does not give an opinion on it. However he is required to consider if any information in it is inconsistent with the financial statements.

c. The auditor needs to clarify any inconsistency. Normally any inconsistency will be resolved and documents amended.

d. If amendments are not made the auditor *may* need to qualify his report on the financial statements or include a statement on the matter in his report.

e. SAS 160 has similar requirements for all other documents and information which accompany audited financial statements.

f. SAS 600 also covers misstatements in the other documents and information. Serious misstatements may require the auditor to seek legal advice on what to do and possibly to resign.

g. Interim statements now consist of several summarised and other statements in accordance with the ASB statement. The auditor may be asked to report on the interim accounts. In practice many interim reports are not reviewed by the auditors.

h. The report covers a small range of requirements including accounting policies used and whether any material modifications may be required to the financial statements.

Points to note

13. a. The auditor's report usually contains a statement like:

'We have audited the financial statements on pages ... to ...'

Auditors must take great care to see that the pages concerned cover all the statements subject to audit examination and opinion and only those statements. Cases have been known of the auditor's report apparently covering a colour photograph of Miss Bilston Boilerhouse 20-7.

b. The annual report and accounts of a public company consists of a number of separate statements and schedules, some of which are, and some of which are not, subject to audit opinion. However it can also be viewed as a unitary whole. When viewed as a whole a view may be given of the results of the period or the state of affairs at the end of the year, which is different from the view given by the accounts which form a part of the whole.

It is therefore desirable for, and SAS 160 requires that, the auditor to examine all other statements and if individually or collectively they give a different view from the accounts, he has a duty to feel put upon enquiry and to investigate the differences.

Case study

Alice is engaged on the audit of Miss Lead PLC a manufacturer of fashion dresses. She has read the proposed directors' report and chairman's statement. She finds that:

1. The directors' report, in discussing developments, states that the company intend to close down the factory at Liverpool and shift production to a newly built extension at the Bolton factory. The accounts include £48,000 as the unamortised cost of the plant at Liverpool. The factory there is leasehold with only one year of the lease to run.

2. The dividend per share is stated in the directors' report to be 4.5p against 4.0p in the previous year and the directors' report makes much play on the increase. In fact the final dividend has gone from 4.0p to 4.5p but the total dividend has gone from 6.3p to 6.2p.

3. The chairman's statement states that the company is poised for a large increase in turnover and profit. Alice has seen the budgeted accounts and forecasts for the next year and further projections in a long-range forecast and plan. These show a short-term decline in business and profit and a very slow recovery in the long term.

The company turnover is £6 million, profits are about £450,000 and net assets £4 million.

The directors have lost the confidence of institutional shareholders and fear a take-over bid.

Alice has discussed these items with the board and they adamantly refuse to make any changes.

Discussion

a. What should Alice do about these items?

b. Draft the audit report assuming nothing else was wrong.

Student self testing questions *Questions with answers apparent from the text*

1. a. What statements appear in an annual report and accounts? (1)

   b. What is the auditors' duty towards:
      - The chairman's statement. (6)
      - The directors' report. (4)
      - Cash flow statements. (5)
      - Interim accounts. (7)

Exercise

Julia, the manager in charge of the audit of Chaotic PLC is reviewing the draft annual report of the group. Among other matters she notes:

a. The general tenor of the directors' and chairman's reports are optimistic but the accounts show a downward trend in profits and this is confirmed by the medium term forecasts prepared for the Board by consultants.

b. The financial statements include a stock of Thingies valued at £640,000 at cost. The chairman's statement states that production of Thingies has ceased as they were loss making. Further enquiries by Julia, indicates that the stock will be sold as a job lot to Opp PLC at a substantial loss.

c. The directors' report states that Subsida Ltd was sold for £3 million to Poke PLC, giving a profit of £0.5 million. However the accounts include a provision for £1.3 million for a series of payments to Poke to compensate them for lower than expected profits earned by Subsida, as agreed in the sale contract.

d. The directors' report states without amplification that 'Successful conclusion of the development of the Whatsit, a new product, will bring substantial profits to the group'. Julia knows that prototypes have been plagued with faults and that a competitor will certainly beat Chaotic to the market.

e. For three months during the year, George Goon was a director of the main group board, having been a director of a subsidiary for several years. He resigned shortly before the year end before pleading guilty to drug smuggling offences. His name does not appear in the list of directors nor is his remuneration included in the directors' remuneration.

The board adamantly refuse to change any of these matters in the report and accounts. What should Julia's firm do, given that the profit of the group is shown as £6.1 million before tax.

Some auditing problem areas

1. The auditor has a duty to all users of the financial statements he is auditing, to see that a true and fair view is given. We now deal with two problem areas: firstly related parties and then reservation of title.

53 Related parties

Introduction

1. Many entities are quite autonomous and deal at *arms length* with all persons and entities that they have contact with. They pursue their own *self interest* at all times. However some entities are not like that all the time. Some deal with persons or entities who are connected with them and transactions between them may not then be at arms length or in the interests of the reporting entity. For example the Adam family (primarily Adam himself) own all the shares in both Cain Ltd and Abel Ltd. For reasons of his own (perhaps inheritance tax reasons) Adam decides that Cain Ltd should transfer a freehold property to Abel Ltd at a nominal price unrelated to market price. In this case, Abel Ltd has gained something and Cain Ltd has lost something, not as a result of ordinary commercial dealing but as a result of dealings with Abel Ltd under the influence of Adam. Both Adam and Cain Ltd are *related parties* of Abel Ltd.

If a reader of the financial statements of Abel Ltd or Cain Ltd wants to get a true and fair view of the affairs of these companies, that reader must be informed about the transaction described above. What is required is disclosure of all dealings with related parties. The ASB issued FRS 8 *Related Party Disclosures* in October 1995 after a very long gestation period. The gist of FRS 8 is that it requires disclosure of:

– information on transactions with related parties
– the name of the party controlling the reporting entity and, if different, that of the ultimate controlling party.

2. The accounting standards are FRS 8 and IAS 24: *Related Parties Disclosures*. The Statement of Auditing Standards are SAS 460 and ISA 550 *Related Parties.*

The auditor's duties re related parties

3. SAS 460 requires that the auditors should:
   a. plan and perform the audit with the objective of obtaining sufficient *audit evidence* regarding the adequacy of disclosure of related party transactions and control of the entity in the financial statements
   b. when *planning* the audit, assess the *risk* that material undisclosed related party transactions may exist
   c. review for completeness, *information* provided by the directors identifying material transactions with those parties that have been related parties for any part of the financial period

d. be *alert* for evidence of material related party transactions that are not included in the information provided by the directors

e. obtain sufficient appropriate audit evidence that material identified related party transactions are *properly recorded and disclosed* in the financial statements

f. obtain sufficient appropriate audit evidence that disclosures in the financial statements relating to *control of the entity* are properly stated

g. obtain written *representations* from the directors concerning the completeness of information provided regarding the related party and control disclosures in the financial statements

h. consider the implications for their *report* if:

-   they are unable to obtain sufficient appropriate audit evidence concerning related parties and transactions with such parties; or

-   the disclosure of related party transactions or the controlling party of the entity in the financial statements is not adequate.

Risk

4. It is the directors' responsibility under FRS 8 to identify, approve and disclose related party transactions and, to that end, they should implement adequate accounting and internal control systems. The auditors can then acquire an understanding of such systems. However the directors may not implement such systems or they may wish to hide transactions with related parties. Directors have been motivated in such matters by intentions to defraud the company (for example by extracting assets from it) or shareholders (for example by window dressing the financial statements) or the tax authorities (for example by transfer pricing to put profits in low tax countries) or national governments (for example by circumventing exchange control restrictions). There is therefore a risk that auditors may fail to identify some related party transactions.

5. In the planning stage of an audit, the auditors should assess the risk that there will be undisclosed related party transactions. In many audits the risk will be small but in others it will be large. The work the auditors can be expected to do depends on the degree of risk identified. There is an *inherent risk* that all relevant related party transactions will not be identified. However SAS 460 makes clear that the auditors cannot be expected to find a needle in a haystack.

6. There are some situations where the auditors need to be especially vigilant and enquire more deeply:

a. where obvious risks exist. For example the company is one of several owned by a resident in a tax haven and the auditors know from past experience that transactions are entered into that are not motivated by purely commercial considerations

b. where there is *control risk,* that is, where the control environment is weak

c. where the management style does not place a high priority on financial statement disclosure.

In general auditors can, in the absence of high risk circumstances, rely upon the representations of the directors. However the auditors must undertake all audits with a proper degree of *scepticism* and be alert at all times to the possibility of undisclosed related party transactions.

Information provided by directors

7. Directors should provide representations to the auditors and this should then be checked. There are various ways of doing this:

   a. reviewing minutes and statutory books (e.g. register of directors' interests)

   b. reviewing large or unusual transactions especially around year ends

   c. reviewing loans received and made, and the bank letter

   d. reviewing investment transactions

   e. reviewing prior year papers

   f. reviewing pension and other trusts

   g. reviewing affiliations of directors and senior managers with other entities

   h. reviewing returns to tax authorities, Companies House, the Stock Exchange, regulatory agencies and others

   i. reviewing correspondence with lawyers.

8. In the course of the audit, staff will be constantly alert to matters which may reveal an undisclosed related party. Such instances may include unexpected prices, unexpected contract terms, transactions lacking commercial logic, and transactions where substance differs from form. Such transactions after date are especially important.

9. The auditors must obtain evidence that the recording and disclosure in financial statements is appropriate. They may need to enquire more closely into disclosed transactions, and obtain third party confirmations.

Control of the entity

10. In most instances this is not a problem. But in some cases it is and then the auditors should obtain appropriate evidence. In some cases the ultimate controlling party is unknown. This seems surprising but the use of tax havens and offshore ownership chains designed to confuse regulatory and tax authorities is not uncommon. If the ultimate controlling party is not known then that fact should be disclosed.

Qualified reports

11. In a few cases the auditors may conclude that they have insufficient evidence on this subject. This is a *limitation of scope* and may require a qualified opinion or, rather unlikely, a disclaimer of opinion. If the auditors conclude that the disclosure is not adequate then they may issue a qualified opinion or an adverse opinion. They may also consider giving, in their report, the information which should have been given in the financial statements.

Summary

12. a. A true and fair view often requires the disclosure of related party transactions and of controlling parties.

   b. FRS 8 and SAS 460 appeared in late 1995.

   c. The auditors have a duty to see that the provisions of FRS 8 are carried out and to obey the prescriptions of SAS 460. However they are not required to find a needle in a haystack.

   d. The auditors need to assess the risk of inadequate disclosure and act accordingly.

e. The directors are primarily responsible for the disclosure of related party and owner-ship matters and the auditors should obtain written representations from them.

Points to note

13. a. Related parties can be of many kinds – owners, directors, 'shadow' directors, key management, persons who tend to act in concert, families of the others.

   b. Some persons and entities are not considered to be related parties for these purposes. For example regulatory bodies, banks, major customers or suppliers despite the fact that they may have considerable influence over the conduct of the company's affairs. Related party transactions like directors' emoluments do not come into the definition either but, of course, The Companies Act 1985 has required their disclosure for many years.

   c. Pension funds and pension fund trustees are related parties. This is in the wake of the Maxwell and Daily Mirror Group affair.

   d. A general requirement for the disclosure of related party transactions is new with FRS 8. However there are many specific requirements by the Stock Exchange for listed companies and in The Companies Act 1985 for all companies (see sections 231, 232, 741 and schedules 4 to 7).

   e. This whole area is fascinating and we shall see how it works out over the next few years.

Case study 1

Convoluted Ltd is a company dealing in rare metals internationally. It has 40 employees (25 in the UK). It is owned by Joe King Ltd, a company registered in the Cayman Islands and is known to deal with several other UK and overseas companies also owned by that company. The company has four directors who are all UK residents and who do not own any shares in the company.

The company has a pension scheme with employee and employer trustees and is heavily indebted to its bankers.

The auditors are Chancy & Co. who are newly appointed.

Discussion

   a. List some possible related parties of this company.
   b. From the auditors' point of view what risks are there that all the requirements of FRS 8 may not be met?
   c. Set out a section in the overall audit plan covering the requirements of SAS 460.
   d. List some possible substantive tests on the subject of related party transactions and ultimate control.

Case study 2

Obtain some annual reports and accounts of public companies. Explore and report on the related party and company control matters.

Student self testing questions *Questions with answers apparent from the text*

1. a. Why are related party transactions and ultimate ownership important to the true and fair view? (1)

b. What are the two main sources of authority in this area? (2)

c. List the requirements of SAS 460. (3)

d. What are the risks that auditors undertake in this area ? (4-6)

e. How might an auditor seek confirmation of directors' representations and assess their completeness? (7)

f. What matters might give concern to an auditor in preparing the auditor's report? (11)

Examination questions

1. Your firm has recently been appointed auditor of Ripley Manufacturing PLC. Ripley Manufacturing PLC is quoted on the London Stock Exchange and the directors own less than 5% of the company's shares.

   You have been asked by the senior in charge of the audit to carry out work in relation to directors transactions with the company, which are required to be disclosed in the company's annual accounts.

   Required:

   a. List and briefly describe the work you would carry out to check if the company has made any loans or quasi-loans to a director, or entered into any guarantees in connection with a loan to a director. (7 marks)

   b. List and briefly describe the work you would carry out to check if there are any:

      i. directors' service agreements with the company.

      ii. options granted by the company to enable directors to purchase shares in the company at a fixed price at a future date. (5 marks)

   c. List and briefly describe the investigations you would carry out to determine whether any director has had a material interest in a contract with the company (other than those described in part b. above). (6 marks)

   d. List and describe the work you would carry out and the matters you would consider if your investigations revealed that Ripley Manufacturing PLC had purchased all the shares in Lowdham Engineering PLC for £4,000,000. One of the directors of Ripley Manufacturing PLC owns 50% of the shares of Lowdham Engineering PLC. (4 marks)

   e. A partner of your firm has asked your advice on another transaction, in which Ilkeston Electrical Ltd purchased all the shares in Nuthall Distributors Ltd for £40,000. Nuthall Distributors Ltd was owned by the two directors of Ilkeston Electrical Ltd, and all the shares in Ilkeston Electrical Ltd are owned by these two directors and their families. You are required to list and describe the work you would carry out and the matters you would consider in relation to the purchase of Nuthall Distributors Ltd by Ilkeston Electrical Ltd. (3 marks)

   (ACCA) (Total 25 marks)

54 Reservation of title

Introduction

1. In 1976, the case of *Aluminium Industrie Vaassen BV* v *Romalpa Aluminium Ltd* (the Romalpa case) made the business community aware of the idea of selling goods subject to reservation of title. It is possible to sell goods under a contract of sale whereby ownership does not pass until the goods are paid for.

2. This departure from the normal contract of sales creates recording and reporting problems for the parties involved and for their auditors.

3. This chapter considers these from the point of view of accounting, reporting and audit.

Accounting treatment

4. The treatment recommended by the accounting bodies is to record 'Romalpa' sales as if they were ordinary sales, that is, the sales are recorded as they are invoiced and the realisation convention is followed. This is an example of the accounting convention of substance over form. Other examples of this convention include hire purchase, group accounts, and some leasing transactions.

5. This treatment is appropriate for 'Romalpa' sales but not for goods sold on consignment or goods sold on sale or return where a sale will only be made on fulfilment of some agreed event such as the resale of the goods by the consignee.

Disclosure in accounts – buyers

6. The matter is only relevant if creditors include a *material* amount owed to suppliers who have sold the goods subject to reservation of title. Such creditors are in effect secured and the Companies Act and the true and fair view require disclosure of secured creditors. In fact it is not entirely clear, if the Companies Act does require disclosure of creditors secured in this way. As the accounts are drawn up on the going concern convention, disclosure of matters which are relevant only in liquidation seems unnecessary.

7. However it is customary to disclose the amount of creditors which are secured in this way. This creates practical difficulties in that:

    a. Purchases and creditors subject to reservation of title are not normally distinguishable from the general run of purchases and creditors.

    b. It is not always clear if a particular sale is subject to a reservation of title which will stand up in a court of law.

Disclosure in accounts – sellers

8. So far as vendors are concerned, the matter is only relevant in improving the collectability of debts. Any review of the required provision for bad and doubtful debts will need to consider this point.

Audit work – purchasers

9. The following work will need to be done on *all* audits:

    a. Ascertain what steps the client takes to identify suppliers selling on terms which reserve title.

b. Ascertain what steps the client has taken to quantify such liabilities.

c. If it is apparent that there are *material* liabilities to such creditors then:

   i. if the liabilities are quantified in the Accounts (usually this is just a note to the accounts) then review and test the procedures which have produced the figure.

   ii. if the directors consider that exact quantification is impracticable (this is often the case) and have estimated the amount or made a general note that such liabilities exist to a material amount, then review and test the information given.

   iii. consider generally if the information given is sufficient.

d. If it appears that there are no material liabilities of this kind, then verify that this is so by reviewing the terms of sale of major suppliers.

e. Obtain formal representations from the directors that there are no material liabilities of this sort, or if there are, that they have been adequately disclosed.

Summary

10. a. Goods can be sold subject to reservation of title.

b. Such sales are called 'Romalpa' sales.

c. The convention is to record such sales as if they were ordinary sales under the accounting convention 'substance over form'.

d. In a Balance Sheet, if creditors include a material amount secured by reservation of title, this fact should be disclosed and, if possible, quantified.

e. The auditor has a duty to apply procedures to ensure that adequate disclosure of such liabilities has been made.

Points to note

11. a. This subject has proved popular with examiners.

b. In practice, a supplier may have difficulty in law in establishing that the subject matter of his debt were sold subject to reservation of title. Liquidators tend to refuse to accept that any debts are secured by reservation of title.

c. Legal doubts exist over the extent to which an unpaid seller can trace or identify his interest in the goods if the goods have become indistinguishable from similar goods not secured, transformed by incorporation in a product (e.g. eggs made into a cake) or sold.

Case study 1

Baloo is engaged on the audit of the accounts of Bagheera Bearing Ltd who trade in industrial bearings. The time is March 2007 and the accounts are for the year ending 31.12.2006. Baloo notes that most of Bagheera's suppliers supply on reservation of title contracts.

Debtors of Bagheera include £26,000 from Akela Ltd. A receiver was appointed to Akela on 26.2.2007 and no dividend is likely to be paid to unsecured creditors. Invoices to Akela have been marked 'These goods are sold on the understanding that title to them passes to the purchaser only on payment of the sum due'. Turnover of Bagheera in 2007 was £340,000.

Discussion

a. Outline the audit work to be done re reservation of title and the creditors.

b. The directors have declined to make a provision against the debt due by Akela. What should Baloo do?

Student self testing questions *Questions with answers apparent from the text*

1. a. How should reservation of title transactions be treated in financial statements? (4)

   b. What audit work should be done on creditors in connection with reservation of title? (9)

   c. What audit work should be done on debtors in connection with reservation of title clauses?

55 Current issues

Introduction

1. Auditing is a fast changing discipline and this chapter is about issues that are currently exercising the profession. There are a surprisingly large number of current issues! By the time you read this there will be new issues so it is very important to read the professional press and student periodicals.

Influences on auditing

2. Developments that change the face include the following items. Some of them will be pursued in more detail later in the chapter. The current influences are:

   a. Statute law – new Companies Acts are rare but statutory instruments changing company law are frequent and other Acts of Parliament also influence auditing. Examples of recent changes include the extension of audit exemption and The Limited Liability Partnerships Act 2000. Both of these are likely to have a profound influence on the auditing profession.

   b. APB and IAPC Statements of Auditing Standards and other guidance on auditing matters. New standards and guidance seems to come daily as the board and committee deal with a backlog of issues and respond to changes elsewhere. Make sure you are up-to-date!

   c. The Accounting Standards Board and the IASC issue new material frequently and the UITF also make pronouncements. All these need to be known by auditors. The latest buzz word is convergence whereby UK and international accounting and auditing standards will be changed to be more like each other.

   d. The professional bodies make new pronouncements and issue new guidance on many issues including ethical and auditing issues.

   e. Corporate governance has become a large issue and the Combined Code on Corporate Governance has caused much upset amongst listed companies and their auditors.

f. Scandals such as the BCCI collapse and the Maxwell affair and many large company failures shortly after clear auditors' reports have led to doubts about the competence and integrity of audit firms.

g. The Securities and Exchange Commission has recently pronounced on professional independence and this has led to a debate on the issue which may have repercussions for some time.

h. The European Community have very different company law and auditing regimes and the conflict between international and UK standards and EC standards will cause some changes to all.

i. The costs of auditing and the international nature of many large clients have led to concentration among audit firms.

j. New opportunities for auditing type work have developed. These include environmental and social auditing, value for money auditing and assurance reporting of various types.

k. The economics of auditing have led to changes in practice. The business risk approach is a new development. It has been suggested that auditors now spend too much time on their computers doing analyses and too little talking to people and getting to grips with real things and real documents. Audit firms are perhaps more interested in making money than they once were.

l. We now live a much more litigious society and auditors now have to practise more defensive auditing to avoid being sued. This may get in the way of desirable innovations.

m. The profession is self-regulated. There is much debate about the need for external and independent regulation. This argument applies to many other professions and spheres of activity

n. The legal status of audit firms is now an issue. Should they be partnerships, limited companies or limited liability partnerships?

o. The global economy has led to auditing becoming more international. This has led to the need for harmonisation of practices in all countries. The auditing profession also needs to become international.

p. Firms have found ways of using computers in their work and the universal use of CISs has changed the face of auditing.

q. E-commerce may yet become a dominant way of doing business.

Independence

3. Independence is both something that is a matter of fact but it is also something which is a matter of appearance. It is important to be independent but it is also important to appear to be independent. In recent years auditing firms have seen auditing almost as a loss leader, and they have seen auditing as giving access to a client so that the client can be sold all manner of additional services, all of which are the really lucrative services. Some large firms have sold off their consultancy arms (at immense profit for the partners) but other work is still the meat of practices.

Independence seems an obvious idea but is actually hard to define. The SEC has suggested four principles on independence:

    a.   An auditor may not have a mutual or conflicting interest with the client.

    b.   An auditor may not audit his own firm's work.

    c.   An auditor may not function as management or as an employee of the audit client.

    d.   An auditor may not act as an advocate for the audit client.

4.   There are some advantages and disadvantages attached to auditors taking on other work for their client.

The advantages are:

    a.   In economic terms, an extensive knowledge of the client will enable the auditor to offer her services to her client in a context which she already understands.

    b.   The auditor will not need to obtain large amounts of background knowledge before conducting the other work.

The disadvantages of an auditor offering other services are:

    a.   The auditor will be perceived as not being fully independent.

    b.   The auditor will in many cases be auditing his or her own work.

    c.   Effectively much of this kind of other work involves management functions.

    d.   Some of the work may effectively involve acting as an advocate for the client.

Ethics

5.   The professional bodies require strict adherence to the ethical codes and have considerable enforcement mechanisms. Necessarily ethical codes should be obeyed in the spirit as well as the letter but often are not. The fundamental principles of the code should be adhered to at all times and can be mentioned in many auditing exam answers. Despite the existence of the codes and enforcement mechanisms there is a probability that external regulation may replace self-regulation. The problem with self-regulation is that it is not seen as independent. Professions are often introverted and close ranks and protect their own. Large firms are not easily disciplined by their peers and new rules are often compromises between public needs and commercial requirements of the audit firms.

The profession

6.   The accounting and auditing profession has undergone many changes in recent years. There are now three tiers – the very big firms, the medium sized firms and myriad small ones. The big five have become big mainly by mergers and are now giant international enterprises with many thousands of staff members. There is talk of still more mergers. Listed companies nearly always use the large firms as their auditors.

7.   In the past audit firms were all partnerships. However it is now possible to incorporate and some firms have done so. It is probable that many firms will register under the new The Limited Liability Partnerships Act 2000 and will have limited liability but with a partnership structure.

Information technology and auditing

8.   The laptop computer is now essential equipment for an auditor. Useful packages that can be used on it include:

    a.   File interrogation packages e.g. to search sales ledgers.

b. Audit programme generators.

c. Checklist generators.

d. Spreadsheets for calculations, listings etc.

e. Word processors to generate documents and store audit working papers and reports.

f. Relational databases.

g. Reference information over the Internet – all regulations and rules governing auditing and accounting can be searched together with all the world's information on any matter.

h. Systems documentation.

i. Risk analysis software.

j. Trial balance processors.

k. Time management software.

Automating procedures

9. The benefits in automating audit procedures include:

a. Files are kept in a more compact form.

b. Systems designed for optimal auditing are adhered to by audit staff.

c. Automatic generation of audit plans, programmes, schedules and procedures.

d. Instant availability of information on a wide range of audit related subjects.

e. The creation of data for audit examination or analytical review that is not readily available from client records.

f. Savings due to more efficient working.

g. Better compliance with audit firm procedures and SASs.

h. Better PR as clients expect and demand that their auditors are up to date and efficient.

i. Freeing audit personnel to think rather than merely go through procedures.

j. Creation of networks such that on line supervision becomes possible.

k. Rapid sharing of information.

10. The disbenefits include less time spent on traditional auditing involving people, objects and client records, a certain rigidity of approach and severe problems if the laptop fails to work or is stolen.

E-commerce

11. Let us look at some terminology:

a. E-commerce: conducting business over the Internet by electronic rather than paper-based methods.

b. EDI – electronic data interchange: a standard method of exchanging documents, such as invoices, between companies that may have incompatible hardware and/or software. Electronic form filling and transmission is far quicker than manually completing a form and then posting it.

c. SET - Secure electronic transmission an extension of EDI so that monies can be transferred primarily through credit card payments.

Each of these new technologies raises risks for firms engaged in using them and, by extension, for their auditors.

12. Some of the risks are:

a   Systems breakdown – many companies are now so dependent on IT that a systems breakdown can have going concern implications.

b. Viruses – computer viruses can spread very rapidly and can cause systems failure.

c. Failure of Internet service provider or of web-based outsourcing supplier. It is suggested that companies will in future have their records, including accounting records, kept by service companies and the data will be interchanged via the web.

d. Confidentiality – data which may be commercially sensitive may be obtainable by hackers or by other means when systems are widely dispersed in and beyond the company.

e. Integrity – data may become corrupted or be unauthorised or duplicated or lost when it is held entirely by electronic means.

f. Health and safety – continuous exposure to computer screens may damage employees' health and lead to actions for damages.

g. Compliance with the law – there are some regulations which must be complied with including the Data Protection Act 1998.

h. Competition – the web is a universal provider of information including product information. In addition suppliers can easily supply goods across national boundaries. International business can easily be mediated through the net. I can, for example, buy books more cheaply from web-based booksellers in the USA than in the UK.   This has implications for many businesses that formerly had quasi-monopoly positions.

i. Fraud – the complexity and anonymity of modern IT systems make fraud a possibility and its detection more unlikely. The ability, even if heavily protected, for access to information by customers and others makes fraud very possible.

j. Money laundering – similarly, money laundering is facilitated by modern IT systems.

k. Lack of audit trail – the trail of paper tracing all transactions is gradually reducing and the paperless office, while far from present yet, is in sight. Integrity of data collection, authorising, collection and transmission is thus more relevant.

l. There is a lack of appropriate technical skills.

m. Investment needs to be at a high level and continuous. Again bringing going concern problems.

n. Selling on-line through the Internet is a new way of doing business. At the time of writing it has not become nearly as important as it was expected to become but it is undoubtedly here to stay.

These technologies represent rapid growth and major competitive and market changes – risk of breakdown of systems, loss of control and going concern problems.

13. E-commerce and indeed all forms of advanced computerisation of complex systems present a number of challenges to the auditor. These include:

a. The need for technical expertise in the audit firm.

b. Whether to accept or continue audit engagements. As we have seen e-commerce presents great risks to companies which engage in it. Some auditors may feel they do not have the skills to tackle such audits or may feel that they would prefer not to accept the audit risks involved.

c. The going concern problem needs more attention than usual.

d. Internal audit is especially important in these areas (if the client has an internal audit department – listed companies should have) and the audit needs to have particular regard to this function.

e. Some parts of the system may be outsourced (e.g. to ISPs or in connection with Secure Electronic Transmission of funds).

f. The focus of controls may be different. Most systems concentrate on recording and storage of transactions. In e-commerce the focus may be on the actual execution of the transactions.

g. Audit firms may be involved in an advisory or consultancy role in setting up systems for clients engaging in e-commerce. This may imply a conflict of interest in carrying out the audit. Can an auditor make a dispassionate assessment of controls she has herself been instrumental in applying?

h. In the early stages of e-commerce, the auditor may find that analytical review is not an option as the business is changing so rapidly.

Carrying out the audit

14. In many ways the procedures required in carrying out audits on clients engaging in e-commerce are the same as those used on any other audit. A possible approach could be:

a. Consider whether the audit should be accepted or continuation of the engagement be accepted.

b. Assign staff with appropriate technical expertise to the audit.

c. Obtain a very detailed knowledge of the business and especially of the risks facing the client.

d. Evaluate the risks to the auditor of the particular audit.

e. Examine and assess the overall control environment.

f. Examine and assess the specific controls in force – auditing round the computer is often impractical in these situations and understanding and testing the computerised controls and using the computer as an audit tool are both necessary.

g. Examining and assessing the controls in place in connection with outsourced processing.

h. Liaising with and assessing the internal audit function.

i. Pay special attention to going concern. Ensure the client has some form of business continuity planning in the case of systems failure.

Financial reporting and web sites

15. Many companies now put their financial statements on the web (look at some!). This can present problems for the auditor. However there is a Bulletin 2001/1 *The Electronic Publication of Auditors' Reports*.

The points to note are:

The Companies Act requirements for the publication of financial statements and associated documents such as the auditor's report must be adhered to. Under The Companies Act 1985 (Electronic Communications) Order 2000, companies can now fulfil their reporting obligations to shareholders in this way. Problems associated with this for auditors are:

a. Identifying audited information by page numbers may not apply.

b. The distinction between audited and unaudited information may not be clear.

c. Audited information can easily be changed.

d. The use of hyperlinks may mean that linked information may be changed and readers can switch between audited and unaudited information without this being clear. (Such hyperlinks should state that the reader is passing from audited to unaudited information.)

e. Overall the auditor must be sure that he is not linked or associated with unaudited information.

16. The letter of engagement should include:

a. Acknowledgement that the report may be published on the web.

b. Note that the responsibility for these rests with the directors.

c. Establish that the company should advise the auditors of any intended electronic publication before it occurs.

d. State that the auditors reserve the right to withhold consent to publish their report electronically if the financial statements or auditors' report are published inappropriately.

e. Note that the directors are responsible for the controls over, and the security of, the web site.

f. State that the examination of the controls over the maintenance and integrity of the web site is not part of the auditor's duties but can be added if required.

17. The auditors' procedures should include checking the information by reviewing the process by which the financial statements are published electronically are derived form the *manually signed accounts*, checking that the two versions are identical and checking that the format does not distort the overall presentation e.g. by highlighting some data.

The auditor's report should identify the financial statements that have been audited. It may be desirable to name these individually instead of using page numbers. It should also identify the nationality of the accounting and auditing standards applied as the web is international. It should limit the auditor's association with any other information in the annual report and accounts.

Summary

18. a. Auditing is a dynamic discipline and change is now rapid.

b. New material emanates from statutes, the ASB and IASC, the APB and IFAC, UITF, corporate governance, professional bodies, regulation and technological change.

c. Independence is an important topic especially in relation to other work.

d. Audit automation and new audit techniques such as risk analysis are current issues.

e. E-commerce is a coming issue as are electronically published financial statements.

Points to note

19. a. It has been possible for accountants to incorporate their businesses since 1989. However only about 100 accountants firms have done so. The Limited Liability Partnerships Act 2000 may lead to many firms registering under it. The benefits are limited liability and the retention of partnership status. There will be financial disclosure requirements on the downside and possibly tax benefits on the upside. A problem of structure is the international nature of many firms and the differing structural possibilities in other countries.

b. Auditing is a surprisingly dynamic discipline. Students are advised to keep up to date by reading the professional press and the business pages of the newspapers can help as can reading annual reports and accounts, either in manually signed format or electronic format.

c. The question of auditor independence is a difficult one due to the conflicting professional and commercial instincts of auditors. Regulators want more independence (= not doing other work) and auditors want more work other than auditing. The use of business risk assessment in auditor is a way of adding other work.

d. Computers and the web are changing the face of auditing. An important point to note us that they greatly increase the need for auditing.

Student self testing questions

1. a. List some influences for change in auditing. (2)
   b. List principles on independence. (3)
   c. List advantages and disadvantages of auditors' taking other work. (4)
   d. What Act may have a big effect on the liabilities of accounting firms? (7)
   e. List some computer packages that are useful in auditing. (8)
   f. List the benefits of automating auditing. (9)
   g. List the risks involved in e-commerce. (12)
   h. List some challenges for auditors in e-commerce. (13)
   i. List some procedures for use by auditors in e-commerce. (14)
   j. What are the problems for auditors when clients publish their financial statements on the web? (15)
   k. What should be included in the letter of engagement when electronically published accounts are issued? (16)
   l. What special items should then be included in the auditors' report? (17)

Case study 1

Partisova Ltd is a large private company owned by Hamish and his immediate family. He is the chairman and chief executive and there are four other employee directors. The turnover is £3 million per annum. The company trades in non-ferrous metals with extensive business in Eastern Europe. The auditors are Tichy & Co., a small firm run by Joe Tichy. Hamish has largely computerised the business with the help of Tichy who is a golf partner as well as the auditor. Hamish wants more advice and assistance from Tichy as business gets more difficult.

Discussion

What are the issues raised by all this?

Case study 2

Dist PLC are retailers of electrical appliance parts with numerous branches. They are wholly computerised with substantial retailing on the web and EDI with suppliers and large customers. They have decided to publish their annual report and accounts on the web.

Discussion

What effect will all this computerisation have on business risk, audit risk, audit procedures and then auditor's report?

56 Environmental matters and auditing

Introduction

1. All enterprises in the twenty-first century face a climate of rapid change and escalating regulatory requirements. Among the major changes occurring are environmental obligations both legal and moral (known as constructive obligations). In recent years there has been the green movement together with many pressures on business and other organisations to respond to very public issues including:

    man-induced climatic change

    the greenhouse effect

    a need for waste management

    a need to avoid polluting the earth, water and air

    a need for recycling

    a need for a safe and clean environment.

2. Some very public occurrences have worried the public including radiation leaks, the burial of atomic waste, Chernobyl, Three Mile Island, depletion of the ozone layer, and, in my home territory the effects of noise, traffic flow and contaminated air of open cast mining. My readers can probably cite many others.

3. The importance of environmental matters has affected auditors in that environmental matters can constitute considerable risks to some audit clients and environmental matters can, in some circumstances, lead to the risk of material misstatement in financial statements. There is an International Auditing Practices Statement 1010 *The Consideration of Environmental Matters in the Audit of Financial Statements.*

4. The professional bodies consider that as environmental matters increase in importance, there will be a growth in the investigation of and reporting of environmental matters.

This will probably mean more opportunities for professional firms in auditing environmental statements. The last edition of this book included a chapter on environmental auditing but it is omitted this time on space grounds. It may be that the future will see a need for environmental auditing in this book.

Environmental matters and the audit

5. Some major considerations are:
   a. Material environmental matters can present major risks to some clients and can lead to possible misstatements in the financial statements.
   b. Responsibility for environmental matters, their recognition, measurement and disclosure, is with the management.
   c The main possibilities for misstatement in financial statements include:
      i. The introduction of environmental laws and regulations which may involve impairment of assets.
      ii. Failure to comply with legal requirements may require accrual of remediation, compensation or legal costs.
      iii. Fines, damages and legal costs may need to be accrued for violations.
      iv. Some companies (including waste management companies, chemical manufacturers etc.) may incur environmental obligation as a direct result of their core operations.
      v. Constructive obligations may occur from publicly stated environmental policies. These may not be legal obligations but may be just as binding.
      vi. Contingent liabilities may need to be disclosed in some circumstances.
      vii. Initiatives to abate environmental damage may cost a great deal but may not enhance the value of fixed assets.
      viii. Vicarious liability may reside in a client as a result of the environmental damage caused by a previous owner of a site.
   d. Some of the SASs and ISAs which may be relevant in this area include:
      i. knowledge of the business
      ii. risk assessments and internal control
      iii. consideration of laws and regulations
      iv. using the work of an expert
      v. audit of accounting estimates.
   e. In some extreme cases environmental matters can lead to abandonment of going concern in whole or in part. An example of this is if a company was obliged to cease production of some environmentally polluting product altogether.

Knowledge of the business

6. The auditor's knowledge of the business needs to be sufficient to enable the auditor to identify and obtain an understanding of the events, transactions and practices related to environmental matters that may have a material effect on the financial statements and the audit. Clearly the auditor will be aware of the environmental risks of mining, extractive, chemical and other industries. But equally any business that is subject to environ-

mental laws, may have vicarious liability or processes that may have an environmental impact should be considered in environmental terms.

Risk factors

7. The auditor needs to assess the business and inherent risks attached to environmental matters in connection with a client where knowledge of the business indicates a risk exists.

Internal control

8. It is the management's responsibility to design and operate internal controls on all aspects of the business including environmental issues. Some companies with high exposure to environmental risk factors may have a separate sub-system for internal controls on environmental matters. This may conform to the ISO standard re *environmental management systems (EMS).*

9. In all audits including those with environmental problems, the auditor needs to assess the control environment sufficient to assess directors' and management's attitudes, awareness and actions regarding internal controls and their importance in the entity.

10. Control procedures should be in place to:

    a. Monitor compliance with the entity's environmental policies as well as all relevant laws and regulations.

    b. Maintain an appropriate environmental information system.

    c. Identify potential environmental matters.

Consideration of laws and regulations

11. It is the management's responsibility to ensure adherence to laws and regulations but as environmental matters connected with laws and regulations may cause misstatements in financial statements, the auditor needs to be aware of any potential misstatement.

12. The auditor's approach here may be:

    a. Use existing knowledge of the business.

    b. Enquiries of management as to policies and procedures on environmental matters.

    c. Enquiries of management as to environmental laws and regulations that may have a fundamental effect on the entity and its financial statements.

    d. Discuss with management the policies or procedures adopted for identifying, evaluating and accounting for litigation, claims and assessments.

Using the work of an expert

13. It is possible that the client employs an expert in environmental matters to conduct an environmental audit. His work is obviously useful to the auditor and the SAS or ISA precepts on using the work of an expert should be followed in assessing the work done and its utility to the auditor

Substantive procedures

14. The auditor may well adopt procedures such as:

    a. Consider risks.

b. Obtain evidence through enquiry of management, seeking corroborative evidence wherever possible.

c. Consider any reports by experts or environmental auditors.

d. Consider the work of internal audit.

e. Review correspondence with lawyers and regulatory agencies and any prosecutions.

f. Examine any media comment.

g. Obtain management representations.

h. Review all the evidence and consider any implications for the auditor's report. This may include a possibility of qualifications due to uncertainty, inadequate disclosure or going concern doubts.

Publicity and annual reports

15. Environmental factors can be very important to some companies and for them, any information on environmental matters may need to be made public. The reasons for this are many and various and include:

a. To ensure investment by ethical investors. Many persons now only invest in 'ethical' companies and unit trusts and other investment vehicles exist to satisfy this demand. Companies all want a high share price and so need to court all potential investors. Hence there is a need to be, or appear to be, ethical in environmental and other ways. Other ways may include paying reasonable wages in developing companies or not employing child labour or even not opening on Sundays.

b. As a part of a marketing strategy. Companies may have a marketing advantage over competitors if they are known to be environmentally clean and thus have products which appeal to green consumers.

c. To appear to be committed to innovation and change, and responsive to new factors.

16. The obvious medium for making public relevant information about a company's policies, systems and achievements in environmental affairs is the company's annual report and accounts. Many companies now include an environmental statement in their annual reports. Auditors need to read this as with all data in annual reports and follow the precepts in SAS 160 or ISA 720. However other publicity possibilities arise. These include:

a. In advertisements and in public relations exercises.

b. By requiring all suppliers to complete a comprehensive environmental questionnaire (and ensuring this procedure is known to the public).

c. By stating that the company has BS 7750 on its stationery etc. Or perhaps that all our production sites in the EC participate in EMAS on all its stationery and literature. Look out for this.

Implications for company auditors

17. Audit firms may well see environmental audit as a new opportunity and an extension to the services presently offered to clients and the public. However there are immediate implications for annual audits as you may have realised in reading this chapter so far. These implications include:

a. Environmental factors may have an impact on asset values.

b.   Environmental factors may have created actual or contingent liabilities.

c.   Environmental factors may have implications for future capital expenditure and cash flows, that may impinge on the viability of the company as a going concern.

d.   Environmental factors may create fundamental uncertainties about the assets and liabilities of a company and its future which may lead the auditor to consider whether he can say the accounts show a true and fair view. The Statement of Auditing Standard on Auditors' Reports on Financial Statements deals with this matter but current auditing standards require qualified auditors' reports where there is material uncertainty.

e.   Balance sheet items such as secured loans may not be secured if land values are affected by environmental factors.

f.   Insurance cover may not be adequate and hence contingent liabilities may exist which are uninsured.

g.   Comprehensive legislation exists in many areas requiring environmental action. Breaches of these may not be apparent to auditors but may lead to undisclosed liabilities. Auditors may consider Section 389A of the Companies Act 1985 which makes it an offence to knowingly or recklessly make a statement to the company's auditors which conveys information to them which they require, or are entitled to require, that is misleading, false, or deceptive.

Social issues

18. There is much interest in social issues as they affect corporate affairs. Companies try to make it clear that they have good social policies in areas like employment, remuneration or treatment of disabled people. Statements often appear in annual reports and accounts on these matters. There has been some recent publicity about the use of child labour in developing countries by major UK companies or by suppliers to UK companies.

19. These issues are interesting to company auditors but are unlikely to lead to misstatement in financial statements. However three points may be made:

a.   Auditors need to read statements made in annual reports on social matters. If these statements contain information which is inconsistent with the financial statements or are misleading (but the financial statements are correct) then the auditor may need to include an explanatory paragraph in her report as required by SAS 160.

b.   Undisclosed liabilities may exist because of breaches of employment law and fines may be payable or damages may be awarded in the courts or tribunals.

c.   Opportunities exist for auditing firms to find work in investigating and reporting on social matters.

Summary

a.   Environmental matters have become very important in daily life and, for some companies, can lead to misstatements in financial statements.

b.   Management are responsible for dealing with and reporting on environmental matters.

c.   There are many opportunities for environmental matters to lead to misstatements in financial statements.

d. Auditors need to consider the impact of environmental matters on items in the financial statements.

e. Social issues can also be important but rarely lead to misstatement in financial statements.

Points to note

a. The government in the UK and in other countries have introduced much legislation to assist in improving or conserving the environmental and many agencies and regulatory bodies now have statutory powers to require companies to take action.

b. Environmental audits are not just an investigation into the interaction of a company with its environment and with legal requirements but rather an investigation into policies and systems and how well practices and procedures fulfil policies.

c. Some public companies include information on environmental matters in their annual reports. Examples include the water companies, British Airways, Body Shop and others. Check any accounts you see for this element.

d. Auditors need to be very alert to environmental factors in some audits but they are a factor in all audits now.

e. Some legislation imposes personal liabilities on directors and managers in the case of infringement of environmental legislation.

f. The public now expects ever rising standards in the environmental area and this subject may loom large in all areas of human activity in the near future. Auditing will be heavily affected.

g. It is important to realise that BS 7750 is not a set of environmental performance guidelines. Rather it is a standard framework for management activities in the environmental area.

h. Environmental auditing or verification as a set of procedures is not very different from the audit of financial statements.

i. This is a very fast moving area. Watch out for changes in the near future!

j. Many of the auditing standards and practice statements are relevant in considering environmental matters. These include SASs 120, 130,160, 210, 300, 420, 500, 520 and 600 and ISAs 250, 310, 400, 540. 570, 610, 620, 720 and 1010.

Case study 1

Sludgy PLC are a quoted company heavily engaged in the waste disposal industry and engage also in some open cast mining in land reclamation projects. The company sees itself as performing an unpleasant duty which the rest of the public are unwilling to do for itself. The company has inevitably acquired a reputation for being environmentally unfriendly and has noticed that the share price has fallen despite good profits and excellent prospects.

Discussion

1. Suggest factors which may have caused the company's reputation and fall in share price.

2. Suggest an action programme for improving the company's public image.

3. What possible misstatements may occur in the financial statements as a result of environmental factors?

4. How might the auditor approach the audit?

Case study 2

Wednesfield Widget Manufacturing Ltd operate from their old freehold factory on a site in a manufacturing estate in Wolverhampton which dates back to the nineteenth century. Their plant is old but is regularly maintained to a good standard. They have certification under ISO 9000 but not under BS 7750. The auditors are Wurried & Co. who are aware that the company has asked for a loan from the bank to be secured on the freehold premises.

Discussion

a. Indicate some green policies the company may adopt.

b. What environmental factors may affect the audit?

c. How might Wurried & Co. incorporate environmental factors in their audit?

Student self testing questions

a. List some major considerations re environmental factors and the audit. (5)

b. What internal control issues concern environmental matters? (10)

c. What might be the auditor's approach to environmental laws and regulations? (11, 12)

d. What substantive procedures may an auditor adopt? (14)

e. List the implications of environmental matters form auditors. (17)

f. What social issues may concern an auditor? (19)

57 Auditing theory

Introduction

1. Auditing is a practical subject. It is something that people do. How it is done today is a result of a long history of marginal changes and responses to new commercial and legal developments over the centuries with the most rapid progress in the last few years. There is no real body of theory in the way that there is, for example, in accounting. In accounting there are a few recognised conventions (going concern, accruals etc.) which underlie all accounting and enable applications to be made to new situations in a coherent and consistent manner. Many attempts have been made to develop theories of auditing with a small range of underlying principles but, currently, we are still managing with the large range of discrete prescriptions provided by the Auditing Practices Board.

2. This final chapter reviews some thoughts on auditing theories and principles including the auditing postulates of Mautz and Sharaf.

Enduring principles of auditing

3. The APB in the Audit Agenda identified eight enduring principles of auditing. These are:

a. **Integrity.** If auditors did not behave with integrity (honesty, adherence to moral principles) and be seen to behave that way, then their reports would not be believed and the whole audit process would have no value. Clearly, in the UK, auditors do behave with integrity although at the margin, there may be some accommodation to client wishes when lucrative work other than audit work is performed and when there is a fear of loss of the audit fee. Partly, conforming to integrity requirements is because of the innate morality of accountants but also because of strict regulation and fear of litigation.

b. **Independence.** If auditors are not independent of the entity being audited or are not seen to be so, then their reports will not be believed and again the whole audit process will have no value. Essentially, auditors must be objective, give their opinions without fear or favour and be unaffected by conflicts of interest or pressures from any source. UK auditors tend to carry on work additional to the audit and their independence is by no means total. Your author believes that attempts to distance the auditors from the directors by such means as their relations with the company being mediated through an audit committee of non-executive directors are not much more than cosmetic. Ultimately auditors will need to be truly independent of commercial clients in the same way as they are with local authorities.

c. **Competence.** If auditors are not competent, then the whole audit process is of no value. In general UK auditors are seen as competent but a number of recent events including company failures, criminal trials and civil litigation have given rise to some doubts in the minds of the business community. The government have legislated for competence (Companies Act 1989 Sections 24 et al.), the professional bodies have encouraged it (difficult exams, approved training, post qualifying education, practising certificates with inspections, etc.) and the Auditing Practices Board have issued numerous prescriptions. An interesting idea is that competence is constantly being improved but at the same time economics have dictated that the time spent on auditing is constantly being reduced even though modern laws, accounting systems and structures are steadily becoming more complex.

d. **Rigour.** This word implies that auditors should apply strictness in conducting their work and in forming their opinions. Auditors should apply a degree of professional scepticism to their work, should assess the risks involved and should obtain sufficient reliable evidence on all matters from a range of sources. The evidence from negligence cases is that auditors do not always apply sufficient rigour especially in complex cases, where clients are dominated by single individuals and in the valuation of subsidiary companies.

e. **Accountability.** Auditors should act in the best interests of shareholders whilst having regard to the wider public interest. The Audit Agenda suggests that where these responsibilities conflict, auditors should generally place the interests of the shareholders first except where this could materially damage the interests of the public. It is difficult to think of specific instances of such conflicts of interest but your author tends to the view that auditors would be more highly regarded if the public interest always prevailed.

f. **Judgement.** Auditors should apply sound professional judgement. Specific areas where judgement is required include assessment of reasonable assurance, material, misstatement and risk.

g. **Communication.** There are two strands to this. Firstly auditors should openly disclose all matters necessary to a full understanding of their opinion and secondly they should make disclosure to the proper authorities of matters they should disclose in the public interest. The former is met by the long standard form of audit report which I imagine is read by nobody. The latter is a new departure and is too new to assess as yet. Auditors tend to be constrained by fears of suits for defamation and by a natural tendency to confidentiality.

h. **Providing value.** Clearly auditing should be conducted with a minimum of resource input and with a maximum of utility to the business community. There is a trade off here and some auditors would assert that despite massive improvements in auditing techniques (e.g. risk and materiality assessments, use of analytical review) audits are often conducted too cheaply. The Audit Agenda suggests that value can be achieved in providing greater benefits to the shareholders, in innovating new services as well as in more economical auditing. This seems to conflict with the principle of independence.

Postulates of auditing

4. These are matters which are assumed to be true and are taken for granted. It is often considered that it is useful to examine a discipline and to see what, if any, are its postulates. This was done by Mautz and Sharaf in their 1961 book *'The Philosophy of Auditing'* and I commend this book to you. Their eight postulates are:

a. **Financial statements and financial data are verifiable.** This is an unspoken assumption by all auditors who otherwise would not attempt to verify the assertions in the accounts they are auditing. Sometimes facts are not strictly verifiable (for example the outcome of contentious litigation) and auditors content themselves with statements of the circumstances which can be verified.

b. **There is no necessary conflict of interest between the auditor and the management of the entity.** If this was not so, auditors would not believe the answers given to their questions and, given the complexity of modern businesses, would find conducting an audit impossible. It is this basic assumption which leads auditors to consider whether they should accept a new client where the integrity of the client is suspect.

c. **The financial statements are free from collusive and other unusual irregularities.** Auditors are expected to uncover material misstatements in financial statements caused by fraud or other irregularities but collusive fraud is often impossible to discover by auditing procedures. Consequently readers of financial statements are entitled to assume that the auditors have uncovered any material misstatements except those caused by collusive fraud. If there were a requirement to uncover such frauds the audit would become impossible or, at the least, require many more detailed and expensive procedures than are currently performed.

d. **The existence of a satisfactory system of internal control eliminates the probability of irregularities.** Auditors are entitled to rely on satisfactory internal controls as evidence of many assertions (e.g. on the completeness of sales or the accuracy of stock taking). If this postulate was not a fundamental principle of auditing they would not do so. It is interesting that SAS 300.8 requires that regardless of the assessed levels of inherent and control risk, auditors should perform some substantive procedures for financial statements assertions of material account balances and transaction classes.

e. **Consistent application of generally accepted accounting principles results in fair presentation of the results and position.** Auditors need some criterion for their assessment of the fairness of the view given by financial statements and the GAAPs supply it. If they did not then there would be no standard by which fairness could be judged.

f. **In the absence of clear evidence to the contrary, what has held true in the past for the entity will hold true in the future.** If this were not so the auditor would be unable to accept the value of debts, the value of fixed assets , the saleability of stock, the effectiveness of internal controls, the integrity of management and many other matters.

g. **When examining financial data, the auditor acts exclusively in the capacity of auditor.** This is tied up with notions like independence, useful economic function and social responsibility to the public. In the past, many auditors assumed that activities like preparing financial statements, extracting balances and preparing schedules was the same as auditing. This postulate is fundamental and yet the necessary independence of mind is still a difficult problem for many auditors.

h. **The professional status of the independent auditor imposes commensurate professional obligations.** This means that members of the professions have higher duties than economic self interest. However it is not always clear to whom professional duties are owed. Are they to the public at large, to the client company or to the shareholders? However it is certain that the professional accounting bodies impose very onerous duties on their members.

Fundamental auditing principles

5. You will appreciate that there is no agreed list of fundamental auditing principles. Here nonetheless is my list:

a. **Professional status:** independence, integrity, rigour in approach, competence, observance of ethical code, observance of the prescriptions of the law and of the Auditing Standards.

b. **Judgement:** of inherent risk, control risk, detection risk, of what constitutes material misstatement, of what constitutes reasonable assurance.

c. **Evidence:** evidence is made available to auditors, auditors have unrestricted access to required evidence, direct evidence is preferred, evidence for any assertion is collected from several sources, auditors are not biased in assessing evidence, evidence is assessed with an appropriate degree of scepticism, anomalies are probed with tenacity, auditors see for themselves.

d. **Communication:** auditors report their audit opinion without fear or favour, they also report matters which they are required to, to the proper authorities, they report in language which is clear, unequivocal and which can be understood by its recipients.

6. The Auditing Practices Board (APB) have published an auditor's code. This sets out nine fundamental principles of accountability, integrity, objectivity and independence, competence, rigour, judgement, clear communication, association and providing value. These ideas should be clear from Para. 3 except association. This means that auditors allow their reports to be included in documents containing other information only if they consider that the additional information is not in conflict with the matters covered by their report and they have no cause to believe it to be misleading.

Summary

7. a. Auditing as a discipline lacks any agreed set of fundamental principles or propositions.

    b. The Audit Agenda contains a list of enduring principles of auditing.

    c. Mautz and Sharaf suggested a list of postulates of auditing.

Points to note

8. a. It is desirable that all auditors follow at all times the various principles I have enumerated in this chapter. In practice auditors are constrained from doing so by a range of influences:

    – the desire for lucrative work in addition to the audit

    – the desire to keep the audit

    – a natural desire to please immediate contact groups especially the directors

    – a desire for a peaceful life

    – a desire to produce the audit as economically as possible so as to make a profit and to avoid losing the audit to competitors

    – the accounting standards are not as rigid a set of criteria for fair view as might be desired and so acceptance of some bending of the rules is inevitable.

    b. On the other hand auditors are now pushed to conform to the principles by:

    – fear of litigation

    – practice regulation and inspection

    – more specific rules (e.g. the Auditing Standards) which have to be followed

Case study 1

Sheinton Military Vehicles PLC have new auditors Thrusting & Co., who won the audit by submitting the lowest tender. They have agreed to assist the company with a range of taxation and consultancy services in IT and management. On the first audit Francis, the clerk in charge of the audit, finds a number of doubtful matters:

a. The company have illegally exported a number of vehicles to a country which is subject to trade sanctions. The chief executive explains that the law has not been broken as the export has actually been to a neighbouring country which is not embargoed.

b. The tax department of Thrusting have advised that the transfer pricing policies of the company broke the tax rules in several countries and that there was a possibility of investigations by those countries with large potential liabilities. The chief executive assures Francis that the tax authorities concerned will not pursue these matters as he has friends in high places.

c. The company have exported vehicles to a particular country where, so a junior manager in the client told Francis, they are used in a particularly brutal oppression of minorities. The chief executive told Francis that the use of the vehicles was nothing to do with them. Think, he said, of the jobs of Sheinton's employees. Francis remembers that a questioner at the last AGM was assured that the company's vehicles were not used in this way.

d. The shares in Sheinton rose in April last year as a result of buying by an unknown institution in a tax haven. This was just before Sheinton bought another company in another tax haven with an exchange of shares. Later the share price fell again as a result of selling by the unknown institution. Francis has been told that this matter should not be investigated as it is not relevant to the audit objectives.

e. Material sums have been paid to a subsidiary in a tax haven by the main operating company. These are described as management services and the accounts of the subsidiary show a small profit and have been audited by a small firm in the tax haven. The chief executive says that Francis should have no problem as he can net off the turnover in the consolidation. The major expense in the subsidiary's accounts is simply cost of sales.

Discussion

Relate this affair to the material in this chapter.

Student self testing questions *Questions with answers apparent from the text*

1. a. List the enduring principles of auditing. (3)
    b. List the postulates of auditing. (4)

Index

References are to chapter and paragraph